DATE DUE

JY 19 04			
SE 17 05			
GAYLORD			PRINTED IN U.S.A.

PARACELSUS

STUDIES IN THE HISTORY
OF
CHRISTIAN THOUGHT

EDITED BY

HEIKO A. OBERMAN, Tucson, Arizona

IN COOPERATION WITH

HENRY CHADWICK, Cambridge
JAROSLAV PELIKAN, New Haven, Connecticut
BRIAN TIERNEY, Ithaca, New York
ARJO VANDERJAGT, Groningen

VOLUME LXXXV

OLE PETER GRELL (ED.)

PARACELSUS

PARACELSUS

THE MAN AND HIS REPUTATION
HIS IDEAS AND THEIR TRANSFORMATION

EDITED BY

OLE PETER GRELL

BRILL
LEIDEN · BOSTON · KÖLN .
1998

Library of Congress Cataloging-in-Publication Data

Paracelsus : the man and his reputation, his ideas and their
  transformation / edited by Ole Peter Grell.
    p.   cm. — (Studies in the history of Christian thought, ISSN
  0081–8607 ; v. 75)
    "Earlier versions of most of the chapters in this volume were
  originally presented in a symposium held at the University of
  Glasgow in September 1993 entitled The transformation of
  Paracelsianism"—Pref.
    Includes bibliographical references and indexes.
    ISBN 9004111778 (hardcover : alk. paper)
    1. Paracelsus,1493–1541.   I. Grell, Ole Peter.   II. Series.
  B785.P24P34   1998
  199'.404—dc21   98–25297
                                                              CIP

Die Deutsche Bibliothek - CIP-Einheitsaufnahme

Paracelsus : the man and his reputation, his ideas and their
transformation / ed. by Ole Peter Grell.
Leiden ; Boston ; Köln : Brill, 1998
  (Studies in the history of Christian thought ; Vol. 85)
  ISBN 90–04–11177–8

ISSN   0081-8607
ISBN   90 04 11177 8

PRINTED IN THE NETHERLANDS

CONTENTS

PREFACE

I should like to thank Professor Heiko Oberman for accepting this volume for publication in the Series. Earlier versions of most of the chapters in this volume were originally presented in a symposium held at the University of Glasgow in September 1993 entitled: *The Transformation of Paracelsianism*—to celebrate the quincentenary of Paracelsus's birth. The symposium was organised by the Director of the Wellcome Unit for the History of Medicine at the University of Glasgow, Dr. Johanna Geyer-Kordesch, Dr. David Weston, Keeper of Special Collections, Glasgow University Library, and Professor Friedrich Niewöhner, Herzog August Bibliothek, Wolfenbüttel. A generous grant from the Wellcome Trust to the Wellcome Unit for the History of Medicine at the University of Glasgow, and additional financial support from the Herzog August Bibliothek, Wolfenbüttel, Germany, made the symposium possible and thus provided the foundation for the present volume.

It should be noted, however, that most of the chapters in this volume were ready for publication in 1994, and accordingly the contributors have been unable to include a number of relevant works in their footnotes which have appeared since.

Finally, I should like to thank Ms Tamara Hug for her expert skills in bringing all the chapters into a unified format and likewise Mr Howarth Penny for his help in collating the three indices of the volume.

Ole Peter Grell
Cambridge, 22 April 1998

LIST OF CONTRIBUTORS

Herbert Breger, Leibniz-Archiv, Hannover, Germany.

John Christie, Division of History of Philosophy of Science, University of Leeds.

Andrew Cunningham, Wellcome Unit for the History of Medicine, University of Cambridge.

Allen G. Debus, Department of History, The University of Chicago, U.S.A.

Ute Gause, Department of Theology, University of Siegen, Germany.

Carlos Gilly, Bibliotheca Philosophica Hermetica, Amsterdam.

Dietlinde Goltz, Institute for the History of Medicine, University of Tübingen, Germany.

Ole Peter Grell, Wellcome Unit for the History of Medicine, University of Cambridge.

Francis McKee, Wellcome Unit for History of Medicine, University of Glasgow.

Bruce T. Moran, Department of History, University of Nevada, U.S.A.

Stephen Pumphrey, Department of History, University of Lancaster.

Hartmut Rudolph, Berlin-Brandenburgische Akademie der Wissenschaften, Leibniz-Edition, Potsdam.

Heinz Schott, Institute for the History of Medicine, University of Bonn, Germany.

Hugh Trevor-Roper, Lord Dacre, Didcot, Oxfordshire.

INTRODUCTION

THE ENIGMA OF PARACELSUS

Ole Peter Grell

Today, more than five hundred years after his birth Paracelsus and Paracelsianism remain surprisingly popular. This has been the case more or less continuously since the mid- to late-sixteenth century. Then as now Paracelsus's name remains associated with novelty. In German speaking areas in particular more people are likely to have heard of Paracelsus than any other medical figure in history, including such prominent men as Hippocrates and Harvey. Only the major religious reformers such as Luther, with whom Paracelsus was and has repeatedly been compared can muster similar or greater popularity among important figures from the early modern period.

It is, however, something of an enigma that this should be the case when it is borne in mind that it is far from clear what exactly Paracelsus contributed to natural philosophy and medicine. But perhaps it is exactly this enigma which has made Paracelsus so attractive to such a variety of people throughout history who all want to claim him as a forerunner or advocate for their particular ideas. Undoubtedly the vagueness of Paracelsus's Hermetic/neo-Platonic natural philosophy has made him particularly well-suited for the projections of later periods.

The scholarly and historical significance of Paracelsus, or as he was properly named, Theophrastus Bombastus von Hohenheim, and his ideas is probably best illustrated by the fact that he merits major entries in the recent *Dictionary of Scientific Biography* (1974), as well as the newly published *Oxford Encyclopedia of the Reformation* (1996). Even for a man born at the turn of the fifteenth century, when the world and the way we look at it had yet to be split into totally separate disciplines, this is a considerable achievement. Together, however, these entries give us an idea of Paracelsus's uniqueness, providing us with a measure of how widely his interests ranged, covering fields such as theology, natural philosophy, medicine, chemistry, cosmology, astrology and occultism, and to what extent he has preoccupied later periods' historians.

The fact that Paracelsus proved so important in such a variety of fields may go some way in explaining the difficulty we have in pinpointing this elusive man and his ideas. Still, the haziness surrounding his life is, of course, to a large extent rooted in the shortage of information relating to his upbringing, education, and career. Thus, Paracelsus appears to have been educated by his father who practised medicine. He does not seem to have received a formal secondary schooling while later he may have studied at various Italian universities and he may have acquired a lower medical degree from Ferrara. Little or nothing is, in other words, certain about his education. Initially he seems to have travelled widely as a military surgeon, in the Mediterranean and Middle East in the service of the Venetian Republic, and later in Scandinavia, possibly serving the Danish king Christian II. Lacking social connections, not to mention proper academic credentials, Paracelsus developed a deeply anti-authoritarian and iconoclastic outlook which served to make him a highly volatile individual. He remained single, and according to his apprentice, Oporinus, avoided the company of women altogether while behaving in an eccentric manner. Not surprisingly he found it difficult to settle in any one place for long, constantly falling foul of his friends and running into trouble with the local authorities who more often than not wanted rid of him as quickly as possible.

Similarly Paracelsus's thirst for new knowledge and experience caused him to travel widely which furthermore guaranteed that his views were developing and constantly changing, while he himself remained in opposition to 'established knowledge' and repeatedly clashed with lay and ecclesiastical authorities wherever he went.

It is somewhat paradoxical that Paracelsus was named after one of the most prolific and famous members of the Peripatetic school, Theophrastus, considering the fierce criticism he was to subject scholastic Aristoteleanism to throughout his life. Likewise, his self-conscious adoption of the nickname Paracelsus from around 1527—surpassing the famous Celsus, who early in the first century A.D. had written a comprehensive encyclopedia covering the whole of medicine—not only refers to his own encyclopedic interests and attempts to comprehend the whole of natural philosophy and medicine, but also to the fact that Celsus had been a layman writing for other laymen, and not an academic exclusively writing for the learned world. This was an ambition Paracelsus firmly shared and emulated by writing in vernacular German, thus attempting to communicate with a much broader and less educated audience than the university trained elite he so despised.

This elusiveness about the person Paracelsus also extends to his ideas. Only few of his works were published by himself or during his lifetime. Apart from his surgical work, *Grosse Wundartzney*, published in Augsburg in 1536 Paracelsus had hardly published anything except a couple of pamphlets on the pox and two so-called *Practica* astrological forecasts of a prophetic and apocalyptic nature, by the time of his death in 1541. Were we to write about Paracelsus on that basis alone, he would look like a totally different man from the one which has been reconstructed on the basis of the vast *corpus* of works edited and published a generation after his death by Adam von Bodenstein and others *post* 1564. But the problems do not stop there. The provenance of the texts published a generation after his death is often far from clear, and many scholars consider a fair number of them to be pseudo-Paracelsian—written by others in imitation of Paracelsus. That still leaves the question unanswered to what degree editors such as Bodenstein, Michael Toxites and Gerard Dorn interfered with Paracelsus's work, rewriting or cleaning incomplete and contradictory texts before printing them. Before any transformation took place Paracelsianism was, in other words, a long way from being a clear-cut set of ideas, and it may well have been thoroughly revised even prior to the great 'Paracelsian moment' around 1570.[1] It is small wonder historians have struggled, and continue to struggle, with both this man and his ideas.

In the first section of this volume dealing with the historical Paracelsus, four complementary, but different historiographical approaches to Paracelsus and Paracelsianism are offered, which provide new and cautious ways of dealing with what Andrew Cunningham has so vividly labelled the 'thin and the fat Paracelsus'.[2] The 'thin', being the unadorned or historical Paracelsus—the 'fat', being the embelished or anachronistic Paracelsus emerging from the writings of later historians.

In his review of the recent Anglo-American historiography on Paracelsianism Stephen Pumfrey concludes that Paracelsianism has

---

[1] For Paracelsus, see W. Pagel, *Paracelsus. An Introduction to Philosophical Medicine in the Era of the Renaissance*, Basel 1958; for the publication of the writings of Paracelsus, see also H. Trevor-Roper, 'The Paracelsian Movement,' in his *Renaissance Essays*, London 1985, 149–99.

[2] See below Chapter 2.

acquired too loose connotations to provide a useful concept for historical analysis. Pumfrey rejects the three dominant historiographical interpretations: First, the existence of a Paracelsian school or followers of Paracelsus, because it assumes that a core of Paracelsian practices and concepts existed, thus failing to deal with the constantly changing nature of Paracelsianism. Second, the equation of Paracelsians with chemical philosophers. This disregards the fact that Paracelsian was a term used by those who wished to marginalise others whom they considered philosophically dangerous and that chemists resisted the term. Third, the iatrochemist seen as a Paracelsian, which makes Paracelsians out of all those who used or defended chemical remedies. This definition, however, brings together strange bedfellows such as mystics, quacks, court physicians and moderate Galenists, while jettisoning all ideological, philosophical and social differences.

The fact we find few natural philosophers in the early modern period who profess to be Paracelsians while the term simultaneously was being generously used by those who wanted to stigmatise their opponents as religiously, politically and philosophically unsound, makes it impossible to discuss Paracelsianism without 'a dialectical consideration of that opposition'. As pointed out by Pumfrey it is amazing that Paracelsianism was able to generate such significant support in the late sixteenth and early seventeenth centuries, when bearing in mind the vigorous religious and political opposition it faced. It is somewhat paradoxical that it should do so within the princely courts so despised by Paracelsus himself, who considered any physician who took up such a position as having betrayed his obligation to use his expertise for the common good.[3] We clearly need further research in order to understand how and why Paracelsianism made this transformation.[4]

Taking his departure in the many and contradictionary roles and reputations of Paracelsus, while simultaneously pointing to the paradox that Paracelsus's motto: 'Let him not be another's, who can be his own', appears deeply ironic when seen in the context of the historiography surrounding him, Andrew Cunningham focusses on what

---

[3] See C. Webster, 'Paracelsus: medicine as popular protest', in O.P. Grell and A. Cunningham (eds.), *Medicine and the Reformation*, London 1993, 57–77, especially 66.

[4] See below Chapter 1.

he terms the thin and the fat Paracelsus. Metaphorically speaking the thin Paracelsus is the historical man who lived in the first half of the sixteenth century and who can only be properly understood via a proper historical analysis. The figure who will materialise from this approach may be complex, but not contradictory. For Cunningham the fat Paracelsus represents 'the Paracelsus-es of all the different historical reputations.' In other words the fat Paracelsus is an anachronistic figure who does not tell us much if anything about the historical man, but rather a lot about the particular group or society which promoted each particular and fat Paracelsus. Emphasising that even a preoccupation with the writings of Paracelsus is far from guaranteeing that a thin rather than a fat Paracelsus will emerge, Cunningham proceeds to present us with two fat versions of Paracelsus: one a mystic/occultist from the late nineteenth century, the other a Jungian from the early twentieth century. Both were embodied in editions and translations of Paracelsus's work and had their own modern occult and Jungian agendas. Finally, Cunningham draws our attention to the significance of the reputation Paracelsus had among his contemporaries. Referring to the epithets given to him by his apprentice, Oporinus, Cunningham asks what they meant in the sixteenth century, pointing out that it is time that we reclaim Paracelsus in his proper historical context

Similar conclusions are reached by Dietlinde Goltz who argues that scholars in the twentieth century have *not* done justice to Paracelsus. Reviewing the vast, primarily German literature on Paracelsus published during the last hundred years, she asks why Paracelsus has received so much attention. Such interest, she argues, is neither merited by his personal life nor his work. Turning to the image of Paracelsus which emerges from the last hundred years of research into him and his work, she emphasises six significant and contradictionary traits. First, that a fair number of authors directly imitate the unusual literary style of Paracelsus, often despite recognising it as confused and incomprehensible. Second, Paracelsus tends to be idolised as a great German, as well as a physician, despite the fact that little is known about both his life and his medical practice. Third, he is generally portrayed as the great proto-scientist and the inventor of a number of new disciplines, unbeknown to him, such as psychotherapy, balneology, and parapsychology, just to mention a few. Fourth, Paracelsus is supposed to have re-established the link between medicine and nature, nature's healing power, despite his

stated preference for chemically prepared drugs which contained
primarily heavy metals and minerals. Fifth, his relationship with his
father is idealised and seen as resting on their mutual love and admiration, based solely on a single reference from Paracelsus himself
telling us only that he learned a lot from his father who never left
him during his childhood. Sixth, Paracelsus's crude criticism of contemporary university based medicine is uncritically accepted. Several of these points are also included in Andrew Cunningham's list
of contradictionary roles allocated to Paracelsus by later historians.
Rather than focussing on these anachronistic features and paradoxes
and their historical significance, Dietlinde Golz seeks to explain
why Paracelsus has been idolized so much more than other famous
physicians such as Hippocrates and Harvey. Once more Goltz points
to the significance of the language used by Paracelsus. His style appeals to our emotions, the grammatical structure may be clear while
the message remains unclear, but the sermon imagery adopted by
him, and a style similar to that found in the early German Lutheran
Bible, has a deeply convincing and truthful ring about it. Similarly,
as pointed out by Charles Webster, the similarities in both style and
argument between the works of Paracelsus and the evangelical protest literature from the 1520s, would have guaranteed that its language alone would have convinced a growing number of German
evangelicals.[5]

The choice of Paracelsus as an icon for those seeking an idol is
further facilitated by the fact that he is so relatively easy to idolize.
Little stands in the way of creating a fictitious image because so
little is known about Paracelsus's personal life, not to mention his
medical practice, especially taking into consideration the high ethical demands he imposed on medical men in general. Add to that
his marginalization by the intellectual elite of his day and a picture
of the unrecognized or misunderstood genius emerges, which it is
easy to accept, especially when Paracelsus's argumentative character
and paranoia is ignored, as has often been the case. Even if the historical biography is recognised as a particular danger area by most
historians, where the writer easily comes to identify subconsciously
with his subject and to impose his own dreams and ambitions on
the historical character, the case of Paracelsus is clearly extreme and,

---

[5] Webster, 'Paracelsus', 55–77.

as emphasised by Goltz, a new critical assessment of the man in his historical context is needed.[6]

Some of this revisionist work has already been undertaken by scholars such as Hartmut Rudolph and Charles Webster. Both Webster and Rudolph have emphasised the importance of the Reformation context for understanding Paracelsus and his ideas.[7] Likewise both consider his theological, as well as his natural philosophical and medical works as part of a whole, without which we cannot fully comprehend Paracelsus. As pointed out by Webster 'any realistic assessment of Paracelsus must recognize the unity of his vocation as apostle, prophet and healer'.[8] Similarly, Paracelsus's critique of the medical establishment is closely linked to the anticlericalism and popular protest of his day while he himself presented his alternative system as an extension of the scriptural piety which was commanding growing support within the rapidly expanding number of evangelical supporters.

Considering Paracelsus's close links with several of the leading reformers of the day and his fierce critique of the Catholic Church and the pope, it is somewhat paradoxical that so many scholars continue to emphasise that Paracelsus died as a Catholic. Why should Paracelsus have chosen to leave the Catholic Church? After all, he had enough difficulties with lay and ecclesiastical authorities as it was, and in order to avoid further difficulties he deliberately avoided publishing his theological works which contained his most pronounced criticisms of the Catholic clergy, the indulgences, the sacraments and the fasts all which he described as the makings of Antichrist, a name he repeatedly used for the pope.[9] The relevance of my query is borne out by the fact that the most fervent critic of the Church during the Reformation period—Luther—did not leave the Catholic Church— it left him—excommunicating him in January 1521. Despite the fact that Paracelsus was critical of most of the leading reformers and

---

[6] See below Chapter 3; for the need of a re-assessment, see also Andrew Cunningham in Chapter 2 below.

[7] See for instance C. Webster, 'Paracelsus Confronts the Saints: Miracles, Healing and the Secularization of Magic', in *Social History of Medicine*, 1995, no. 07/03, 403–21 and H. Rudolph, 'Paracelsus' Laientheologie in traditionsgeschichtlicher Sicht und in ihrer Zuordnung zu Reformation und katolischer Reform', in P. Dilg and H. Rudolph (eds.), *Resultate und Desiderate der Paracelsus-Forschung*, Stuttgart 1993, 79–98.

[8] Webster, 'Paracelsus', 74.

[9] See Webster, 'Paracelsus Confronts the Saints', 406.

their theology, hostile as he was to any formal ecclesiastical structure while being much closer to spiritualist outsiders of the Reformation such as Sebastian Castillio,[10] it nevertheless has to be borne in
mind that his fiercest and most virulent attacks were on the Catholic Church and the pope. Likewise, it is significant that Paracelsus,
despite his disagreements with many of the Protestant leaders, not
only respected, but was close to several of them. Thus in March
1525 he wrote a letter to his 'Christian brethren' Martin Luther,
Johannes Bugenhagen and Philip Melanchthon where he included
his commentary on the first five chapters of the gospel of St.
Matthew.[11] Two years later he was patronised by the Basle reformer
Johannes Oecolampadius who was instrumental in promoting him
as municipal physician and professor of medicine at the university.
In 1531 Paracelsus resided in St. Gallen, most likely under the patronage of the humanist physician and reformer of the city, Joachim von
Watt, known as Vadianus. While there, Paracelsus finished his *Opus
Paramirum*, the first major statement of his chemical pathology, which
he dedicated to Vadianus.[12] Thus the links between Protestantism
and Paracelsianism, so evident towards the end of the sixteenth century, was already in evidence during his lifetime. Rather than seeing Paracelsus as some sort of dissenting Catholic we should take
him for what he was: an evangelical dissenter who felt at home
among the reformers who, like him, were questioning authority.

Finally, in the last chapter in the historiographical section, Herbert
Breger explores the differences in character and personality between
Paracelsians of the seventeenth century such as Jan Baptist van

---

[10] For Castillio and the spiritualist outsiders of the Reformation who supported a
tolerant and anti-doctrinal approach in religious matters see O.P. Grell & B. Scribner
(eds.), *Tolerance and intolerance in the European Reformation*, Cambridge 1996, 1–12 and
passim.

[11] See H. Rudolph, 'Einige Gesichtspunkte zum Thema Paracelsus und Luther'
in *Archiv für Reformationsgeschichte*, 72, 1981, 34–54; see also H. Rudolph, 'Theophrast
von Hohenheim (Paracelsus). Arzt und Apostel der neuen Kreatur', in H.-J. Goertz,
Radikale Reformatoren, Munich 1978, and H. Dopsch, 'Humanismus, Renaissance und
Reformation—Paracelsus und die geistigen Bewegungen seiner Zeit', in H. Dopsch
et al. (eds.), *Paracelsus (1493–1541) 'Keines anderen Knecht...'*, Salzburg 1993, 249–58.

[12] See E. Rosner, *Hohenheims Weg von St. Gallen nach Ausburg (1531–1536)*, Vienna
1977. It is noteworthy that some reformation historians have been uncomfortable
with the close association between Paracelsus and some of the reformers. See for
instance Gordon Rupp, *Patterns of Reformation*, London 1969, 375–76, who wonders
whether Paracelsus was summoned to St. Gallen to treat a former burgomaster
with the approval of Vadianus, or whether the reformer suspected him of being a
charlatan.

Helmont, Johann Rudolph Glauber and Johann Joachim Becher, and mechanists such as Robert Boyle, Newton, Huygens and Leibniz, as a possible explanation of their conflicting views on nature, 'science' and society. Where the mechanists tended to be cautious and generally conservative individuals, the Paracelsians appear to have been radical and rebellious. Likewise, the mechanists concentrate on facts and empirical evidence in their writings, renouncing rhetoric and emotions which in turn are so significant in the works of the Paracelsians. Breger concludes that historians should attach far greater importance to the psyche and character of Paracelsians in the explanation why these men chose the natural philosophical outlook they did and not the competing world-view of the mechanists which was simultaneously on offer in the seventeenth century.[13]

The five chapters in the second part of this volume deal with the religious, social, and political implications of Paracelsianism. Carlos Gilly emphasises the significance of Paracelsus's spiritual and eirenic Christianity, opposed to all formal ecclesiastical structure, which was at odds with both pre-Tridentine Catholicism as well as with mainstream Protestantism. He explains why and how it went underground. Paracelsus evidently avoided publishing his theological works in order not to become a target for both Catholics and Protestants, while his later editors and publishers deliberately avoided discussing his religious views. This should not surprise us, bearing in mind that their enterprises took place in the age of confessionalism. Leading a clandestine existence, theological Paracelsianism naturally joined up with other marginalised religious groups such as the followers of Caspar Schwenckfeld and Sebastian Castillio, who shared its apocalyptic and millenarian expectations. By the beginning of the seventeenth century, when excerpts of Paracelsus's theological works first began to be published, Paracelsus was portrayed as a great prophet and proclaimer of an imminent golden age. It is noteworthy that the majority of Paracelsus's works published during these years were his prophesies and *Practica*. Furthermore this is also the period when Paracelsus came to be seen as the founder of a new religion of two lights, grace and nature, labelled *'Theophrastia Sancta'*. This was a term coined by the Paracelsian/Rosicrucian Tyrolean schoolmaster Adam Haslmayr, who considered the *'Theophrastia'* to be the only true form

---

[13] See below Chapter 4.

of Christianity which had hitherto only been practised in concealment until resurrected by Paracelsus. For Haslmayr it was the 'living
word of God', to be found in 'the inner being' of Man, and far more
important than the 'external characters' or text of the Bible, which
mattered. Rejecting the external vestiges of Christendom, Haslmayr
advocated 'a church of the spirit', while uniting the theology of
Paracelsus with that of Valentin Weigel.[14]

Closely connected to Gilly's chapter are the two chapters by
Hartmut Rudolph and Ute Gause. Rudolph offers an analysis of
Paracelsus's concept of the Eucharist which Paracelsus set out in no
less than twenty separate texts. Considering the importance of the
Eucharist to the theological debate of the Reformation, Paracelsus's
position on this particular topic is of considerable interest, especially
when it is borne in mind that most of his writings on this topic go
back to the early 1530s—the crucial years of the sacramental debate.
Paracelsus rejected the elevation of the Host, using a terminology
identical to reformers such as Bucer, Zwingli, and Oecolampadius;
he also rejected the idea of transformation of the bread and wine,
pointing out that the body and blood of Christ can only be relished
in faith. Bearing in mind that it was the Basle reformer Johannes
Oecolampadius who sponsored Paracelsus's appointment as municipal physician and professor of medicine in Basle in 1527, and that
Oecolampadius was among the first of the South German and Swiss
reformers to adopt a symbolic interpretation of the Lord's Supper,
a subject he wrote on repeatedly, it is hardly surprising that Paracelsus, at least at an early stage of the development of his eucharistic
views, was strongly influenced by the Basle reformer. Furthermore
Oecolampadius appears to have been generally attracted to the views
of spiritualists such as Paracelsus and Caspar Schwenckfeld.[15]

Having identified this proximity to the Swiss Reformation in
Paracelsus's early writings on the Eucharist, Rudolph emphasises the
futility of charting Paracelsus's views within the denominational landscape of the Reformation, instead he points to the significance of
Paracelsus's anthropology which is in evidence not only in his theological works, but throughout his whole *opus*, including his works

---

[14] See below Chapter 7.
[15] For Oecolampadius, see *The Oxford Encyclopedia of the Reformation*, Oxford 1996,
3, 169–71 and K. Hammer, 'Der Reformer Oekolampad, 1482–1531' in H. Oberman
(ed.), *Reformiertes Erbe*, 1, Zurich 1992, 157–170. See also Rupp, *Patterns of Reformation*,
3–46.

on medicine and natural philosophy. These views Rudolph finds in much closer correspondence with the ideas of neo-Platonic Renaissance philosophers such as Ficino and Pico della Mirandola, rather than the theology of reformers such as Bucer and Zwingli. This is, of course, an interpretation which underlines the unity of Paracelsus's whole authorship and brings together his theological writings with his works on natural philosophy under the heading of what Rudolph describes as 'magical dynamism'.[16]

Ute Gause analyses what means Man, according to Paracelsus, had on offer to acquire knowledge about God. Gause points to the two different scholarly traditions in this particular domain. One, interprets Paracelsus as a 'Christian Magus' who thinks knowledge of God can be acquired through his creation—nature—the other, sees him as both a natural philosopher and religious thinker, while denying that knowledge about Christ can be obtained through nature, and emphasises instead the significance of special revelation or grace. She finds support for both approaches in Paracelsus's early theological writings and his *Astronomia magna*, but underlines that 'heavenly magic' or revelation has, in her opinion been overrated by most scholars as a means of gaining knowledge for Paracelsus.[17]

By the late sixteenth century Paracelsianism was no longer a primarily German concern. Hugh Trevor-Roper demonstrates how it came about that Paracelsianism became aligned with French Calvinism and thus helped create a chiliastic Reformed ideology which was so dominant within the Protestant camp during the first phase of the Thirty Years War. Paracelsianism, according to Trevor-Roper, became Protestantised, more by default than because it had any positive Protestant content. The fact that it was rejected as part of the general neo-Platonic, Hermetic philosophy of the Renaissance by the post-Tridentine Catholic Church—Paracelsus's works were put on the Index in 1599—served to make it appealing to Protestants.

Paracelsianism was brought back to France by medical students who had studied at German and Swiss universities. Back in France the Huguenots became the recognised promoters of Paracelsianism, who for political and religious reasons internalised its apocalyptic and millenarian outlook, despite Calvin's hostility to such ideas. As

---

[16] See below Chapter 8.
[17] See below Chapter 9; see also U. Gause, *Paracelsus (1493–1541). Genese und Einfaltung seiner frühen Theologie*, Tübingen 1993.

such it became an important component of international Calvinism
not only during the first phase of the Thirty Years War, but also
during the first two decades of the seventeenth century leading up
to the war.[18] With the defeat of the Elector Palatine in Bohemia in
1620 and the sack of Heidelberg in 1622, the alliance between Calvinism and Paracelsianism was finally broken, even if some millenarian Paracelsians such as Samuel Hartlib and Amos Comenius found
a new home in England during the Civil Wars and Interregnum.
Their religious and political expectations ended in disappointment,
and resulted in what Trevor-Roper terms 'the last act of Paracelsian separation' where chemistry separated itself from the apocalyptic
and religious strait-jacket, in which Paracelsus and his disciples
had locked it.[19]

Not surprisingly the vast amount of Paracelsian publications and
editions which were published in the second half of the sixteenth
century generated a near equivalent number of works deeply hostile
to Paracelsianism. Among the leading exponents of such views were
the Coburg physician, chemist, and schoolmaster, Andreas Libavius.
Libavius's polemical writings against Paracelsianism easily dwarf the
colossal text for which he is best known, the *Alchemia* (1597). Bruce
Moran puts the question why Libavius should have spent a considerable part of his life on a polemic which today strikes us as highly
unproductive. Rather than simply a concern to determine what was
good or bad medicine, Moran suggests, what motivated Libavius in
his writings was his ambition to promote a particular vision of the
world, governed by virtue and upright moral character. Physical
truth, according to Libavius, should be found in causes rather than
in revelation, as claimed by his Paracelsian opponents. This had to
be expressed in a clear and grammatically correct language, as opposed to the hazy and useless language of secrecy used by the Paracelsians. The Paracelsians, on the other hand, condemned Libavius
and those who shared his views, for using a secret language too—
in their case the subtlety of scholastic philosophy. This, however,
was not an argument restricted to the merits of good or bad language, but about who were to control learning—the anti-Paracelsians

---

[18] As pointed out by Carlos Gilly below in Chapter 7 the alliance between
Calvinism in general and millenarian and apocalyptic Paracelsianism in its Rosicrucian form was never as clear cut, in Germany at least, as portrayed by scholars
such as Francis Yates, see her *The Rosicrucian Enlightenment*, London 1972.

[19] See below Chapter 5.

within the academic institutions of the day, or the Paracelsians who could draw on support from within the princely courts where they primarily operated. In other words, what Libavius spent a considerable part of his life on was a defence of traditional academic power and influence against the threatening and undermining tendencies of the Paracelsians who, more often than not, operated within princely courts and thus were much closer to the centres of power.[20]

In the third and final section of this volume, dealing with the philosophical and medical aspects of Paracelsianism, Allen Debus argues for the significance of Paracelsianism and chemical philosophy in the medical and 'scientific' debate of the seventeenth century, as opposed to astronomy and the physics of motion which primarily have come to take centre stage in what has been termed 'the Scientific Revolution'. Debus provides an overview of the diffusion of Paracelsian chemical thought in the sixteenth and early seventeenth centuries. Emphasising its geographical origin in Central Europe, where Paracelsus worked and where his early followers published his manuscripts, Debus like Trevor-Roper points to France as the first place outside its birthplace to demonstrate serious interest in Paracelsianism.[21] It commenced in earnest in the debate over the medicinal qualities of antimony which had been promoted by the Paracelsian physician from Montpellier, Louis de Launay, and eventually declared a poison by the Parisian faculty of Medicine in 1566. The interest in Paracelsian, chemical medicine was then continued by a succession of royal physicians beginning with Roch le Bailif in the 1570s and including the famous Paracelsians Joseph Duchesne and Theodore de Mayerne. They were all vigorously opposed by the conservative, Galenic, Parisian Medical faculty and the extensive debate involving Joseph Duchesne during the first years of the seventeenth century resonated across Europe and caused the energetic anti-Paracelsian Andreas Libavius to treat this conflict in two books. Like Trevor-Roper, Debus emphasises the religious agenda in the debate, conducted as it was primarily between Calvinist Paracelsians and Catholic Galenists.

In England the reception of Paracelsianism was a far more gradual and uncontroversial process. Initially it found strong support among leading surgeons such as John Banister and William Clowes, while

---

[20] See below Chapter 6.
[21] See below Chapters 10 and 5.

in the 1580s it was promoted by Thomas Moffett, a prominent
Fellow of the London College of Physicians. In the early seventeenth
century it found a forceful supporter in Theodore de Mayerne, who
had settled in London and become royal physician to James I following the death of the French king, Henri IV, in 1610. The fact
that England did not possess eminent medical schools such as those
in Paris and Montpellier in the late sixteenth and early seventeenth
centuries goes a long way in explaining the relatively easy ride chemical innovations faced here, especially when it is borne in mind that
the levels of religious tension were no way near to the frictions experienced in France, at least not until the outbreak of the English Civil
War in 1642.

In Spain and Portugal post-Tridentine Catholicism and fear of
Protestantism led Philip II to pursue an isolationist cultural policy.
Books were to be licensed by the Spanish Inquisition, while Spanish
students were ordered to return home from foreign universities with
the exception of a few Italian universities which were considered con-
fessionally sound. This policy guaranteed that Spanish universities
did not keep pace with the rest of Europe. The Spanish *Index* had
already taken note of Paracelsus's heterodoxy as early as 1585 and
in 1632 he was declared a Lutheran and most of his work was out-
lawed. When these policies were finally abandoned in the 1660s it
resulted in a considerable and delayed interest in iatrochemistry in
the late seventeenth century which reflects the concerns of the sixteenth century rather than the Enlightenment.[22]

Finally, Debus shows how Paracelsian chemical medicine influenced
physicians in the Ottoman Empire from around 1640. Numerous
manuscript copies of Ibn Sallum's work *New Chemical Medicine invented
by Paracelsus* (1640) appear to have circulated among Turkish physicians. Paracelsian ideas seem to have been of far greater consequence
within the Ottoman Empire than were the ideas of Copernicus or
the mechanical philosophers. As Debus points out this may well be
explained by the greater emphasis on religion within the Ottoman
Empire of the early modern period. This in turn might well have
benefitted the positive reception of Paracelsianism while hindering
the competing philosophy of the mechanists.

In his chapter on the introduction of Paracelsianism into late sixteenth century Denmark, Ole Peter Grell assesses the role and signi-

---

[22] See below Chapter 10.

ficance of the highly influential work, *Idea medicinæ*, by the Paracelsian Peter Severinus, the Dane. Severinus's highly eclectic variety of Paracelsianism is seen as a deeply urbane, Hippocratized variant which proved acceptable to both lay and ecclesiastical powers in the age of confessionalism. Both the writing and life and career of Peter Severinus differed dramatically from that of Paracelsus. In its Severinian form Paracelsianism was transformed into a non-confrontational correction to Galenic medicine with most, if not all heterodox religious aspects removed. The subsequent professors of medicine at the University of Copenhagen, Caspar Bartholin and Ole Worm, in the main continued to espouse and teach a Severinian type of Paracelsianism and Worm made sure that it remained untainted by the dangers of religious heterodoxy inherent in early seventeenth century Rosicrucianism.[23]

John Christie deals with 'the Paracelsian body', focussing upon the body of the early modern practitioner and its agency in chemical practice. As such it is the actual activities in the Paracelsian laboratory, rather than the results, which Christie draws attention to, and which have tended to be forgotten or marginalized in historical writings. He emphasises that there is no single Paracelsian body, but a plethora of bodies, in some cases split according to gender and 'according to a male over female hierarchy'.[24]

Christie reminds us that it is important to remember that Paracelsians in their alchemical experiments needed a sophisticated sensory approach where the role of smell, taste and colour were of the highest significance. Here time was of the essence in affecting the physical or bodily activity in the laboratory, not to mention the successful outcome of any experiment. In this context it is noteworthy that Paracelsus and his followers adopted popular contemporary concepts such as prophetic, eschatological and Providential time. Thus, Paracelsus considered the successful coming together of physician and patient as totally dependent on Providence, without which no healing could be successful.

Apart from being temporal the Paracelsian body was also itinerant not only in geographical but also in social and political terms.

---

[23] See below Chapter 11; see also O.P. Grell, 'The Reception of Paracelsianism in Early Modern Denmark: from Peter Severinus, the Dane to Ole Worm', *Medical History*, 1995, 39, 78–94.
[24] See below Chapter 12.

It gradually moved from the margins of society, away from the high-ways and the inns, where it had threatened vested interests, to the princely courts, where it found protection from those who in turn wanted rid of it. Furthermore, the Paracelsian body was dirty and sweaty as a result of its hard manual work with furnaces and flasks. As opposed to the sterile and unproductive activities of the Aristotelian scholars within the universities, the alchemical body was both skill-ful and productive, producing new medicine for the benefit of Man.[25]

Paracelsus called the archeus of the stomach, which served to separate nutrition from poison, the 'alchemist within'. His ideas proved highly influential on the development of digestion theory in the seventeenth century. In his chapter on 'the Paracelsian Kitchen' Francis McKee looks at how such theories played a role in the chang-ing world of the seventeenth century kitchen. Citing some of the emblems from the Paracelsian physician Michael Maier's work *Atalanta Fugiens*, McKee emphasises how domestic, everyday work such as washing and cooking fish were used as models by the Paracelsian natural philosophers and alchemists. In conjunction with the dev-elopment of digestion theory among Paracelsian physicians such as Maier, Sir Kenelm Digby, and Jan Baptist van Helmont, a new literary genre—the cookery book—developed. Based on La Varenne's influential cookery book *La Cuisinier Français*, McKee points to major changes in continental cookery in the first half of the seventeenth century: the arrival of boullion and sauces being added to dishes, innovations which may well have resulted from the debate about chemical philosophy and the process of digestion.

Two of the most influential cookery books published in England in the early seventeenth century were published by the Paracelsians Hugh Plat and Gervase Markham. In many of the English cookery books of this period, which were all aimed at women in charge of large households, the distinction between diet and disease was blurred, and they accordingly contained substantial sections on cures and included numerous medical receipts. McKee draws attention to the fact that elaborate distillations for both domestic and medical pur-poses were emphasised by Paracelsian cookery writers in particular.[26]

Rather than seeing Paracelsus as a precursor of psychosomatic me-

---

[25] *Ibid.*
[26] See below Chapter 13.

dicine Heinz Schott takes the opposite view, namely that modern psychosomatic medicine in a secularized form reflects much of the occult, magic and religious content of Paracelsus's writings. Paracelsus's views on the role of magnetism and imagination in what he himself termed 'the invisible diseases' were fairly common ideas in the early sixteenth century and are, as already stressed by Walter Pagel, proof of the influence on Paracelsus of the neo-Platonic ideas of Ficino and Pico della Mirandola. Schott, however, is of the opinion that the influence of the cabbala on Paracelsus's thinking on these subjects has been underemphasised.[27] For Paracelsus the attractive power of the magnet is a symbol of, and metaphor for, the power of imagination. He is also unique in his emphasis on the power of the magnet and the significance of magnetic healing as part of natural magic. For three hundred years after his death imagination and magnetism continued to be major topics of interest for natural philosophers. Increasingly imagination came to be seen as deeply significant for psychosomatic interaction, while magnetism, however, gradually· came to be considered more of a natural law. Despite the fact that Mesmerism with its 'animal magnetism' was not inspired by Paracelsian ideas, it eventually linked up with such concepts when it became part of the Romantic Revival in the early nineteenth century. The role of faith and 'invisible powers' in healing has, in other words, retained its prominence within medicine despite the dominance of science from the late nineteenth century onwards, and much of what Paracelsus wrote about imagination and magnetism remains with us in one form or another.[28]

This volume, revisionist as it is, does not resolve the enigma of Paracelsus or fully explain the peculiar popularity of Paracelsianism through the ages. Much remains to be done, even if some important historiographical steps have been taken in the first section of this volume. The other two sections offer important insight into particular aspects of Paracelsus's ideas and the effects of Paracelsianism in its particular historical settings, emphasising its fluidity and often contradictionary nature. It is somewhat bizarre that when Paracelsian ideas finally won through towards the end of the sixteenth century it was within the princely courts so despised by Paracelsus. In effect

---

[27] For this see Raphael Patai, *The Jewish Alchemist*, Princeton 1994, especially parts six to eight.
[28] See below Chapter 14.

the natural philosophy of an outsider and anti-establishment character had by then been annexed by the establishment. What was
intended for the benefit of the common man came to serve the privileged. However, it still remains an open question how Paracelsian
this often sanitised Paracelsianism was.

PART ONE

THE HISTORICAL PARACELSUS

CHAPTER ONE

THE SPAGYRIC ART; OR, THE IMPOSSIBLE WORK OF SEPARATING PURE FROM IMPURE PARACELSIANISM: A HISTORIOGRAPHICAL ANALYSIS

Stephen Pumfrey

I   Liber prologi in vitam beatam:[1] *introduction*

The vitality of Paracelsianism within the mainstream of the Scientific Revolution has become an established orthodoxy. The current state of scholarship has more than answered George Sarton's 1955 request for such histories. No longer dying on the margins as mystical pseudo-science, Paracelsianism is now, thanks largely to the work of Walter Pagel and Allen Debus, the confident living subject of studies, such as are in this volume, of its growth and transformation.[2]

Recent monographs have certainly expanded the sphere of its influence. To Lindroth's Swedish Paracelsians, we can now add the Poles studied by Hubicki. Bruce Moran's very recent publications have anatomised German courtly networks, and Jole Shackelford has found Danish ones. We might expect Catholic lands where the Inquisition was powerful to be infertile territory but, while Iberia still seems to be so, Giancarlo Zanier has contended that 'contrary to widespread belief, *Italian* Paracelsianism was not a phenomenon limited to a few virtuosi.' The most recent research by Debus has even found Islamic discussions of Paracelsianism.[3]

---

[1] The Latin subheadings are only allusions to Paracelsian works and terms. No more direct relevance is implied.

[2] For Sarton's agenda-setting, see Allen G. Debus, *The English Paracelsians* New York 1965, Preface, 9. The seminal work in English for modern Paracelsian studies was, of course, Walter Pagel, *Paracelsus. An Introduction to Philosophical Medicine in the Era of the Renaissance*, Basel 1958. The extent and importance of Paracelsian influences in the Scientific Revolution have been established beyond doubt in the magisterial Allen G. Debus, *The Chemical Philosophy. Paracelsian Science and Medicine in the sixteenth and seventeenth Centuries*, 2 volumes, London 1972. The 1993 Glasgow symposium at which this chapter was presented was called, of course, 'The Transformation of Paracelsianism 1500–1800; Alchemy, Chemistry and Medicine'.

[3] Sten Lindroth, *Paracelsismen i Sverige till 1600-tallets mitt*. Lychnos Bibliotek, no. 7,

It is, perhaps, time to reassess what was this Paracelsianism which historians consider was transformed, and why it was transformed. This chapter begins with a critical review of recent, largely Anglophonic historiography. It concludes from the review that Paracelsianism has acquired a loose extension, in some cases too loose to perform useful analytical work. It suggests that this is because the sixteenth and seventeenth century actors themselves routinely used the label 'Paracelsian' as a marginalising term for dangerous philosophy and philosophers. This allows us to look more closely at the concerns (religious, intellectual and social) that were raised by the popularity of 'Paracelsian' chemical philosophy, and finally to draw conclusions about some of the factors, which we will insist were ideological, that controlled its transformation in the early modern period.

Given Paracelsus's reputation as a religious, political and intellectual radical, and (thanks to Oporinus)[4] as an immoral drunkard, it is not surprising that few writers acknowledged him as their master. This means that Paracelsianism is largely an historians' construct, an influence or evolving tradition loosely based on Paracelsus's innovations, which we deploy to make sense of an eclectic, otherwise chaotic period in the history of science and medicine. Whilst that does not mean, of course, that it is a mere invention, students of the recent historiography can be forgiven for feeling confused about questions such as: what was Paracelsianism? or, what were the defining features of a Paracelsian? The confusion only deepens when we turn back for answers from historians to contemporaries.

Uppsala 1943; Wlodimierz Hubicki, 'Paracelsists in Poland', in Allen G. Debus, *Science, Medicine and Society in the Renaissance: Essays to honour Walter Pagel*, 2 vols. London 1972, vol. I, 167–176; Bruce T. Moran, 'Court Authority and Chemical Medicine: Moritz of Hessen, Johannes Hartmann, and the Origins of Academic Chemiatria', *Bull. Hist. Med.*, 63, 1989: 253–274; Bruce T. Moran, 'Prince-practitioning and the Direction of Medical Roles at the German Court: Maurice of Hesse-Kassel and his physicians', in Vivian Nutton (ed.), *Medicine at the courts of Europe, 1500–1837*, London 1990, 95–116; Jole Shackelford, 'Paracelsianism and Patronage in Early Modern Denmark', in Bruce T. Moran (ed.), *Patronage and Institutions: Science, Technology and Medicine at the European Court, 1500–1750*, New York 1991, 85–110; Giancarlo Zanier, 'La Medicina Paracelsiana in Italia: Aspetti di un'accoglienza particolare', in *Rivista di storia della filosofia*, 4, 1985, 627–653. Quotation from 627; For Islam, see Debus Chapter 10 below.

[4] For Oporinus's calumnies, see Pagel, Paracelsus, 30.

II Tria prima: *three historiographical Paracelsianisms*

a. *The follower*

Reviewing the scholarship of recent decades shows historians using three overlapping orders of Paracelsian, each of which carries a different conception of his transformation. In the first place, historians of science and medicine have often used it in a literal sense to suggest a follower of Paracelsus. This relies on the simplistic concept of the influence of great men and their works, and is thus less frequent today. Nevertheless it is apparently justified by contemporary references to a Paracelsian sect or, as Johann Weyer wrote, the 'Paracelsist school (for that is what they want to be called)'.[5] The usage implies that there was an essential core of Paracelsian concepts and practices. Paracelsians are therefore located according to their conformity to the core doctrines (although commentators have always found it difficult to agree about what these were).[6] It permits the identification of species such as the semi-Paracelsian. Graham Rees has argued that Francis Bacon was a semi-Paracelsian, because his cosmology was 'de-deified' thereby 'stripping Paracelsian cosmogony from its Biblical and metaphysical roots'.[7] Similarly, because J.-B. Van Helmont is considered to have made Paracelsianism more acceptable to mainstream 'new philosophers' such as Robert Boyle, by shaving it of some mysticism and supplementing it with experiment, he is considered a 'moderate' or 'ambivalent' Paracelsian.[8]

---

[5] Johann Weyer, *Witches, Devils and Doctors in the Renaissance: Johann Weyer, De Praestigiis daemonum*. Transl. John Shea. In *Medieval and Renaissance Texts*, vol. LXXIII, Binghampton, N.Y. 1991, 154; for problems with the concept of historical influence, see Quentin Skinner, 'Meaning and Understanding in the History of Ideas', *History and Theory*, 8, 1969, 3–52.

[6] This paper primarily discusses problems raised by current historiography, but the problem existed *ab initio* because of the problematic corpus of Paracelsian texts. As is well known, few were published in Paracelsus's lifetime, and scholars are still divided over which of the later sixteenth-century texts are pseudo-Paracelsian records or works by early adherents. Furthermore, editors 'improved' the coherence of Paracelsus's writings, which were often incomplete and contradictory. It is therefore unavoidable partially to select the 'central doctrines' of an author described by Owsei Temkin as 'the elusive Paracelsus'. See Pagel, Paracelsus, 90f. As Andrew Cunningham shows in Chapter 2 below, readers reliant upon modern selections and translations have to be doubly vigilant.

[7] Graham Rees, 'Francis Bacon's Semi-Paracelsian-Cosmology', *Ambix*, 22, 1975, 81–101. Quotations from 101.

[8] See for example W. Pagel, 'Van Helmont's Concept of Disease—To Be or not

Our first meaning, then, prepares us to recognise an interpenetration of heterodox Paracelsianism with the more sober aspects of the Scientific Revolution, but also prepares us to see a core which, in the seventeenth century, half-hearted and moderate disciples dilute and displace. The transformation thus conceived is one fundamentally of decline.

It is true that much of the religious symbolism, mystical occultism, arcane language and more extraordinary claims of some sixteenth-century Paracelsians became less evident in the seventeenth century, as perspectives and practices which they had advocated were developed by later writers who resisted the label 'Paracelsian'. Thus, whilst contemporaries used the first, essentialist meaning (as we saw), it has proved too strict to be useful in capturing the historical significance of developments in Paracelsian natural philosophy. Allen Debus in particular has led the way in identifying that significance (retrospectively, but legitimately) to lie in the establishment of a tradition of 'chemical philosophy'—i.e. the belief that many natural phenomena are produced by irreducibly chemical causes or principles, and which require (al-)chemical analysis to be understood.

b. *The chemical philosopher*

Thus a second order broadens the term to equate Paracelsians with 'chemical philosophers'. Debus's monumental two volume work, *The Chemical Philosophy*, definitively laid out the chief agents, works, ideas and techniques of this tradition. But great caution is needed before accepting the extension, as some recent studies of Paracelsianism have clearly done.[9] Are chemical philosophers the same as Paracelsians? On the one hand, yes: the subtitle of Debus's *opus magnum* is, after all 'Paracelsian Science and Medicine in the sixteenth and seventeenth Centuries'. Furthermore, its personnel are largely those who have appeared in his preceding *English Paracelsians* and the subsequent *French Paracelsians*.[10] On the other hand, no: because non-

---

to Be? The Influence of Paracelsus', *Bull. Hist. Med.*, 46, 1972, 419–454, esp. 438. For a recent study of the influence of Helmont on English science, see Antonio Clericuzio, 'Robert Boyle and the English Helmontians', in Z.R.W.M. von Martels, *Alchemy Revisited: proceedings of the international conference on the history of alchemy in the University of Groningen, 17–19 April 1989*, Leiden, no date, 192–199.

[9] See, for example, the studies of Hubicki and Zanier, 'Medicina Paracelsiana'.

[10] Debus, *English Paracelsians*; Allen G. Debus, *The French Paracelsians: the chemical challenge to medical and scientific tradition in early modern France*, Cambridge 1991.

Paracelsians, drawing on Arabic and scholastic Aristotelian traditions, metal-working, vulgar alchemy, mechanical philosophy and even Galenic physic, can now be enrolled by historians as chemical philosophers, on the basis of a non-Paracelsian interest in chemical principles or (a commonly used sign) chemical medicines and analysis. This results in a much less cosmosophical but still very plastic usage. It permits us to construct an historically significant 'transformation of Paracelsianism', from Paracelsus himself, through both sides of arch-antagonisms such as that between Libavius and Croll, or between van Helmont and Fludd,[11] and on to Boyle and Georg Stahl. It therefore also legitimates the conclusion that Paracelsian ideas and practices developed as an integral part of any 'scientific revolution'. We might deem this broadened usage more helpful to an understanding of the *longue durée*, but does it lead to a more useful understanding of Paracelsianism?

c. *The iatrochemist*

A third, and final order of Paracelsians can be discerned in the literature, which differs from the second in that it does not demand of its members *any* obvious philosophical commitment. Many studies of early modern Paracelsianism focus on iatrochemistry as the key area of growth and debate. Here the touchstone of Paracelsians is their use, development or defence of chemical remedies. As with the previous two usages, this has justification if we accept that chemical medicines were Paracelsus's enduring legacy. The iatrochemical test generates a third set of Paracelsians, differing from the second because the chemical *philosopher* must be assumed to have had a distinctive world-view, differentiating him from a mechanical, magnetic, Hermetic or peripatetic philosopher and from the unlearned. For him, natural processes had to be understood not mechanically or formally but chemically, through ontological principles (such as the *tria prima* or *semina*) which were not operationally reducible to those of other philosophies. One would expect such chemical *philosophers*

---

[11] For Libavius and Croll see Robert Multhauf, 'Medical Chemistry and "The Paracelsians"', in *Bull. Hist. Med.*, 28, 1954, 101–25, and his 'The Significance of Distillation in Renaissance Medical Chemistry', in *Bull. Hist. Med.*, 30, 1956, 327–345, esp. 343–5; for van Helmont and Fludd see Allen G. Debus, *The chemical philosophy: Paracelsian science and medicine in the sixteenth and seventeenth centuries*, 2 vols.: New York 1977, vol. 1, chs. 4, 5.

to echo Daniel Duncan who, writing in 1683, argued that chemistry was *not* an *art*, because, far from being contrary to nature, nature herself operated chemically.[12] By contrast, our third order of Paracelsians explicitly enrols all those prepared 'to take good medicines from anywhere',[13] irrespective of what they believed about any *modus operandi*. As we shall see, this included Galenists and others who violently denounced the chemical philosophies which had originally provided explanations. By ignoring debates of medical philosophy, and by sticking to pharmaceutical practices, which undeniably increased in popularity, our third usage creates not so much a transformation of Paracelsianism but its imperial advance from the margin to the mainstream.

One cannot deny that these three conceptions of Paracelsianism achieve their historical purposes in constructing, respectively, a continuing influence, an emerging discipline and a replicated practice. Although we have emphasised the differences, historians have tended to conflate the concepts, to inflate the numbers, and hence to deflate the analytical currency, with a resulting confusion about how contemporaries understood the school of Paracelsianism. Its dormitory certainly now houses some odd bedfellows. Between the historian's sheets we find coupled together quack healers and court physicians, moderate Galenists and mystical Fluddeans. Thereby covered up are the philosophical, ideological and social differences which often provide telling insights into the transforming boundaries of early modern science and medicine.

It may be instructive at this point to draw a parallel with the historiographical fate of the related 'Hermetic tradition'. Frances Yates's identification of Hermeticism and Allen Debus's of Paracelsianism as ignored, 'pre-scientific' yet significant factors in the evolution of early modern science were simultaneous and much-needed challenges in the 1960s to an unduly positivist history. By the 1970s allegedly Hermetic influences had been detected in many quarters, from well-known occultists like John Dee to heroes of the Scientific Revolution such as William Gilbert and Francis Bacon. The grounds for such detections varied from evidence of a close reading of the *Hermetica*, through the mere mention of Hermetic *prisci theologii* such as Orpheus, to a vague similarity between a natural philosopher's practice and

---

[12] Debus, *French Paracelsians*, 135.
[13] Debus, *English Paracelsians*, 70.

aspects of Hermetic writings.[14] This promiscuity has led Brian Copenhaver to his cogent critique. He reproves recent scholars for equat-
ing Hermeticism with what he will have us call simply occultism,
and he shows how much so-called Hermeticism is actually an eclectic Neoplatonism. Whilst this might seem from our chronological distance to be scholastic quibbling, it has important implications for
historical understanding. Copenhaver is surely right to conclude by
denying that 'our modern conceptions of Hermetism have yet become
clear and stable enough to guide us reliably through the thickets of
seventeenth-century controversy.'[15]

From our survey of recent historians' conceptions of Paracelsianism,
we might suspect that the same can be said for them. As we shall
see, conceptions based on the prescription of chemical remedies and
even on a commitment to chemical principles have the unfortunate
consequence of guiding us away from, rather than through the most
significant thickets of controversy. Furthermore, they do not prove to
be clear and stable.

III   Mysterium Magnum: *the historically invisible Paracelsian*

In our search for those more stable categories through which to
understand early modern Paracelsian controversies, an attractive strategy is the recovery of contemporary deployments of the terms. This
approach superficially offers a more reliable fourth order of Paracelsians, but in fact produces the reverse of a stable conception. The
records are full of claimed sightings (or rather accusations) of Paracelsianism, and descriptions of the beliefs and practices of Paracelsians,
but these were generally resisted or denied by their targets. There
were, in fact, very few professing Paracelsians.

It has been said that attempts to make a 'distinction between true
and false Paracelsians [were] a familiar theme in the [seventeenth]
century.'[16] These attempts give us a good entrée to our review. In
1610 Francis Anthony, who has been portrayed as a Paracelsian of

---

[14] For an example of loose usage, see Peter J. French, *John Dee. The World of an
Elizabethan Magus*, London 1972, ch. 4.
[15] Brian P. Copenhaver, 'Natural magic, hermetism and occultism in early modern science', in David C. Lindberg and Robert S. Westman (eds.), *Reappraisals of
the Scientific Revolution*, Cambridge 1990, 261–301. Quotation from 288.
[16] Debus, *English Paracelsians*, 141.

the first order[17] was attacked by the English college of Physicians'
censor, Matthew Gwinne, a Paracelsian of the third order. Gwinne
distinguished between 'chemiatri' or 'Galeno-Chymici', whom he
approved, and 'chymici'—false doctors like Anthony. In a later list
Gwinne anatomised his chymici into 'Mountebanks, Empiricks, quack-
salvers, [and] Paracelsians (as they call themselves)'.[18] For these and
many other English physicians, Paracelsians (there were no good
ones) were chemical artists with dangerous, unfounded claims to expertise in physic.

Similar attacks on Paracelsians were made throughout Europe,
and Gwinne probably derived his categories from Libavius. In an
early work Libavius called all Paracelsians chemical impostors: 'The
Paracelsian profession will be philosophical when whores are chaste
virgins and sophisms are indubitable truth itself'.[19] But who are
Libavius's Paracelsians? Problems arise when we turn to those whom
Libavius approved. Hannaway noted the paradox that Libavius detested Paracelsians, and yet defended the Huguenot physicians to
the French court, Duchesne and Mayerne, when they were opposed
by the Galenists of the Sorbonne medical faculty.[20] Duchesne and
Mayerne are of course central members of historians' Paracelsian
traditions, however defined. But, by 1606, when Libavius intervened
in the Paris dispute, he had a more complex set of categories. There
were Galenists, Chemiatri and Paracelsians. Chemiatri (who are not
Paracelsians) are further divided into the good and the bad. The
good are undisruptive compromisers between old and new medical
practices, who number Avicenna and Arnold of Villanova among
their esteemed predecessors. Bad chemiatri (and Libavius is thinking
of Oswald Croll) pursue the novelties of occult, spiritual philosophy,
which, while they present it as (and perhaps believe it to be) a syn-
cresis of all medical wisdom, actually subverts the discipline. The
third class, of Paracelsians, are irredeemable—deluded, absurd and
cacomagical. So Duchesne escapes as a good chemiatrus, Croll is
reproved as a bad one, but Libavius presents neither of these key
chemical philosophers, nor himself (of course) as a Paracelsian.

---

[17] Debus, English Paracelsians, 142, notes that he was '[a] self-styled Paracelsian'.
[18] Debus, English Paracelsians, 143–5.
[19] Quoted in Owen Hannaway, The Chemists and the Word: The Didactic Origins of
Chemistry, London 1975, 91 n. 60.
[20] Ibid., 82.

If we have listened too long to quasi-'Paracelsians' of the conservative, compromising sort who upheld the medical establishment, we should turn to central actors like Duchesne and Van Helmont. Duchesne is a prime candidate for the historians' first category, the follower, and yet he still denied that he was a Paracelsian: Paracelsians were 'common chemists' who 'have no philosophy'—a recurring charge that provides a key to the disputes.[21] Van Helmont is similar, admitting an admiration of Paracelsus whilst remarking that it was his enemies who consigned him to the school of Paracelsians.[22]

It is not surprising to find many learned critics making Duchesne's charge that 'Paracelsians' were dangerous healers and writers because they were insufficiently 'philosophical'. Certainly, as Kocher showed for England, some unschooled irregulars adopted the name to aggrandise their popular remedies.[23] But we have not, regrettably, arrived at a stable conception simply through the elimination, as 'quacks', of bad Paracelsians. Given Paracelsus's own denunciation of book-learned philosophy and his valorisation of 'experience' (both attitudes that supported the empirics), it was inevitable that some sympathetic and respected chemical philosophers responded to the occultist intellectualising of a Croll or a Duchesne by making too much philosophy the sign of a Paracelsian. One such was the 'Paracelsian' founder, with official patronage, of the Jardin des Plantes, Guy de la Brosse. According to Guerlac's study, de la Brosse 'expresses a cautious respect for Paracelsus', but 'deals harshly with those other followers of Paracelsus he enumerates': Croll, Duchesne, Gerard Dorn and others including, incredibly, Libavius. They are 'Souffleurs', a sect afflicting medicine who 'take Paracelsus as their patron and call themselves "Paracelcistes."' His main criticism was that 'most [Paracelsists] have entered the shop of this artist [Paracelsus] without ever stoking the furnace', and immediately begin to speculate, writing books which are 'well received by contemplative and lazy persons

---

[21] Duchesne produced a typically 'Paracelsian' spagyric commentary on Genesis, believed in the *tria prima* and adopted a characteristically iatrochemical medical practice. For this, and his view on Paracelsians, see Debus, *Chemical Philosophy*, vol. II, ch. 5, esp. 306, 318.

[22] *Ibid.*, 310.

[23] Paul H. Kocher, 'Paracelsian Medicine in England: the First Thirty Years (ca. 1570–1600)', *J. Hist. Med.*, 2, 1947, 451–480. For a discussion of Paracelsianism which assumes the easy identification of quackery, see L.R.C. Agnew, 'Quackery', in Allen G. Debus (ed.), *Medicine in seventeenth-century England*, London 1974, 313–325.

who cite them as authorities.'[24] Thus, while de la Brosse is more like the practically oriented *chymicus* whom physicians and court occultists alike branded as Paracelsian, he names just those systematisers as the true, and truly dangerous Paracelsians.

Before 1650 most philosophers treated as suspicious if not dangerous any philosophy which dismissed the superior learning of the ancients, and they preferred the authority of tradition over the genuinely new. Paracelsus emphatically broke with tradition, and yet learned chemical philosophers resisted charges that they encouraged such a dangerous break by re-describing themselves (and even Paracelsus himself) not as a new school, but as bearers of an ancient wisdom. Jacques Gohory was one of the earliest exponents of this strategy.[25] In England Robert Bostocke neutralised Paracelsus's rejection of learned elites in general by presenting his Paracelsianism as the pre-Galenic 'Auncient Phisicke'.[26] Later Duchesne, like Croll before him, denied that there could be a school of Paracelsus because, insofar as Paracelsus was valuable, he was an *adeptus* who had only revived an ancient philosophy.[27] To these difficult cases we could add Michael Maier, Robert Fludd and many others.

It is perhaps significant that most of the above were not primarily professional doctors, but non-scholastic natural philosophers associated with Protestant court circles. They were a group marked by their eclecticism, and it is their wide-ranging interests in occult philosophy which makes problematic their mobilisation within a Paracelsian tradition. One solution is to describe them, as Owen Hannaway described Croll, as Hermetic Paracelsians, or Paracelsian Hermetics.[28] But when we recall Copenhaver's critique of Hermeticism, it would seem that to avoid our problem by recourse to a sub-group of Hermetic Paracelsians is to find ourselves in a deeper hole. Just as Copenhaver disputed Westfall's wisdom in calling Henry More a Hermetic, when More endorsed Casaubon's exposure of the

---

[24] Henri Guerlac, 'Guy de la Brosse and the French Paracelsians', in Allen G. Debus (ed.), *Science, Medicine and Society in the Renaissance: essays to honour Walter Pagel*, 2 vols.: London 1972, vol. I, ch. 16. Quotations from 187, 186.

[25] Debus, *Chemical Philosophy*, 146.

[26] *The Difference between the Auncient Phisicke, first taught by the godly forefathers, consisting in unitie, peace and concord; and the latter Phisicke proceeding from idolators, ethnickes and heathen: as Gallen and such other . . . By R.B. Esq.*, London 1585. The British Library catalogue adds '[i.e. Robert Bostock]'.

[27] For Duchesne, see Debus, *French Paracelsians*, 57; for Croll see Hannaway, *Chemists and the Word*, 5.

[28] Hannaway, *Chemists and the Word*, 56.

Hermetic corpus,[29] so we should worry about the contradiction between historians' alacrity in identifying actors as Paracelsians and the same actors' vigorous denials.

We are forced to conclude that a search for stable criteria for a fourth order of Paracelsians, built out of contemporary perceptions, fails. In early modern Europe Paracelsians, like cannibals, savages and other demonised categories, seemingly lived over the hills. This is not to say that there was no agreement at all. At one end of a spectrum of monstrous Paracelsians, the unlearned druggist was reviled by strict Galenist and chemical philosopher alike, and for similar reasons. At the other end lay the fanciful elaborator of Paracelsian cosmosophy, but apparent agreement here concealed deep differences. For the Galenist, as later for the mechanist, *any* talk of microcosms or *archei* was dangerous nonsense, whereas the chemical philosophers each winnowed their particular wheat from Paracelsian chaff. Thus Paracelsianism functioned as a labile category of otherness, everywhere on the increase and threatening the intellectual order. It did so either because of its subversive philosophy or, when it suited, its lack of philosophy. In each case, the critic of Paracelsianism, whether a 'Paracelsian' or not, was anxious to show that his philosophy was the safe and necessary one.

Res ipsa?: *an empty set of Paracelsians?*

Any concept of Paracelsianism, then, is going to be manufactured, its tradition of Paracelsians constructed, and its members selected by the historian. In this case the conclusion is more than a banal truism of historiography: it reflects the fact that the actual historical set of professing Paracelsians is largely an empty set. This is not always the case: we easily identify members of the sets of Galenists, of mechanical or experimental philosophers, or of Catholics and Calvinists— because these are professed categories of identification. We cannot so easily identify early modern quacks, witches, atheists, puritans—and Paracelsians—because these are ascribed categories of marginalisation.

Even when we move from general historiographies to excellent fine-structured studies of Paracelsians, the problem remains of identifying groups using labels which were primarily deployed by enemies. Here we can consider Charles Webster's article 'Alchemical

---

[29] Copenhaver, *Natural Magic*, 288.

and Paracelsian medicine'.[30] He wished to broaden Debus' focus upon English physicians, which suggested that in England our third, pragmatic kind of Paracelsian preponderated. Webster contended that 'the vernacular medical literature [gives] as little insight into the degree of interest in the medical philosophy of Paracelsus as they would into the level of understanding of Aristotle'.[31] He found both erudite and mechanical Paracelsianism 'incubated' by a 'wider alchemical movement', as it was in central Europe. Clearly one cause of this disagreement was what counts as Paracelsianism, and hence where to look for it and how 'philosophical' it was.

Webster's later monumental study of early seventeenth-century English Paracelsians,[32] despite its careful attention to specific meanings and contexts, has itself been criticised for reasons which relate to our problem. In 1989 Peter Elmer identified English Paracelsians in a way which explicitly differed from both Debus and, in particular, Webster.[33] Elmer defines them by their 'tendency . . . to conflate religious and medical concerns' by 'investigat[ing] medical phenomena which might be associated with the operation and function of the soul', through 'an ecstatic communion . . . between man and nature', indeed a democratic, learned ignorance.[34] These religious ideologists are very like one of Webster's puritan groups but, crucially for Elmer, they are sectaries not puritans because for Elmer puritans upheld, along with Anglicans, a lack of concern with Galen's paganism, a respect for professional medical hierarchies, and traditional separation of the sciences from theology. Elmer concludes that what he sees as Webster's "Puritan-science" hypothesis remains largely unproven'.[35]

Here we have not one but two terms, Paracelsian and puritan, which were largely used by contemporaries for marginalisation but which, when given positive membership by historians, produce different

---

[30] In Charles Webster (ed.), *Health, medicine and mortality in the sixteenth century*, Cambridge 1979, 301–334.

[31] *Ibid.*, 320.

[32] Charles Webster, *The Great Instauration: Science, Medicine and Reform. 1626–1660*, London 1975.

[33] Peter Elmer, 'Medicine, Religion and the Puritan Revolution', in Roger French and Andrew Wear (eds.), *The Medical Revolution of the Seventeenth Century*, Cambridge 1989, ch. 1.

[34] *Ibid.*, 17, 28. He further characterises them, 20, 25, as democratisers of knowledge, and 'iatrochemists who prided themselves on their learned ignorance', for many of whom book-learning was abhorrent.

[35] *Ibid.*, 17, 31, 45.

accounts of the origins of modern science. This is not to say that historians should desist from such attempts. How else can we work? But it is to say that one must be aware of how particularly constructed is a category, tradition or influence such as Paracelsianism, and to insist that no unproblematic account can be given of 'the transformation of Paracelsianism'.

IV *Preliminary conclusions*

We can draw three conclusions from this analysis of usage. First, after thirty years of scholarship Paracelsianism, like Hermeticism, seems ripe for re-assessing, and specifically for anatomising. We must be more attentive to the historical work which the concept and label performed, although we cannot hope to find one clear usage. Our first order, of Paracelsians committed to a doctrinal core, will not survive as the equivalent of Copenhaver's clarified Hermeticists. There are neither sufficient numbers, nor sufficient agreement about core Paracelsian doctrines.[36]

Secondly, there are good reasons for dissolving also our third order of pragmatic de-ideologised iatrochemists. This category might, tautologically, be used to chart the extent of use of chemical medicines, but Paracelsianism should not be reduced to mere practice. Hannaway considers that such reductionism was the flaw in Robert Multhauf's study of Croll. It divorced Croll's practice 'from its supposedly Paracelsian ideology', so that 'in these purely practical terms Multhauf sees Libavius as an ally of Croll'.[37] If, as we have suggested, philosophical and ideological concerns crucially determined many of the responses to Paracelsianism, then the third order cannot guide us through thickets of controversy which it does not even recognise.

The third conclusion is a suggestion that we make a virtue out of a necessity, and focus on the agonistic field in which the label Paracelsian was demonologised and resisted. We might explore parallels with recent histories of atheism and other largely empty sets of otherness such as witchcraft.[38] Just as contemporary anti-atheistic

---

[36] See the discussion in n. 6 above.

[37] Hannaway, *Chemists and the Word*, 69, 82. Hannaway's reservations refer to the works of Multhauf cited in n. 11.

[38] On 'atheism' see Michael Hunter and David Wootton (eds.), *Atheism from the Reformation to the Enlightenment*, Oxford 1992; on witchcraft see Brian Levack, *The witch-hunt in Early Modern Europe*, London 1987, ch. 2.

discourse tells us little about 'real' early modern atheists (of whom there were few if any),[39] but provides instead a mirror to fears of threats to moral order, so might we use a history of Paracelsianism, real and imagined, to perform a similar function in the narrower field of natural philosophy.

V Medicina philosophica: *reinstating ideologies of knowledge to the history of Paracelsianism*

The third conclusion points again to a need to emphasise the philosophical, religious and ideological debates which Paracelsianism occasioned. One obvious objection to such an emphasis is that this is to see ideology where contemporaries saw only effective and ineffective medicine. The objection has most force in the case of English iatrochemists, whom Debus famously argued were compromisers. 'The great majority of English physicians ... readily accepted those of the new remedies which proved their worth, but few concerned themselves with the deeper and more occult aspects of Paracelsian thought.'[40] Leaving aside Webster's observations that Debus's group of medical men does not exhaust English interest in Paracelsianism, let us agree that its members showed a practical acceptance, but let us ask what kind of acceptance that was.

The question has to be answered in the context of efforts among early modern physicians to secure their position and status. We know that physicians throughout Europe were concerned about the advance, within an expanding medical marketplace, of irregular and unorthodox healers, many of whom were identified as 'Paracelsians'. Recent articles by Harold Cook and John Henry have reminded us that physicians defended their position at the top of the hierarchy by invoking philosophical criteria. Central to the physician's understanding of his role was his training in natural philosophy.[41] Even

---

[39] Indeed Febvre's influential view was that there could be no proper history of irreligion before the late seventeenth century. See Lucien Febvre, 'Aux origines de l'esprit moderne: Libertinisme, naturalisme, mécanisme', in his *Au coeur religieux du XVIe siècle*, Paris 1957, 337–58. For a discussion of this strong thesis of the empty set of atheism, see Wootton in Hunter and Wootton, *Atheism*, 16–17.

[40] Debus, *The English Paracelsians*, 80.

[41] Harold J. Cook, 'The new philosophy and medicine in seventeenth-century England', in David C. Lindberg and Robert S. Westman, *Reappraisals of the Scientific Revolution*, Cambridge 1990; John Henry, 'Doctors and healers: popular culture and the medical profession', in Stephen Pumfrey, Paolo L. Rossi & Maurice Slawinski,

the late seventeenth-century iatromechanist Christopher Merrett could define a physician in terms little different to those of a sixteenth-century Galenic textbook:

> The word Physician, derived from the Greek '*phusikos*', is plainly and fully rendered by the word *Naturalist*, (that is) one well vers'd in the full extent of Nature, and Natural things; hereunto add the due, and skillful preparation and application of them to Mens Bodies, in order to their Health, and prolongation of Life, and you have a comprehensive Definition of a Physician.[42]

Similarly, it was the lack of natural philosophy which was used to marginalise the hated empiric. As Eleazar Dunk explained,

> by an Empirike is, as you know, understood a Practitioner in Physicke, that hath no knowledge in Philosophy, Logicke, or Grammar: but fetcheth all his skill from bare and naked experience. Ignorance then is the difference whereby these men are distinguished from other Physicians.[43]

Although Duchesne was no Galenist, he expressed broad agreement, with a Paracelsian twist. He dismissed 'common chemists' as ignorant operators who, when they dared to prescribe their chemicals as medicines, were acting as empirics. Only those, added Duchesne, who 'reduce things to principles . . . and discourse on the properties of Nature [are] properly called Physicians or Natural Philosophers but because they use their hands, one may also properly call them mechanics and artisans.'[44]

Thus, according to physicians of all traditions, whilst they prescribed drugs according to natural philosophical principles, empirics administered them in ignorance of the institutes of physic. Even when an empiric prescribed identically to a physician, he was still to be condemned because of his dangerous ignorance of the philosophical cause and effect behind his treatment.

As long as most physicians agreed around Galenic principles, the criteria for philosophical physic were clear. The physician employed the proper discourse of 'elements, temperaments, humours, spirits,

---

Science Culture and Popular Belief in Renaissance Europe, Manchester 1991, 191–221, esp. 194.

[42] [Christopher Merrett], *The Character of a Compleat Physician, or Naturalist*, 1680?, 2–3, cited in Cook, *New Philosophy*, 414.

[43] Eleazar Dunk, *The Copy of a Letter written by E.D. Doctour of Physicke to a Gentleman, by whom it was published*, 1606, 20–1. Cited in Cook, *New Philosophy*, 409.

[44] Debus, *French Paracelsians*, 52–3.

parts of the body, faculties and actions.'[45] But when Galeno-Aristotelian
understandings of the body were challenged by Neoplatonic, Hermetic,
or generally occultist physicians like Duchesne, as well as by iatro-
mechanists, the eclectic climate of early seventeenth-century philosophy destroyed the consensus. Physicians could now pick and choose
their natural philosophical principles but, to be physicians, they still
had to make a choice. Cook observes that an additional erosion of
the criteria was the shift from physic to medicine—an important distinction difficult to preserve in Anglophonic historiography. This shift
was one from the holistic treatment characteristic of Galenism to
quick-fix drugs[46] and other more interventionist techniques, partially
in response to market preferences for a more 'Paracelsian' approach.

   This might be interpreted as an abandonment by physicians of
their ideological claim that a natural philosophical barrier separated
them from the so-called Paracelsians. The historians' third order of
pragmatic iatrochemists in fact depends upon such an interpretation.
But recent social history of medicine shows that physicians actually
attempted to reinforce the distinction. Although, as Pagel and Debus
rightly noted, Galenists easily appropriated chemical medicine, they
did so by insisting that it worked Galenically, not 'Paracelsically',
and certainly not because an ignorance of causes did not matter.
There were, in any case, non- and pre-Paracelsian traditions, especially Arabic ones, from which Galenists could claim that chemical
practices, including the emblematic Paracelsian use of mercury drugs,
derived.[47]

   Furthermore, genuine conciliators such as Guinther, Sennert, Gwinne
and de Sorbait had little difficulty incorporating into Galenism enough
Paracelsian principles to make their use appear orthodox. Thus,
Sennert granted that (Paracelsian) homeopathic principles were appropriate for the preservation of health, whilst upholding Galenic allopa-
thy in the field of pathology. Paracelsus's *tria prima* could be explained
reductively as stable, physiologically significant mixtures of the four

---

[45] Cook, *New Philosophy*, 408.
[46] Indeed the English word medicine (as opposed to physic) derives from the
Latin *medico*, to drug. See Cook, 398.
[47] This is a major burden of Webster's article, *Health, medicine and mortality*. On
316 he concludes that 'a receptivity to Paracelsianism is not surprising in view of
the debt of Paracelsus to late medieval alchemy.' For a more general exposition
see B.J.T. Dobbs, 'From the Secrecy of Alchemy to the Openness of Chemistry',
in Tore Frangsmyr (ed.), *Solomon's House Revisited: the organisation and institutionalisation
of science*, Canton, MA 1990, 75–94.

elements. In the absence of blind trials, Galenic, or later iatrome-chanical, physicians naturally filtered conflicting empirical evidence surrounding the efficacy of new remedies through their medically informed and natural philosophical understandings of the likely physiological effects.[48]

We can conclude that the test of philosophical rectitude remained a crucial one for all physicians. Galenists who defended chemical remedies surely did so not because they had become methodological pragmatists, and certainly not because they had come to espouse Paracelsianism, but because they had managed to accommodate them within an orthodox philosophy of the body. Learned chemical physicians similarly defended the remedies through philosophy, albeit based on very different Paracelsian principles. And so, of course, did 'unlearned' Paracelsians, although their 'philosophies' did not win learned recognition. Many, like John Webster, and Paracelsus himself, argued that their more spiritual philosophy should replace the vain and 'humane' philosophy of the schools. It must be emphasised, as it is by Cook, that whilst the rise of self-styled 'non-metaphysical' new philosophers and empiricists carried the risk of turning a Paracelsian empiric like Webster into a true physician, the socio-political reality was that new ideological barriers were found to protect the empiricist philosopher from the merely empiric enthusiast and quack. Recent historians of medicine properly question antagonistic labels such as 'quack' and ask instead why their discourse, and even that of the more erudite court Paracelsians, generally failed to move them from the margin to the centre.[49]

For Galeno-chymical reconcilers like Sennert, it was not chemical

---

[48] Witness the classic early Paracelsian debates over the use of mercury and antimony upon patients, many of whom subsequently died. Antimony was (is) a known poison which caused vomiting, and Galenists like Grevin wished to see it proscribed on those grounds. Defenders like de Launay argued for a safe purgative effect on the Paracelsian grounds that it was administered only after alchemical extraction of its spiritual essence—a paradigm case of theoretical incommensurability. For a discussion see Debus, *English Paracelsianism*, ch. 1. For Guinther, see Debus, *Chemical Philosophy*, vol. 1, 145; for Sennert see Pagel, *Paracelsus*, 322f.; for Gwinne, see Debus, *English Paracelsians*, 142–3; for de Sorbait see Erna Lesky, 'Paul de Sorbait, (1624–1691), Anti-Paracelsian and Harveian', in Debus (ed.), *Science, Medicine and Society*, vol. II, ch. 20. See especially 6.

[49] See R. Porter, 'The language of quackery in England, 1660–1800', in P. Burke and R. Porter (eds.), *Language and Society*, Cambridge 1986. See also W.F. Bynum and Roy Porter, *Medical Fringe and Medical Orthodoxy 1750–1850*, London 1987, esp. chs. 2, 6. Compare Agnew, *'Quackery'*.

practices *tout court* which had to be resisted, but chemical philosophy. This was because, for Sennert, chemical philosophy transgressed
those hierarchies of knowledge which he, like Libavius before him,
believed were essential to good order and to true belief. Sennert was
quite explicit:

> it is not for Chymists, as such, to dispute of principles, but for Physitians
> and Philosophers. And Chymistry doth but only bring some observa-
> tions and experiments by working from which the Physitian and
> Philosopher makes conclusions.[50]

Sennert did not merely fear the trespass of chemists into the domain
of philosophy. A greater danger was that chemists pressed on into
the domain of the divine,

> for because they think they have reformed or perfected all Philosophy
> and Physick, they stay not there, but proceed to Divinity, and mix
> prophane and holy things together.[51]

Francis Bacon made similar criticisms for different reasons.

> The school of Paracelsus ... find the truth of all natural philosophy
> in the Scriptures; scandalising and traducing all other philosophies as
> heathenish and profane ... Neither do they give honour to Scripture,
> as they suppose, but much imbuse them. For to seek heaven and earth
> in the word of God ... is to seek temporary things among eternal.[52]

Such comments highlight two recurrent and well-known strands of
attack upon Paracelsians. First, that their philosophy was false, absurd,
speculative and mystical; secondly, following on seamlessly, that it
conflated philosophy and religion, which was deemed to be wrong
even if the natural philosophy and theology had not been themselves
patently dangerous.[53] These were the associations that made so
resistible the label of 'Paracelsian' or, the label supplied by Mr. Culpeper's ghost, 'Mathematical, Mystagogical, Chymical-Rosicrucean.'[54]

---

[50] Debus, *Chemical Philosophy*, vol. I, 195.
[51] *Ibid.*, vol. I, 196.
[52] Francis Bacon *Works* (eds.) J. Spedding et al., London, 1857–59, vol. 6, 486.
Also cited by Rees, *Bacon's Carmology*, 90.
[53] This is reminiscent of the Catholic church's position on Copernicanism. Of
two Copernican doctrines, it declared the motion of the Earth 'foolish and absurd
in philosophy', but the centrality of the Sun 'formally heretical'. See Giorgio de
Santillana, *The Crime of Galileo*, Chicago 1955, 121.
[54] Cited from F.N.L. Poynter, 'Nicholas Culpeper and the Paracelsians', in Allen
G. Debus, *Science, Medicine and Society in the Renaissance: Essays to honour Walter Pagel*,
2 vols., London 1972, vol. 1, 218.

VI *A Philosophia Sagax of the Macrocosm and Microcosm*

Even in debates about iatrochemical practice then, questions of ideology and theology were ever present. Although it is impossible in a short chapter to categorise adequately the heterogeneous issues which divided antagonists, an important set is captured by Michel Foucault's notion of a Renaissance episteme of resemblance—his short-hand term for the concepts of microcosm and macrocosm, spiritual magic, theory of signatures, and a doctrine of language which gave words an equal reality to things.[55] In the second half of this chapter, we shall suggest that these were the central issues raised by the spectre of Paracelsianism. Of course, its development within the more general occult Renaissance episteme of resemblance, by learned chemical philosophers and by Paracelsus himself, meant that Paracelsianism did not uniquely raise these issues. Rather, contemporaries judged that it raised them acutely and irresponsibly.

Until the era of Debus and Yates, historians of science treated Renaissance occultism as rather bizarre, so that, while it was not ignored, neither was it tackled adequately. Henri Guerlac, for example, wrote of an inexorably 'progressive emancipation from the more speculative aspect of [Paracelsian] doctrine.'[56] Guerlac was right in that the progressive marginalisation of the more cosmosophical aspects of Paracelsianism does indeed constitute its major transformation. But because we can no longer be satisfied with his assumption of its inevitability and progressiveness, historians now have to re-open the question of why that marginalisation occurred.

Recently, of course, historians have sought more fully to replace Paracelsianism in its context. Debus undertook the vital, in his words 'internalist', task of presenting Paracelsians 'from their point of view', although it was not until Hannaway's Foucaultian study of Libavius and Croll, *The Chemists and the Word*,[57] that the extent of chemical philosophers' conflict over the episteme of resemblance became fully appreciated. But Hannaway's snapshot of a dispute in progress could

---

[55] Michel Foucault, *The Order of Things. An Archaeology of the Human Sciences*, London 1970, ch. 2, 17–45. A major problem with Foucault's account, which draws heavily upon Oswald Croll, is his assumption that it typified all Renaissance discourse.

[56] Guerlac, *Guy de la Brosse*, vol. I, 179. Debus also lamented that the neo-Platonic strain in Paracelsian writings 'had the unfortunate effect of stamping mysticism as well as experimentalism on these men'. See Debus, *English Paracelsians*, 42.

[57] Debus, *English Paracelsians*, xii; Hannaway, *Chemists and the Word*.

not also deal with its resolution. Since then, a variety of historians such as Westman, Ormsby-Lennon, Jan Golinski and, most recently, Massimo Luigi Bianchi,[58] have all focused on the rise and, more significantly, the fall of this historically circumscribed, literally baroque system of representing nature. This body of work has gone a long way towards recovering the contemporary plausibility of the episteme of resemblance in certain circles, despite its difference from modern, classificatory scientific rationalism.

Such sympathetic approaches have in turn provoked Brian Vickers' intervention. In several recent articles, he re-states the case for a fundamental divide between occult and scientific mentalities, where Paracelsianism and Paracelsian reifications of metaphor in particular, fall on the wrong side.[59]

Indeed, Vickers presents Paracelsians as key antagonists, vanquished in the end-game of a long debate over the proper relation between signifiers and signifieds. Vickers sees the debate as contested between conventionalists (construed as right reasoners, stretching from Aristotle to the new seventeenth-century scientists), and occultists—anthropocentric thinkers (stretching from the early Platonists to 'Paracelsians'), who abused metaphor and collapsed distinct levels of representation into a web of resemblance.

In Vickers' binary anthropology conventionalist scientists do indeed explore analogies as suggestive of natural connections, but crucially also attend to disanalogies in order to analyse and differentiate. Occultists, however, had a mystical commitment to a holistic universe, grounded in belief in a single divine archetype from which all levels of reality—physical, spiritual and verbal—emanate and interconnect. Thus occultists collapsed analogy into metaphor and then into identity, reifying the figurative into expressions of a deep symbolic

---

[58] Robert S. Westman, 'Nature, art and psyche: Jung, Pauli, and the Kepler-Fludd polemic' in Brian Vickers (ed.), *Occult and Scientific Mentalities in the Renaissance*, Cambridge 1984, 177–229; Hugh Ormsby-Lennon, 'Rosicrucian Linguistics' in Ingrid Merkel and Allen G. Debus (eds.), *Hermeticism and the Renaissance: Intellectual History and the Occult in Early Modern Europe*, London 1988, 315–332; Jan Golinski, 'Hélène Metzger and the Interpretation of Seventeenth Century Chemistry', in *History of Science*, 25, 1987, 81–97; Massimo Luigi Bianchi, *Signatura Rerum: Segni, Magia e Conoscenza da Paracelso a Leibniz*, Rome 1987.

[59] 'Analogy versus identity: the rejection of occult symbolism, 1580–1680', in Brian Vickers (ed.), *Occult and Scientific Mentalities in the Renaissance*, Cambridge 1984, 95–163; 'On the Function of Analogy in the Occult', in Ingrid Merkel and Allen G. Debus (eds.), *Hermeticism and the Renaissance*, 265–292.

order.[60] Vickers isolates Paracelsians as 'the most remarkable instances of reification' or 'a good example of the limitations of . . . thinking in images'. He deems that an 'error . . . lies in arguing that the occult sciences in the Renaissance were productive of ideas, theories and techniques in the new sciences'.[61] Interestingly, Walter Pagel evaluated Paracelsus's thought very similarly, except for the last point where Pagel, like Debus, was concerned to prove that 'mystical' Paracelsianism nevertheless had very fruitful scientific consequences, especially in the work of Sennert, Van Helmont and other moderates.[62]

Patrick Curry has presented cogent criticisms of Vickers' account of the decline of Paracelsianism, which need not be rehearsed here. We should note that Vickers relies on an anthropological dichotomy between closed, primitive and open, scientific modes of thought which its originator has described as 'ripe for the scrap-heap'.[63] In 1987 Jan Golinski showed how a similar dichotomy underlay Hélène Metzger's account of the replacement of Paracelsian with mechanical chemistry. However, even if we accept such anthropological models, it does not help us to explain historically why the episteme of resemblance was found wanting when and where it was.[64] But Vickers' work, even if it is not explanatory, provides valuable evidence that contemporaries *did* respond as though the intellectual order depended upon the defeat of Paracelsian ideologies of resemblance and metaphor. He cites Sennert writing of Oswald Croll and the Marburg school.

> Hence we may gather that the Analogie of the great and little world is extended too large by the Chymists, because they make not an analogie, but an identity. . . . Therefore, the soul that loves truth is not satisfied with similitudes only, but desires solid demonstrations.[65]

As we saw earlier, Sennert's worries about this philosophical error were underscored by the connection he saw with theological heresy. Van Helmont put it starkly.

---

[60] Vickers, *Mentalities*, 121–32.

[61] *Ibid.*, 126–7.

[62] Pagel, *Paracelsianism*, 52–3.

[63] Patrick Curry, 'Revisions of Science and Magic', in *History of Science*, 23, 1985, 302–325. The quotation, from Robin Horton, is cited on 306.

[64] Nor, we should note, did Foucault, whose model of epistemic shifts and ruptures has the effect of foreclosing the possibility of continuous historical explanation. See Jan Golinski, 'Hélène Metzger and the Interpretation of Seventeenth Century Chemistry', in *History of Science*, 25, 1987, 81–97.

[65] Quoted by Vickers in *Mentalities*, 141, 142.

> I being a Christian, could not admit of Microcosmical Dreams, as they
> have been delivered by *Paracelsus*! That is, by literally and not metaphor-
> ically understanding them.[66]

Francis Bacon put it more starkly still:

> By mixing the divine with the natural, the profane with the sacred,
> heresies with mythology, you [Paracelsus] have corrupted, o you sac-
> rilegious impostor, both human and religious truth.[67]

Martha Baldwin has recently found that, whilst the Jesuit colleges
permitted study of vulgar alchemy, its occult and Paracelsian forms
were considered a danger to religion.[68] A particular sticking point
for the religiously orthodox was the cabalistic doctrine that words
could effect cures through their power of resemblance with the things
they named. Lesky has shown how this alleged power of words was
what a compromising Galenist like Paul de Sorbait could not take
from his 'Paracelsians'. His concern was widely shared: '*An verborum
et characterum vis sit?*' [is there power in words and images?] was a
frequent *quaestio* debated in medical schools—the right answer being
that there was not.[69] But why was Paracelsian resemblance theory
so controversial and, eventually, defeated? Answers to this question
would resemble in microcosm those to the question of why magical
world views in general were marginalised in the seventeenth century.

VII   Paragranum: *identifying key transgressions*

In this historiographical review, we must limit ourselves to recent
scholarship which helps to explain the distaste reserved particularly
for 'Paracelsianism'. Three lines of enquiry throw direct light on our
suggestion that Paracelsianism be considered as a term of stigmati-
sation which exposes contemporary fears about intellectual order.

---

[66] *Ibid.*, 146.

[67] *Ibid.*, 133.

[68] Martha Baldwin, 'Alchemy in the Society of Jesus', in Martels, *Alchemy Revisited*,
182–7.

[69] Erna Lesky, 'Paul de Sorbait (1624–1691), Anti-Paracelsian and Harveian', in
Debus (ed.), *Science, Medicine and Society*, vol. II, ch. 20. See 5.

a. Lux Naturae: *epistemology*

Paracelsus's texts suggest a subversive epistemology. Hannaway noted that the very anthropocentric Paracelsian version of microcosm/macrocosm theory of knowledge stressed not merely the occultist's view (that man, by virtue of his unique position as the synthesis and embodiment of the divine creative archetype, was the focus of resemblances and powers) but, more importantly and radically, that man thereby 'possessed within himself all knowledge and all power of nature', an inner knowledge 'awakened by a process of sympathetic attraction, between the object . . . and its microcosmic representation within man himself', which Paracelsians called 'experience'. Of course, 'experience' was an endlessly contested term in seventeenth-century natural philosophy. But, as Hannaway shrewdly observed in passing, Paracelsian understandings of empiricism differed from others in this crucial respect: 'Man was no *tabula rasa* who acquired knowledge by the operation of the reasoning mind on the evidence of sensory observation.'[70] Rather, Everyman had knowledge of nature inscribed in his very being.

Paracelsus himself exploited the destabilising, democratising consequences of such an empiricism for established learning. Indeed he deplored university education because it impeded the natural, illuministic capacity for knowing. And, as Charles Webster and others have established, various radical groups later deployed against learned physic this populist epistemology of quasi-ecstatic cognition, based on man as a microcosm and on nature as an open book.[71] Since their philosophy found little support among the learned, they were castigated as unphilosophical empirics.

This was not, of course, an *essential* Paracelsian epistemology. It certainly did not suit the interests of learned occultist Paracelsians, who depended upon offering their patrons an *esoteric* wisdom. Hannaway gave the example of Oswald Croll, who reinstated nature as a cryptic text requiring immense learning for its decipherment. But it was not orthodox scholarship, and so Libavius still regarded Croll as 'part of those intellectual and cultural forces which threatened the very fabric of the society which sustained him.' Croll's 'learning' broke

---

[70] Hannaway, *Chemists and the Word*, 25.
[71] Webster, *Great Instauration*, 32, 'Elmer', *Medicine, Religion*.

the constraints of the traditional disciplines, in Libavius's case those of Philippo-Ramism.[72]

These very different empiric and learned-occultist versions of 'Paracelsian' cognition show that conservative resistance to Paracelsianism must be read in the context of a wider debate about how new, post-Aristotelian discourses of natural knowledge were to be constructed which would be effective, yet safely disciplined. The radically individualistic, indeed literally enthusiastic, approach of many Paracelsians was intolerable to early modern polities.

b. Opus Paramirum: *safety at work beyond wonder*

The second fruitful area of recent scholarship takes us on from boundary disputes primarily about philosophy, to boundary disputes between humane and divine learning which, as we saw, were of greater moment. It confirms that opponents often rejected Paracelsianism because it seemed to make that boundary particularly problematic. Some of the most intellectually disturbing Paracelsians were, as we have seen, those who took to extremes Biblical justifications for chemical interpretations of nature. These writers developed a thoroughly cosmotheological chemical philosophy, in which they read *Genesis* as the description of God's 'spagyric', alchemical act of creation. As Betty Jo Dobbs has recently reminded us, this was by no means a uniquely Paracelsian strategy. Indeed 'the widespread chemical philosophy of the sixteenth and seventeenth centuries' was part of a wider 'assimilation of alchemy to Christianity'.[73] Consequently, Paracelsianism had consequences for religious controversies which contemporaries did not, and historians cannot, ignore.

The recent surveys of Piyo Rattansi and especially Charles Webster, in his *From Paracelsus to Newton*, are both attempts to foreground such religious issues.[74] Writing against the grain of scientific revolution historiography, Webster in particular stresses the continuing, and in many respects unchanging dialectic between science and religion from

---

[72] Hannaway, *Chemists and the Word*, ch. 6; for Libavius's deployment of scholarly criteria in polemics against Paracelsians other than Croll, see Bruce Moran, Chapter 6 below.

[73] Dobbs, *Secrecy of Alchemy*, 77.

[74] P.M. Rattansi, 'Art and Science: the Paracelsian vision', in John W. Shirley (ed.), *Science and the Arts in the Renaissance*, London 1985; Charles Webster, *From Paracelsus to Newton: Magic and the making of modern science*, Cambridge 1982.

1500 to 1700. Webster's Paracelsians are characterised by their attempts to express close relations between the spiritual and the physical during a long period when 'the magic of prophecy lost none of its force since the time of Paracelsus, nor the dream of a spiritual magic which would restore human power over nature'.[75] And, as his final chapter on demonic magic makes clear, Paracelsians were constantly accused of unacceptable transgressions of consensual lines between science and religion.

But the decades around 1600 were very unpropitious ones for a more spiritualised natural philosophy. In what many historians take to be an intensely critical period in European intellectual life, the boundaries which ordered intellectual discourse were dissolving, and hence being the more vigorously defended. We have already noted the physicians' mobilisation of 'true philosophy' against Paracelsian empirics, but the boundary between philosophy and theology was more important. Novel and spectacular cures especially posed problems for a classificatory boundary between the natural and the miraculous. Recent work such as that by the late D.P. Walker and Stuart Clark shows how an ideological squeeze on wonder-workers led to a particular focus on the heresies of alleged 'Paracelsians'.[76]

It is no coincidence that the most intense 'Paracelsian' debates were concurrent with the most intense phase of developments in demonology and witch-hunting. Indeed, to dismiss a healer as a Paracelsian was often to accuse him or her, as Paracelsus himself was accused, of using diabolical cures. Whether a cure was adjudged natural or diabolical depended, of course, upon what philosophy of nature was applied, and who had the authority to apply it. Stuart Clark has shown how closely demonology was tied to natural philosophy. Demonologists were fond of quoting Peter Martyr, who insisted that 'the devil had only two "bridles": one was the will of God, the other the *boundary of nature*.'[77] Catholic and Protestant apologists generally agreed that the devil performed, on a witch's behalf, not miracles but mirables (i.e. wonders). These might surpass the skill of even the best magician, but they were still natural. As

---

[75] Webster, *Paracelsus to Newton*, 34.
[76] D.P. Walker, 'The Cessation of Miracles', in Merkel and Debus, *Hermeticism and the Renaissance*, 111–124; Stuart Clark, 'The rational witchfinder: conscience, demonological naturalism and popular superstitions', in Pumfrey et al., *Science, Culture*, 222–248.
[77] Clark, *Rational Witchfinder*, 223 (emphasis supplied).

D.P. Walker put it, 'the Devil cannot break the laws of nature, but can only move things about with superhuman speed . . . and perhaps speed up natural processes . . . [but the] limitation was by no means clear cut, since no one could be quite sure what the laws of nature were.'[78] The uncertainty was especially marked in the decades around 1600, although most judges vigorously denied that the laws embraced the extraordinary powers attributed by Paracelsus to the micro-cosmic human body and to macrocosmic Creation. The necessity of refutation, however, was what sustained many of the Paracelsian debates.

Although Paracelsianism was deplored and its texts censored by orthodox Catholicism, it most exercised Protestant commentators. This was not merely because most Paracelsians flourished in Protestant states, but also because Protestant theologians developed a doctrine of 'the cessation of miracles'. Walker has shown how Protestants developed a position that the age of miracles had ended, partly to counter their use by Catholic apologists as signs of divine endorsement of Tridentine doctrine, but also to suppress Reformed extremists who laid claim to powers of exorcism and miraculous healing. Protestant theologians therefore were particularly vigilant towards claims of miraculous or wondrous cures, which they were anxious to interpret as stumbling blocks in the path to true religion, strewn by the Devil, superstitious Papists and their allies.[79]

These concerns were at their height at the turn of the century. In a climate of intense religious anxiety, conservative theologians and natural philosophers required firm and undisputed boundaries between the normal-or-natural, the wondrous-or-preternatural and the genuinely miraculous-or-supernatural. Paracelsian philosophers not only disputed but dangerously blurred these boundaries with their claims to produce remarkable natural effects by spiritual means, and they were attacked from at least two sides.

One side is exemplified by the physician, Reformed theologian and demonologist Thomas Erastus. As Pagel noted, Erastus made Paracelsus's spiritualisation of nature the opening and major part of his attack. He carefully repaired boundaries, insisting that 'Nature admits of no miracle', before reclassifying much of Paracelsianism as

---

[78] Walker, *Cessation of Miracles*, 116.
[79] Clark, *Rational Witchfinder*, 111–4.

witchcraft.[80] Yet from the other side, Erastus' antagonist, the witch-craft sceptic and Protestant court physician Johann Weyer, equally condemned the 'Paracelsist school' for encouraging the *false* belief in witchcraft. For Weyer, Paracelsians promoted superstition because, being ignorant of effective, orthodox, Galenic medicine, they dreamed up supernatural explanations of those natural diseases and cures which lay beyond their limited philosophical understanding.[81]

Attempts to demarcate the merely natural from the diabolically preternatural also controlled the debate, which Allen Debus made famous, about the controversial weapon salve, a cure often attrib-uted to Paracelsus.[82] The weapon salve was attacked by Catholics and Protestants, Aristotelians and mechanists alike. Few, however, disputed that it worked. The question was one of causation. The occultists Robert Fludd and Rudolf Göckel both wove explanations out of ideas of magnetic sympathy.[83] Their naturalistic defences pro-voked a typical response from Fludd's bugbear, the Anglican parson William Foster. Foster regarded the salve as the devil's work, and was surprised to find support coming from Rudolf Göckel in Marburg. He knew Marburg to be a centre of Protestantism, but perhaps not as the vibrant centre of occult and chemical philosophy which Bruce Moran's work is uncovering. Consequently Foster wrote that

> Rodolphus Goclinius is so full of characteristicall superstitions and magical cures, that I am ashamed that any such cures should come from one reputed to be a Protestant.[84]

We can conclude, then, that some of the more significant transfor-mations of Paracelsianism were occasioned by disputes in religious ideology about the proper relations between science and religion. These disputes were by no means exclusively occasioned by Para-celsianism, but it would seem that the high profile and radical views

---

[80] For a discussion of Erastus's *Disputationes de Medicina Nova Paracelsi*, see Pagel, *Paracelsus*, 311–322.

[81] Weyer, *Witches*, 156–7.

[82] Allen G. Debus. 'Robert Fludd and the Use of Gilbert's "De Magnete" in the Weapon Salve Controversy', in *J. Hist. Med. and Allied Sci.*, 19, 1964, 389–417.

[83] Stephen Pumfrey, 'William Gilbert's Magnetic Philosophy 1580–1684: the Creation and dissolution of a discipline'. Unpublished Ph.D. dissertation, University of London 1987, ch. 2.

[84] Revd William Foster, *Hoplocrisma-spongus; or, A sponge to wipe away the Weapon-salve. A Treatise wherein it is proved that the cure . . . is Magicall and Unlawfull*, London 1631, 36.

of some so-called Paracelsians turned it into an emblematic ragbag of orthodox fears.

Disputes such as that surrounding the weapon salve clearly raised what can be described, conveniently if anachronistically, as 'the proper relations between science and religion'. To avoid anachronism, we must be careful not to assume that Paracelsians were especially guilty of conflating the two areas. It is true that contemporaries accused them of being so, but all early modern natural philosophy developed through intimate relations and accommodations with theology. All agreed that the Book of Revelation and the Book of Nature were parallel texts. When writers like Bacon or Sennert complained that Paracelsians and others tended to 'mix the sacred and the prophane', the real complaint was, not that they were being mixed, but that the mix was an illegitimate one which threatened the established order of the disciplines.

c. Elias Artista: *Typology and the relation between science and religion*

The problem of how to renegotiate the relationship between science and religion, in ways which moved away from Thomist Aristotelianism but which did not simply spiritualise nature, was surely one of the most difficult accomplishments of the Scientific Revolution. Mechanical philosophers, drawing on arguments from design and on God's voluntary sustenance of the laws of nature, emerged with the most powerful solution. They generally excluded from their discourse echoes of the occultist episteme of resemblance. Paracelsian cosmotheology was made to look nonsensical or, in Robert Boyle's word 'unintelligible'.

Some recent work suggests that, far from being the result of an inevitable emancipation of reason, this exclusion in natural philosophy was divorced from, and even in contradiction with other intellectual traditions. Here it is worth returning to Dobbs's article. Having discussed spagyric creation theology, she moves on to chemical philosophers' use of typological interpretation. This connection puts the transformation of Paracelsianism into the exciting and under-explored context of typological theology. Seventeenth-century theologians continued to assume that God was progressively revealing his divine plan. Early men, such as Adam and Noah, were read *metaphorically* as adumbrations of Christ the anti-type. 'The future revelation [she explains] will be fuller, but *since the overall plan remains the same*, the type will necessarily bear resemblances and analogies to the antitype yet to come.'[85] This is a central doctrine which, at the very least, lent encouragement to advocates of an episteme of resemblance. After all, typological readings of the book of nature were explicitly sanctioned, from Augustine onwards, by the assumption that nature and scripture were 'literally identical in structure, and this parallel text metaphor came ever to the fore in early modern Europe'. A persistent example was the analogy made between the seven days of creation, and seven stages of natural history, a use of typology still of central importance to Thomas Burnet in 1684.[86] Yet alchemical typology and resemblances were little different. 'Elias Artista', a figure whom Pagel showed was common in Paracelsian discussions, was one specific type who exemplified the progressive revelation of alchemical wisdom.[87] Linden and Nicholl have also shown that religio-alchemical typologies were standard devices in early modern literature, which fed off this conventional theology.[88]

So, at the same time as established theologians and their natural philosophical allies were driving out Paracelsian resemblance theory, a very similar world-view continued to underwrite much orthodox exegesis. Why, then, could the natural world not be Paracelsian? We must surely conclude that these negotiations were more political and religious than natural philosophical or empirical. It may even be that Paracelsian controversies assisted the decline of the typological universe. Paul Korshin, in his *Typologies in England, 1650–1820*, finds that the long tradition began to lose its theological application in the late seventeenth century because of England's spectacular 'intermingling of religion and politics'. Views changed to make, in the words of one commentator, *'typical or allegorical reasoning . . . weak and enthusiastical.'*[89] There are intriguing parallels between Korshin's study

---

[85] See Northrop Frye, *The Great Code: the Bible and Literature*, New York 1982; Jean Daniélou, *From Shadows to Reality. Studies in the Biblical Typology of the Fathers*, London 1960, and Paul J. Korshin, *Typologies in England 1650–1820*, Princeton 1982. An influential Puritan example was Thomas Taylor, *Christ Revealed: Or . . . A Treatise of the Types and Shadows of our Saviour*, London 1635: reprint ed., Delmar, NY 1979.

[86] Thomas Burnet, *The Theory of the Earth: Containing an Account of the Original of the Earth . . .*, London, 1684. See the discussion in Dobbs, *Secrecy of Alchemy*, 82–3.

[87] Walter Pagel, 'The Paracelsian Elias Artista and the Alchemical Tradition', reprinted in Walter Pagel, *Religion and Neoplatonism in Renaissance Medicine*, ed. Marianne Winder, London 1985, XI, 1–6; Dobbs, *Secrecy of Alchemy*, 83–6.

[88] Stanton J. Linden, Alchemy and eschatology in seventeenth-century poetry', in *Ambix*, 31, 1984, 102–124; Charles Nicholl, *The Chemical Theatre*, London 1980.

[89] Korshin, *Typologies*, 77, 116.

and recent accounts which relate the demise of English Paracelsianism to its association with enthusiasm from the 1630s to 1650s.[90] Whilst one cannot generalise from Restoration England to Europe generally, one can conclude that any explanation of the transformation of the metaphorical world of Paracelsianism will not be confined, as Vickers would wish, to an eventual triumph of science, nor to a chronicle of expanding chemical technique, but will be related to context-specific early modern renegotiations of ideologically acceptable boundaries between divine and natural learning.

VIII   *Conclusion*

What this interpretation of recent scholarship suggests is that the sets of ideas and practices stigmatised as Paracelsian were caught up in a transformation not limited to chemical medicine, nor even to natural philosophy. It was one in which conservative universities were losing the power to define and maintain disciplinary boundaries and content. Consequently, old maps of knowledge, particularly the borders between the theological and the natural philosophical, and between the metaphysical and the empirical, were being redrawn in a climate of great tensions in the religio-political order. However the new map was to look, most commentators agreed that Paracelsian versions were philosophically, religiously and politically dangerous innovations.

If our focus on contested ideologies of knowledge is correct, then a confident history of occult chemical philosophy can discard some of its older concepts. The first notion of a Paracelsian school or tradition fails to deal with its Protean character. The second, broadening it into chemical philosophy, elides the historical reality that 'Paracelsian' was an ascribed label of marginalisation which chemists resisted. The third, of identifying it with iatrochemical practice, jettisons all the (ideological) signposts through the thickets of controversy.

We can concur most fully with Jole Shackelford, who has written

---

[90] For two discussions of the way in which 'new philosophers' in England attempted to exclude enthusiasm and Paracelsianism, see Paul B. Wood, 'Methodology and Apologetics: Thomas Sprat's "History of the Royal Society"', *Brit. J. Hist. Sci.*, 13 1980, 1–26; Steven Shapin and Simon Schaffer, *Leviathan and the Air Pump. Hobbes, Boyle and the Experimental Life*, Princeton 1985.

recently that 'Paracelsianism is best thought of as an ideology, ... to which opposition arose on many foundations.'[91] This chapter has put forward reasons why it is impossible to discuss Paracelsianism without a dialectical consideration of that opposition. In contrast to historians who have read early modern Paracelsianism either as self-contained philosophy or as an ideologically neutered chemical practice, we have suggested that it was in large part constituted by its opponents. Given the strength of theological and political opposition, we might well wonder how cosmotheological Paracelsianism ever found significant support. The answer to this question is becoming clearer as scholars like Moran, Shackelford and Trevor-Roper establish the courtly context within which it flourished and declined. These courts, frequently Protestant courts concerned about inter-confessional tensions, often patronized Paracelsian studies as part of the late sixteenth and early seventeenth-century trend of promoting reformed, unifying, spiritual philosophies.[92] When they failed to ameliorate Europe's gathering religio-political crisis (more than a *theologia Paracelsica sancta* was needed to end the Thirty Years' War!), the trend was abandoned. Further investigation of these courtly sites will provide much clearer answers to the question of how early modern Paracelsianism was transformed, and will do so because it links it to ideology and to the wider intellectual concerns of early modern Europe.

---

[91] Shackelford, *Paracelsianism and Patronage*, 82.

[92] See, for example, R.J.W. Evans, *Rudolf II and His World: A Study in Intellectual History*, Oxford 1973; Bruce T. Moran, *The alchemical world of the German court: occult philosophy and chemical medicine in the circle of Moritz of Hessen (1572–1632)*, Sudhoffs Archiv, Beihefte H. 29, Stuttgart 1991; Karin Figala and Ulrich Neumann. 'Michael Maier (1569–1622): New Bio-Bibliographical Material', in Martels, *Alchemy Revisited* 34–50; Hugh Trevor-Roper, 'The Court Physician and Paracelsianism', in Vivian Nutton (ed.), *Medicine at the courts of Europe, 1500–1837*, London 1990, 79–95.

CHAPTER TWO

PARACELSUS FAT AND THIN:
THOUGHTS ON REPUTATIONS AND REALITIES

Andrew Cunningham

I *Paracelsus contradictory*

I am proposing the historiographical category of the fat and the thin. I hope it will be recognised that while my account of this category begins in Paracelsus, the concept of the fat and the thin is a general historiographical one which could perhaps be put to useful work to help understand the relation between reputations and realities in the case of other historical figures. The fat and the thin is a concept which closely concerns the transformations of Paracelsus and of Paracelsianism.

I was relieved to discover that the elusiveness of Paracelsus is not something that has only been experienced by me. Forty years ago, that most eminent historian of medicine, Owsei Temkin, published an article 'On the elusiveness of Paracelsus', and in it he pointed out that 'two of the greatest historical figures of the medical past are also amongst its most elusive ones'.[1] These two are Hippocrates and Paracelsus. This elusiveness is indeed quite remarkable, especially since I believe we can say that Hippocrates and Paracelsus are two of the only three characters from the history of medicine whose names are known universally, to the man in the street (the other, I hazard, would be Pasteur).

Was there one man called Paracelsus? I asked myself. Or were there many men called Paracelsus? For I found that Paracelsus was variously claimed as:

A SUCCESSFUL PHYSICIAN   A FAILED PHYSICIAN

A PRACTICAL PHYSICIAN   A SPIRITUAL PHYSICIAN

A CHEMIST   AN ALCHEMIST

---

[1] Owsei Temkin, 'The elusiveness of Paracelsus', *Bulletin of the History of Medicine* 1952, 26, 201–217, see 201.

A MAGICIAN OR MAGUS	A SCIENTIST (*or* someone turning magic into science)
A PROPHET	A MADMAN
AN OPPONENT OF THE ANCIENTS	A HUMANIST (that is, a Renaissance follower of the Ancients)
THE HIGH POINT OF MEDIEVAL NATURAL PHILOSOPHY	THE BEGINNING OF MODERN SCIENCE (*or* the bridge between the two)
A FULLY POLITICISED SOCIAL-REVOLUTIONARY	AN OTHER-WORDLY MYSTIC
A MAN OF HIS TIME	A MAN FOR ALL TIMES

And in addition to these roles, he also had reputations among historians as an *astrologer*, as an early *biologist* and *biochemist*, *mineralogist*, *anthropologist*, even *psychiatrist*.

What is particularly striking about these roles is not just that they are multiple, but that so many of them are mutually contradictory. We get to the ridiculous position where, in the classification still used by the history of science journal, *Isis*, Paracelsus supposedly contributed at the same time, *and with the same writings*, to Science and Pseudoscience: he was simultaneously both Scientist and Pseudo-Scientist!

Paracelsus's motto is said to have been: 'Let him not be another's, who can be his own' (Alterius non sit qui suus esse potest). This sounded to me like a statement about preserving one's personal identity, and this question of Paracelsus 'being himself' led me (eventually) to ask: Who was this man? What did he really think and teach? Why, given how incomprehensible I found his writings and the writings by some historians about him,[2] did he have such a persistent reputation? And what was it 'really' a reputation for? The 'real' Paracelsus and his supposed achievements all eluded me. I should stress that this was not a problem about the notorious difficulty or obscurity of Paracelsus's *language*, but about getting a rounded view of Paracelsus from the writings of historians, even if one also had recourse to the writings of Paracelsus himself.

---

[2] I should mention that the fundamental work on Paracelsus with which I had to wrestle at the time was that of Walter Pagel, *Paracelsus: An Introduction to Philosophical Medicine in the Era of the Renaissance*, Basel 1958.

I did at one time think that the problem was one of my own limited vision, rather than something to do with either Paracelsus, or with other historians. Perhaps his multiple historical reputations simply reflect the multi-faceted nature of Paracelsus' personality, the universality of his message, the profundity of his doctrines, the diversity of his achievements? Perhaps this is the point of an enigmatic historical character such as Paracelsus, this is what makes him so 'great', that he is available to and seemingly 'speaks to' later generations? Perhaps it requires the work of many historians for us to be able to see the different facets of his reality? Hence the historian interested in the political history of the sixteenth century can discover the political Paracelsus who is not evident to the historian of chemistry who, by contrast, finds Paracelsus the proto-chemist, someone not evident to the political historian? Perhaps only if all such accounts are taken together can we perceive the true Paracelsus in all his complexity?

But I realized (again, eventually) that in fact this is not the case: issues of anachronism render some of our current representations of Paracelsus completely invalid. For in the centuries subsequent to Paracelsus we have separated-out, or marked off, disciplines of knowledge in a way alien to Paracelsus' time. Hence he has become a supposed 'contributor' to a range of fields which, by our modern categories of knowledge, are contradictory, and which did not exist as categories of knowledge in his own time. And he has been given separate reputations in each of these histories. That is, it is us, with *our* subject-divisions, who have created a multi-faceted and contradictory picture of Paracelsus, and one which in many respects simply cannot be authentic. Amongst the many important new distinctions and contrasts in the domain of knowledge that have been made since Paracelsus' time, there are those between religion and science, as incompatible and mutually exclusive areas; between science and magic, similarly seen as incompatible; between the supposed 'rational man of the Renaissance', and the mystic of the sixteenth century; the fundamental distinction between 'medieval' and 'modern', with all the judgemental force involved in making such a contrast; the distinction between science and (popular) politics, and our customary belief that these are properly distinct and unrelated domains; the distinction between chemistry and alchemy, and the view that the history of chemistry must show a new rational science here replacing an old mystical art—that sense must oust nonsense. Moreover, a host of new sciences have been created since Paracelsus's time, including a number to which Paracelsus has been described as a contributor: such as mineralogy, biology, anthropology, all created in the early nineteenth century; psychiatry, created at the end of the nineteenth century; and biochemistry, created in the twentieth century. In particular, we have completely lost *natural philosophy* as a coherent and meaningful category of knowledge and enquiry, which is one within which Paracelsus was working, at least some of the time.

In addition, the multiple reputations of Paracelsus are in part due to our perfectly natural desire, especially when creating a *new* discipline, to have founding fathers. The desire of historians of chemistry in the 19th century, for example, to have a suitable transitional figure to bridge between 'alchemy' and chemistry, between medieval and modern, drew their attention to Paracelsus, and created for him the role of father of modern chemistry.[3]

So the world of knowledge, the map of the disciplines, has completely changed since Paracelsus' day. Yet historians and others have been eager to give Paracelsus some roles as a proto-practitioner of modern disciplines, disciplines quite unknown in Paracelsus' own time, logically impossible though such roles are. And many writers on Paracelsus have generally ignored the categories of knowledge which existed in Paracelsus' day, and not sought to characterise him as a man of his time.

The problem about this attribution of 19th and 20th century activities to Paracelsus, is not just that we thereby have only a partial view of the historical rounded figure, but that we produce for ourselves a view of Paracelsus that logically could not have been the case. We distort the history if we try and make it fit inappropriate categories—no matter how we bolster our work with direct citation of Paracelsus's own works and words. If, for instance, we seek the chemist in Paracelsus, we find in him a 19th or 20th century man,

---

[3] This view of the historic role of Paracelsus in the history of chemistry continues today. J.R. Partington in his multi-volume work, *A History of Chemistry*, London 1961, says 'From our point of view, he [Paracelsus] represents a step forward from alchemy. He administered a rude shock to the conventional alchemists, and by his blustering profusion of abusive rhetoric he pushed aside their unintelligible jargon by one even less comprehensible but more modern and in nearer relation to reality' (vol. 2, 123). Similarly, in his recent survey history of chemistry, (*The Fontana History of Chemistry*, London 1992), W.H. Brock sees the mid-sixteenth century as the time during which 'alchemy had been transmuted into chemistry' (28), and for his story Paracelsus still plays the role of intermediary between (medieval) alchemy and (modern) chemistry, by employing 'an empiricism that was controlled by Christian and Neoplatonic insights' (45).

something which, no matter how talented he was, he could not possibly have been, because he was a sixteenth century man.

So the real issue here is that of recognising which questions about Paracelsus are legitimate and historically valid, and which ones are not. All of which leads me to the fat and the thin.

II   The fat and the thin

There are two parallel iconographic traditions for Paracelsus, which originate from his lifetime. One shows him thin, hatless, bald, simply dressed, and with an expression which is neither smile nor scowl, but looks like the face at rest. This is the portrait by Augustin Hirschvogel of 1538, and claims to show Paracelsus at age 45. The other shows him fat, hatted, with hair showing below the hat (and presumably continuing under the hat), richly appareled, and with an expression which might be a smile. This derives from a painting at the Louvre, now attributed to the school of Q. Metsys, produced c. 1528–30. Later representations of Paracelsus come primarily from these traditions, taken as models.[4] Strikingly, over the centuries, in subsequent representations, the thin Paracelsus seems to get thinner, while the fat Paracelsus gets fatter.

This is interesting in itself and for what it says about historical

---

[4] My information here is built on the twenty-one engravings and other portraits held in the Wellcome Institute, London, as described in Renate Burgess, *Portraits of Doctors and Scientists in the Wellcome Institute of the History of Medicine*, London 1973, 271–2. The portraits listed there, deriving from originals from the period of Paracelsus's lifetime, appear to divide into four traditions, which might be built on just two representations:

   1. *thin* A. (Burgess numbers 10–11), bald, from original in the State Library, Vienna, 1538, by Hirschvogel; this is my 'thin' Paracelsus. B. (Burgess numbers 12–16, and 20) bald with sword, earliest listed appearance 1587; this looks to me like a development of number 1A, so I count it also as in the tradition of the 'thin' Paracelsus.
   2. *fat* A. (Burgess number 19) with a hat and furred coat, derived from a drawing, sometimes known as 'a young man with slouch hat' by the younger Holbein, 1526; this might be the origin of the tradition of the 'fat' Paracelsus (see Pagel, *Paracelsus*, 7 n. 13). B. (Burgess numbers 1–9) with hat, from a Louvre painting, c. 1528–30, attributed to school of Q. Metsys; also sometimes known as 'the Hollar version': my basic 'fat' Paracelsus. This has also been attributed to Jan Van Scorel (1495–1562); see Pagel, *Paracelsus*, 90.

Burgess numbers 17–18 are a quite different representation of Paracelsus, with a clipped beard, and which dates from the 17th century. Number 21 is a twentieth-century image of Paracelsus. I have heard that there is an article by Walter Pagel on this general theme, but I have not been able to locate it.

Paracelsus. Etching by Augustin Hirschvogel (1538). Courtesy of Wellcome Institute Library, London.

Physick Proffeſsor at Basil.

Philip Theophraſtus PARACELSUS *He died at*
Saltzburge Anᵒ. Dom: 1540. aged
47 yeares.

W. Marſhall ſculpſit.

Paracelsus. Line engraving by W. Marshall after J. Payne. Derived from School of Q. Metsys
(c. 1528–30). Courtesy of Wellcome Institute Library, London.

perceptions of Paracelsus. But here I want to use the existence of these parallel iconographical traditions as a motif for a treatment of Paracelsus' historical reputations, and the relation between his reputations and his realities.[5] That is, we can take the existence of an iconographical tradition of a 'thin' Paracelsus as representing Paracelsus stripped of all his accreted reputations—the 'real' Paracelsus, as it were, the one who lived. Given the nature of the picture itself one might risk a joke, and regard this as 'the bald truth'.[6] This thin Paracelsus must, of course, be constructed basically from the original (Latin and German) printed writings of Paracelsus himself, in all their abundance, and from related contemporary materials, and it is an image still under construction by historians. There *was* a historical Paracelsus who lived, and this Paracelsus is being reached by proper historical exegesis and is turning out to be a very complex figure, though not a self-contradictory one.

The parallel existence of an iconographical tradition of a 'fat' Paracelsus, can be taken by us to represent the Paracelsus-es of all the different historical reputations. Again, to risk another joke, given the picture of the fat Paracelsus, we could regard these fat Paracelsus-es as presenting 'the embellished truth', as long as we bear in mind that while clothes embellish and present a certain image of a person, they at the same time conceal the body beneath. And hats are ideal for concealing the bald truth.

We all of us come to the study of Paracelsus initially with some image or other about him in our minds: that he was, for instance, an alchemist, a magician, a scientist, a popular political figure, a man of the middle ages, and so on. These are the fat Paracelsus-es. Fat Paracelsus-es are all later creations. These images we bring to our work are ones which have been created, unconsciously and unself-

---

[5] For this vocabulary of 'fat' and 'thin' I am initially indebted to Johanna Geyer-Kordesch's comments on my original paper at the Glasgow conference, and to the subsequent table-talk of Allen Debus. The present considerations have been developed since then.

[6] Jokes in academic papers are very risky so, to avoid misunderstanding, I must stress that I am *not* saying that the illustration of the thin Paracelsus is a true likeness, and the fat one is not; I am not at all concerned with the issue of the relative authenticity (if any) of these images to the historical Paracelsus. Perhaps neither of them correspond to his true likeness. For present purposes it doesn't matter. What matters is what images they were *meant* to convey, and what images they *did* convey, to the viewer (these not necessarily being the same), especially the later viewer who could not have seen Paracelsus in person.

consciously, by people later than Paracelsus. Most of the historical literature of over three hundred years on Paracelsus is doing such work: making fat Paracelsus-es of one kind or another. Even the most scrupulous of historians can bring to their work on Paracelsus (or any other historical figure) an agenda which leads them to find *in* Paracelsus (or whoever) what they brought *to* him.

Every time people write about Paracelsus, the Paracelsus they think they are describing is the thin Paracelsus, the Paracelsus who really lived. But in fact this is not necessarily the case. For finding the thin Paracelsus is very difficult indeed, for the simple reason that fat Paracelsus-es keep getting in the way and making it not only difficult but very often impossible to see the thin one. And new images of Paracelsus are unwittingly being constantly created by ourselves as historians, in the very act of seeking to find something in Paracelsus and his work which is relevant to the agenda of historical research we ourselves are engaged on.

Of course it does not feel as though we are creating new fat Paracelsus-es as we labour to read and understand the writings of Paracelsus and his contemporaries. Indeed, the act of reading Paracelsus's own writings and of deploying them in our writings about him, make us feel that the opposite is true: that we are reading and thus listening to the true Paracelsus, and in our writings we are revealing the true, thin, Paracelsus to our audiences. Yet always there is the problem of the selectivity we unwittingly practise: our eagerness to see in what Paracelsus wrote what we want to find, plus our willingness to believe that Paracelsus must have meant what we want him to have meant.

These historical reputations, the multiple reputations Paracelsus has had in all the periods since his day, including today, are just as valid reputations as the thin Paracelsus, and are also historical Paracelsus-es. For these varied fat Paracelsus-es had and have important roles within the collective imaginations of the societies in which they are created, roles which are usually far more important to those societies than the figure of the 'true', thin, Paracelsus.

Each fat Paracelsus does important ideological and psychological work in the society or group which promotes and projects him, and in this sense any fat Paracelsus is more important generally than the thin one. These fat Paracelsus-es are not false Paracelsus-es: they are just different from the 'thin' Paracelsus, Paracelsus the historical figure who actually lived. Moreover, of course, the reputations are *also* themselves historical realities.

The existence of fat Paracelsus-es raises questions of *why* Paracelsus was chosen to be 'fattened up' at a particular time and by particular people? And these questions are, of course, not in any way questions about the thin Paracelsus and his time, but about the time when, and the society in which, each particular fat Paracelsus was created.

The basic historiographic points at issue (and they are very basic) are two. First, unless we are very careful and alert to what we are doing in our historical studies, we confuse one or other fat Paracelsus for the thin one. That is, we attribute characteristics, goals, achievements, beliefs, and so on, to the thin Paracelsus which are in fact from our present, and thus construct fat Paracelsus-es which serve our later purposes—but which we mistakenly take to be true about the historic ('thin') Paracelsus. This can lead to our history-writing being simply self-serving and indeed simply circular, as we reinforce the image of Paracelsus that we bring with us by bolstering it with layers of authentic historical information and quotation from the writings of Paracelsus; such work may simply further obscure from view the thin Paracelsus rather than make him more visible. I should stress that the encounter with the historical texts of Paracelsus will not, in itself, ensure that we are dealing with the thin, rather than our preferred fat, Paracelsus. Quite the reverse: prejudice or preconception can withstand any number of encounters with the evidence and remain unscathed, as my examples will show. One could, I suppose, make the joke that inside every fat Paracelsus there is a thin Paracelsus trying to get out. But in fact we will only find the thin Paracelsus if we go deliberately looking for him, and without preconceptions about his proper shape.

The other basic historiographic point comes from my own experience in trying to understand the historical reputations of Paracelsus. It is this: unless and until we can distinguish between the fat and the thin, then we simply go round in circles asking absurd questions which try and cope with the apparent contradictions in Paracelsus— such as 'how much was Paracelsus a medieval mystic, how much a modern scientist?'—questions which derive simply from historical reputations Paracelsus has been given, rather than from Paracelsus the historical figure in his own time.

It is inevitable that round the thin Paracelsus fat Paracelsus-es

would gather. And this is the case with all historical figures later
thought to be important: fattening-up is a recurring, natural, historical process which happens to celebrated figures of the past when
they are needed to achieve latter-day purposes, and in the course of
which they are given new pasts, new historical reputations.

It may be that the thin Paracelsus, whenever we might succeed
in reconstructing him in his completeness, will be ultimately of interest only to historians. But that should be an incentive to us. The
picture of the thin Paracelsus is, of course, what the best practice
of historians working on him is bringing to light.

III   *The occult Paracelsus*

So: there are many fat Paracelsus-es. Paracelsus today has many reputations *simultaneously*, each of which has its own *historical* origin and
its *modern* reason for surviving and being promoted/celebrated by
historians and others. I cannot, of course, hope to look at the source
and function of all these, especially since some of them are still in
the course of being made, such as Paracelsus the theologian, or
Paracelsus the political activist. But I will look at the making of one
particular reputation, the most dominant one still current, and at
the version of it which has been with us and developing for a century or more now: Paracelsus as occultist/mystic.

My questions here will be: why does Paracelsus have such a large
reputation today as an occultist, and especially why has his 'occult'
medicine been more studied than his practical medicine? and, why
do we have texts (translations) which promote this view? These are
questions about fat Paracelsus-es, how and why Paracelsus was historically *given* certain reputations, not questions about what kind of
occultist the thin Paracelsus 'really' was. That would be an enquiry
of a different kind. I present two little case-studies.

To illustrate the source and force of Paracelsus's recent reputa-
tion as an occultist, I take as my first example late 19th century
Britain. As far as Paracelsus studies are concerned, this is when the
English-speaking world received its first extensive set of transla-
tions of the works of Paracelsus, made from the Latin edition of
Geneva of 1658.[7] Two volumes, each of 400 pages of translation,

---

[7] Something of this story has been told by Charles Webster, 'The nineteenth

were produced, and a hundred years later these two volumes are still the largest source of Paracelsian works available in English, having been reprinted in the 1960s. This project was a product of the occult revival of 19th century England.[8] The Paracelsus that this translation/edition gives us is therefore, as one might expect, an occult Paracelsus.

The co-ordinator of this substantial translation exercise was Arthur Edward Waite (1857–1940). The period c. 1820 to c. 1910 in Europe has been called by James Webb, 'The flight from reason'.[9] In splendidly robust fashion Webb argues that the new views of the world portrayed by the 'new science' of the 19th century elicited, as its counterpart, a 'crisis of consciousness' [sic], a crisis in which resort to the occult, in a myriad of ways, was central:[10] the 'new science' (together with the 'new politics' of bourgeois nationalism and liberalism) had as their counterpart what one might call a 'new occultism'. This occultism included Spiritualism, 'hypnotism, magic, astrology, water-divining, "secret" societies', and others.[11] As far as Britain was concerned such occult concerns began around 1848 and peaked in the 1880s.

All these occult obsessions were lived out, one after the other, by Arthur Edward Waite. In 1880 Waite was in his early twenties. He had left Catholicism as a young man, through the rather unusual route of reading Robert Chambers' *Vestiges of Creation*, but did not abandon the search for the mystical 'One'.[12] Waite was a life-long mystic, looking for Fairy land or 'Faërie'—an early work of his was *The Heart's Tragedy in Fairyland*—and he had 'a bee-filled bonnet'.[13] He always hoped that research into the occult and occult practices

---

century afterlife of Paracelsus', in Roger Cooter, ed., *Studies in the History of Alternative Medicine*, London 1988, 79–88, but the historiographic points he makes are different.

[8] Despite their date of publication, the appearance of these volumes had nothing at all to do with 1893 being the 400th anniversary of Paracelsus' birth.

[9] James Webb, *The Flight from Reason* (vol. 1 of *The Age of the Irrational*), London 1971. On these matters see also, for instance, Bruce F. Campbell, *Ancient Wisdom Revived: A History of the Theosophical Movement*, University of California Press 1980. I am grateful to my former colleague Perry Williams for guidance here.

[10] *The Flight from Reason*, xiii.

[11] *The Flight from Reason*, xiv.

[12] Indeed, according to Waite, it was in reading Chambers' book that 'the whole cosmos began to move about me, spelling out living oracles, of which Church, and Rome especially, had never conceived', *Shadows of Life and Thought*, London 1938, 48–9.

[13] *Shadows of Life and Thought*, 128.

and their histories would help him in his 'lifelong Quest' (as he called it) for mystical union. Waite was able to make a living out of his concern with the history of the occult and the mystical, for he luckily fell in with two publishers keen to put out occult works (though a lot of their stock went unsold); and when they all failed him, Waite became London manager of Horlick's Malted Milk (itself a drink with proverbial restorative powers!), and wrote their advertisements and pamphlets.

Waite's life-long Quest was intense, but sceptical: he was always hoping that 'another explosive might be placed [by himself] astutely in the camp of fond believers'.[14] In particular what Waite believed was that scholarly work on the *history* of each these traditions would serve to sift the authentic truths from the bogus later accretions in each of these traditions, and this historical work is what he devoted his life to: history will take us to the mystical truth. It should be noted that while Waite is here dealing in terms of the 19th century sense of 'history' in which some development or progress is to be perceived, he is actually expecting *degeneration* over time from some pristine original to have happened.

His autobiographical work, *Shadows of Light and Thought* (1938), reveals his personal life-route through the mystical and occult: he went via Spiritism (or Spiritualism), which did not satisfy him and which disillusioned him by its rampant trickery; he tried Theosophy, as did many many others, for this was the time of Madam Blavatsky and Anna Besant; Occult Science attracted him in turn, including Alchemy; so did Magic, especially the works and approach of the Frenchman Eliphas Lévi (Alphonse Louis Constant, 1810–78); Rosicrucianism lured him in its turn, and here as always he is sympathetic to the 'real' Rosy Cross and its mysteries, but full of doubt about the drivel put forward by its modern day advocates. The Order of the Golden Dawn called him next, and then Esoteric Freemasonry; he found in most cases that after the necessary historical research he could, unlike most members, reach the true mysteries, and receive 'that life in the heart, that secret of light in the mind which no one tells to another, because it cannot be put into words'.[15] Waite talked to the trees (or rather, he listened as they talked to him),[16] he was

---

[14] *Shadows of Life and Thought*, 100.
[15] *Shadows of Life and Thought*, 162.
[16] *Shadows of Life and Thought*, 68.

fascinated by Animal Magnetism and Hypnotism, he earnestly sought
out the history of the Holy Grail, and toyed with Tarot cards, always
believing that one or other of these would be the true key to the
mystic route to 'pure being which is the Life of the Soul in God'.[17]

By the 1890s (that is, after his work on Paracelsus), he claimed
that he was weary of all the false prophets and the widespread ignorance of the occult shown by his contemporary practitioners of the
occult. Yet still he cherished

> the vague feeling . . . that something was lying *perdu* beneath the cesspools
> and ashpits of so-called occult science. It was the notion presumably
> of a Higher magia, with Jacob Böhme and a dozen lesser but reputed
> names as apologists, if not as champions.[18]

It was in this commitment to occult seeking that Waite enthusiastically directed the translation and publishing of the works of Paracelsus.
For Paracelsus was, for him, a potential source of the 'Higher magia'.

The man who personally financed the translation and publication
of the Paracelsus edition was Fitzherbert Edward Stafford-Jerningham
(1833–1913).[19] His was an old Catholic aristocratic family. The Hon-
ourable Stafford-Jerningham succeeded his brother as Lord Stafford
in 1892; this brother, though officially declared lunatic in 1862,[20]
had held the title since 1884. Lord Stafford was another convert to
the occult world, and was using up the family fortunes by trying to
make gold by alchemical transformation, and in this was obviously
an undeclared lunatic. Stafford needed certain texts translated to
help his transmutations, initially the *Lexicon Alchemiae* of Martinus
Rulandus, and this is why he employed Waite. When Waite had
had the translation made, Stafford wanted it printed—in an edition
of one, just for his own use. Waite's view of the general project
was that

> what was wanted was a working canon of distinction between those
> alchemists who were dealing with a supposed physical operation and
> those who used the symbolical language of Alchemy in a spiritual or
> transcendental sense.[21]

---

[17] *Shadows of Life and Thought*, 195.
[18] *Shadows of Life and Thought*, 145.
[19] His grandfather had succeeded in having the old barony restored in 1829, the
previous baron, Lord William Howard, having been executed for treason in 1680
as one of the 'five popish lords' involved in the Titus Oates affair.
[20] See *Burke's Peerage*.
[21] *Shadows of Life and Thought*, 131.

For Lord Stafford he produced English versions of a number of alchemical works, including *The Triumphal Chariot of Antimony* by Basil Valentine. And then, in 1894, appeared 'the *magnum opus* of the whole incredible adventure, being my edition of *The Hermetic and Alchemical Writings of Paracelsus*', and for this Waite had to work against time 'so that the Earl might not wait unduly'. And although, according to Waite, at the time 'seekers were few indeed' for the work of Bombast von Hohenheim, this edition has nevertheless been of great influence in subsequent years.

The first volume is devoted to works of Paracelsus which could fit under the title of 'Hermetic Chemistry', such as *The Aurora of the Philosophers* and *Concerning the Nature of Things*. The themes of the second volume are 'Hermetic Medicine' and 'Hermetic Philosophy', with 'Hermetic Medicine' including texts such as *The Archidoxies* and *Alchemy the Third Column of Medicine*, but also including several texts on how to prepare alchemical medicines. The emphasis on hermeticism and alchemy will be evident, as will the omission of all the practical medical treatises of Paracelsus, such as the surgical works.

What Paracelsus appears from this set of volumes? Obviously this Paracelsus is an alchemist. Thus Lord Stafford the practical alchemist wanting the transmutation of metals had his Paracelsus here, with recipes he could follow. But Paracelsus is also presented as an alchemist concerned (as Waite put it in his Preface) with 'the development of hidden possibilities or virtues in any substance, whether by God, or man, or Nature'.[22] And so Waite also had his Paracelsus here, a Paracelsus who is an alchemist at the spiritual and transcendental level rather than at the material level, indeed who is a spiritual alchemist, using 'the symbolical language of Alchemy in a spiritual or transcendental sense'. And, on the medical side, this edition presents Paracelsus the *spiritual* physician, with his Great Elixir and his Universal Medicine: but deliberately excludes Paracelsus the *practical* physician with his 'many formidable treatises on surgical science, and on the causes and cure of diseases'.[23] For, to Waite, even Paracelsus' prescriptions 'were not to be literally understood, even when they were apparently the ordinary formulae and concerned with the known

---

[22] *The Hermetic and Alchemical Writings of Aureolus Philippus Theophrastus Bombast, of Hohenheim, called Paracelsus the Great, Now for the First Time Faithfully Translated into English,* by Arthur Edward Waite, 2 vols., London 1894, repr. New York 1967, vol. 1, Preface, xxii–xxiii.

[23] *The Hermetic and Alchemical Writings,* vol. 1, Preface, xxii.

materia of medicine'.[24] *All* was spiritual and to be understood spiritually. To put it bluntly, Waite's Paracelsus was a Paracelsus who
had been engaged on a spiritual journey, and not a sixteenth century one but a *19th* century spiritual journey, taking him through
Spiritualism, Theosophy, Occult Science, Alchemy, the Magic of
Eliphas Lévi, Rosicrucianism, and the Order of the Golden Dawn,
and who was about to move on to Esoteric Freemasonry and the
lore of the Tarot cards. Late-nineteenth century occultism is built
into the selection of the texts, into the interpretation of them, into the
very translation itself, and into the characterisation of Paracelsus
the historical man. In particular, Waite imported from Eliphas Lévi
the view that Paracelsus was restoring an ancient occult medicine.[25]

One can see, thus, how *this* occult Paracelsus was the construction of modern, 19th century British, occultists. A similar state of
affairs seems to have obtained in the early years of this century in
both France and Germany, where editions of the translated works
of Paracelsus were produced under the auspices of mystic and occult
publishers.[26]

There is another occult Paracelsus, a different and more famous
one, created shortly after, and which is still flourishing into the present day, and this tradition, too, produced a set of translated texts
of Paracelsus, seeming to offer unobstructed—if assisted—access to
Paracelsus the man speaking. This is the Paracelsus which emerges
from the work of Carl Gustav Jung and his circle, and Jung's 'analytical psychology'.

Jung's encounter and fascination with alchemy is very well known,
and is integral with his working-out and presentation of his 'analytical psychology'. Jung was the son of a Lutheran pastor. Always religious in outlook from his childhood, and working on psychic (hypnotic)
phenomena for his thesis, from around 1910 Jung became completely

---

[24] *The Hermetic and Alchemical Writings*, vol. 1, Preface, xxii.

[25] Lévi says, 'This truly universal medicine is based upon a spacious theory of
light, called by adepts fluid or potable gold . . .', *The History of Magic, Including a Clear
and Precise Exposition of its Procedure, its Rites and its Mysteries*, translated by Arthur
Edward Waite, London 1913, 340.

[26] Hans Kayser, ed., *Schriften Theophrasts von Hohenheim gennant Paracelsus*, Leipzig,
'Bücher der deutscher Mystik', 1921, in which brief passages from Paracelsus are
assembled under various headings; Grillot de Givry, *Oeuvres Complètes de Paracelse,
Traduites pour la Première Fois du Latin et Collationnées sur les Editions Allemandes*, 2 vols.,
Paris, in the 'Classiques de l'Occulte' series, 1913–4.

fascinated by the mythical, spiritual, and mystical traditions, and this interest was a significant factor in his break with Freud in 1913.[27] In his autobiography Jung records some telling moments in this respect. In 1910 Freud 'adopted' Jung as his intellectual heir, and urged Jung to defend the sexual theory. Jung said, 'Against what?', and Freud said 'Against the black tide of mud of occultism'.[28] Jung went out and explored the occult. So the period of Jung being made the heir is the period of Jung beginning to split from Freud—and it was precisely over the rational/occult distinction! One can see, therefore, how very important the occult dimension was to Jung and to his analytical theories. Jung, of course, interpreted this event as Freud denying his mystical (feminine) side; Jung says that Freud had dreams that Jung wanted to kill him (Freud), the father figure. So each interpreted the event according to their pre-existent theories.

Astrology Jung took up at a time when it was becoming of great interest in the German speaking world,[29] but his interest in alchemy seems more unusual. Jung's own deep interest in Paracelsus seems to have begun in 1928,[30] and was thereafter very committed, and not only did he seize the opportunity of twice giving major public lectures on Paracelsus (in 1929 and 1941), one of them on 'Paracelsus the physician', but he wrote another important essay on him too, 'Paracelsus as a spiritual phenomenon' (published in 1942). Of this essay Jung wrote in his autobiography:

> Through Paracelsus I was finally led to discuss the nature of alchemy in relation to religion and psychology—or, to put it another way, of alchemy as a form of religious philosophy. This I did in *Psychology and Alchemy* (1944). Thus I had at last reached the ground which under-lay my own experiences of the years 1913 to 1917; for the process

---

[27] See George B. Hogenson, *Jung's Struggle with Freud*, University of Notre Dame Press 1983, esp. Part 2, 'From Freud to Mythology', 15–40.

[28] C.G. Jung, *Memories, Dreams, Reflections*, orig. German edition, 1962; tr. by Richard and Clara Winston, 1967; London, reprint, 1983, 173. The claim has been made that Freud's psychoanalysis was deeply influenced by mysticism, but mysticism from the Jewish tradition, not the alchemical tradition as in the case of Jung; see David Bakan, *Sigmund Freud and the Jewish Mystical Tradition*, Princeton 1958.

[29] Ellic Howe, *Urania's Children: The Strange World of the Astrologers*, London 1967, esp. chapter 5, 'The German revival'. For the British story, see now also Patrick Curry, *A Confusion of Prophets: Victorian and Edwardian Astrology*, London 1992.

[30] 'Light on the nature of alchemy began to come to me only after I had read the text of the *Golden Flower*, that specimen of Chinese alchemy which Richard Wilhelm sent me in 1928. I was stirred by the desire to become more closely acquainted with alchemical texts'; Jung in *Memories, Dreams, Reflections*, ch. 7, 230.

through which I had passed at that time corresponded to the process of alchemical transformation discussed in that book.[31]

So Jung equates his own personal psychic journey and spiritual trans-mutation with the alchemical transmutations of Paracelsus: that is to say, in Jung's view, Paracelsus and his work had, at a higher or more universal level, prefigured Jung himself and *his* work. And in writing so extensively on alchemy in later years, once he had had the initial insight or vision, Jung's general aim was

> to demonstrate that the world of alchemical symbols definitely does not belong to the rubbish heap of the past, but stands in a very real and living relationship to our most recent discoveries concerning the psychology of the unconscious. Not only does this modern psycholog-ical discipline give us the key to the secrets of alchemy, but, conversely, alchemy provides the psychology of the unconscious with a meaning-ful historical basis.[32]

With his essentially religious and spiritual attitude to psychological phenomena, and having found in Gnostic writings the prototype of the 'archetype',[33] in Paracelsus and alchemy Jung then found the prototypes of neurosis and transference, much of dream symbolism, and the role of the therapist who 'confronts the opposites with one another and aims at uniting them permanently'.[34] The Jungian ther-apist is an alchemist. Conversely of course for Jung, Paracelsus the alchemist must have been an early Jungian therapist.

And Paracelsian alchemy is for Jung more than just a metaphor or model for psychic transformations:

> As the alchemists, with but few exceptions, did not know that they were bringing psychic structures to light but thought that they were explaining the transformations of matter, there were no psychological considerations to prevent them, for reasons of sensitiveness, from lay-ing bare the background of the psyche, which a more conscious per-son would be nervous of doing.[35]

---

[31] Jung, *Memories, Dreams, Reflections*, 236.

[32] C.G. Jung, *Mysterium Coniunctionis: An Inquiry into the Separation and Synthesis of Psychic Opposites in Alchemy*; first German edition 1955, 1956; English translation by R.F.C. Hull, Princeton 1963, repr. 1977, xiii.

[33] The whole concept of the 'archetype', so central to his developed theories, Jung took in 1919 from the *Corpus Hermeticum* (God is 'the archetypal light'). Jung, 'Archetypes of the collective unconscious', *Collected Works*, vol. 9, 4; Jolande Jacobi, *Complex/Archetype/Symbol in the Psychology of C.G. Jung*; original German edition, Zurich 1957, English translation by Ralph Manheim, New York 1959; see 34.

[34] *Mysterium Coniunctionis*, xv.

[35] *Mysterium Coniunctionis*, xvii.

So alchemy for Paracelsus—at least in Jung's view—'was not sim-ply a chemical procedure as we understand it, but far more a philo-sophical procedure, a special kind of yoga, in so far as yoga also seeks to bring about a psychic transformation.'[36]

All this is delightfully and necessarily circular in argument. Jung thinks he finds *in* Paracelsus and alchemy certain truths about psy-choanalysis, 'truths' he is in fact projecting *onto* Paracelsus and alchemy. And then he uses these 'truths', deriving ultimately from his psy-choanalytic thinking, to interpret Paracelsus the historical figure as an alchemist-who-is-really-a-psychoanalyst. This is, of course, the only way one can find a twentieth century psychoanalyst in the sixteenth century: by putting him there, and claiming he was not aware of what he was 'really' doing. 'None of the alchemists ever had any clear idea of what [their] philosophy was really about', writes Jung,[37] who from his superior position knows the truth: they were really psychoanalysts!

Why Jung chose Paracelsus as his model, apart from the fact that both were Swiss and Paracelsus was the most famous of German-speaking physicians in history, I have not been able to determine. But it was, I suppose, important for Jung that Paracelsus was some-one from well before the 'atomistic, mechanistic views of the late nineteenth century' which Jung disliked and which he associated with Freud.[38]

The actual set of Paracelsus texts in German which projected this view of Paracelsus, using Paracelsus' own words—and which were then translated from German into English—was produced by Jolande Jacobi. Jacobi was one of the group of loyal female disciples that Jung attracted round himself, and who have been recently well described as his 'Valkyries'.[39] She came from a Hungarian Jewish family, and left them behind her when she went to work with Jung in 1938, at the age of nearly 49. She had religious and mystical inclinations, eventually converting to Catholicism. She became an analysand of Jung, and eventually became a Jungian analyst herself.

---

[36] 'Paracelsus the Physician', paragraph 28; see the English translation by R.F.C. Hull (1966) reprinted in *The Spirit in Man, Art and Literature*, London 1966.

[37] 'Paracelsus as a Spiritual Phenomenon', 231 of the original German edition; see *Collected Works*, vol. 13, 186, translated by R.F.C. Hull.

[38] The quotation is from Jolande Jacobi, *The Way of Individuation*, tr. R.F.C. Hull, London 1967, 3.

[39] See the chapter 'Jolande Jacobi: Impressionist', in Maggy Anthony, *The Valkyries: The Women Around Jung*, Longmead, Shaftesbury, Devon 1990, 55–63.

She has been described as 'the disturber of the peace, the one with
the vision of Jung's greatness who wished to present him to the world
in a big way; an extrovert who grated on the nerves of the very
introverted circle of people around Jung'.[40] Her sharp tongue put
her at odds with others of Jung's circle, and her fiery temper led to
disputes with Jung himself. The end of one such dispute has passed
into the lore of Jungian analysts: to his great surprise, another analyst saw Jacobi being thrown out of Jung's office after she had had
a row with Jung, and she went down the stairs on her bottom, bump,
bump, bump.[41] But, whatever this apparent rebellion against Jung
might mean, when she applied herself to the task of expounding and
popularising the works of Jung, Jacobi is found to 'stick closely to
Jung's words and ideas, simply clarifying him':[42] she became the great
populariser of the Master's works, and her writings on, from and
about him are still in print.

So in this context it is quite significant that in introducing her
earliest essay at popularising Jung, *The Psychology of C.G. Jung*, first
published in 1940, Jacobi was to quote Paracelsus in her Introduction.
Following the 'inner path', Jacobi claims, equips the individual to
turn to the 'outer path' to 'fulfil the claims of life in the collectivity':

> Within and without he will be able to affirm his personality. 'The
> world was created imperfect' says Paracelsus, 'and God put man into
> it in order to perfect it'.[43]

And her second work promoting the Jungian vision was in fact
the book of Paracelsus texts: *Paracelsus: Selected Writings*, which first appeared in German in 1942 with the more revealing title of 'Living
Heritage'.[44] This volume is put together from paragraphs and short
passages from Paracelsus' writings, illustrating various themes, such
as 'Credo', 'Man and the Created World', 'Man and his Body', 'Man
and Works', 'Man and Ethics', 'Man and Spirit', 'Man and Fate',
and 'God the Eternal Light'. By this technique we get, for instance,

---

[40] *The Valkyries*, 55.
[41] *The Valkyries*, 59.
[42] *The Valkyries*, 60.
[43] This passage is introduced into the 4th English edition of 1944, and is the
only appearance of Paracelsus in this work; this passage was obviously introduced
by Jacobi after she had completed her next book, the one on Paracelsus.
[44] Originally published as *Theophrastus Paracelsus: Lebendiges Erbe*, Zurich 1942;
English translation by Norbert Guterman, Princeton 1951, second edition 1958,
reprinted 1959.

a smoothly flowing 'Credo' from Paracelsus, outlining succinctly his beliefs, and using only his own words. But it is a 'Credo' which Paracelsus did not write as a 'Credo': in other words, the 'Credo' is a Jacobi construct. It is also, of course, a Jung construct. How far it represents any 'Credo' that Paracelsus himself might have written, must remain an open question.

And this is where it gets really interesting, because only a couple of years later, in 1945, Jacobi compiled a similar work from the writings of Jung himself, in part as a 70th birthday gift. This is *Psychological Reflections.*[45] Among the headings Jacobi uses here are 'Recognition of the soul', 'Man in his relation to others', 'Between good and evil', 'The life of the spirit', 'The way to God'. The two works are, in some ways, interchangeable (at least in the eyes of a non-believer in either alchemy or Jungian analysis, like myself), and many of the texts within them could be quoted as characterising either Paracelsus or Jung, so close has the identification of the two become in the eyes of Jacobi the Jungian student and, I suggest, in the eyes of Jung himself.

So here are two 'fat' occult Paracelsus-es: one a late 19th British one, one a mid-20th century Swiss one, with different occult visions, serving different occult interests, yet each built authentically, it would appear, on genuine Paracelsus texts, and each producing—making accessible—Paracelsus texts which reinforce that vision and place it at the door of the historical Paracelsus. There is nothing like a translation or edition of texts to have this kind of effect! There are probably other occult Paracelsus-es too: to each occultist his occult Paracelsus.

None of this is to deny that there *is* indeed of course an enormous and enormously significant occult dimension to Paracelsus—to the thin Paracelsus, that is. It is just to point out that the *construction* of the later *reputation* (or, more properly, reputations) of Paracelsus as an occultist was made by people whose first interest was in their own spiritual view of the occult or in their own view of psychical life, not in retrieving the true historical 'thin' Paracelsus. The *only* Paracelsus they were each interested in was *their* 'occult' one. We have seen two occult Paracelsus-es here: someone whose alchemy

---

[45] Originally published as *Psychologische Betrachtungen: Eine Auslese aus den Schriften von C.G. Jung*, Zurich 1945; second edition, 1949; English translation mostly by R.F.C. Hull, London 1953.

was a mystical spiritual adventure and whose 'true' medicine was also wholly spiritual, the other someone whose alchemy was truly a process of psychological and psychoanalytical self-liberation. It is perhaps not surprising, therefore, that these occult Paracelsus-es do not mesh particularly well either with each other or with other Paracelsus-es, those constructed in pursuit of different interests.

Incidentally, tracing the origins of these occult Paracelsus-es did help me understand why I had originally found Paracelsus so antipathetic: the answer lay in the fact that I cannot stand modern occultism, so I simply detested the historical Paracelsus presented through the distorting lenses of modern occultisms. It was, of course, before I learnt to distinguish between the fat and the thin Paracelsus-es. What was particularly liberating for me was to discover that even a deeply scrupulous scholar such as Walter Pagel, whose writings on Paracelsus had seemed so authoritative but which I had found so deeply irritating and intellectually impenetrable, had an agenda of his own when he drew our attention to Paracelsus as being a most significant figure in the history of medicine; but once one recognised the agenda, even Pagel's Paracelsus was another fat figure.[46]

IV   *Thin Paracelsus*

In writing about the 'elusiveness' of Paracelsus, Owsei Temkin wrote that 'The literature on Hippocrates and Paracelsus is abundant just because it is provoked by so many unanswered questions', questions, he implied, about the historical Paracelsus. I beg to differ. We have seen a little of how malleable the reputation of Paracelsus has been over the centuries, how open to interpretation, how available the thin Paracelsus has been for fattening. Paracelsus has multiple reputations because of the multiple later interests of others, who have had an interest in co-opting him to their side.

Is there anything about the historical, the thin, Paracelsus which makes, or made, him particularly attractive/available for these many imposed roles, these multiple after-lives, these 'subsequent performances' (as Jonathan Miller might term them)? That is, why have

---

[46] The nature of Pagel's Paracelsus has been explored by T.M. Stokes, 'Walter Pagel as an historian of medicine', unpublished M. Phil. essay, Cambridge Wellcome Unit.

later people so often chosen Paracelsus, rather than anyone else, on whom to foist such varied roles? A possible answer might be that Paracelsus had many roles for his contemporaries. And here, in closing, I want to raise the question of the meaning of certain distinctive features of Paracelsus' reputation in his own day and shortly after—beyond his involvement with magic and his possible pacts with the Devil—and which have needed explaining or explaining away by later admirers intent on characterising Paracelsus in their own images.

I call to attention six aspects of his contemporary reputation:[47]

1. his excessive drinking
2. his excessive travelling
3. his constant raging against authority
4. his dirtiness
5. his madness
6. his lack of sexual reputation—indeed the rumour that he was a eunuch or had been castrated.

I am not concerned here with the validity of these reputations, but with their existence and their association with the Paracelsus who lived: I am calling on the principle that gossip like this must, at some level, correspond to something about the real person, or have been seen as a possible thing which might be true of this person, or it couldn't 'stick', as gossip must do if it is to be believed.

The point I am centrally interested in here is this, which I have not been able to find dealt with in the literature: what was the *sixteenth* century meaning of such reputations? Although the tradition of work on Rabelais begun by Mikhail Bakhtin has opened up such questions, and for the very period of Paracelsus,[48] I have not found the meanings of these particular reputations dealt with. We know that today reputations for drunkenness, dirtiness, rootlessness, raging, raving, and not having sex, are not desirable, and they would tend to undermine the validity of what one preached. One or two historians have claimed that these are simply slanders put about by Paracelsus' enemies, and these characterisations would certainly work

---

[47] Most of these derive from the account of Paracelsus' assistant, Johannes Oporinus, in a letter dating from 1555; the letter is translated in Henry M. Pachter, *Paracelsus: Magic into Science*, New York 1951, 154–6.

[48] Mikhail Bakhtin, *Rabelais and his World*; original Russian version, 1965; English translation by Helene Iswolsky, Cambridge, Mass. 1968; Carol Clark, *The Vulgar Rabelais*, Glasgow 1983.

like that today. In a Romantic interpretation—a kind of interpretation which was of course created long after Paracelsus' own day—by contrast, these characteristics serve, in the eyes of admirers of Paracelsus, to make him into a romantic genius. If we take just the drinking, then Eliphas Lévy, for instance, the fully romantic French magician of the 19th century, to whom Paracelsus once appeared in a dream, interpreted Paracelsus' drunkenness in just this way—as revealing the true spiritual and magical gift of Paracelsus. 'The marvellous Paracelsus', he calls him, 'always drunk and always lucid, like the heroes of Rabelais':[49]

> To strive continually against Nature in order to [achieve] her rule and conquest is to risk reason and life. Paracelsus dared to do so, but even in the struggle itself he employed equilibrated forces and opposed the intoxication of wine to that of intelligence. So was Paracelsus a man of inspiration and miracles.[50]

In other words, like a true magical adept, Paracelsus kept himself balanced between the opposing forces by keeping himself drunk.[51]

Paracelsus' reputation as someone immune to sexual temptation, and possibly as castrated, may possibly be linked to either the Christian ascetic tradition or to his magical interests. The Greek Church Father, Origen, castrated himself to achieve greater commitment to the kingdom of heaven,[52] the medieval scholastic and priest, Peter Abelard, also castrated himself. Similarly there is a tradition of a mythical figure, embodied in the character of Klingsor, whose (self-?) castration gave him superior magical powers.[53] Paracelsus and those gossiping about him may not have known about any of these. But was

---

[49] *Transcendental Magic*, 11.

[50] *Transcendental Magic*, 266.

[51] Another post-Romantic interpretation puts Paracelsus' drunkenness down to simple excess, typical of a genius: Giordano Bruno supposedly said (according to Henry Pachter):

> Who after Hippocrates was similar to Paracelsus as a wonder-working doctor? And, seeing how much this inebriate knew, what should I think he might have discovered had he been sober?

As quoted by Pachter, *Paracelsus: Magic into Science*, 297, without reference.

[52] Joseph Wilson Trigg, *Origen: The Bible and Philosophy in the Third Century*, London 1985, 53–4.

[53] In Wolfram von Eschenbach's *Parzival* Klingsor is unmanned by a jealous husband; in Wagner's *Parsifal* he is understood to be self-castrated. I am grateful to Martin Preston for information on these points.

there possibly a *sixteenth* century image of castration as leading to greater purity, holiness or power with respect to nature?

Of course, if we knew the 'real' Paracelsus, he would be firmly placed in his time, historicised, and limited to his time: and hence he would be less famous, less available to be all the things we want him to be. I come back to Paracelsus' supposed motto: 'Let him not be another's, who can be his own'. He has been everyone else's: is it time for him to be his own man?

CHAPTER THREE

PARACELSUS AS A GUIDING MODEL – HISTORIANS AND THEIR OBJECT

Dietlinde Goltz

I *Preliminary Remark*

This chapter contains the results of a study of the relationship between historians dealing with Paracelsus and the object of their research. For this purpose, I consulted the medical writings of Paracelsus[1] and also used the scholarly historical literature on Paracelsus of the last one hundred years as a source.[2] This literature comprises monographs purporting to be scholarly contributions as well as articles published in learned journals whose authors hold, by and large, an academic degree. Most of these authors hold academic posts in universities. I believe this preliminary remark to be necessary in order to avoid any misconceptions that I might have based my analysis on 'yellow press' statements on Paracelsus.

II *Introduction to the subject matter*

The history of medicine certainly does not suffer from any shortage of outstanding personalities. For some 200 years now, Paracelsus has been counted amongst history's great doctors,[3] and for more than 100 years, the number of writings on Paracelsus has exceeded the

---

[1] See the edition by Karl Sudhoff (ed.), *Theophrast von Hohenheim, genannt Paracelsus. Sämtliche Werke.* 1. Abteilung. Medizinische ... Schriften, 14 vols., Munich/Berlin 1922–33.

[2] A complete record and analysis of this literature is neither possible nor necessary here.

[3] It was only from the Romantic period onwards that Paracelsus came to be seen in a positive light; see the detailed study by K. Goldammer, *Paracelsus in der deutschen Romantik. Eine Untersuchung zur Geschichte der Paracelsus-Rezeption und zu geistesgeschichtlichen Hintergründen der Romantik*, Salzburger Beiträge zur Paracelsusforschung 20 (henceforth *SBP*), Vienna 1980.

literature on any other physician.[4] In addition, literature on Paracelsus reaches beyond the field of history of medicine and, to a remarkable degree, is read by educated people. We are thus justified in terming Paracelsus—besides Hippocrates—the physician of the past whose name is most widely known in the German speaking countries.

Why is it that Paracelsus, in contrast to Hippocrates, Harvey, Haller or Virchow, despite the facts that his writings never became official textbook teaching material and the medical reform which he so vociferously advocated was never realised, has been the focus of attention of so many biographers and historians, many of whom have dedicated their whole working lives to him? What is the reason for the immense popularity of Paracelsus, to whose name everybody seems to be able to attach some concept or other? Why are there so many clinics and chemist's shops named after Paracelsus in the German speaking countries, while only few such institutions are named after other medical celebrities? Why is it that seminars on Paracelsus are still particularly popular with medical students?[5]

It is a striking phenomenon that a historical personality whose merits are rather modest in comparison with other famous physicians[6] meets with so much attention. I shall demonstrate that any explanation based on the significance of the person or his works fails to hit the core of the matter.

There must be reasons for the popularity of Paracelsus as a historical subject and for the distinct traits of the image of Paracelsus which I will elaborate on in the following. And it is, without a doubt, the task of the historian to trace such reasons and to present them— even though they may be in evidence to a greater or lesser extent also within ourselves in our capacity as historians working on Paracelsus.

Section III presents a selection of six conspicuous and contradictory traits—or over emphasized aspects—of the Paracelsus image,

---

[4] See the bibliography by K.-H. Weimann, *Paracelsus-Bibliographie 1932–1960 mit einem Verzeichnis neu entdeckter Paracelsus-Handschriften (1900–1960)*, Kosmosophie 2, Wiesbaden 1963 and the continuation by R. Dilg-Frank, 'Paracelse, philosophe de la nature et de la religion: Bibliographie 1960–1980', in *Paracelse—Cahiers de l'Hermétisme*, Paris 1980, 269–80.

[5] For the 'marketing' of the name Paracelsus, see R. Blaser, 'Paracelsus als Aushängeschild' in *Die ganze Welt ein Apotheken. Festschrift für Otto Zekert*, SBP 8, Vienna 1969, 1–6.

[6] W. Pagel, *Das medizinische Weltbild des Paracelsus. Seine Zusammenhänge mit Neoplatonismus und Gnosis*, Kosmosophie 1, Wiesbaden 1962, 1–32 provides an assessment of Paracelsus and his work which remains valid; for his major achievements, see in particular 29–31.

after which I will put forward some attempts at interpretation (IV).
Section V examines the problem based on Paracelsus's own writings, and the conclusion (VI) answers the question for the point and
purpose of this study, as well as discussing some of the results of my
analysis.

III   *Striking traits of the Paracelsus image*

While browsing through literature on Paracelsus, the reader quickly
comes to realise that a substantial number of authors adopt the style
of language and speech of Paracelsus to a greater or lesser degree,
sometimes culminating in downright imitation. I am not talking about
works such as E.G. Kolbenheyer's Paracelsus novel[7] which are termed
'adaptations', but about writings which claim to be scholarly analyses. This phenomenon can be found again and again in the literature of the last 100 years.[8] I am not familiar with other cases in
which historians writing about topics or persons adjust to the historical language of their subject or imitate the diction of their hero.
In some cases the authors went as far as creating neologisms which

---

[7] See E.G. Kolbenheyer, *Paracelsus. Romantrilogie*, Munich 1941. The individual
parts of the trilogy were published in 1917, 1921, and 1925 respectively; see also
K. Goldammer, 'Paracelsus-Bild und Paracelsus-Forschung. Wissenschaft und populäre Elemente in der Literatur', *Nova Acta Paracelsica* (henceforth *NAP*) 10, 1982,
109–27 and A. Weuthen, 'Zum Paracelsus-Bild des 20. Jahrhunderts', *Beiträge zur
Geschichte der Pharmazie* 38, 1986, 58–60.

[8] See F. Gundolf, *Paracelsus*, Berlin 1927, E. Zeller, *Paracelsus. Der Beginn eines
deutschen Arzttums*, Halle (ca. 1935), R. Thiel, *Männer gegen Tod und Teufel*, Berlin 1936,
A. Reitz, *Die Welt des Paracelsus. Leben und Gedanken des ausgezeichneten Doktors der Medizin
Theophrastus von Hohenheim, genannt Paracelsus*, Stuttgart 1937; in particular G. Sticker,
Paracelsus. Ein Lebensbild, Nova Acta Leopoldina, New Series, 66, Halle 1941,
F. Weinhandl, *Paracelsus-Studien*, ed. S. Domandl, *SBP* 10, Vienna 1970, S. von
Waltershausen, *Paracelsus am Eingang der deutschen Bildungsgeschichte*, 2nd. ed., Leipzig
1942, F. Werle, 'Die kosmische Weltanschauung des Paracelsus', *NAP* 4, 1947,
12–29, K. Goldammer, *Paracelsus. Natur und Offenbarung*, Heilkunde und Geisteswelt
5, Hannover 1953, E. Bloch, *Vorlesungen zur Philosophie der Renaissance*, Frankfurt 1972,
58–68 (Paracelsus), H. Schipperges, *Paracelsus im Licht der Natur*, Stuttgart 1974, *idem*,
'Paracelsus. Arzt in seiner Zeit—Arzt an der Grenze der Neuzeit', *Anstösse* 2, 1982,
40–46, *idem, Paracelsus. Das Abenteuer einer sokratischen Existenz*, Sokratische Weisheit 3,
Freiburg 1983, *idem, Die Entienlehre des Paracelsus. Aufbau und Umriss seiner Theoretischen
Pathologie*, Veröffentlichungen aus der Forschungsstelle für Theoretische Pathologie
der Heidelberger Akademie der Wissenschaften, Berlin/Heidelberg 1988, L. Müller-
Salzburg, 'Der Teil und das Ganze in Hohenheims Gedankenwelt', *SBP* 25, 1987,
146–79. See also L. Braun, 'Paracelsus und der Aufbau der Episteme seiner Zeit'
in *Festschrift für Otto Zekert*, *SBP* 8, Vienna 1969, 7–18, *idem, Paracelsus. Alchemist—
Chemiker—Erneuerer der Heilkunde. Eine Bildbiographie*, Zurich 1990 and others.

they considered to be Paracelsus-type German, which, however, have probably never been used in German-speaking regions. Paracelsus is said to be *'stürzig gleich einem jungen Strom'* ('precipitant like a young stream'), and a *'beginnlicher Forscher'* (a 'beginning researcher'). In *'kampfsüchtigen Läuften'*[9] ('struggle-keen rambles'), for example, he is said to have explored 'European regions in flowering relaxation' (in *'blühender Gelassenheit durchs europäische Gebreite'*), only to write down the 'findings of the day' (*'die Findungen des Tages'*) in the evenings.[10] In other sources he is said to act *'selbstig-schöpferisch'* ('self-creatively') and also *'naturforscherlich'* ('natural-scientifically') within a 'nature-bound world-feeling' (*'naturisches Weltspüren'*),[11] and he is said to show the 'sharpened sightability of a creator working spiritually in the dark' (*'die geschärfte Sichtigkeit des in nächtlicher Stille geistig Schaffenden'*).[12] Other linguistic 'peculiarities'[13] include words such as *'Ähnelungen'* ('similarities'), *'unbehilfliche Formen'* ('unhelpful forms'),[14] 'wunderbarliche Männer' ('wonderfully men')[15] and *'gesichtige Nachgründer der Natur'* ('sightful recreators of Nature').[16]

This activity of creating and imitating language seems even stranger as, at the same time, Paracelsus is reproached for a language which is 'confused, roundabout, almost abrupt' and 'often completely incomprehensible'[17] or 'not yet really very expressive'; his 'expressive clumsiness'[18] is emphasised, and it is claimed that Paracelsus's contemporaries found it hard to understand his language and that he was unable to make himself understood properly. This argument is epitomised in the claim that Paracelsus was unable to correctly understand his own terminology.[19] Why, we have to ask ourselves, do researchers

---

[9] Gundolf, *Paracelsus*, 14 and 28.
[10] Zeller, *Paracelsus*, 21 and 19.
[11] Gundolf, *Paracelsus*, 31, 131, 65.
[12] Goldammer, *Paracelsus*, 28.
[13] F. Spunda, *Paracelsus. Menschen, Völker, Zeiten. Eine Kulturgeschichte in Einzeldarstellungen* 6, Vienna/Leipzig 1925.
[14] Gundolf, *Paracelsus*, 30, 16, 65.
[15] F. Strunz, *Theophrastus Paracelsus. Idee und Problem seiner Anschauung*, Deutsche Geistesgeschichte 2, 2nd. ed., Salzburg/Leipzig 1937, 11.
[16] Zeller, *Paracelsus*, 41.
[17] *Ibid.*, 7.
[18] Goldammer, *Paracelsus*, 29f.
[19] K. Goldammer, 'Aufgaben der Paracelsusforschung', in J. Telle (ed.), *Parerga Paracelsica. Paracelsus in Vergangenheit und Gegenwart*, Heidelberger Studien zur Naturkunde der frühen Neuzeit 3, Stuttgart 1992, 8, 14, 22. A few scholars praise Paracelsus's language, see R. Netzhammer, *Theophrastus Paracelsus. Das Wissenswerteste über dessen Leben, Lehre und Schriften*, Einsiedeln/Waldshut/Cologne 1901, 99 (*'der gewandte Schriftsteller'*—'the skillful writer'), and B. de Telepnef, 'Glossen zum Paragranum oder

mimic a language which they believe to be confused, roundabout, clumsy and unsuitable for understanding the subject matter?[20]

My second point is the completely exaggerated and therefore immediately obvious[21] idealisation of Paracelsus as a person, usually phrased in a surge of superlatives. He is termed the 'most important unfinished in the history of medicine'[22] and the 'most significant figure of the northern Renaissance',[23] and he is seen as a 'powerful personality'[24] or a 'powerful storm'.[25] He is considered to be a 'real'[26] or 'prophetic genius'[27] and an 'ingenious spirit',[28] and he is even termed the 'bearer of light for mankind'.[29] Some see in him 'predominantly a metaphysician'[30] or a 'worldly-wise thinker',[31] while others regard him as a 'fanatical fighter for truth'[32] with 'a proud sense of freedom'.[33] Of

---

Viersäulenbuch', *NAP* 3, 1946, 16 (*'die plastische, neu und herrlich klingende deutsche Sprache'*—'the malleable, new and magnificient German language'); for Paracelsus's language and how it was assessed by his contemporaries, see the detailed study by J. Telle, 'Die Schreibart des Paracelsus im Urteil deutscher Fachschriftsteller des 16. und 17. Jahrhunderts', in R. Dilg-Frank (ed.), *Kreatur und Kosmos. Internationale Beiträge zur Paracelsusforschung*, Stuttgart/New York 1981.

[20] See in particular Gundolf, *Paracelsus*, who deliberately imitates Paracelsus's language and describes it as 'dark and violent speech' (*'dunkles und heftiges Sprechen'*) which is characterized by a 'struggle with expression' (*'Kampf mit dem Ausdruck'*, 13) and is 'often unclear and disjointed' (*'oft unklar im Sagen, oft ordnungslos im Verknüpfen'*, 14). Gundolf considers Paracelsus to be 'heavy-tongued' (*'schwerzüngig'*, 44). The textual logic is perceived by Gundolf to be 'heavy-handed and phrased . . . in an awkward way' (*'schwerfällig und umständlich gefasst'*, 128).

[21] Although this idolisation is evident, hardly any scholars refer to it. Only Fritz Hartmann has warned against turning Paracelsus into a figment of one's wishes, see F. Hartmann, 'Paracelsus und die heutige Medizin', *Anstösse* 2, 1982, 48.

[22] E. Rosner, Studien zum Leben und Wirken des Paracelsus in St. Gallen [1977]; *NAP*, New Series 3, 1988, 32. I have not attempted to trace these epithets which Rosner uses repeatedly without any references to the sources.

[23] Cited without a reference by R. Mühler, 'Paracelsus und E.T.A. Hoffmann', *SBP* 11, 1972, 117.

[24] *Ibid.*, 118.

[25] C.G. Jung, *Paracelsica. Zwei Vorlesungen über den Arzt und Philosophen Theophrastus*, Zurich/Leipzig 1942, 9, 10: 'Paracelsus is an ocean' (*'Paracelsus ist ein Meer'*).

[26] Zeller, *Paracelsus*, 12.

[27] H. Hartmann, *Paracelsus—eine deutsche Vision*, Berlin/Vienna 1941, 25.

[28] *Ibid.*, 109.

[29] G. Sticker, *Paracelsus*, 77.

[30] Goldammer, 'Aufgaben', 11.

[31] *Ausstellungskatalog Paracelsus-Gedächtnis-Ausstellung zur Feier der 400. Wiederkehr des Todestages. . . .* Published by Gauamt für Volksgesundheit Württemberg. Stuttgart 1941, 3.

[32] Anon., *Vom Wirken berühmter Ärzte aus vier Jahrhunderten. Theophrast von Hohenheim (Paracelsus)—William Harvey—Leopold Auenbrugger—Carl Gustav Carus.* (Extracts of their works) Ludwigshafen 1936, 11.

[33] J. Hemleben, *Paracelsus. Revolutionär, Arzt und Christ.* Frauenfeld/Stuttgart 1973, 46.

course, he is also termed the 'pioneer for the new',[34] a 'radical reformer'[35] or just an 'adventurer',[36] a 'great speculator'[37] and a 'non-conformist'.[38] These features and epithets are well known and could be multiplied at will.

This type of idealisation maintained its momentum and quality during the Nazi period. For Alfred Rosenberg, for example, Paracelsus represents 'a man with a great longing'; he is a 'lonely prophet . . . with the mark of genius'.[39] His German origins and his (alleged) struggle for a pure German art of medicine, free of foreign influences, were emphasised.[40] This emphasis of the 'German' character of Paracelsus could, however, already be found long before 1933, and not only in Germany but also in Austria and Switzerland, where the particular appraisal of his German origin can be seen even after the War.

Even more striking, however, is the idealisation of Paracelsus as a doctor. Of course, he is universally known the 'great doctor'[41] or the 'courageous doctor' who 'knows no fear'.[42] 'The passion of the doctor' was 'all too strong'[43] within him; he possessed 'unusual abilities as a healer'[44] because he always concentrated on patients rather than illnesses.[45] 'Paracelsus knows', so it is said, 'that the angel lauded him as a doctor'[46] or that 'he was appointed by God to become active as a doctor'.[47] But for everyone, Paracelsus is the 'true doc-

---

[34] Goldammer, *Paracelsus*, 11.

[35] S. Rhein, 'Melanchthon und Paracelsus' in Telle (ed.), *Parerga Paracelsica*, 57, cited by H. Rudolph in Chapter 8 below.

[36] Schipperges, *'Paracelsus'*, 9.

[37] Bloch, *Vorlesungen*, 59: 'He died in 1541 . . . a great empiricist, as well as a great speculator' (*'1541 starb er . . . als grosser Empiriker und gleichzeitig grosser Spekulant'*).

[38] L. Müller-Salzburg, 'Paracelsisches bei Goethe', *SBP* 26, 1988, 51.

[39] A. Rosenberg, *Der Mythos des 20. Jahrhunderts. Eine Wertung der seelisch-geistigen Gestaltenkämpfe unserer Zeit*, 5th ed. Munich 1933, 251; similar ideas can be found at an earlier date, see H.S. Chamberlain, *Die Grundlagen des neunzehnten Jahrhunderts*, 2 vols., Munich 1909, 834, who praises Paracelsus as a 'fearless destroyer of Arab-Jewish quackery' and a 'fanatic mystic', 1058.

[40] See, for example, the titles published between 1933 and 1945 in Weimann, *Paracelsus-Bibliographie*.

[41] F. Strunz, *Theophrastus Paracelsus*, 12 and M. Schad, *Paracelsus. Sein Ringen um eine wirklichkeitsgemässe Medizin*, Vorträge Urachhaus 38, Stuttgart 1987, 5.

[42] H. Hartmann, *Paracelsus*, 45: 'As a true physician he is fearless' (*'Furcht kennt er als wahrer Arzt nicht'*).

[43] R. Weber, 'Reformatio Medicinae und die Heilkunst des Volkes', *NAP* 8, 1957, 106: 'In ihm war die Leidenschaft des Arzt-Seins zu stark'.

[44] Hemleben, *Paracelsus*, 39.

[45] L. Müller-Salzburg, 'Faust und Paracelsus', *NAP* 10, 1982, 133.

[46] Zeller, *Paracelsus*, 16.

[47] A. Vogt, *Theophrastus Paracelsus als Arzt und Philosoph*, Stuttgart 1956, 18; see

tor', whatever picture this characterisation may call to mind,[48] so that the following question was asked as early as 1907: 'Are there more inspired doctors today than he was?'.[49] The ethical standards which Paracelsus puts forward for doctors and which are indeed high,[50] have implicitly—and probably subconsciously—been turned into real characteristics.[51] Only very few authors concede that we know hardly anything about the day-to-day medical practice of Paracelsus.[52] One of the commonplaces with respect to this image of the true doctor is the unequivocal remark that Paracelsus was the first doctor to practice 'holistic medicine', and he is purported to have been the first doctor to 'see man as a whole'. These authors usually fail to mention what type of 'holistic medicine' they refer to, and at the same time they ignore the fact that the pathology of 'humours' which Paracelsus argued against so heatedly is an excellent example of a holistic practice of medicine which was never equalled before and has never been surpassed since in the way in which it tried to integrate human nature and the environment.[53]—

---

also R.J. Hartmann, *Theophrast von Hohenheim*, Stuttgart/Berlin 1904, 102–115, esp. 102–05.

[48] Zeller, *Paracelsus*, 43: 'These helpers of nature, created by God, are the real physicians' ('*Diese von Gott gewollten Helfer der Natur sind die wahren Ärztlichen Menschen*'); Strunz, *Theophrastus*, 66: 'The true physician incorporates the ideal of knowledge and ability' ('*Der wahre Arzt ist das Ideal eines Wissenden und Begnadeten*'), 168; H. Hartmann, *Paracelsus*, 45; see also Spunda, *Paracelsus*, 44f., 50–52 (Paracelsus as a true doctor); Braun, *Paracelsus*, 135; Franz Hartmann, *Die Medizin des Theophrastus Parazelsus von Hohenheim. Vom theosophischen Standpunkte betrachtet*, 2nd. ed. Leipzig [ca. 1922], 34; H.U. Schefer, *Das Berufsethos des Arztes Paracelsus*, Gesnerus, Supplement 42, Aarau/Frankfurt/Salzburg 1990, 43–45 (Paracelsus on true and false doctors).

[49] E. Schlegel, *Paracelsus in seiner Bedeutung für unsere Zeit. Heilkunde, Forschungsprinzipien, Religion*, Munich 1907, 56.

[50] See Schefer's new and comprehensive monograph on Paracelsus as a physician, Schefer, *Berufsethos*.

[51] Noticeable, in particular, in F. Strunz, *Beiträge und Skizzen zur Geschichte der Naturwissenschaften*, Hamburg/Leipzig 1909, rep. Leipzig 1972, 64–66, where initially Paracelsus's standards for physicians are quoted only for the passage to end: 'So much in brief about his personal character' ('*Soweit in ein paar Strichen eine Skizze seiner Persönlichkeit*'); see also A. Moeller van den Bruck, *Verschwärmte Deutsche*, Die Deutschen 3, Minden 1905, 57.

[52] See, for example, H. Hartmann, *Paracelsus*, 92f., 97 and Fritz Hartmann, *Paracelsus und die heutige Medizin*, 47.

[53] See among others Strunz, *Theophrastus Paracelsus*, 186; F. Spunda, *Das Weltbild des Paracelsus*, Vienna 1941, 62f.; F. Werle 'Paracelsus', *NAP* 1, 179; E.W. Kämmerer, *Das Leib-Seele-Geist-Problem bei Paracelsus und einigen Autoren des 17. Jahrhunderts*, Kosmosophie 3, Wiesbaden 1971, 41f.; V. Bazala, 'Paracelsus und die positive Gesundheitslehre' in *Gestalten und Ideen um Paracelsus*, SBP 41, Vienna 1972, 27–35 and G. Harrer, 'Paracelsus und das Ganzheitsdenken in der modernen Medizin, *SBP* 12, 1974, 53–54.

In conclusion, we cannot help but remark that the sometimes rapturous idealisation of Paracelsus as the true doctor[54] is in direct contrast to available sources. A similar discrepancy concerns the continuous admiration of the new medicine alleged to have been inaugurated by Paracelsus and the medical reform said to have been initiated by him, despite the fact that we are fully aware that he never managed to realise it even in rudimentary form.

Thirdly, I will now highlight some of the other merits[55] which have been attributed to Paracelsus. It enhances the image of the 'great precursor and initiator of modern chemical medicine'[56] and of the perfect and true doctor to be hailed as a 'great scientific pioneer',[57] for example as the 'discoverer of psychosomatics',[58] of psychotherapy[59] and—what could be more obvious—of the unconscious.[60]

---

[54] See Zeller, *Paracelsus*, 42–78 (Chapter on 'Medical man'—'*Der Ärztliche Mensch*'); Spunda, *Paracelsus*, 50–52; Strunz, *Theophrastus Paracelsus*, 27f., 66f., 74: 'this doctor is without doubt a genius . . . Nothing of greater significance can hardly be said about a physician' ('*Dieser zweifellos geniale Arzt . . . Bedeutenderes kann über einen Arzt kaum gesagt werden*').

[55] I have limited myself to brief examples. A comprehensive survey, even without commentary, would fall outside the scope and size of this Chapter.

[56] Jung, *Paracelsica*, 65; above Jung, however, stated that it was 'difficult to find any other fundamental, medical discoveries which could be traced back to Paracelsus' ('*schwer, anzugeben, welche sonstigen ärztlichen Entdeckungen grundsätzlicher Natur auf Paracelsus zurückführt werden könnten*'), see 12.

[57] Strunz, *Theophrastus Paracelsus*, 27; Jung, *Paracelsica*, 177: 'pioneer of empirical psychology' ('*Bahnbrecher der empirischen Psychologie*'); H. Haberlandt, 'Paracelsus im Lichte moderner naturwissenschaftlicher Forschung', *NAP* 7, 1954, 195; Blaser, *Paracelsus*, 27; S. Domandl, 'Agrippa von Nettesheim, Faust und Paracelsus—drei unstete Wanderer', *SBP* 26, 1988, 17: 'lonesome pioneer' ('*einsamer Bahnbrecher*'); K. Greiner, *Paracelsus im Lande seiner Väter*, *SBP* 2, Salzburg 1961, 3. Braun cautiously questions the term 'pioneer', although he then proceeds to use similar characterisations, see L. Braun, *Paracelsus und die Philosophiegeschichte*, *SBP* 5, Vienna 1965, 5f.

[58] Müller-Salzburg, *Faust und Paracelsus*, 133; I. Betschart, 'Paracelsus und die moderne Psychologie', *NAP* 8, 1957, 39.

[59] Strunz, *Theophrastus Paracelsus*, 46; J. Strebel, *Paracelsus. Zur vierten Jahrhundertfeier seines Todes 1541–1941*, Luzern 1941, 15: 'Within psychiatry solutions can only be found once more if the discipline, which is at a dead end, reaches back to Paracelsus' ('*In psychiatrischen Fragen können erst wieder Lösungen erzielt werden, wenn die heutige Psychiatrie, die in engen Sackgassen steckt, auf Paracelsus zurückgeht*'); Jung, *Paracelsica*, 177; L. Birchler, 'Lionardo und Paracelsus', *NAP* 5, 1948, 43. These alleged merits of Paracelsus have, however, not been accepted within the history of psychiatry, see F.G. Alexander and S.T. Selesnick, *Geschichte der Psychiatrie. Ein kritischer Abriss*, Zurich 1969, 118–120. Neither are they mentioned by H.F. Ellenberger in his monograph on 'the discovery of the unconscious', *Die Entdeckung des Unbewussten*, 2 vols., Bern/Stuttgart/Vienna 1973.

[60] R. Allendy, 'La psychiatrie de Paracelse', *NAP* 2, 1945, 121, 124f.; I. Betschart, 'Der Begriff "Imagination" bei Paracelsus', *NAP* 6, 1952, 57; D. Brinckmann, 'Paracelsus und das anthropologische Problem der Übertragung', *NAP* 8, 1957, 46,

He, the 'father of balneology'[61] is, of course, also the 'founding-father of geriatrics' and the first geriatrician[62] as well as the 'first military doctor',[63] and he has, of course, also earned eternal merit as parapsychologist.[64] Less frequently, he is termed a 'creator of a new epistemology'.[65] Again and again, however, he is called a precursor or initiator of 'modern chemical medicine' or celebrated as 'the founder of scientific chemistry'.[66] He is supposed to have laid the foundations of 'scientific research which works on strictly experimental and systematic principles'[67] and is therefore quite logically honoured as 'the first and foremost proponent of the mechanist view of the world'.[68] There is hardly any direction of medicine which Paracelsus is not said to have initiated or discovered, and there is hardly any scientific discovery which Paracelsus is not supposed to have made or at least foreseen.[69] It is precisely this role of Paracelsus as the

---

and P. Marty, 'Paracelsus, der Retter der Geistesumnachteten. Ein paar Gedanken zum Hohenheimer als Psychopathologen', *NAP*, New Series 1, 1987.

[61] H. Hartmann, *Paracelsus*, 104; Strebel, *Paracelsus*, 15; *idem*, 'Paracelsus als Begründer der allgemeinen und speziellen Balneologie. Ein Kommentar zur paracelsischen Lehre von den Heilquellen (De Thermis)', *NAP* 5, 1948, 121–34; *idem*, 'Über Heilpflanzen und Heilbäder in der Balneologie Hohenheims und über seine korrigierenden Zusätze zu den Heilbädern', *NAP* 5, 1948, 135–38; Schad, Paracelsus, 12: 'He was definitely the first balneologist' (*'Er ist gewissermassen der erste Badearzt gewesen'*).

[62] E.F. Scheller, *Langlebigkeit mit Paracelsus-Arzneien. Versuch einer Geriatrie nach Paracelsus*, Heidelberg 1977, inside cover and 91.

[63] H. Hartmann, *Paracelsus*, 173.

[64] P.G. Frei, 'Parapsychologisches bei Paracelsus', *NAP* 7, 1954, 121–32.

[65] Goldammer, *Paracelsus*, 65. Hemleben, *Paracelsus*, 95, on the other hand, states: 'Paracelsus is not weighed down by any epistemology' (*'Paracelsus ist durch keine Erkenntnistheorie belastet'*).

[66] Strebel, *Paracelsus*, 15, 21; *idem*, 'Stand und Aufgaben der schweizerischen Paracelsus-Forschung', *NAP* 1, 1944, 29; Jung, Paracelsica, 65, 38; H. Hartmann, *Paracelsus*, 20, 46; Vogt, *Theophrastus*, 42.

[67] H. Hartmann, *Paracelsus*, 87.

[68] De Telepnef, 'Glossen', 19; Anon., *Vom Wirken*, 9f.

[69] Not only did he reach beyond his own time, but even measured by todays standards Paracelsus was a superior scientist, see, for instance, A. Dyk, 'Zur Krise unserer Gegenwart', *SBP* 25, 1987, 85: 'With this standpoint Paracelsus has reached far beyond his own time' (*'Mit einem solchen Standpunkt hat Paracelsus weit über seine Zeit hinausgegriffen'*). J.D. Achelis, *Paracelsus: Volumen Paramirum (Von Krankheit und gesundem Leben)*, Jena 1928, 3: 'He answers the questions inherent in his time before they are even asked . . .' (*'Er antwortet auf die immanenten Fragen seiner Zeit, noch ehe sie gestellt sind . . .'*); Birchler, 'Lionardo und Paracelsus', 43: 'Leonardo and Theophrastus were way ahead of their time in their scientific knowledge' (*'Lionardo und Theophrastus waren in ihren naturwissenschaftlichen Kenntnissen ihrer Zeit unendlich voran'*); Strebel, *Paracelsus*, 15: 'Paracelsus is way ahead and above many of todays disciplines' (*'Vielen heutigen Disziplinen ist Paracelsus auch jetzt noch turmhoch überlegen und meilenweit voraus'*); see also Schlegel, *Paracelsus*, 70.

'first', as 'founder', as 'renewer', as 'pioneer' and as 'first proponent', as 'creator' and 'fundamental thinker' of so many and such diverse disciplines which strikes the observer as unreal, because the 'real' creation of so many and such diverse scientific areas by one and the same human being contradicts any form of historic experience.

The fourth point concerns the role of nature, which is of prime importance in the works of Paracelsus.[70] Here again, we encounter a more or less intense idealisation of nature and of the relationship between nature and medicine. Returning medicine to the foundations of nature and singling out the 'light of nature' as the physician's guiding motive is seen to be the most important act of Paracelsus.[71] The assignment of a crucial role to the light of nature has even been regarded as the 'most significant act in the history of ideas', which would assure Paracelsus eternal fame.[72]

Nature is considered to be the 'God's means of expression'.[73] It is portrayed as an active, non-malignant force. It is wise and becomes the ever benign and ever healing principle.[74] In this function, Nature is the instructor of the physician. Its healing powers lie hidden in herbs which nature allows to grow and whose proper use it teaches doctors.[75] In this way, nature is endowed with a special healing power visibly embodied in plants. As everybody naturally assumes that Paracelsus was in unique possession of such knowledge, because this was revealed to him by nature,[76] he was hailed as a naturopath, and

---

[70] For the concepts of nature and the light of nature, see E. Metzke's excellent work, 'Erfahrung und Natur in der Gedankenwelt des Paracelsus' (1939) in *Coincidentia oppositorum. Gesammelte Studien zur Philosophiegeschichte*, Forschung und Berichte der Evangelischen Studiengemeinschaft 19, Witten 1961, 20–58.

[71] For the 'light of nature' (which has its origin in scholastic thought), see Jung, *Paracelsica*, 46–52, 67; see also Strunz, *Theophrastus Paracelsus*, 40f., 70–75; F. Medicus, 'Paracelsus in der philosophischen Bewegung seiner und unserer Zeit, *NAP* 1, 1944, 53–61 and *idem*, 'Das Problem der Erkenntnis bei Paracelsus, *NAP* 5, 1948, 2–6; Schipperges, *Paracelsus*, 59–68; Braun, *Paracelsus*, 55–64.

[72] Jung, *Paracelsica*, 24.

[73] Strunz, *Theophrastus Paracelsus*, 41; Spunda, *Paracelsus*, 73f.

[74] See Strunz, *Beiträge und Skizzen*, 48–50, 64f.; Gundolf, *Paracelsus*, 19f.; Spunda, *Paracelsus*, 134; Medicus, 'Paracelsus', 53–55; Bazala, 'Paracelsus', 28f.; I. Betschart, 'Die Signaturenlehre des Paracelsus', *NAP* 9, 1977.

[75] Reitz, *Paracelsus*, 48, 51; Vogt, *Theophrastus*, 90f.; Schipperges, *Paracelsus*, 179–191, especially 188f.

[76] *Austellungskatalog*, 68: 'Paracelsus had a deeper insight into the healing power of plants' (*'Paracelsus hatte eine tiefere Einsicht in die Heilkraft der Pflanze'*); see also Achelis, *Paracelsus*, 25f., and W.F. Daems, 'Die Idee der Heilpflanze bei Paracelsus', *NAP*, New Series 3, 1988.

is often quoted by adherents of naturopathic societies as an authority still today.[77] In the course of all this approval for Paracelsus it is easy to overlook that he clearly preferred medicines containing heavy metals and other mineral preparations all of which, even with minimal doses, can only be termed toxic.[78] There can be no question that today we live much healthier lives without the chemical naturopathy of Paracelsus.—A certain contradiction also exists, by the way, between two different ideal views of Paracelsus: between Paracelsus as the great naturopath and Paracelsus the experimental chemist and founder of chemistry. The first Paracelsus obtains the foundations of his therapy more in the form of revelations of a divine and benign nature, while the other Paracelsus finds his therapeutic foundations himself in his own experiments which were carried out with scientific precision.

The relationship between Paracelsus and his father is portrayed in the same rapturous terms and with the same enhanced significance as his relationship with nature. The only source available is a passage of Paracelsus which tells us that his father never left him and that he, Paracelsus, had also learnt a great deal from him.[79] This information is then exploited to reconstruct a father-son-relationship characterised by deep love. We are told how the father took the little boy's hand during a walk and pointed out medicinal herbs and later explained the illnesses during visits to the sick.[80] Even Karl

---

[77] See, for instance, *'Der Naturarzt'*, no. 11, Giessen 1987, 3; no. 3, 1989, 3; *'Reformrundschau'*, no. 5, 6–8, Bad Homburg 1991.

[78] See in particular the regulations with ingredients and applicable dosages contained in the *Liber Praeparationum* in *Paracelsus. Sämtliche Werke*, 1. Abteilung, 3, 311–359; with regard to the destillations, 'reductions' and 'purifications' prescribed there, the final products are not likely to have been any less toxic than the materials from which they were made; see, for instance, the dropsy prescription from 'The Eleven Treatises of the Origins ... of Individual Diseases' (*'Elf Traktat von Ursprung ... einzelner Krankheiten'*) ibid., 1. Abteilung, 1, 8f.

[79] In the second book of the 'Grosse Wundarznei' written in 1536 (i.e. after his father's death), Paracelsus writes: 'From childhood days I have dealt with these things and learned from well-informed people ... first of all Wilhelmus von Hohenheim, my father, who never left me, and besides him there are a large number ... who have made great efforts, such as the Bishop Scheit von Settgach ...' (*'von kintheit auf hab ich die ding getriben und von guten underrichtern gelernet ... erstlich Wilhelmus von Hohenheim, meinen vatter, der mich nie verlassen hat, demnach und mit sampt im ein grosse zal ... die sich gross gemühet habent, als bischof Scheit von Settgach'*), see *Paracelsus. Sämtliche Werke*, 1. Abteilung, 19, 354.

[80] See for instance F. Lejeune, *Theophrast von Hohenheim. Paracelsus.* Berlin 1941, 22: 'There was a beautiful relationship full of trust and with a like-minded scientific endeavour between the two.' (*'Ein schönes Verhältnis voller Vertrauen und gleichgerichteten*

Sudhoff, whose declared intention was only to describe what 'could be proven from records', claims that the father had introduced the son to the botany of the Alps, 'which was thriving there amongst shrubs, in the woods and on meadows', 'as early as his time in Einsiedel'.[81] This seems to me as if a modern researcher was trying to construct a sociology of the German family using gravestone inscriptions as primary sources. This point is also important as it shows that a relationship is idealised about which we know nothing but a few words uttered by Paracelsus after his father's death. This is striking and induces us to look for a possible background.

The sixth and last point is even more curious. It concerns the adoption and imitation of Paracelsus's invectives against orthodox contemporary medicine by almost all authors dealing with the subject. Paracelsus's evaluation is accepted as a valid assessment of historical facts. It is well known that the polemic arguments of Paracelsus in this area reached a peak which was way higher than the none too reticent attempts at vilification by his opponents. His abuse is not only adopted in all seriousness as far as its contents are concerned but also verbally. And the brighter the colours which are used to paint the model Paracelsus, the darker and contemptible the picture of the traditional medicine of the 16th century. It is said that the 'medicine of his [Paracelsus's] day was in a poor state',[82] medicine knew 'only thin and confused writings';[83] it was determined by 'a mentally inert dogmatic system and schoolboy's wisdom',[84] which was not based on experience[85] but only dealt with the 'stale doctrines of antiquity'.[86] It is even claimed that medical instruction in

wissenschaftlichen Strebens bestand zwischen beiden.'); Bittel on the other hand, stressed as early as 1944 that we know nothing about his childhood and adolescence, K. Bittel, 'Die Kindheit Theophrats in Einsiedeln', NAP 1, 1944, 37–44; see also Blaser, 'Paracelsus und Arzttum', 15.

[81] K. Sudhoff, Paracelsus. Ein deutsches Lebensbild aus den Tagen der Renaissance, Leipzig 1936, 13, 7: 'I have consciously rid myself . . . of all romantic decoration, of allusions and suspicions.' ('Ich habe mich bewusst frei gemacht . . . von allem romantischen Beiwerk, von Ausdeutungen und Vermutungen').

[82] R. Netzhammer, Theophrastus Paracelsus. Das Wissenswerteste über dessen Leben, Lehre und Schriften, Einsiedeln/Waldshut/Cologne 1901, 75: Paracelsus 'the impetuous demolisher of the rotten house of medicine' ('der ungestüme Niederreisser des verlotterten medizinischen Gebäudes').

[83] Gundolf, Paracelsus, 10; H. Hartmann, Paracelsus, 19: 'mere book-learning' ('reine Buchlehrsamkeit'); see also idem, 60f., and L. Englert, Paracelsus. Mensch und Arzt, Berlin 1941, 20–24.

[84] Ausstellungskatalog, 3.

[85] Englert, Paracelsus, 22f.

[86] Anon., Vom Wirken, 9: 'Fed up with the stale textbook wisdom of late antiq-

Ferrara had nothing whatsoever to do with the art of healing.[87] Medicine at the time was nothing more, it is claimed, than a 'thought-less mixing of the prescriptions of the Galenic tradition',[88] and the pharmacies of the 16th century are described by today's authors as no less than institutions for the systematic defrauding of patients.[89] It is therefore only logical to lump all apothecaries together and call them a 'money-grabbing gang'.[90]

I do not need to stress how unreal and wrong this picture is that the majority of historians writing on Paracelsus would like to make us accept of 16th century medicine. One might discard these views by pointing out the lack of education of such historians and igno-rance of the context in which Paracelsus stood. But even if we assumed that this was the case, we would still have to realise that ignorance of the historical context does not, of necessity, have to lead to such a level of condemnation. It is therefore safe to assume that other reasons may be at stake here, which must be uncovered.

IV *Some Attempts at Interpretation*

This concludes the series of striking traits in the picture of Paracelsus which were cited by way of example. I will now try to assess the deeper-lying motivation of the historian in portraying and eval-uating Paracelsus as a historical personality in this rather than any other light.[91] Generally speaking, wishes and fantasies which all of

---

uity and with its reinterpretation in the syllogistic, hair-splitting reasoning of Arabism, he felt an urge to draw from the sources of free observation of nature.' (*'Überdrüs-sig geworden an der abgestandenen Lehrweisheit der Spätantike und ihrer Umbildung in der syl-logistischen Haarspalterei des Arabismus, drängte es ihn, aus den Quellen freier Naturbeobachtung zu schöpfen'*).

[87] Englert, *Paracelsus*, 19, points out after describing a medical lecture in Ferrara: 'This had nothing whatsoever to do with the art and skill of healing.' (*'Mit Heilkunde und Heilkunst hatte das alles nicht das geringste zu tun'*).

[88] *Ausstellungskatalog*, 68.

[89] Englert, *Paracelsus*, 46: 'Likewise the conditions for the manufacture of drugs were deplorable and almost beyond our conception. Together with the apothecaries the doctors well and truly exploited the sick.' (*'Denn auch auf dem Gebiet der Arzneiherstellung waren die Misstände jener Zeit für uns fast unvorstellbar. Die Apotheker beuteten im Verein mit den Ärzten die Kranken regelrecht aus.'*) This practice is then described in detail. See also Strebel, *Paracelsus*, 13 and idem, 'Nachwort mit Kommentaren zu Hohenheims erster Monographie in der Weltliteratur über Gewerbe-Krankheiten und Gewerbe-Hygiene.' *NAP* 5, 1946, 99.

[90] Netzhammer, *Theophrastus Paracelsus*, 54.

[91] I am aware that the following can only be a draft outline. Considering that

us harbour when we approach a historical subject and which we all
seek to satisfy and act out are the most powerful motivation for those
who see Paracelsus as an ideal figure, and who then try to present
this idealised figment as a real-life historical personality. And indeed,
this need to create such an idealised figure seems to exist on the
part not only of historians dealing with Paracelsus but also on the
part of their readers.

In the case of Paracelsus it would be possible to argue an idealised view of the father and of the physician. However, this argument must be taken one step further by suggesting that he was
endowed with those traits of character which the authors would like
to boast themselves. This process is really quite simple: We project
all our wishes for grandiose characteristics—for example the qualities of a 'true physician' as well as the wishes for greatness and
omnipotence which have been passed down unconsciously from our
childhood years—onto the historical figure of Paracelsus. By means
of a parallel identification process, also subconscious, with this vehi-
cle for our ideal ego, a large proportion of the ideal features attributed to him then falls back on ourselves. As adepts, we shine, so to
speak, in the light into which we have placed our master.[92]

We therefore have to come to realise that the idealised figure
'Paracelsus' is therefore nothing more than a figment of our own
wishes for perfection and greatness which we believe we cannot ful-
fill in any other way. His model personality, his true physicianship
and the scientific achievements which are said to break the barriers
of human limitation are therefore nothing but figments of our own
imagination.

It is certainly true that such projections are widespread mental
mechanisms which are of the utmost importance for the psychological development of children, in particular.[93] What is really at the
core of the matter, however, is the degree of amalgamation between

---

nothing, to my knowledge, has yet been written on these issues and taking into
consideration their significance for research into Paracelsus and Paracelsianism, I
have decided to publish these results in their preliminary form. As such, I hope
they may inspire others.

[92] On projective identification, see for example J. Sandler (ed.), *Projection, Identification,
Projective Identification*, London 1989. In the psycho-historical literature, the examination of motives and working-procedures of historians have yet to be described.

[93] See Sandler, *Projection*, and the earlier study by W. Loch, 'Identifikation und
Projektion', in *Über Begriffe und Methoden der Psychoanalyse*, Bern/Stuttgart/Vienna 1975,
71–90.

the self and the elected model figure. If this bond is too tight, and if it occupies too large a section of the self, there is a danger of losing any form of insight into reality. The idealisation could be ignored, as it is all too obvious. It makes itself felt, however, in incorrect historical conclusions, the cause of which is not immediately realised.

I will use the last one of the points mentioned just before as an example. In this case, the idolisation of Paracelsus has led to a situation where opinions about the orthodox medicine of the sixteenth century were taken over unchecked, as historical circumstances are seen with the ideas of the guiding model. If this approach is accepted, a historical-critical assessment of Paracelsus's evaluations is no longer possible and no longer necessary. In contrast, the adoption of his deprecations exalts the ideal figure in manifold ways and therefore at the same time our self-esteem, which is inextricably linked to it. An idealised personality like Paracelsus cannot—taking this approach— have erred concerning the state of medicine of his time. An assessment which does justice to reality is therefore no longer possible, because the opinion of Paracelsus, in whichever way it has been interpreted, has taken the position of the critical reflection of one's own self. On the basis of the moral perfection and absolute scientific authority attributed to him, it only seems legitimate and logical if his views are adopted as the most fitting in every situation.

This idealisation has other consequences which are not obvious at first sight. If, for example, circumstances are encountered which might disturb the ideal image, authors prefer to ignore them, not to notice them or even to deny them altogether. Paracelsus's social revolutionary tendencies and his demands for free treatment of the poor and for the renouncement of private money and property in the name of charity are not mentioned in most works.[94] This side of Paracelsus does not, understandably, seem so likeable to many critics. The way in which less glorious traits of character of Paracelsus are dealt with—such as, for example, his alcoholism, is indicative of

---

[94] This, for instance, applies to Netzhammer, *Theophrastus Paracelsus*, where such a reference is even lacking in the chapter on 'The Physician's Virtue' (*'Des Arztes Tugend'*), see 120–22 and to Schipperges, *Paracelsus*, and *idem*, *Paracelsus. Das Abenteuer einer sokratischen Existenz*, Sokratische Weisheit 3, Freiburg 1983, and Spunda, *Paracelsus*. Often only a slighting reference is made, see, for instance, Hemleben, *Paracelsus*, 34; see also K. Bittel, 'Ein Sozial-Programm bei Paracelsus', *NAP* 3, 1946, 77–85; however Goldammer has edited a number of socio-ethical and socio-political writings, see K. Goldammer (ed.), *Paracelsus. Sozialethische und sozialpolitische Schriften*, Tübingen 1952, see in particular the Introduction and 101–02.

this denial. And here, it is not immediately obvious that such omissions or emphatic denials are really based on the idealisation of Paracelsus and on the identification with this model figure.

If one last proof was required that we are really dealing with ourselves here and no longer with Paracelsus, I would refer you to a not insignificant number of publications entitled 'Paracelsus and . . .', such as the article 'Paracelsus and the Soul of Technology'. Paracelsus is mentioned in the title of the book and once in the first paragraph, while the remaining 30 pages of the article make do without any mention of him.[95]

Allow me to just mention briefly that the adoption or imitation of the language of Paracelsus should also be understood as an act of identification with the model. If you *speak* like him, you will *be* like him. The fascination which emanates from his language and induces us to imitate it may therefore be an expression of the wish to have as powerful an effect on others as Paracelsus had with his 'real' language.

The idealisation of nature is also based on subconscious fantasies and wishes. Its characterisation as wise and never damaging is probably due to the longing, present in every human, for a good and nourishing mother who only gives and does not demand anything in return.[96] Paracelsus's nature seems be able to satisfy this longing best. Unless reflected, this longing leads to an interpretation of Paracelsus's concept of nature which does not correspond to the sources.

The ideal view of an untroubled and harmonic father-son relationship, which is not borne out by the sources, presents a similar situation. This points to the authors' own wishes for such a portrayed relationship.

There are a good deal more peculiarities in the handling of Paracelsus by historians, one of which is, for example, the marked

---

[95] D. Brinckmann, Paracelsus und die Seele der Technik', *NAP* 2, 1945, 129–71; see also G. Harrer, 'Paracelsus und die Psychopharmaka', *SBP* 22, 1981, 163–68; F. Stadler, 'Paracelsus und die Musik in Salzburg', *SBP* 23, 1984, 118–27; and H. Sucker, 'Wie finden wir einen Weg zu einer neuen Chemie und Pharmazie', *NAP*, New Series 3, 1988, 13–25.

[96] Paracelsus himself alludes to this image; see his book on the Birth of Sensitive Objects (*'Buch von der Gebährung der emfindlichen Dinge'*), *Paracelsus. Sämtliche Werke*. 1. Abteilung, 1, 262f., 266f.; *De generatione hominis, ibid.*, 1, 297; *Opus paramirum, ibid.*, 9, 179f., 190f., 196.; *Das Buch paragranum* (1st revision), *ibid.*, 8, 70–72, 85f., 108. Paraphrases on the 'maternal character of nature' can also be found in Achelis, *Paracelsus*, 35f.

emphasis of his Faust-like character and his connections to Goethe's 'Faust' tragedy.[97] And it would also be helpful to examine those aspects of the 'Paracelsus' theme more thoroughly which researchers prefer to concentrate on in order to determine the reasons for this preference. One of the answers might lie in the longing for a completely new type of medical art, for a turnaround in the art of healing, which is widely seen to have a reference point on Paracelsus and his call for a new art of medicine.[98] Another subject which merits examination is the role played by Paracelsus's sense of mission in the imaginations of his historians. The way that historians deal with historical criticism of Paracelsus by authors of past centuries is another point meriting attention. Any criticism of Paracelsus seems to be beyond conception in the 20th century.[99] This is probably the most important reason for the lack of historical-critical biographies and ergographies of Paracelsus. These points merit a much more detailed examination and explanation than has been possible in the context of this preliminary examination and within the space available.

I would now like to move on to look at the discussed problem from the point of view of Paracelsus, as the question has not yet

---

[97] Paracelsus's 'Faust-like' character is stressed by almost all scholars in such a way that the reader might be tempted to believe that Paracelsus was 'Faust himself'; see Gundolf, *Paracelsus*, 12; F. Spunda, *Das Weltbild des Paracelsus*, Vienna 1941, 7–20; Jung, *Paracelsica*, 55, 66; Brinkmann, 'Mythos und Logos', 166f.; Birchler, 'Lionardo und Paracelsus', 41; Zeller, *Paracelsus*, 5, 11; Vogt, *Theophrastus*, 17; Blaser, 'Paracelsus und Arzttum' 14, 29; Müller-Salzburg, 'Faust und Paracelsus', 128–46; *idem*, 'Paracelsisches bei Goethe', *SBP* 26, 1988, 51, 65; Englert, *Paracelsus*, 34; the first section in H. Hartmann, *Paracelsus*, 15–52 is entitled 'A Faust-like fate' ('*Ein faustisches Lebensschicksal*'); Bloch, *Vorlesungen*, 58–68; Thiel, *Männer*, 49; Betschart, 'Paracelsus und Goethe', 180–89; S. Domandl, 'Agrippa von Nettesheim, Faust und Paracelsus—drei unstete Wanderer', *SBP* 26, 1988, 9–15.

[98] See the anonymus introduction to the journal *Anstösse* 29, 1982, 40: 'The cathwords NATURE—ART OF HEALING—RELIGION—INITIATIVES FOR A NEW MEDICINE make it clear that the interest in Paracelsus is not solely based on the history of medicine, but has to be seen within an, as yet, undeveloped holistic medicine which takes the dimensions of nature, the environment and religion seriously. ('*Die Stichworrte NATUR—HEILKUNDE—RELIGION—ANSTÖSSE FÜR EINE NEUE MEDIZIN machten deutlich, dass die Beschäftigung mit Paracelsus nicht lediglich medizinhistorisch begründet war, sondern unter der Perspektive einer neu zu entwickelnden ganzheitlichen Medizin stand, die die Dimensionen von Natur, Umwelt und Religion ernstnimmt.*').

[99] The only 'learned study' with which I am familiar (15 pages) is H. Magnus, *Paracelsus, der Überarzt. Eine kritische Studie*. Abhandlungen der Medizin 16, Breslau 1906, who warns against turning Paracelsus into a 'superdoctor' and pleads for a more realistic assessment of his merits. Magnus, however, did not enquire into why Paracelsus had been turned into a 'superdoctor'. His criticism, however, has been generally ignored.

been answered why Hippocrates, Harvey, Hufeland or Virchow have
not been endowed with a similar ideal of the self.

V   *The part played by of Paracelsus in creating the idealised picture*

The endowment of a human being with charismatic properties such
as an absolute moral integrity and scientific perfection, and his recognition as an undisputed authority is, indeed, only one side of the
proverbial coin. A guiding model in the shape of an idealised picture comes into existence not only due to the activities of those who
create it; the person so styled must also possess certain abilities, and
there must be certain circumstances which are conducive to creating a stable relationship between an idol and its following.[100] We
therefore also have to ask how Paracelsus meets the wishes and fantasies of his historians.

The first and perhaps most important area where Paracelsus assists
the transfer of our emotions and phantasms to his own person is his
language. In *Corpus Hippocraticum*, for example, we find the following statement: 'The body of man comprises blood, phlegm, yellow
and black bile, and these humours constitute the nature of his body,
and due to these humours man falls ill or is healthy. Man is well
when these humours are present in the right proportion in terms of
effectiveness and quantity. . . .'[101] This is certainly a speculative, but
clearly phrased scientific statement which can be verified or falsi-
fied, but which in any case one can deal with *rationally*, because it
appeals to our reason and not to our feelings. Paracelsus's sentences,
on the other hand, almost invariably appeal directly to our emotions. They target our irrational levels. Their contents only appear
to be clearly expressed, while in reality they are only indirectly accessible to reason.

The effect on the emotions is initially triggered by the sound of

---

[100] See also the work by I. Schiffer, *Charisma. A psychoanalytic look at mass society*,
Toronto 1973.

[101] Hippocrates, *De natura hominis*, 4,1; here cited from the German translation
of Kapferer, *Die Werke des Hippokrates. Die hippokratische Schriftensammlung in neuer deutscher Übersetzung*. Stuttgart/Leipzig 7, 1934, 20f. The Greek text is reproduced in
J. Jouanna, *Hippocrate: La nature de l'homme*. Edité, traduit, et commenté, Berlin 1975,
172f.; Polybos is considered to be the author of this work, see Grensemann, *Der
Arzt Polybos als Verfasser hippokratischer Schriften*, Mainz 1968 and Jouanna, *Hippocrate*,
55–59.

the language, which is reminiscent of the familiar Lutheran Bible German and evokes associations of a religious dimension. Utterances made in this language just cannot be wrong—this is the first message. They seem truthful, original and wise, and, quite irrespective of what is said, they trigger emotional reactions rather than rational deliberation.

It is not only the pure sound of the language, however, that so effectively appeals to the reader, but also the contents. At first sight, what is said seems to convey clear and comprehensible information. This clarity, however, is limited to the grammatical structure. A famous example shall serve to illustrate this. At the beginning of the *Paragranum* we read the following sentence: 'So nun aus der natur der arzt wachsen sol und muß, und in im und von im und aus im ist nichts, alles aus und in der natur, so ist es von nöten, das er aus der natur geboren werd und nit zu Leipzig oder zu Wien . . . die natur lernt den arzt, nit der mensch'.[102] ('So now the physician shall and must grow from nature, and within him and from him and out of him is nothing, · everything is from and in nature, and so it is necessary that he is born from nature and not from Leipzig or Vienna . . . nature teaches the doctor, not man.') These are sentences which are easily understood but which at the same time somehow sound wise and profound. The difficulties only come about when we try to rationally deal with this statement, because it is then that we notice very quickly that Paracelsus does not mention here nor anywhere else what he understands by 'nature' at this point or how he imagines this process of birth from earth or the education of doctors by nature as the teacher to actually take place.

Unless we are aware of the precise historical background of such statements by Paracelsus and if we leave our own rational sphere, we find that these sentences—and especially those quoted most frequently for their alleged conciseness and profound contents—are but mere sermon-style rhetoric or empty words which can be filled by every reader at will with his own ideas and phantasms. At this point, Paracelsus extends his whole hand to those historians keen to transfer their ideal of self-hood to him. This is what differentiates Paracelsus from Hippocrates, Harvey, Virchow and other famous physicians.[103]

---

[102] *Paracelsus, Sämtliche Werke.* 1. Abteilung, 8, 140.

[103] Another observation springs to mind, in connection with the fascinating effects of language, which points to a further reason for the popularity of Paracelsus in

External factors, which are not located in the personality of
Paracelsus, also favour the idolisation of Paracelsus and the transfer
of certain phantasms to him. The lack of any sources concerning
his childhood naturally lends impetus to attempts to project images
of an ideal childhood and of an ideal father-son relationship stem-
ming from the imaginations of the authors themselves onto the blank
screen of Paracelsus's childhood. The lack of any material on the
kind and type of his activities as a physician stirs the imagination in
a similar way. The high ethical demands imposed by Paracelsus on
doctors are all too quickly taken to represent real-life features of
Paracelsus himself, on the basis of which the ideal of a true physician can easily be reconstructed or confirmed.

Of the further circumstances concerning Paracelsus which con-
tribute to him becoming a charismatic figure, I will finally mention
the image of the great malunderstood or misunderstood which he
draws himself quite well and willingly. He often stresses, for example, that he was not recognised anywhere due to his poor apparel
and his travelling mode of life.[104] Such obvious injustice, a deficit of
this or another type, always serves to increase the degree of charisma
which is assigned to the otherwise shining hero, because it brings
him down to earth.[105] It is not, however, a question of real pity
extended to Paracelsus, when the poor and little understood genius

---

the Romantic age. Romanticism was also the period in which the language of
Paracelsus came to be seen as 'historical' and different from the well-known classical German language. While Paracelsus's language still sounded very much like
the spoken vernacular of his day, he himself had been termed a 'waffler' etc. Now
that his language came to be considered 'historical' and therefore related to the
favoured 'medieval' vernacular, it increasingly met with approval, even to the extent
of direct imitation. See W. Artelt, 'Wandlungen des Paracelsusbildes in der Medizingeschichte', *NAP* 8, 1957, 33–38, and K. Goldammer, 'Paracelsus-Bild und Paracelsus-
Forschung. Wissenschaftliche und populäre Elemente in der Literatur', *NAP* 10,
1982, 109–27, who, however, both ignore the linguistic aspect. We should, however, remind ourselves that the glorification of Paracelsus shown and analysed here
never had any effect outside German-speaking countries.

[104] See for instance the Preface to the 2nd book of the *Grosse Wundarznei* (1536)
in Paracelsus. Sämtliche Werke. 10, 224f., the Prologue to *Liber Archidoxis, ibid.*, 3,
93, and the *Sieben Defensiones, ibid.*, 11, 123–60.

[105] Schiffer, *Charisma*, 29–34 ('The charisma of imperfection'); Lejeune's statement
Paracelsus, 58, is indicative of this tendency: 'Paracelsus has contributed so much to
progress and reason that he may be excused if in some respects he has been unable
to go beyond of the prejudice of his time. This does not detract from his achievements. Is this not true for other great men? And finally is it not true for us too?'
(*'Paracelsus hat so viel, so unendlich viel Vernünftiges und Fortschrittliches gebracht, dass man
ihm wohl verzeihen dürfte, wenn er im einen oder anderen nicht aus den Voreingenommenheiten
seiner Zeit herausfand. Das verkleinert ihn nicht im geringsten. Ist es anderen grossen Männern
nicht ebenso gegangen? Und schliesslich, geht es uns nicht auch so?'*).

is stressed,[106] but self-pity and, in particular, the wish to be restored to one's own rightful place and to have one's merits recognised—which is what has happened to Paracelsus today. For all their pity with the 'poor misunderstood', authors overlook, however, that Paracelsus was a person with paranoid tendencies and an argumentative character.[107] We therefore will have to examine very carefully whether he was really rejected because of his poor apparel only or whether things did not really look quite different.

VI   Concluding remarks

To end with, I will raise the question of what purpose such an analysis can really serve. This question is quite justified, and one could legitimately raise the objection that in the past, academics managed to get by without such studies on the background motives of historians, and that this is a field which could be left to psychologists, who enjoy looking for our unconscious motives.

I believe, however, that things are not quite as simple. The underlying motives examined here have obviously made a tremendous impact on the quality and the result of historical research. I believe that the many and blatant errors which have resulted from the idealisation of Paracelsus to a higher or lesser degree have become clear without me having pointed out every misjudgement. You might object and say: 'Yes, we are aware of the errors, and it is certainly not us who are meant.' This objection, too, is certainly correct and justified.

Nevertheless: The fact that we constantly—starting with our choice

---

[106] Moeller van den Bruck, *Die Deutschen*, 70: 'Accordingly Paracelsus led the life typical of the misunderstood genius of all times.' ('*So war denn Parazelsus' Leben das Typische der grossen Verkannten aller Zeiten.*'); R.J. Hartmann, *Theophrast*, 64, 94, 156f.; Gundolf, *Paracelsus*, 13, 27, 'one of the greatly misunderstood' ('*einer der grossen Verkannten*') 28; Spunda, *Paracelsus*, 37; Strunz, *Theophrastus Paracelsus*, 11, 49, 35, 87; Goldammer, 'Paracelsus-Bild' 121; Müller-Salzburg, 'Faust und Paracelsus', 145; Strebel, 'Gewerbekrankheiten', 92f., 98, 101; de Telepnef, 'Glossen', 21; Netzhammer, *Theophrastus Paracelsus*, 106–110; H. Hartmann, *Paracelsus*, 55–58; *Ausstellungskatalog*, 3f.; Anon., *Wirken*, 10f.; Schad, Paracelsus, 13; H. Werner (ed.), Mikrokosmos und Makrokosmos. Okkulte Schriften von Paracelsus, Munich 1989, 12 (Introduction); O. Zekert, *Paracelsus in der Zeit*, *SBP* 1, Vienna 1960, 20.

[107] Only in Jung, *Paracelsica*, 10f. do we find some short remarks on the psyche of Paracelsus; Müller-Salzburg, 'Faust und Paracelsus', 144, and H. Karcher, 'Paracelsus. Stadtarzt von Basel', *NAP* 1, 1944, 85 have a few critical remarks about Paracelsus's traits of character. Otherwise no attempts have been made in the literature quoted in this chapter to understand or describe the character or mental make-up of Paracelsus in a non-idealised way.

of topic—impose unconscious wishes and phantasms on our subject matter, is true for each and every one of us. I even believe that the study of history is impossible without such a transfer. Descriptions of historical events always constitute more or less subjective assessments, as objective data are often lacking and history cannot be reconstructed in its totality. There cannot, therefore, be an objectively correct and eternally valid interpretation of the figure of Paracelsus and of his work. Coming generations will approach the phenomenon Paracelsus with other wishes and fantasies and make sure that our perception of Paracelsus changes.[108]

The transfer of one's own ideal of the self onto a historical personality is, however, one *extreme of the mental involvement of the historian* which must definitely be avoided, as it entails a massive misrepresentation of history. In order to achieve this aim, it is not really necessary to appeal for help from the field of psychology. This error can be circumvented to a certain degree by recognising it and becoming aware of it. This would be a first step. The second step towards avoiding this error is adherence to the commands of a historical-scholarly methodology, that is adherence to rules like the one that every hypothesis must also be proven or that mere paraphrases of a passage from Paracelsus[109] cannot be allowed to pass as a scholarly result. The recognition of these and other rules which belong to the basic mental equipment of the historian could act as a corrective, and make sure that more justice is done to Paracelsus than has been the case in this century so far.

---

[108] For the 'changes in the evaluation of Paracelsus in the history of medicine', see Artelt, 'Wandlungen des Paracelsusbildes', and Goldammer, 'Paracelsus-Bild', which, however, do not cover the issues discussed here.

[109] Examples of paraphrases of Paracelsus can be found in Sticker, *Paracelsus*, where the language is indistinguishable from Paracelsus's, as is W.A.L. von Brunn, *Paracelsus und seine Schwindsuchtslehre*, Praktische Tuberkulose-Bücherei 26, Leipzig 1941, F. Medicus, 'Das Problem der Erkenntnis bei Paracelsus', *NAP* 5, 1948, 1–17, Schipperges, *Paracelsus* and idem, *Sokratische Existenz*.

CHAPTER FOUR

THE PARACELSIANS – NATURE AND CHARACTER

Herbert Breger

If we are to talk of 'Paracelsians', we should first clarify the meaning of the term. This is particularly important for the second half
of the seventeenth century, the period on which I intend to focus.
The answer is easy for the late sixteenth and early seventeenth centuries: Alexander von Suchten, Gerard Dorn, Oswald Croll and
others were definitely Paracelsians. Those who were merely followers of Paracelsus in the second half of the seventeenth century, without adding much of their own thought, are of little importance to
the historian of science. But what about Jan Baptist van Helmont,
Johann Rudolph Glauber and Johann Joachim Becher? They admired
Paracelsus, and were obviously influenced by him, but clearly they
were also scholars with highly original ideas. It is on these more
complex 'Paracelsians' that I intend to focus.

They exemplify one of the themes of this volume, namely the
transformation of Paracelsianism. It could be entertaining to demonstrate that this theme contains a certain paradox: to assume a
transformation presupposes a certainty about what constitutes a
'Paracelsian'. Although I do not wish to dwell on this tricky question,
I believe that the developments in science during the seventeenth
century should be taken into account. It is, after all, within the
context of these developments that Helmont, Glauber, Becher and
others evolved as 'Paracelsians'. Thus, at the time, the debate between
'mechanists' and followers of Paracelsus formed an important issue
for science. While the historian of science has to keep in mind that
there is no sharp distinction between these schools of thought, it will
be useful to highlight the difference in approach.[1]

Therefore, my starting point is the contrast between mechanists
such as Boyle, Newton, Huygens and Leibniz, and the 'Paracelsians'.

[1] Cf. for example P.M. Rattansi, The intellectual origins of the Royal Society,
Notes and Records of the Royal Society of London, 23, 1968, 129–143; A.G. Debus, Thomas
Sherley's *Philosophical Essay* (1672): Helmontian Mechanism as the Basis of a new
Philosophy, *Ambix*, 27, 1980, 124–135.

There is no need to outline their differing concepts of nature, as they have often been described. However, in reading the long tracts written by both Paracelsians and mechanists, one gets the vague impression that there is a more profound difference between them than just their views on nature. Having had an interest in the contrast between Paracelsians and mechanists for some time, I believe that this difference does exist, and that it deserves to be explored within the framework of the history of science.

In 1656, Henry More declared that the Paracelsians were all suffering from melancholy.[2] They were followers of 'delirous Fancies', and of 'the wildest Philosophical Enthusiasms that ever were broached by . . . Christian or Heathen'. The charges of melancholy, enthusiasm and an inclination towards flights of fancy are evidently based on certain assumptions about character. Is it true then that there are certain differences in personality between the mechanists and the Paracelsians? And if there are, can they be related to their conflicting views on nature, science and society?

We know very little about the personalities of seventeenth-century scientists. The private letter, i.e. one mirroring the writer's personality and baring his emotions to a friend, was almost unknown at the time, and so was the personal diary containing intimate reflections on life. The autobiographies of Cardano and Cellini present the well-known image of Renaissance individuals, and accounts of Paracelsus's life and his writings suggest that, like them, he, too, was prone to emotional outbursts. Nevertheless, these writings do not tell us anything about Paracelsus the man, as the autobiography was only developed much later, by Jean-Jacques Rousseau and Karl Philipp Moritz. As far as I am aware, none of the memoirs written by seventeenth-century scientists are of that kind. In his booklet *Eine Kindheitserinnerung des Leonardo da Vinci*, Sigmund Freud demonstrates how brilliant insights can be gleaned from a sketchy autobiography. However, I do not wish to apply this risky strategy, so I need to choose a different methodology.

It is true that biographies can yield some information. Paracelsus, like many of his followers, lived a restless life. He spent it wandering from town to town, and repeatedly got into trouble with the

---

[2] T.H. Jobe, The Devil in Restoration Science: The Glanvill-Webster Witchcraft Debate, *Isis*, 72, 1981, 349. By the way, J.Ch. Adelung takes a similar view in his *Geschichte der menschlichen Narrheit*.

authorities and high-ranking persons. Alexander von Suchten was accused of being a heretic and an atheist. He lost his position as personal physician to the king of Poland, and two of his adversaries demanded that he be subjected to torture. Jan Baptist van Helmont was imprisoned for some time, and his manuscripts were confiscated. He was not allowed to publish for twenty years, and the Spanish Inquisition proclaimed him guilty of circulating 'monstrous, super-stitious nonsense of the school of Paracelsus, that is, of the Devil himself'.[3] He was persecuted, then, because he was a Paracelsian. There is, however, the possibility that he only became a Paracelsian because he already had a certain inclination to be rebellious.

Others preferred to conform to the prevailing political order and to enjoy a quiet life. Like Paracelsus, Johann Joachim Becher wan-dered from town to town throughout his life, but he was never per-secuted for being a Paracelsian. On the contrary, he was accorded a friendly welcome at every court. He would then usually be given a position at court, and the prince would expect him to fill the coffers of the treasury. However, in the outcome Becher would always have to leave the court in haste.

Glauber, on the other hand, informs his readers that he had never cared to earn his living in the service of lords and princes, but rather by his own efforts, and he explicitly refers to the Paracelsian motto 'Alterius non sit qui suus esse posset'.[4] John Webster was a non-conformist, and during the Civil War he served as a physician and a chaplain in the Parliamentary Army.

Compared to these, the biographies of most mechanist scientists[5] differ significantly. Admittedly, the persecution of Galileo is like that of Paracelsus, but it is debatable whether Galileo was actually a mechanist—since mechanism in the strict sense only started with Gassendi and Descartes. However, at this point I am only explor-ing some ideas rather than going into detail on dogmatic issues. So, for the moment, I prefer not to exclude Galileo downright, and to leave this question open.

The mechanist scientists active during the second half of the sev-enteenth century tended to be cautious. They were successful in their

---

[3] W. Pagel, Helmont, in: J.B. van Helmont, *Aufgang der Artzney-Kunst*, vol. 2, München 1971, Appendix, XIII.

[4] J.R. Glauber, *Theutschlands Wohlfahrt*, part 1, Amsterdam 1656, 96.

[5] Things are more complicated for the mechanist philosophers, because Hobbes as well as Spinoza came into trouble with the authorities.

professional careers, and in a number of cases there is evidence that they deliberately avoided public discussion of topics that were liable to get them into trouble. Newton's concept of the Trinity is the most striking example, but his refusal to publish his writings on alchemy is also relevant in this context. Descartes, too, refrained from publicising some of his ideas in order to avoid conflict with the Catholic church. He lived according to his motto 'Bene vixit qui bene latuit', expressing a different sentiment to Paracelsus's 'Alterius non sit qui suus esse posset'. As for the biographies of Huygens, Mariotte, Boyle, Leibniz, Wallis and others, they do not give the impression that these scholars were rebels, nor that they would fight recklessly for an idea without regard for the outcome.

It is well known that both the Royal Society and the Académie des Sciences avoided the discussion of political and theological matters; they deliberately limited themselves to debates that would not alarm the political and ecclesiastical authorities. It is true that there was a minor controversy about theology in the early days of the *Journal des Scavants*, but then the editor was dismissed, and his successor acted more cautiously. Robert Hooke and, to a lesser extent, Johann Bernoulli could be quoted as further exceptions. Both were involved in several disputes, and one gets the impression that, unlike Newton or Leibniz, they may have enjoyed them. However, neither Hook nor Johann Bernoulli had any quarrel with either the secular or the church authorities, and their disputes within the scientific community did not damage their careers.

Besides biography, the writings of Paracelsians and mechanists provide another source of information. Again, there is a striking contrast. Generally speaking, the mechanists concentrate, or at least claim to concentrate, on facts. Descartes's mechanical explanations are stated quite boldly, and most are simply wrong. Nevertheless, he has a characteristic habit of stating his facts concisely, giving an apparently plausible interpretation, and then moving on to the next topic.

True, Henry More and Joseph Glanville not only believed in witchcraft, but they were eager to prove its existence. However, neither can be considered a prominent scientist, and both claimed to prove their theories by empirical evidence. Generally speaking, Edme Mariotte's careful and concise description of facts and his avoidance of 'heretical' topics are characteristic for the mechanist approach.

Robert Boyle carried this tendency to an extreme, and he had no qualms about boring his reader with extensive accounts of facts.

Leibniz, himself a mechanist, praised Boyle for his approach, although he suggested that it would be useful to draw the occasional conclusion from all those data.[6]

Thomas Sprat[7] pointed out that the Royal Society rejected all amplifications, digressions and 'swellings of style' in favour of brevity and a natural style. Some mechanists not only listed facts, but they also elaborated mathematical solutions, and often dealt predominantly with mathematics. Obviously, they chose the most cautious presentation of facts possible in science and natural philosophy. It can be said in general that the habit of concision and the almost complete renunciation of rhetoric are traits common to all mechanists. If one counts Galileo among them, he is again the exception, making extensive use of rhetorical strategies.

In contrast to the mechanists, the Paracelsians are conspicuous by their lack of concision. They tend to repeat themselves, but they never appear to be satisfied with their own formulations. They believed that truth could not be expressed fully in words, and that every verbal communication could only contain an approximation of the truth. As a result, their descriptions are overly expansive, and yet the reader is left with the abiding impression that there was more to be said on the subject. The Paracelsians were fond of examples, metaphors and digressions. Often these were not, it seems, deliberately used rhetorical devices, but rather reflections of the writer's attempt to evoke particular images in his reader's mind.

In their certainty that truth cannot be expressed completely, the Paracelsian texts bear a certain resemblance to the writings of the mystics. Twenty years ago, Michael Polanyi coined the term 'tacit knowledge', and we have been aware since then that there is a category of knowledge, on which we regularly rely, that cannot be expressed fully in language. Take the example of riding a bicycle. If one tries to express in language how this is done, one will always use too many words and yet fail to convey the whole experience.

Given the nature of seventeenth-century medicine and chemistry, it is plausible that experts had a certain 'tacit knowledge' or 'know-how' at their disposal, which could not be expressed perfectly in

---

[6] G.W. Leibniz, *Sämtliche Schriften und Briefe* (Academy edition), series III, vol. 3, Berlin 1991, 373.

[7] *The History of the Royal-Society of London*, London 1667, 113, compare also 100−109. My kind thanks to Lord Dacre for this indication.

words.[8] For a Paracelsian, a good text on nature's secrets always had to imply more than it revealed. John Webster[9] admits that a certain passage in Paracelsus is 'very dark, and hard to understand', but he assures the reader that it conceals a deep meaning. A young student of medicine or chemistry would spend several years training with an experienced master, thereby acquiring the know-how that could not be expressed in a book. Paracelsian writings must be seen against this background. They were of an occasional nature and were not intended to be the most authoritative source of information. This source would be either one's own experience or the fruits of a long apprenticeship with an expert.

It is obvious that the Paracelsians, unlike the mechanists, consider the role of this 'tacit knowledge' of paramount importance for both science and religion. Thus, if mystical experience, or something very much like it, is acknowledged, the teachings of the established church cannot be the whole of God's truth.

There is a further cause for the diffuse quality of the Paracelsians' writings: in their opinion nature was full of secrets whose disclosure was imminent. These high expectations are obviously based on religious enthusiasm and utopian thought.[10] Paracelsians do not view nature as some kind of mechanical clock, but rather as a sealed treasure-chest. Consequently, they do not believe that it is sufficient to communicate what they know—and in fact they always confess to knowing little compared to the knowledge that will be revealed in the future. Instead, it is more important for them to communicate a sense of expectation, astonishment and surprise. This will enable the readers to pay the necessary attention to common phenomena and to look at nature with due respect. Thus they would learn about God's goodness, as he begins to reveal the secrets of nature to them, and finally they would make their own discoveries.

The Paracelsians claim that it is in particular the most mundane, common phenomena that are full of secrets and wonders. Glauber writes that the best and most important things in medicine and chemistry are those that are easiest to make, with the least amount of

---

[8] The same has been claimed for the twentieth century by M. Polanyi, *Personal Knowledge*, London 1962; H.L. Dreyfus & S.E. Dreyfus, *Mind over Machine*, New York 1986.

[9] *Metallographa*, London 1671, 118, 326.

[10] Cf. H. Breger, *Elias artista—A Precursor of the Messiah in Natural Science*, in: E. Mendelsohn/H. Nowotny (eds.), *Nineteen Eighty Four: Science between Utopia and Dystopia* (= *Sociology of the Sciences*, vol. 8), Dordrecht, Boston, Lancaster 1984, 49–72.

work.[11] In another tract he states that good things are taken for granted and therefore not respected.[12] There is an obvious parallel between these ideas and the radical political ones held by several Paracelsians: in both cases the common and well-known phenomena may reveal surprising secrets.

When looking at Paracelsian writings, another contrast to the mechanists becomes obvious. Whereas the latter rarely provide any information about themselves in their scientific writings, the former do so extensively. The mechanists attempt to give the impression of not being subjective entities—a fiction still in use among scientists today. In reading the Paracelsians, on the other hand, one is often given the impression that the author is melancholic, and this condition is sometimes described as a source of invention and inspiration.[13] On the reverse side of melancholy lie high expectations and utopian thought, and Johann Joachim Becher writes: 'We are such that we always look to impossible things and that we esteem the impossible, whereas we despise those things that are true, easy and according to the due course of nature.'[14]

A number of Paracelsians, in particular Glauber and Becher, take a moralist point of view. Compared to the past, they claim, men have become worse. Friendship, love and honesty have become rare. Men do not search for the truth, but for their own advantage, they even cheat each other, etc. So the writings of the Paracelsians contain a considerable amount of mourning, disappointment and unfulfilled longing for a better society. These moralistic remarks are often bolstered by autobiographical detail. Thus Glauber and Becher, for instance, considered themselves innocent victims of their cruel enemies. They convey the firm conviction of having been hurt by others for no apparent reason.

Psychologists have been investigating narcissism for the past decades.[15]

---

[11] J.R. Glauber, *Glauberus concentratus*, Amsterdam 1668, 68. Similar statements are made in B. Figulus, *Thesaurinella Olympica*, Frankfurt/Main 1908, 165; *Nodus Sophicus Enodatus*, no place given, 1639, fol. A II r° and v°.

[12] J.R. Glauber, *Von den drey anfangen der Metallen*, no place given, 1666, 85.

[13] J.J. Becher, *Närrische Weißheit*, Frankfurt/Main 1682, 11; G.W. Leibniz, *Sämtliche Schriften und Briefe* (Academy edition), series III, vol. 2, 270.

[14] J.J. Becher, *Chymisches Laboratorium, oder Untererdische Naturkündigung*, Frankfurt/Main 1680, 540.

[15] H. Kohut, *The Analysis of the Self*, New York 1971.—The terminology of this discussion among psychologists has already been mentioned by Dietlinde Goltz in Chapter 3 above, although in a different context. I think this coincidence is not by chance. In both cases scholars project their feelings on the object they are investigating.

The narcissist tends to see himself mirrored in all his relations to other people, and is particularly inclined to feel hurt. Furthermore, he has a tendency to admire others and to long for admiration from others, as well as an inclination to draw an unrealistically sharp borderline between good and bad. Finally, a very high self-esteem allied to occasional bouts of self-accusation is characteristic. I am well aware that psychic structures can change significantly over three centuries, and I am not claiming that twentieth-century psychological profiles can easily be superimposed on the seventeenth century. I believe, however, that Paracelsian authors can display traits characteristic of the narcissistic character, whereas mechanists tend to elide any recognisable individual characteristics.

The complete absence of emotional content in mechanist writings is a striking fact that calls for some explanation. According to a widely accepted view, lack of emotion and absence of prejudice are essential requirements for scientific objectivity. In 1938, Gaston Bachelard published *La formation de l'esprit scientifique. Contribution à une psychanalyse de la connaissance objective*. According to this intriguing book, scientific progress relies on the gradual elimination of emotion in the interpretation of phenomena. Thus it resembles the development from the naively of childhood towards the reflectiveness of adult age. It seems to me, however, that this model is too simple.

It is well known that sometimes scientists cling stubbornly to preconceived ideas to great profit: Kepler's development of his planetary laws, and the discovery of energy conservation by Helmholtz, Joule and Mayer are two of many possible examples. Every scientist needs a motive for his research, at least for long-time projects and when trying to move beyond the conclusions of his predecessors. It is true that no scientist should allow his emotions or preconceived ideas to interfere with his results, or he may find himself rejected by the scientific community. However, we have learned from the philosophical discussions of the last few decades that the difference between 'correct' and 'incorrect' scientific statements is not easily defined—even though there is a difference. Scientists refer explicitly or implicitly to views of nature or to methodologies, such as the mechanistic world view. But why do distinguished scientists such as Newton, Leibniz, Laplace, Ampère, Lord Kelvin or Helmholtz adopt one world view rather than another? The question has rarely been discussed by historians of science, let alone by philosophers of science.

Why do some scientists see nature as a mechanical clock, and

others consider it analogous to a living organism? Why are the former satisfied, if they can explain a natural process in terms of pres-
sure, motion and the impact of particles, whereas for the latter the
explanation needs to involve semen, birth, growth and maturation?
Generally speaking, both systems were wrong, but how are we to
understand the gratification the scientists derived from the respective explanations? Certainly, some general theories in cultural history
attempt to answer this question by reference to the general mental-
ity of an era, the *Zeitgeist*. But how are we to explain why, during
the same period, prominent scientists adopted mutually contradictory
world views?

One could attempt to answer these questions by using the classical concept of projection. This implies that the process of gaining knowledge requires the scientist to project his view of nature on
to the world. In doing so, he will achieve results by the controlled
procedures of experimental science. If his projections are such as
to allow successful scientific progress, he will become a prominent
scientist, i.e. he will only then become an object of study for our
discipline. Van Helmont, Glauber and Becher all proved that the
Paracelsian projection of nature remained productive until the end
of the seventeenth century.

If we adopt the hypothesis of projection, one immediate conclusion
can be drawn. Every human being must define his relationship to
that part of nature which is his own body, including his natural instincts. Does he perceive the unrestrained actions of his instincts and
emotions as positive, and does he believe, therefore, that too much
control over them would be objectionable? Or does he consider his
instincts and emotions dangerous unless controlled by reason? Does
it fill him with joy to contemplate the growth of plants, or the birth
of animals or children? Or, on the contrary, is he more fascinated
by the function and regularity of a mechanical clock?[16] Many similar questions could be asked. If the projection hypothesis is valid,
we should expect to find certain parallels between a scientist's personality and the kind of projection that is a tacit part of his work.

I have argued above that the Paracelsians often gave free rein to
their emotions, and also that they were often of a stubborn, independent and rebellious nature. The mechanists present quite different

---

[16] Cf. J.A. Comenius, *Opera omnia*, vol. 15/I, Prag 1986, 92.

characters. Thus Descartes writes: '*Ma troisiesme maxime estoit de tascher tousiours plutost à me vaincre que la fortune, et à changer mes désirs que l'ordre du monde.*'[17] The mathematician and physicist John Wallis writes in his autobiography:

'It hath been my Lot to live in a time, wherein have been many and great Changes and Alterations. It hath been my endeavour all along, to act by moderate Principles, between the Extremities on either hand, in a moderate compliance with the Powers in being, in those places, where it hath been my Lot to live, without the fierce and violent animosities usual in such Cases, against all, that did not act just as I did, knowing that there were many worthy Persons engaged on either side. And willing . . . if things could not be just, as I could wish, to make the best of what is.'[18]

When Leibniz was thirty years old, he stated that he would never be seen extremely cheerful or sad. He said he felt grief and joy only to a moderate extent, and that laughter changed his face more often than it moved his spirit.[19] In one of his philosophical works he writes: '*Qui Deum amat, amat omnes. Quisquis est sapiens, amat omnes*'.[20] The rationalist foundation of this concept of love is evident. Harmony, reconciliation and the idea of truth as the sum total of individual perspectives are fundamental tenets of his philosophy. He was not fond of argument, and preferred to learn from a new book rather than criticise it.[21]

Self-control was a central issue in the seventeenth and eighteenth centuries. Saint-Simon records that, during his long life, Louis XIV rarely flew into a rage, believing that emotions did not become a king.[22] In his book *Über den Prozeß der Zivilisation*, Norbert Elias explores changes in upper-class behaviour, arriving at the conclusion that control of the emotions increased markedly from the Middle Ages to the beginning of the twentieth century. Quite a number of his examples are taken from the Renaissance and the seventeenth century.

---

[17] R. Descartes, *Œuvres*, vol. VI, eds. Adam/Tannery, Paris 1965, nouvelle édition, 25.

[18] Ch. Scriba, 'The autobiography of John Wallis', *Notes and Records of the Royal Society of London*, vol. 25, 1970, 42–43.

[19] Cf. K. Müller/G. Krönert, *Leben und Werk von Leibniz*, Frankfurt/Main 1969, 2.

[20] G.W. Leibniz, *Philosophische Schriften*, ed. Gerhardt, vol. 7, Berlin 1890, 75.

[21] G.W. Leibniz, *Philosophische Schriften*, ed. Gerhardt, vol. 7, Berlin 1890, 526.

[22] L. de Saint-Simon, *Mémoires complets*, ed. La Bédollière, vol. XIII, Paris 1856, 77.

Albert O. Hirschman's work[23] charts the introduction of a theory of the passions into social philosophy during the seventeenth and eighteenth centuries. He explains that a man ruled by his passions was seen to be unpredictable and therefore dangerous, while one who had sublimated his passions into social concerns could be an ally and could help stabilise society. This concern for reliability and rationality is reminiscent of the fascination the mechanical clock held for the mechanists. There is a conspicuous difference between them and the Paracelsians in matters of causality and calculation, and concerning the concept of natural law. According to Paracelsus, material things are always individually 'different': 'The water is always water, but it is different in every fountain.'[24] The perception of the uniqueness of all natural objects suggests that nature is always subject to change.

For seventeenth-century mechanists, God was the legislator of nature and therefore the guarantor for her regularity, but Paracelsus doubted whether God's providence was stable and immutable, 'because God himself may be made uncertain'.[25] Leibniz agreed with Paracelsus insofar as he, too, considered all things to be unique, but he insisted that there were strict and immutable laws, and explained how the principles of causality and individuality could be combined. To renounce the principle of causality would have been absolutely impossible for Leibniz, and in this respect he is in agreement with the other mechanists.

Nevertheless, there were often severe difficulties with the replication of experiments. Thus Mariotte wrote to Leibniz, referring to a procedure for the production of steel: '*Vous scavez Monsieur, qu'il faut très peu de chose pour changer les effects, et qu'encore qu'on nous ayt enseigné fidèlet un secret on a peine à y bien réussir dans les premières espreuves.*'[26] In one of his letters to Brand, the discoverer of phosphorus, Leibniz says essentially the same.[27]

Robert Boyle, too, was concerned by this problem, and he discussed it in his tract *On the Unsuccessfulness of Experiments*. Thus the

---

[23] *The passions and the Interests*, Princeton 1977.
[24] Paracelsus, *Sämtliche Werke*, I Abteilung, ed.: Sudhoff, vol. 2, München, Berlin 1930, 309.
[25] Paracelsus, *Sämtliche Werke*, I Abteilung, ed.: Sudhoff, vol. 12, München, Berlin 1929, 393.
[26] Leibniz, *Sämtliche Schriften und Briefe* (Academy edition), series III, vol. 2, Berlin 1987, 683.
[27] *Ibid.*, p. 558.

mechanists do not doubt the validity of the principle of causality, although they admit their problems with experiments in chemistry. They express no emotion in their writings, but they reveal a certain feeling of unease when a process is not yet under control, i.e. when a process cannot be replicated.

The Paracelsians, on the other hand, do not claim that nature is acting in accord with immutable laws. They treat such empirical evidence with remarkable calmness, even indifference. Johann Joachim Becher, for instance, published a collection of chemical experiments, accompanied by a note stating that the reader would find that some processes worked, while others did not. Fittingly, the title of the book is *Chymischer Glücks-Hafen*, or *The Chemical Pot of Luck*. Thus chemistry shades into lottery. Becher pursues the fundamental role of change in nature even further: in his book *Närrische Weissheit und weise Narrheit*, he attempts to prove that the rational and the irrational are inseparably connected,[28] using evidence taken from science and technology.

Becher's attack on the mechanists' worship of rationality is seconded by a noteworthy remark by Glauber.[29] In the very beginning, he writes, God's spirit hovered over the waters and made them pregnant, thereby creating the world. To the mechanists, this must have seemed extremely crude. It was clear to them that the world had been created by rational means, and it was also clear that God had employed his powerful intellect for that purpose.

In her book *The Death of Nature. Women, Ecology, and the Scientific Revolution*, Carolyn Merchant refers to the difference between Paracelsians and mechanists in her examination of the changing representation of nature as a woman. She writes that the metaphors used in representing nature changed significantly in Early Modern times. Around 1500, nature was thought of as a nourishing mother to be respected and not hurt, whereas by 1700 she had become a disorderly woman, to be subdued, assaulted and even raped. This change is likely to have had an effect on the role of women in society, as well as on the exploitation of nature by an industry based on science. The key element in Merchant's argument seems to be that nature is a cipher for 'woman' and no more than that. (I disagree with the expression 'no more than that'.)

---

[28] Breger, Becher, Leibniz und die Rationalität, in: *Johann Joachim Becher (1635–1682)*, eds. G. Frühsorge/G.F. Strasser, Wiesbaden 1993, 80–84.
[29] *Theutschlands Wohlfahrt*, part 3, Amsterdam 1659, 147.

The change between 1500 and 1700 described by Merchant might be at least partly due to the tendency towards increased control of the emotions. Certainly, control of the emotions may go hand in glove with the subjection of 'disorderly' women. Possibly it was believed that a man's control over his emotions was threatened by the presence of a woman.

What happened then when our seventeenth-century scientists met women? There are no known cases of violence or rape, and it seems rather that the mechanists avoided women. For example, a few years after his mother's death, Newton suffered a severe nervous breakdown. At the time, he blamed Locke for bringing him into contact with a woman, and one gets the impression that he felt threatened.[30] When Fermat offered Descartes his friendship, Descartes replied that the letter brought him as much pleasure as if it had been written by a mistress for whom he had been longing passionately.[31] Writing at the end of the nineteenth century, Ferdinand Rosenberger[32] pointed out that many of the prominent seventeenth-century mechanist philosophers and scientists were not married.

There are some exceptions to this general rule. Galileo was not married, but he had a mistress and three children. However, when he left Padua, he dismissed the mother of his children, taking care to marry her to someone of suitable social rank. The only other exceptions I am aware of are Guericke, Tschirnhaus, Hudde, Wallis and the two Bernoullis, who were all married. It appears that Tschirnhaus considered his married state a problem; he did not like his friends to tell Huygens about it, but later, he felt obliged to write to Huygens justifying his marriage.[33] One has to keep in mind, though, that, as a nobleman, Tschirnhaus was in an unusual position within the scientific community. Since he could not eschew his social position altogether, marriage was an economic requirement for the continuation of his mathematical, optical and philosophical research.

Assuming a historical process of increasing self-control, one could

---

[30] A.R. Hall, *Isaac Newton—Adventurer in Thought*, Oxford, Cambridge (Mass.) 1992, 243.

[31] R. Descartes, *Œuvres*, eds. Adam/Tannery, vol. 2, Paris 1898, 280.

[32] *Die Geschichte der Physik*, vol. 2, Braunschweig 1884, 245.

[33] *Briefe an Ehrenfried Walther von Tschirnhaus von Pieter van Gent*, ed.: Reinhardt, (Wissenschaftliche Beilage zu den Programmen des Realgymnasiums zu Freiberg Ostern 1911), Freiberg 1911, 17; Ch. Huygens, *Œuvres complètes*, vol. 8, Den Haag 1899, 461–463.

be tempted to argue that there were no women whom the mechanists would consider suitable. The reason would be that they themselves were ahead of their times in this process, and educated women with a comparable amount of self-control were rare in the seventeenth century. I doubt whether this is true, though. Molière's comedy *Les femmes savantes* seems to imply that there were educated women around. The same seems to be implied in a mocking remark about a woman who refused to marry unless the prospective husband proved the quadrature of the circle.[34] Here I have been using the attitude towards women as a kind of litmus-test for the hypothesis.

Patterns of illness may provide another touchstone. Johanna Geyer-Kordesch investigates such patterns among the Enlightened and among religious enthusiasts in the eighteenth century. She finds remarkable differences between the two groups, and demonstrates that they were related to the general ideas held by them respectively.[35] It seems plausible that habits of illness can tell us something about people's attitudes towards their bodies and their health, as well as about their general views on nature and on the relation between matter and the immaterial soul.

It was generally accepted in the Paracelsian tradition, of which van Helmont is the most prominent example, that emotional disturbances could cause bodily illness. This discovery may be based on the greater importance attributed to emotions by the Paracelsians. One also needs to take into account the possibility that, because of their personality type, the Paracelsians were more susceptible to psychosomatic illness. (There is also an obvious connection between this hypothesis and the Paracelsian use of magic.) However, not enough is known about this field of research. According to a dissertation presenting a nosological portrait of Leibniz,[36] he was in severe pain from gout in his later years. In order to desensitise his nerves, he gripped his legs in a vice.[37] This seems to reflect a rather

---

[34] *Journal des Sçavans*, 4 march 1686, Amsterdam 1687, 80–81; Leibniz, *Sämtliche Schriften und Briefe* (Akademie-Ausgabe), Berlin, Leipzig 1950, series I, vol. 4, 590.

[35] J. Geyer-Kordesch: Cultural habits of illness. The Enlightened and the Pious in eighteenth century Germany, in: *Patients and Practitioners*, ed. R. Porter, Cambridge 1985, 177–204.

[36] E. Görlich, *Leibniz als Mensch und Kranker*, Dissertation Medical College Hannover 1987.

[37] J.G. von Eckhart, 'Lebensbeschreibung des Freyherrn von Leibnitz', in: Ch.G. von Murr, *Journal zur Kunstgeschichte und zur allgemeinen Litteratur*, part 7, Nürnberg

'mechanistic' attitude towards his body. I cannot say more on this topic here, though, as I have not yet collected a sufficient number of data regarding attitudes towards illness.

This is also true for a final topic I should like to mention. In his study on Leonardo da Vinci, Sigmund Freud pays particular attention to the absence of a father in Leonardo's early years. Both Wallis and Leibniz were six years old when their fathers died, and Newton's father died even before his son's birth. It may be possible to provide some psychological interpretation for the mother-child relationship in these situations, but I prefer not to fill the gaps in our evidence by conjecture. Nevertheless, it seems to me that the relation between the personalities of these scientists and their difference concepts of nature merits further investigation.

1779, 198. Cf. also the report of Pascal's sister on Pascal: G. Perier, La vie de Monsieur Pascal, in: B. Pascal, Œuvres, vol. 1, Paris 1908, 69–70.

PART TWO

THE SOCIAL AND RELIGIOUS PARACELSUS

CHAPTER FIVE

PARACELSIANISM MADE POLITICAL 1600–1650

Hugh Trevor-Roper

One great difficulty about Paracelsianism, as about any word end-
ing in -ism, is that of definition. Not only did its meaning change
with time: even at its beginning it is indistinct. An amalgam of
medieval alchemy and neo-Platonic ideas developed in a mystical
German context, it was expressed in oracular style and a novel, enigmatic language by an egomaniac genius. However, within this opaque
context it is distinguished from the other contemporary ideological
systems, or nebulae, into which it merged by one important element:
its specific medical and chemical content; and it is this content which
would ultimately vindicate it. And yet before this content could be
detached from the nimbus around it and used critically, the amalgam
had an interesting history. While in Germany it remained amorphous
and unorganised, in France it became associated with a specifically
French religion, Calvinism. It also, together with that religion, became
political, indeed revolutionary. Carried largely by French Huguenots,
it became part of the revolutionary ideology which animated the first
phase of the Thirty Years War.

How did this transformation come about? Initially there was no
necessary connection between Paracelsianism and Protestantism. Paracelsus himself died without breaking with the Catholic Church. He
was not a good Catholic—far from it—but he managed to avoid
frontal collision. Like Erasmus, he preached, though in a more violent form, a doctrine which was independent of formal sectarian divi-
sions. But he preached it mainly in the German lands: that is, in
the same spiritual and intellectual context which produced Luther—
and not only Luther but also those other religious preachers whom
Luther would eclipse: the prophets of the second, more radical
Reformation. As the views of Luther hardened in reaction against
the Peasants' revolt of 1525, Paracelsus, who supported that revolt,
preaching in favour of the peasants of Tyrol, became a part of that
second reformation. However, that was in the future. In the religious fluidity of his own time his ideas, as they were then perceived,

did not challenge conventional pre-Tridentine Catholicism, and his specific medical ideas could be, and often were, adopted by Catholic physicians.

So when they first came to France these ideas had no necessary association with Protestant heresy. The first recorded French Paracelsian, Jacques Gohory, was a Roman Catholic, as were all the members of the little group of medical doctors patronised by Queen Catherine de Médicis. Those were still days of liberal Catholicism at court, or at least at that court, before the polarising events of the 1560's: the last session of the Council of Trent and the outbreak of the French Wars of Religion. Even after that turning-point it was still possible, if one had powerful and independent-minded protectors, to combine Paracelsianism in medicine with Catholicism in religion. I do not know whether Leonardo Fioravanti counts as a Paracelsian— he was certainly respected by Paracelsians—but he was presumably a good Catholic since he prospered in Counter-Reformation Italy and was even ennobled by the Pope. The Medici, in Italy as in France, were patrons of Paracelsianism. Ferdinando II Grand Duke of Tuscany, was a sound Catholic, a client of Spain, but he was also very independent and attracted Paracelsian doctors to his state. One of them was the Portuguese Jew Stephanus Rodericus Castrenis, or de Castro, who made no bones about his allegiance to Paracelsus.[1] Another was the Scotchman Macollo—his real name, I suspect, was McCulloch,—who became one of the Grand Duke's physicians.[2] And of course there was the Grand Duke's brother-in-law, the Emperor Rudolf II, patron of Paracelsian *magi*, astrologers and what not?[3] But he was not regarded as a good Catholic, so perhaps we had better not generalise from him.

The most interesting of the Catholic patrons of Paracelsianism is Ernst von Wittelsbach, Elector of Cologne. Of course there was a streak of heresy in the Wittelsbachs: the senior branch of the family, the Electors Palatine, had been early patrons of Paracelsianism and their successors became Calvinists, indeed the leaders of inter-

---

[1] See, for instance, his *de Meteoris*, Florence 1620.

[2] On Macollo see my *From Counter-Reformation to Glorious Revolution*, London 1992, 33–4.

[3] The interest of the Medici in Paracelsianism persisted. Don Antonio de' Medici, brother of Grand Duke Cosimo II, collected Rosicrucian and alchemical writings in several languages and patronised the Paracelsian enthusiast Adam Haslmayr. See Carlos Gilly, *Adam Haslmayr, der erste Verkünder der Manifeste der Rosenkreuzer*, Amsterdam 1994, 25, 170, 177–8, 204–5.

national Calvinism. But Ernst von Wittelsbach was of the junior, Bavarian branch, a Prince of the Church, a pillar of the Counter-Reformation, a bulwark of imperial power in the Rhineland. Nevertheless he was well known as a patron of Paracelsian writers and it was he who commissioned and financed the first complete edition of the medical works of Paracelsus, published in 1589–91 and edited by his court physician Johann Huser. Huser was a Catholic from Baden who assured his readers that Paracelsus himself was a good Catholic too; otherwise, he said, he would never have vouched for him.[4]

However, these are exceptions. Generally speaking, by that time, Paracelsianism had been Protestantised just as Erasmianism had been—not so much on account of any positive Protestant content as because it had been rejected by the Catholic Church. It was rejected as part of the philosophic package in which is was contained: that is, the neo-Platonic, anti-Aristotelean, Hermetic philosophy of the Renaissance. At the turn of the century, the post-Tridentine Catholic Church, threatened by the Protestantism whose spread it now ascribed, in part, to its own former liberalism, turned against that whole philosophy of Nature out of which Paracelsianism had sprung. It condemned Patrizi, burned Bruno and Pucci, imprisoned Campanella; and in 1599 it put the works of Paracelsus on the index. By this time the Archbishop-Elector had seen the light and withdrew his support: the promised edition of Paracelsus' theological works did not appear.

However, though unpublished, the religious ideas of Paracelsus, were gradually leaking out, or being extracted, from his medical writings, and were being merged, or perhaps confused, with those of Valentin Weigel, Caspar Schwenckfeld, and other German preachers of the second Reformation. Thus, by a double process of Catholic rejection and radical Protestant syncretism, Paracelsianism, from an independent system, neither Catholic nor Protestant, gradually became, in effect, an ill-defined Protestant heresy.[5]

But a heresy of which kind of Protestantism? Paracelsus himself had repudiated Luther as no better than the Pope, and his disciples

---

[4] On Huser see Joachim Telle, 'Johann Huser in seinen Briefen', in *Parerga Paracelsica* (*Heidelberger Studien zur Naturkunde der Frühen Neuzeit III*), 1992.

[5] See Carlos Gilly below in Chapter 7 which documents the continuity of this Paracelsian-Weigelian 'amalgam'.

equally rejected the authority of Calvin; and orthodox Lutherans and
Calvinists, where they had authority, were no less dismissive of him.
Especially perhaps the Calvinists. The established Calvinist Churches
of Geneva, the United Provinces and Scotland knew how to keep
heresy at bay, and the most powerful attack on Paracelsianism, that
of Thomas Erastus, came from the Calvinist university of Heidelberg.
However, about the same time when they were repudiated by the
Catholic Church, Paracelsian ideas found their way into certain
Calvinist societies. Bringing with them the eschatological and apocalyptic ideas of the German second Reformation—ideas repudiated
by both Luther and Calvin—they accepted the discipline of a French
religion. With it, they were politicised and, by politics, were brought
back, as a radical force, into Germany.

The decisive factor in this process was the European policy of the
French monarchy. French kings, though Catholic, were consistently
opposed to the Habsburg monarchies of Vienna and Madrid, and
for this reason were obliged, whatever their personal preferences, to
court the Protestant states on their sensitive northern and eastern
borders. There was thus created, from the Netherlands to Switzerland,
a belt of Protestant cities and principalities which were, to a vary-
ing extent, political and cultural clients of France. French was the
language spoken in the courts of the Prince of Orange in Brussels
or the Hague, of the Electors Palatine in Heidelberg, of the Princes
of Zweibrücken, and of course in the free city of Geneva. And with
French culture came a French religion, the French version of Protestantism, Calvinism. However much the French court, whether Valois
or Bourbon, might oppose the Calvinism of its own Huguenot subjects in France, it was bound to support it in this vital area abroad.
Geneva itself, the source from which the disruptive Huguenots of
France were ideologically sustained, was protected by France against
reconquest by Catholic Savoy. Calvinism, indeed, in those countries,
was a badge of French patronage, replacing Lutheranism as they
accepted such patronage. William of Orange's first and second wives
were Dutch and German, Catholic and Lutheran; his third and
fourth were French Calvinists. Maurice the Learned, Landgrave of
Hesse, like the Elector Palatine, would become a Calvinist as he
moved into the French clientèle. Calvinism was carried into those
countries by French missionaries. In one sense, these men were refugees, fleeing from Catholic persecution in France; in another they
were purveyors of French culture, the articulators of a Calvinist inter-

national directed from France against the opposite Catholic international directed from Spain.

However, the traffic of ideas between France and Germany was not in one direction only. It was mutual. If Calvinism was carried into Germany from France, German ideas, and particularly Paracelsian ideas, were brought back into France from Germany. Medical students from the Huguenot areas of France were unlikely to study, or to be welcome, in the rigidly orthodox university of Paris. Many of them would prefer to go to German or Swiss universities. Many also would serve as medical officers in the armies in Germany. There they would become familiar with Paracelsian ideas and practice, which they would then bring back to France and teach, especially, in the numerous provincial universities which good Catholics like Cardinal du Perron and good Galenists like Gui Patin were so eager to suppress. By 1580 the Huguenots were recognised as the carriers of Paracelsianism in France. Religions and medical heresy went together, and to the orthodox both were subversive, indeed revolutionary. But this did not prevent them from being patronised, as occasion required, even by Catholic kings.

Especially of course when the Catholic king was the ex-Huguenot Henri IV. As the political leader of the Huguenots, Henri had been a patron of revolution. He had been surrounded by Huguenots grandees and he and they had relied on Huguenot Paracelsian doctors. Indeed, he had used one of these doctors—Joseph du Chesne, the famous Quercetanus—as a secret political agent to organise financial support from Calvinist Geneva, Swiss cantons and German princes.[6] Physicians were often used for such purposes: they had the contacts and the cover; they enjoyed privileged access to the great and could be trusted with their secrets; and Paracelsians, in particular, were accustomed to conspiracy.

When Henri became Catholic King of France he did not give up his Protestant *clientèle* or his Paracelsian doctors. This aroused deep suspicion in the established institutions. But the Huguenots also were suspicious of the royal apostate. He had given guarantees, but how long would they last? Like the English puritans under Elizabeth, they were prepared to support the Crown, but not unconditionally. A

---

[6] For Joseph du Chesne's diplomatic activity see E. Rott, *Histoire de la representation diplomatique de la France auprès des cantons suisses* II, Berne and Paris 1902, 405, 465, 472, 581–3.

time might come when they would find themselves betrayed. Therefore they must keep up their revolutionary spirit: they might have
to go it alone. For such a purpose the rigid discipline of orthodox
Calvinism would be necessary. But they also drew on the apocalyptic eschatology of the German radicals, including Paracelsus.

Thus there came into being a kind of triple alliance. At the summit
was the French King, now firmly Catholic but pursuing a Protestant
policy for reasons of state. Supporting him, but conditionally, were
the Huguenot party at home and their Calvinist allies abroad; and
behind them, giving them assurance that great cosmological forces
were on their side—that Antichrist was doomed to fall, that the
prophet Elijah was about to return and transform the world—were
the radical prophets of the German second Reformation. It was an
alliance of convenience, for orthodox Calvinists repudiated such theories; but it was held together by a common fear: fear of Catholic
reconquest supported by overwhelming Habsburg power.

In the first year of the new century this fear, already acute, was
sharpened by an alarming incident. In 1601 (we are told) one Gaspard
Baronius, a nephew of the famous cardinal and church historian,
travelling on a secret mission from Rome to Madrid, defected in
France. He was brought to Paris, to the house of the Duc de Bouillon,
the machiavel of the Huguenot high command. There he handed
over the secret papers which he was carrying. These, we are told,
contained the blue-print for a Catholic 'crusade' to extirpate Protestantism at its very centre and so destroy it throughout Christendom. One of those most alarmed by the de-briefing of Gaspard
Baronius was Agrippa d'Aubigné, the unbending warrior-poet of the
party, who is our source for the story.[7] As he afterwards recalled it,
the signal for this crusade was to be a massacre of the Protestants
of the Grisons of Switzerland. This would be followed by the seizure
of the Valtelline pass through the Alps, which they controlled and
which was vital to Habsburg communications. Then would come
the conquest of Geneva by its old overlord the Duke of Savoy, and
the restoration of the Catholic bishopric. With the passage of time
d'Aubigné's recollection of these documents would become more

---

[7] D'Aubigné recounts the episode in his *Histoire Universelle* (ed. A. de Ruble, Société
de l'Histoire de France, 1886–96) ix, 199–201, and in his *Memoires* (ed. Ludovic
Lalaune, Paris 1869) 130–1. He also alludes to it in his correspondence. Cf. A. Garnier,
Agrippa d'Aubigné et le Parti Protestant, Paris 1928, 113–5.

detailed and exact, but in any case the general message was clear. So was the necessary response. The crusade must be forestalled by a pre-emptive strike. If Henri IV, for reasons of state, were to launch such a strike, so much the better: the Huguenots would then support the Catholic king. But in any case the Huguenot party must be mobilised for their part in the action: prepared politically and spiritually for a struggle that would change the world.

Such is the story told by Agrippa d'Aubigné, who clearly believed it to the end of his long life. Was there any truth in it? I have never seen it confirmed. Perhaps it was fantasy, or propaganda. But that does not matter, for essentially it would be confirmed by subsequent facts. In the very next year the Duke of Savoy attempted to seize Geneva by a sudden attack and was only prevented by a lucky chance. Thereafter opposing leagues, Protestant and Catholic, were formed, Protestant fears became paranoid; and celestial portents were found to correspond with Paracelsian or pseudo-Paracelsian prophecies. In such an atmosphere any incident might precipitate the great cosmological and chemical drama which, as the Paracelsian oracle Oswald Croll wrote in 1609, was now due to break out and in which 'Elias Artista', Elijah the Alchemist, was to come and make all things new.

The expected incident duly occurred in that very year, 1609. It was the dispute over the succession to the sensitively placed Duchies of Jülich and Cleves. Henri IV decided, for his own reasons of state, to intervene with force; the Calvinist international was mobilised; and the Paracelsian prophets believed that their hour had come.

The excitement, and the organisation, of the Huguenot leaders and their foreign allies on this occasion is illustrated by the secret correspondence of Philippe du Plessis-Mornay, the revolutionary propagandist of the 1570's, the friend and counsellor of Henri IV in his Huguenot years, the Platonist philosopher-statesman of the party. Mornay is often seen as a grave counsellor of moderation. But not now. Now he appears as the orchestrator of the Calvinist international, directing, from his citadel of Saumur, a network of active allies and agents in Switzerland, Italy, Bohemia, Moravia, Hungary, Poland. The language that he uses is exalted, messianic: the language not of French reason of state or of orthodox Calvinism but of millenarian eschatology. Henri IV's proposed war, he insists, is the necessary pre-emptive strike against Antichrist. He had been advocating such a strike for three years; now Babylon will fall; a

new age of the world is to begin. Mornay is sending secret agents
in all directions, with false names and double instructions—one set
to be announced, the other concealed. 'The key of the whole business' is the Calvinist minister in Geneva, Jean Diodati. Diodati in
turn is the link with Venice—with the two Servite friars, Paolo Sarpi
and Micanzio Fulgenzio, who are to bring Venice over to Reform:
the friars, he reports, expect 'the infallible ruin of this Antichrist'
within six years at most. Then, from Venice, Calvinism will invade
the Austrian lands. Croatia will soon be won. Meanwhile Mornay
is forging cross-links between Venice and the Hague, Venice and
Heidelberg. In Venice itself Mornay's personal agent is the man who
handles the foreign relations of Paolo Sarpi, 'the soul of Padre Paolo'
as he is called, Pierre Asselineau, a French Huguenot and Paracelsian
physician. The secret agent whom Mornay sends to Oldenbarneveldt
and Prince Maurice in the Hague to persuade them to send emis-
saries to Venice is another physician, Dr. de Licques, the brother
of his factotum at Saumur. Of him I know nothing.[8]

So once again we find physicians as secret agents of the Calvinist
international. I have already mentioned du Chesne. He is now dead:
he died in 1609. His last service to Henri IV were as secret emissary
to the Landgrave of Hesse, Maurice the Learned, the most important West German client of France. Maurice was himself a chemist,
the founder of a chemical laboratory at Kassel, and he too used his
physician, another Paracelsian, Dr. Mosanus, as his secret diplomat
agent. Some of such business was transacted directly between Mosanus
and du Chesne.[9] Another central figure in the German Calvinist
web was the young Elector Palatine, Frederick V. He was guided, or
driven, in politics by Christian of Anhalt-Bernburg who, like all the
Anhalt princes—there were five of them, all Calvinists and allied to
France[10]—was a committed Paracelsian and himself an amateur

---

[8] For Mornay's activity as advocate of a pre-emptive strike from 1606 onwards
and as organiser of the Calvinist international for it, see *Memoires et Correspondance
de Philippe du Plessis-Mornay*, ed. La Fontenelle de Vaudoré et Auguis, Paris 1824,
vols. x–xii.

[9] Correspondence of Mosanus and du Chesne, mainly chemical but referring to
their secret diplomatic activity, is preserved in Kassel (Murhardsche Bibliothek 20
MS chem. 19, 88–133) and in Marburg (Hessisches Staatsarchiv 4a. 39 Nr. 56).
See also Christoph von Rommel *Correspondance de Henri IV avec Maurice le Savant,
Landgrave de Hesse*, Paris 1840.

[10] The eldest of the Anhalt princes, Joachim Georg (of Anhalt-Dessau), who ruled
the whole principality until its re-division in 1605, had served Henri IV as a military commander in the French civil war and acted as his agent to other German

chemist. Anhalt's own physician was the famous Paracelsian Oswald Croll, whom he had used as his secret agent to the Calvinist magnates of Bohemia.

Such was the machinery which was mobilised by Mornay in 1609–10. It never moved into action. As he set out in his coach from Paris for the eastern front, Henri IV was assassinated by a Catholic fanatic, and the whole enterprise was halted. The advocates of the pre-emptive strike were desolated. 'This execrable parricide', exclaimed Mornay, 'has changed the face of the world'. 'That holy work, begun with such zeal', had been frustrated, and from now on he turned from international conspiracy to the defence of the threatened privileges of the Huguenots at home. He became again their advocate, their statesman, their philosopher. But the machinery, though unused, did not rust. The French monarchy might be neutralised, but if another major power could be found to move it, it could be used again.

One obvious patron was the King of England, James I. With the assassination of Henri IV, and the establishment of the ultra-Catholic regency of Marie de Médicis, the French Huguenots looked to England for their support. Some of them chose to emigrate. One of these was Henri IV's last Paracelsian physicians, Theodore de Mayerne. He had been a friend, disciple and colleague of du Chesne. Like him, he had studied in Germany, had cosmopolitan contacts, and political interests. He was a *protégé* and life-long friend of the Huguenot leader, the Duc de Rohan. Even after his emigration to England, where he became chief physician to James I, he remained the trusted physician of Rohan and the other Huguenot grandees. He was a friend of Asselineau in Venice. In England he was closely associated with Pierre du Moulin, 'the Pope of the Huguenots', who was employed as a scribe and a propagandist by James I. The new rulers of France watched both Mayerne and du Moulin with deep, and sometimes paranoid suspicion. In 1615, when the two men visited France together, they waited till Mayerne had left for England and then arrested du Moulin. Three years later, when Mayerne revisited Paris, they were less delicate: the King of England's chief physician

princes. 'All the Anhalt princes' are listed as Paracelsians by du Chesne, who dedicated his *Pharmacopoeia Dogmaticorum Restituta* to Christian of Anhalt-Bernburg. Another of the brothers, August of Anhalt-Plötzkau, was the enthusiastic patron of the Paracelsist and Rosicrucian Adam Haslmayr, see Gilly, *Adam Haslmayr*. Another Ludwig, of Anhalt-Köthen, was the patron of the *Fruchtbringende Gesellschaft*.

was summarily ordered out of the country. This insult, which caused great offence and a diplomatic rupture, was never explained. It can be explained only by the crisis atmosphere of the time.

For we are now in 1618, the year not only of Huguenot revolt but also of the Bohemian revolution, which would lead to the second attempt at a pre-emptive strike against Antichrist. The strike, when it came—the election of the Elector Palatine to the Throne of Bohemia—was the triumph of the high-risk policy of Christian of Anhalt. Were it to succeed, it would alter the balance of the Electoral College, of the Empire, of Europe. It would be a Calvinist triumph, and at first it appeared as such: at the news of the election, the Huguenots resorted to the electoral court at Heidelberg—among them Mayerne's sister, newly married to a young Huguenot activist, the Baron de Jaucourt, also there. It would also be a Paracelsian triumph. The Paracelsians throughout the Empire rejoiced; their enthusiasts gathered in Prague; they saw, once again, the imminent realisation of their prophecies, now given new impulse by the Rosicrucian movement, new confirmation by the stars: for what else could the great comet of 1618 portend? Surely Elijah, Elias Artista, the chemical Elijah of Paracelsus, was now coming to make all things new; and he was to appear in Bohemia, Prague was to be the new Jerusalem. One of those who was in Prague to witness the new epiphany was the greatest Paracelsian of the time, the pupil of the millenarian encyclopaedist of Herborn, J.H. Alsted: Jan Amos Komensky, the famous Comenius. In his more excited moments Comenius would even take on the role of Elijah himself. Another was Paul Felgenhauer, Paracelsist preacher and physician, who would make the same claim.[11] Another was the Paracelsian mystic from Lusatia, Jacob Böhme.

Unfortunately, once again, the pre-emptive strike failed. The Calvinists had hoped that the King of England would support his son-in-law: it was the leader of the French Huguenots, the Duc de Bouillon, who had negotiated the marriage of the Elector, his nephew, to the English Princess Elizabeth. Du Moulin, then presiding over a rebellious Huguenot assembly in la Rochelle, actually wrote to King James urging him to do so. But King James had no intention of backing so rash a venture. So, as in 1610, the pre-emptive strike

---

[11] For Felgenhauer see H.J. Schoeps, *Philosemitismus im Barock*, Tübingen 1952, 18–45.

was frustrated by an event—there an assassination, here a miscalculation—at the political summit. However, this time, it was too late to retreat. The unfortunate Elector, hailed by German and Czech Protestants as the Lion of the North, the answer to prayer, the fulfiller of prophecy, had to go it alone: alone to disaster.

The train of disaster began in Switzerland, in the *sacro macello*. 'The Holy Butchery' of the Protestants of the Grisons. To the Calvinist faithful this was very sinister. Agrippa d'Aubigné naturally remembered the revelations of Gaspard Baronius over which he had brooded for nearly twenty years. According to Baronius, the next step would be the attack on Geneva: that was to be the beginning of the 'crusade', which, was to be launched in 1622.[12] At such a critical hour D'Aubigné decided that his place was at the front. He left France for good, established himself at Geneva, and assumed the task of fortifying the cities of Geneva and Berne against the expected attack. This indeed was exactly what Rome was planning. Calvinist Geneva, wrote the Pope, was the cess-pool of Europe; it had been tolerated so long only as a sump into which Christendom could discharge its filth; now was the time to clean it out; and he called on the King of France and the Duke of Savoy to conquer it and restore it, purged, to its rightful Catholic bishop.[13]

That of course did not happen. Calvinist Geneva was after all, a French protectorate. But otherwise the Catholic *Blitzkrieg* was a great success. Late in 1620, after the decisive battle of the White Mountain, Prague was reconquered. In 1621 Spain entered the war. In 1622 Heidelberg was sacked. By the end of that year the Calvinist International was in ruin. The King of Bohemia was an impotent exile in the Hague. In the Palatinate as in Bohemia Protestantism was crushed. Meanwhile, in France, the Calvinist kingdom of Navarre had been reconquered and recovered for Catholicism. In this universal rout, the idea of a Calvinist Venice leading to the conversion of Croatia had evaporated. The millenarians, the Paracelsians of Europe who had been so triumphant in 1618 were scattered. They hid their heads in Germany, or fled abroad to eastern Europe: Comenius to the estate of Karel Žerotin, Mornay's correspondent in Moravia,

---

[12] The date 1622 for the final show-down with Antichrist was also favoured by Felgenhauer.

[13] See the instructions given by the Pope to his agent Fr. Corona on 18 July 1621, printed in J. Gaberel, *Histoire de l'Eglise de Genève*, Geneva 1858–62, II. ii, 255.

and thence to that of a Calvinist magnate in Poland; his teacher
Alsted from Herborn to the protection of the Calvinist prince of
Transylvania.

In the midst of this *débâcle*, in the winter of 1621–2, Theodore de
Mayerne, returning from a visit to his newly acquired estate in
Switzerland, stopped in Sedan as the guest of his patient, the Duc
de Bouillon, to whom he brought a secret appeal from the trem-
bling senators of Berne. In Sedan he found several old friends who
had taken refuge in that Calvinist enclave. One of them was Pierre
du Moulin for whom France was now unsafe. Another was an
old associate, a Paracelsian alchemist from Orleans, Guillaume de
Trougny, with whom he and du Chesne had formed a secret group
in Paris seeking to perform 'The Great Work' and produce the Philosopher's Stone. At Sedan they now discussed, for the last time, the
problem of Elias Artista, whether, and when, and in what form he
should come.[14]

Was this then the end of the adventure? It was certainly the end of
the Calvinist international, and so the Paracelsians were freed from
the Calvinist, Huguenot embrace. For a time they were atomised
and depoliticised, as many of them, of course, had always been. But
they did not despair. They went to ground, working quietly in small
groups in German courts, cities, academies, laboratories. Others, having witnessed the failure in Bohemia and Germany, looked abroad.
They imagined new centres where they could await, and perhaps
forward, the promised Paracelsian revolution: Utopias, Antilias,
Macarias, in islands off the Baltic coast, or in the Western hemi-
sphere, or perhaps even in that other island, an island of peace in
the universal war, the island in which so many Protestant refugees
were seeking asylum: England.

Unfortunately the rulers of England, at that time were not very
sympathetic to such ideas. English intervention on the Continent,
whether in Germany in support of the Elector, or in France in support of the Huguenots, had been disastrous, and after 1628 Charles I
was determined to cut his losses, break with international Protestantism, and seek to secure his aims by appeasing, not resisting, the
victorious Catholic powers. But there was a strong party in the country eager to reverse this process: to return to the ideals of Queen
Elizabeth, to re-protestantise the Church of England, and even to

---

[14] British Library, MSS Sloane 2083 f. 1, MSS Sloane 693 f. 52.

intervene in the continental war, not merely to restore the electoral family to the Palatinate (the limit of royal policy) but to reverse the disasters of the 1620's and re-create Protestant power: why should that honour be left entirely to the King of Sweden? It was among such men that the refugees found protection and encouragement, and in such circles that the radical Paracelsian and millenarian ideas which had been expressed in Germany and Bohemia were adopted and adapted to English circumstances. It was from 1620, the year of the Bohemian *débâcle*, that millenarian ideas, inspired by Alsted, began their spectacular acceptance in England; it was in the 1630's that the German immigrant Samuel Hartlib, the founding father of all those Macarian and Antilian utopias, set out to use England as his laboratory for a Paracelsian reformation.

How well he used it became clear in November 1640 when the collapse of the 'personal rule' of Charles I presented a sudden opportunity for radical changes in England itself. Then the voices of English aristocrats calling for political redirection and of English clergy calling for a re-calvinisation of the national Church were joined by the voices of Hartlib and his friends and patrons calling for a radical, and in fact, a Paracelsian reformation. So at the very beginning of the crisis we find Hartlib, through his political and clerical allies, calling for his Bohemian friend Comenius to be fetched from exile in Poland to be the prophet and articulator of such a reformation. For Comenius would not be brought to England merely as a pedagogical reformer, to set out his new method of teaching Latin to schoolboys: he was summoned, and came, to inaugurate a new age through a total religious and chemical—i.e. Paracelsian—revolution.

Insular historians looking back at the English Revolution of 1640–1660 tend to see it, especially now, as a plan of limited reform which got out of hand and degenerated through civil war into revolution. But that is to be deaf to these passionate voices. It was 1619 come again. Now as then, as in 1610, behind the political leadership—Henri IV, the Elector Palatine, the temporising parliamentary leaders—behind the Calvinist or Calvinising clergy—the French Huguenots, the German and Bohemian Calvinists, the English 'Presbyterians'—stand the enthusiasts who are convinced that this was no mere political episode or ecclesiastical reform but a great historical climax, a consequence that had long been hanging in the stars. Antichrist is scheduled to fall; all things are to be made new; Christ's second coming is within sight; and if no one has yet spotted Elias

Artista descending from the clouds, John Milton, the pupil of the millenarian Dr. Mede, is there, with his singing robes about him, declaring that 'all creatures sigh to be renewed' and offering himself as a substitute. This is not necessarily Paracelsianism, but it fits into the amalgam of which Paracelsianism is an ingredient, and the chemical content comes from Paracelsus himself.

In 1641 in England, as in 1619 in Bohemia, the excited visionaries expected a sudden, complete victory for the new enlightenment. The old order was to dissolve, and by its dissolution to reveal the new. When this did not happen, when the old order resisted and England, like Germany, was engulfed in a long, untidy civil war, Comenius saw that once again he had miscalculated; so he returned to Eastern Europe: to Poland and Transylvania—the Poland of Suchten and Sendivogius, the Transylvania of Alsted. Perhaps the new dawn would break there. But if their philosophic champion had abandoned them, his Bohemian and German disciples now in England and their English friends, organised by Hartlib, did not despair. Shrugging off their early 'Presbyterian' patrons, they continued their work under the more congenial rule of the Cromwellian 'Independents', combining messianic aspirations with practical medical and chemical studies, publishing the prophecies of Comenius and his Eastern European *protégés*, the chemical and medical works of Paracelsus and his followers, the mystical theology of Jacob Böhme. Cromwell even offered Comenius a refuge in reconquered Ireland; but Comenius had now given up hope of England as the scene of the new theophany: he looked rather to the exhilarating conquests of the new King of Sweden, and then, when those failed, would settle for the patronage of a rich and generous merchant in Amsterdam.

The acceptance, in Puritan England, of Paracelsian medical and chemical ideas, and of the prophetic ideology in which they were entrenched, is well known from the writings of Pyarali, Rattansi and Charles Webster.[15] Paracelsus, Croll and Sendivogius were then names to conjure with. The famous work of Sendivogius, said its English translator, was second only to the Bible as a source of knowledge of God and Nature. Here it is enough to point to the practical consequences. The long civil wars, the years of 'blood and confusion' which followed the failures of 1619 and 1641, and above all the dis-

---

[15] P. Rattansi, 'Paracelsus and the Puritan Revolution', *Ambix*, x, 1963; Charles Webster, *The Great Instauration*, London 1975.

illusion thereby engendered both in central Europe and in England, led to the last great act of Paracelsian separation: the separation of chemistry, the unique contribution of Paracelsus himself, from the messianic religious system into which he and his later disciples had locked it. International Calvinism, the force which had mobilised that system for political revolution, was now discredited, and in the changed intellectual climate after the end of those convulsions revolutionary religion was out of fashion. So the explosive charge was removed from the old amalgam and the combustible ingredients could be separated and rendered harmless. Just as, after the Hussite wars of Bohemia in the 15th century, the quietist Bohemian Brethren became the residuary legatees of the revolutionary Taborites, so, in 17th century England quietist Quakers became the residuary legatees of the revolutionary Fifth Monarchy Anabaptists, and in Germany the Pietists of Halle took up the religious legacy of Paracelsus, leaving his chemical legacy to be developed in its own context, purged of ideology, free from the excitement of politics and revolution.

CHAPTER SIX

MEDICINE, ALCHEMY, AND THE CONTROL OF LANGUAGE: ANDREAS LIBAVIUS VERSUS THE NEOPARACELSIANS

Bruce T. Moran

Paracelsus died in 1541, but 'Neoparacelsus' did not. 'Neoparacelsus' was a name coined by the Coburg physician, chemist, and school-master, Andreas Libavius (c. 1540[?]/c. 60[?]–1616), for a certain Paracelsian physician whose views had lately been debated at the University of Erfurt. Libavius chose the name, one which he extended thereafter to other Paracelsians as well, so as to avoid, he said, the use of a proper name and the appearance of raving against a specific individual or his character.[1] We must, however, not be deceived. Call-ing the character and virtue of Paracelsians into question was pre-cisely the aim of a large number of polemical writings composed by Libavius, writings which, in their number, weight, and measure, alto-gether dwarf the already enormous text for which he is best known, the *Alchemia* (1597).[2]

In fact, only by comparing the first and second editions of the *Alchemia* does one catch a glimpse of how much some of the earlier disputes affected Libavius's chemical and medical thinking. By 1606, the *Alchemia* (now spelled *Alchymia*) included commentaries greatly extending the range of the first 1597 edition.[3] The new narrative was forged from polemic and contained specific reference to names like Johann Graman, Nicolaus Guibert (ca. 1547–1620), and Joseph Michael; each of whom had, by then, inspired independent treatises from Libavius's hand. Given their connection to the publication his-tory of his best known work and their imposing presence on the

[1] *Andreae Libavi Halensis Sax. Med. D. Po. Laur. Physici Rotenburgici ad Tubarim, Neoparacelsica . . .*, Francofurti: Ioannes Saur, impensis Petri Kopffij, 1594, 186–187.

[2] *D.O.M.A. Alchemia Andreae Libavii . . .*, Francofurti: Iohannes Saurius, impensis Petri Kopffij, 1597.

[3] *D.O.M.A. Alchymia Andreae Libavii, Recognita, Emendata, et aucta, tum dogmatibus et experimentis nonnullis; Tum Commentario Medico Physico Chymico . . .*, Francofurti: Iohannes Saurius, impensis Petri Kopffij, 1606.

Libavian shelf, it seems only natural to ask why these texts were written, and for whom. Yet very little attention has ever been granted them. One twentieth century commentator characterized the polemical writings as 'fruitless,' and accused Libavius of wasting 'the greater part of his life' in their pursuit.[4] But surely Libavius did not think he was wasting his time. And just as certainly we would miss something important about the nature and purpose of the greatest part of his medical and alchemical commentary if we avoided the unseemly side of his discourse and failed to ask why it made sense for him to construct it.

Not everyone has fled from these texts. Owen Hannaway, for instance, made the epistemological positions taken by Libavius and one of his best known Paracelsian opponents, Oswald Croll (ca. 1560–1609), the focus of an impressive study, *The Chemists and the Word*.[5] Nevertheless, in confronting the Paracelsian opposition, Libavius took up arms 'against a sea of troubles;' and in that larger setting Croll was just one of many threatening currents. This study will look more broadly at Libavius's attacks against 'Neoparacelsus' and consider a few of the rhetorical strategies which he employed in confronting the Paracelsian opposition. Doing so should bring us face to face with concerns heretofore unnoticed about his most numerous writings and, at the same time, call attention to a wider dimension of the Paracelsian debate. While ostensibly about alchemy and Paracelsianism, Libavius's polemical treatises are equally valuable as grammatical exercises, dialectical demonstrations, and moral sermons. At one level they are true *apologia*, joining language, virtue, and institutional authority in defense of academic wisdom. At the same time, however, they can be read (and I think they were read) as texts with important pedagogic purposes, teaching by example what good argument is, what tastefully constructed Latin looks like, what it is to be morally responsible, especially in regard to one's duty to city or state, and, in at least one treatise, what it is to be a humanist-academic man. Read in this way, Libavius's most numerous writings entail a kind of symbolic strategy for transmitting a particular vision of the social world, and in this regard the stakes, in the war of words

---

[4] Wlodzimierz Hubicki, 'Libavius (or Libau), Andreas,' *Dictionary of Scientific Biography*, ed. C.C. Gillispie, New York 1970–76, vol. 8, 309–312.

[5] Owen Hannaway, *The Chemists and the Word: The Didactic Origins of Chemistry*, Baltimore and London 1975.

between Libavius and 'Neoparacelsus,' were much greater than simply a determination of which medicaments could cure and which could not.

Libavius spent the majority of his professional life as a physician and school teacher. In 1586 he was appointed 'Stadt- und Raths-Schulen Rector' in Coburg, and became professor of history and poetry at the University of Jena in 1588. Three years later he moved to Rotenburg where he was appointed municipal physician and where he became, soon thereafter, inspector of schools. An invitation to become director of the newly founded *Gymnasium Casimirianum Academicum* of the Saxon duke, Johann Casimir, brought him back to Coburg in 1607. The nature of the school is important. Under Libavius's direction the Gymnasium combined classes from the city's Paedagogium with more advanced, university level, subjects. It was a small school, of around eight instructors, including Libavius. Grammar (both Latin and Greek), rhetoric, and Aristotelian dialectic were the backbone of the curriculum. Characteristically, as director, Libavius seems to have emphasized dialectic.[6]

If we look for the locus of that set of dispositions which, more than anything else, inclined Libavius to think and act in certain ways—what has been called a *habitus* by the French sociologist Pierre Bourdieu[7]—we must look to the gymnasium. Here Libavius himself was rigorously trained and here he, as a teacher and director, incorporated its history. A teacher, of course, must also let himself be taught. But within the pedagogical context, Neoparacelsians, who, according to Libavius, possessed no method, whose language was vulgar, and who chose words in order to obscure rather than to reveal the order of nature, could claim no intellectual authority. Their writings he referred to as a cloaca. Their secretiveness was, above all, morally irresponsible and intellectually uncivil. Paracelsian

---

[6] Gottfried Ludwig, *Ehre Des Hoch-Fürstlichen Casimiriani Academici in Coburg, oder Desselben vollständige Histories . . .*, Coburg 1725, vol. 1, 139–157, 412–417; vol. 2, 6–50, 244–245. Also helpful in reconstructing Libavius's professional life are J. Ottmann, 'Erinnerung an Libavius in Rothenburg ob der Tauber,' *Verhandlungen der Gesellschaft Deutscher Naturforscher und Ärzte*, 65, 1894, 79–84. A. Schnizlein, 'Andreas Libavius und Seine Tätigkeit am Gymnasium zu Rothenburg,' *Beilage zum Jahresbericht des Kgl. Progymnasiums Rothenburg ob der Tauber für das Schuljahr 1913/1914*, Rothenburg 1914. J.R. Partington, *A History of Chemistry*, London 1961, vol. 2, 244–270. Hubicki, *Dictionary of Scientific Biography*, vol. 8, 309–312.

[7] Pierre Bourdieu, *Language and Symbolic Power*, ed. and intro. John B. Thompson, trans. Gino Raymond and Matthew Adamson, Cambridge, Mass. 1991.

writers, Libavius observed, should be sent to *Cynosarges*, the gymnasium for the non-native sons of Athens.[8]

Classical rhetoric required paying attention to moral character.[9] Language reflected both virtue and vice and comprised a mirror by means of which one might separate truth from falsehood. Deep within one of his most hostile rebuttals Libavius wondered about what use might come from his Paracelsian battles. They were, he concluded, the means for discovering virtue and vice. For it was among the virtues and vices that one could discern what was genuine and what was not.[10]

Given the connection between virtue, language, and learning, it comes as no surprise that one of the first arguments used by Libavius against the Paracelsians in an essay ostensibly aimed at the Rosicrucians is a moral one. The brothers of the Rosy Cross are Paracelsians in disguise and they, together with their spokesman, Oswald Croll, are guilty of moral cowardice. They use ink not to print words for purposes of clear discourse but, like octopi, to hide behind. Their ideas have lent themselves to all sorts of judgements and have led finally to *discordia in religione*.[11] Indeed, Libavius insists, if this sort of Paracelsian approach to language and knowledge would break into theology and politics hardly anything of either would remain for long. Thus, it is a wonder, he observes, that the author of the *Fama Fraternitatis* (one of the earliest Rosicrucian manifestos) saw fit to complain that 'learned know-it-alls' (*der Überdrang der Nassweisen*) had hindered Paracelsus in the course of his work. It would have been more correct to write that God wished to protect his schools and churches and therefore stood against Paracelsus, the spread of whose thinking would have led to more terrible things than had been caused by the peasant's war itself.[12]

The schools, from Libavius's point of view, *were* in peril, especially where princely interests in occult philosophy influenced university

---

[8] *Pro Defensione Syntagmatis Chymici Contra Reprehensiones Henningi Scheunemanni Paracelsistae... in D.O.M.A. Appendix necessaria Syntagmatis Arcanorum Chymicorum Andreae Libavii...*, Francofurti: Nicolaus Hoffmannus, impensis Petri Kopffij, 1615, 44ff.

[9] Brian Vickers, *In Defence of Rhetoric*, Oxford 1988, esp. chapters 1 and 5; also Vickers, 'Epideictic and Epic in the Renaissance,' *New Literary History: A Journal of Theory and Interpretation*, 14, 1982–83, 497–537.

[10] *Pro Defensione Syntagmatis Chymici Contra Reprehensiones Henningi Scheunemanni Paracelsistae...* 113.

[11] *D.O.M.A. Wolmeinendes Bedencken von der Fama und Confession der Bruderschafft dess Rosen Creutzes...* (Frankfurt: Egenolff Emmeln in verlegung Petri Kopffij, 1616, 5ff.

[12] *Ibid.*, 75ff.

curricula. The unthinkable occurred in 1609 when the German Landgrave, Moritz of Hessen-Kassel (1572–1632), appointed the Paracelsian physician, Johannes Hartmann (1568–1631), to the newly
created chair of chemical medicine at the University of Marburg.
Libavius had nothing against chemical medicine, and claimed to be
no enemy of Paracelsus (at least to the extent that he might find
something worthwhile in his writings). While loathing the horridness
of Paracelsus and Paracelsians, Libavius tolerated authors who made
use of metaphors [*Parabolicos vero autores*] as long as they were otherwise of sound mind, and admitted the harmony of the greater and
lesser worlds.[13] The presence, however, of a mystical Paracelsian like
Hartmann within the institutional walls of traditional Aristotelianism
prompted yet another round of hostile critique.[14]

Hartmann had come to the university by court appointment, but
others with no ties to the academy also boasted of court positions
and noble titles. Besides Croll and Hartmann, Libavius also took
aim at other, lesser known, opponents. Among these, Joseph Michael,
Georg am Wald, Nicolaus Guibert, Pierre le Paulmier, Henning
Scheunemann, and Johann Graman received the brunt of his criticism. In most cases the message was simple. Despite claims to social
and intellectual respectability, these writers only feigned learning and
revealed their ignorance and lack of moral virtue in stylistic inele-
gance and in vulgar inventions of medical terms—names, Libavius
says, which are more monstrous than the things they represent.

Writing a lengthy essay called the '*Liber Antigramaniorum*,' part of an
even lengthier text called the *Neoparacelsica* (1594), Libavius addressed
specifically the thinking of Johann Graman, a Paracelsian *medicus ordi-
narius* at Erfurt. There are some, Libavius complains, who take to
themselves the authority to judge and the power to censure as if
they have not arrived at such faculties from the outside, but have
been born into them.[15] Graman had never been trained in logic,

---

[13] *De Igne Naturae . . .* in *D.O.M.A. Syntagmatis Arcanorum Chymicorum Tomi Secundi . . .*
(Francofurti: Nicolaus Hoffmannus, impensis Petri Kopffij, 1613, 9. Also, *Neoparacelsica*,
496–497.

[14] *De Philosophia Vivente seu Vitali Paracelsi Iuxta P. Severinum . . . ex Repititione I.
Hartmanni* in the section *Examen Philosophiae Novae* of *Appendix Necessaria Syntagmatis
Arcanorum Chymicorum*. See Bruce T. Moran, *Chemical Pharmacy Enters the University:
Johannes Hartmann and the Didactic Care of Chymiatria in the Early Seventeenth Century*,
Madison 1991. Also, 'Court Authority and Chemical Medicine: Moritz of Hessen,
Johannes Hartmann, and the Origin of Academic Chemiatria,' *Bulletin of the History
of Medicine*, 63, 1989, 225–246.

[15] *Neoparacelsica*, 185.

and thus needed to rely upon 'poetic trifles' and a medical philosophy based almost entirely upon personal illumination. Because of their supposedly divine origin, Paracelsus's doctrines could not be tested by anyone, no matter how talented. Libavius preferred the historically mediated to the personally inspired. 'The fame of our times is better known and more exact, and we are more skilled in preparing and treating because past times have collected knowledge and have passed it on as increased treasure.'[16] Rather than revelation, physical truth should be found in causes which Libavius considered the foundation of knowledge. The youth must understand logic which itself discloses the whole, the immutable and the necessary.[17] Knowledge follows not from meditation but from hard analytical work. 'True philosophy,' Libavius writes, 'is not so much an investigation of hidden and unknown things as it is . . . a pounding [of things] to pieces. . . . While [the philosopher] does this, he does not yet know', but strives after knowledge.[18]

That students might understand logic was one of the principal aims of Libavius's polemical writings. 'These things have been said,' he writes, 'so that they might show the youth the worthlessness of Neoparacelsus and his allies.'[19] The method was to recreate Graman's syllogisms and explode them. What remained after the dialectic demolition were only 'crazed stories' told in an incoherent language, or *Gramatica* [a pun on grammar and Graman's name] and with a vocabulary founded in Babylon. 'Stay here boys,' Libavius advises, 'and punish the wisdom of beastly Neoparacelsus,'[20] learn 'to whip him with tough and stinging switches.'[21] Neoparacelsus deserved ridicule for shamelessly trying to seduce the young. Libavius, however, was on to the disguise. 'If we were complete blockheads,' he exclaims, 'whom you could throw to vulcan, you would have nothing to fear; but now those same blockheads are turned into hammers and these will destroy your senses and the fog of your reasoning, and they will drink to (other) boys ridiculing your vanity.'[22] Paracelsians have stolen their nobility, have been morally irresponsible, and have

---

[16] *Ibid.*, 482.

[17] *Ibid.*, 547.

[18] *Pro Defensione Syntagmatis Chymici Contra Reprehensiones Henningi Scheunemanni Paracelsistae . . .*, 36.

[19] *Neoparacelsica*, 586.

[20] *Ibid.*, 635.

[21] *Ibid.*, 637.

[22] *Ibid.*, 637–38.

veiled themselves in the didactically useless language of secrecy. 'If you are real doctors and do not flee from the light [of wisdom],' Libavius asks, 'why do you not teach in the academies? You are occupied at courts where I believe you accomplish more by flattery than by speaking the truth, and advance more by begging than by curing [*mendicando amplius, quam medicando*].'[23]

An insistence upon clarity and openness in chemical language is a rhetorical commonplace among chemical writers of the early seventeenth century. Recent studies have emphasized the social practices of chemical communication during this period and have outlined the economic, religious, and institutional contexts of openness.[24] What the case of Libavius and Neoparacelsus shows us is the way in which the language of secrecy and openness also took shape as a form of moral discourse, a discourse tied, at least in part, to institutional powers capable of legitimizing chemical and medical language. At one point in his diatribe against Graman, Libavius proclaimed that the confusion was all about vocabulary.[25] In another response, he accused Paracelsians of creating their own linguistic and grammatical empire wherein they ruled as tyrants.[26]

Paracelsians too, of course, were ready to condemn secrecy. For many, the subtleties of scholastic philosophy and the Latin constructions upon which they were based amounted to a private language—the province of an academic and social elite.[27] The son of

---

[23] *Ibid.*, 729.

[24] Cf. Jan V. Golinski, 'Chemistry in the Scientific Revolution: Problems of Language and Communication,' in David C. Lindberg and Robert S. Westman eds., *Reappraisals of the Scientific Revolution*, Cambridge 1990, 367–396. See also B.J.T. Dobbs, 'From the Secrecy of Alchemy to the Openness of Chemistry,' in Tore Frängsmyr ed., *Solomon's House Revisited: The Organization and Institutionalization of Science*, Canton, Mass. 1990, 75–94. William Eamon, 'From the Secrets of Nature to Public Knowledge: The Origins of the Concept of Openness in Science,' *Minerva* 23, 1985, 321–347. Pamela O. Long, 'The Openness of Knowledge: An Ideal and Its Context in 16th-Century Writings on Mining and Metallurgy,' *Technology and Culture*, 32, 1991, 318–355. In regard to Libavius, two additional works ought to be compared: Owen Hannaway, 'Laboratory Design and the Aim of Science: Andreas Libavius and versus Tycho Brahe,' *Isis*, 77, 1986, 585–610 and Jole Shackelford, 'Tycho Brahe, Laboratory Design, and the Aim of Science: Reading Plans in Context,' *Isis*, 84, 1993, 211–230.

[25] *Neoparacelsica*, 694.

[26] *Pro Defensione Syntagmatis Chymici Contra Reprehensiones Henningi Scheunemanni Paracelsistae . . .*, 77.

[27] On the Paracelsian use of language see Dietlinde Goltz, 'Die Paracelsisten und die Sprache,' *Sudhoffs Archiv*, 56, 1972, 337–352. Also, Joachim Telle, 'Die Schreibart des Paracelsus im Urteil deutscher Fachschriftsteller des 16. und 17. Jahrhunderts,' *Medizinhistorisches Journal*, 16, 1981, 78–100.

Johann Graman, Georg Graman, advanced his own view of secretiveness by referring to Libavius as 'Hans Schlauraffen' from the school of 'Doctor felt-hat,' a 'Physicaco' with 'rabbit brains not to be cured with hellebore.' To cover up his ignorance, Libavius (who should better be called *Libaffe*) had gotten hold of a fog cap by means of Narristotelian tricks-of-the-air in Narragonia. (This was, of course, all a mockery of Aristotelian studies and the language that served it.) As a result, this man (Libavius) has become one of the 'logiatrics' and 'Grammaticuculi,' and had condemned honest physicians like Georg's father, Johann—a physician who had been taken into ducal service and had served the city of Erfurt. In contrast to such a courtly and municipal vocation, what could Libavius possibly say for himself? He had stayed at home, had remained hidden away in his grammatical pedantry and had accomplished nothing more than playing the role of a Narristotelian Zoilus (Censurer of Homer).[28]

Responding to the younger Graman, as well as to others, Libavius carefully chronicled all the insults, and took precise notice of every abuse hurled his way. Georg Graman he refers to as a new evil spirit [*alastor*] which has crept out of the darkness. He is obscure, however, and of no importance, a 'raging fly,' who calls Aristotle 'Narristoteles,' and a 'horned chicken,' and to whom university professors are simple pedants (literally, 'scholastic foxes' [*vulpes scholasticas*]). But, Libavius adds, 'the Gymnasium of the Duke of Saxony in Coburg, of which I am director, does not admit such fresh students [*beanos*]. They must be removed to the boy's benches . . . Let that ass learn Latin before he opposes himself to learned men.'[29] But Graman had written in Latin, or so he thought. The problem was that his Latin was provincial, not classical.

Libavius chose a similar strategy in answering another critic, Henning Scheunemann. Among other personal insults, Scheunemann had referred to Libavius as a Jackdaw on account of the wordiness of his essays. Libavius responded by accusing Scheunemann of being more ignorant than a Jackdaw and still daring to mix with the learned and eloquent. Because he has not paid attention to the elegance of letters and has never learned to write Latin and Greek without

---

[28] *Hermetica et Jatro-Chemica Morbi Sulphurei Cagastrici Curatio . . . Gestellet und in Druck Verfertigt durch Georgium Graman . . .*, Halberstadt: Jacob-Arnold Koten, 1614, *ad lectorem benevolum.*

[29] *Pro Defensione Syntagmatis Chymici Contra Reprehensiones Henningi Scheunemanni Paracelsistae . . .*, 12–13.

orthographic vice, Scheunemann is well suited to be a Paracelsian. The more he is unskilled and ignorant of literature, the more impertinently he crawls into the Paracelsian furnaces. For his inferior grammar, Scheunemann also deserves to be whipped.[30]

The public flogging of Scheunemann's poor grammar includes a lengthy chapter whose focus is apparently nothing more than a single letter of the alphabet, the letter 'h' and its inclusion in the word 'Art(h)emesia.' But even with Libavius's pedantic tendencies and acknowledging that economy of expression was not one of his strong suits, why lavish so much attention in print on such a seemingly trifling matter? The issue was really not about orthographic propriety at all, of course what mattered was the power of aspiration. Including the 'h' in 'arthemesia,' Libavius finally explains, does not so much affect the sound of the other letters as it mixes with the rough spirit in the person pronouncing them. Paracelsians, he thus concludes, not only deserve punishment for their medical licentiousness but for the destruction of the liberal arts as well.[31]

Latin and Greek were signs of intellectual privilege and Libavius was fully aware of their power when he referred to his commentary on Scheunemann as an *epicrisis*, that is, an examination of candidates for admittance to the ranks of privileged persons.[32] Someone else who was definitely not of that rank, at least on Libavius's reasoning, was another personal adversary, a physician from Lorraine named Nicolas Guibert. Guibert had practiced Paracelsian medicine for forty years before turning to Galen. At the same time he renounced alchemy and mounted an attack on the subject which occasioned a response from Libavius already in 1604. Ten years later Guibert turned up the heat once again in a second attack, which occasioned an equally boiling Libavian response. It was a response with a definite pedagogic and humanist purpose. Writing against Guibert, Libavius notes that he has tempered his writing so as to endeavor always to mix in something which can be useful to diligent youth.[33] Calling to the youth of Guibert's homeland, Lorraine, Libavius writes: 'Come good boys, teenagers, youths. I shall teach you Latin and Greek',

---

[30] *Ibid.*, 35ff.
[31] *Ibid.*, 39ff.
[32] *Ibid.*, 16.
[33] *Vita, Vigor et Veritas Alchymiae Transmutatoriae in Syntagmate Arcanorum . . . Opposita Apologiae, et Tractatibus De Interitu Alchymiae Transmutoriae Nicolai Guiberti . . . in D.O.M.A. Appendix Necessaria Syntagmatis Arcanorum Chymicorum Andreae Libavii*, 133.

which Guibert says he does not understand. 'I will teach you splendid things which that coal burner of yours could never grasp'.[34]

Clearly Libavius intended to emphasize classical learning as appropriate to early education. By the time a child reached the age of fourteen, the canonical age at which a boy might legally marry, most educators of the early seventeenth century considered moral character to have been shaped forever.[35] Guibert had missed something in his youth. Although now an old man, Guibert, Libavius writes, still reeks of the odor taken on as a youth. One who would be a judge of what is true and false must have grown accustomed from an early age to the rules of wise judgement, and not have licked out the stinking pots of crazy people (a reference to time spent in the laboratory with Paracelsian physicians). Guibert had just not been to the right sort of school, and thus had not had the benefit of real experience. 'Experience is not the product of one action, or of one time, or of one man, but of many [people] and of all or most times.'[36] As a result, he had not passed through what Walter Ong described as a linguistic rite of passage, namely training in classical grammar, rhetoric, and dialectic (which, of course, amounts to a kind of moral training).[37] This is what really separated humanist men from vulgar boys, or women, for that matter.

Guibert had squandered his youth amidst the depravities and frauds of the Paracelsians. At last, says Libavius, he has come to the study of legitimate subjects, and now, as if he were an autodidact, passes judgement in matters of scientific principles based on his own opinions. His vision, however, is distorted. He does not understand the force of true arguments. He does not possess those resources of logic which are necessary for civilized debate. He comprehends, says Libavius, neither my Latin nor my Greek. His use of terms is both foreign and barbarous.[38]

One thing that has so far gone by completely unnoticed by those

---

[34] *Ibid.*, 176.

[35] See Steven Ozment, *When Father's Ruled: Family Life in Reformation Europe*, Cambridge Mass., 1983, 144. On methods of education in the sixteenth century see Georg Mertz, *Das Schulwesen der deutschen Reformation im 16. Jahrhundert*, Heidelberg 1902. Also, Gerald Strauss, *Luther's House of Learning: Indoctrination of the Young in the German Reformation*, Baltimore and London 1978.

[36] *Vita, Vigor et Veritas . . .*, 150.

[37] See Walter J. Ong, *Rhetoric, Romance, and Technology: Studies in the Interaction of Expression and Culture*, Ithaca and London 1971.

[38] *Vita, Vigor et Veritas . . .*, 132.

who have commented on Libavius's writings is the extent to which many of those writings are richly packed with Horatian allusions. In his polemics especially, Horace, that elegant middle class poet of Augustan Rome, is always close at hand. Horatian odes, epistles, and satires were, of course, standard examples of sophisticated Latin and grandiloquent invective. They were as well part of almost every course in humanist grammar and poetry, and Libavius made sure that Horace remained accessible to for students at the *Casimirianum*. In particular, Libavius must have found in Horace's *Ars Poetica* a model of linguistic elegance and learning. He also found there a close ally in the struggle over what Horace described in terms of the triad 'authority, right, and the rules of speaking.'[39] In some rather famous passages,[40] Horace advised that the theme of a particular speech should be appropriate to ability (38ff.) and the style to subject matter (73ff.). A speaker's language ought also suit his emotion (99ff.), social rank, age, and occupation (114ff. and 156ff.). Libavius heeded the recommendations and, while ridiculing those inspired by the *idiotos logos*, constructed a style and vocabulary consistent with what he saw as the true subjects of his apologetic discourse—the defense of Galenic medicine and alchemy to be sure, but also the protection of logic and method from the attacks of self-taught enthusiasts, and the preservation of a distinctive language reflecting the authority of traditional institutions.

Guibert's subject, on the other hand, was something vulgar. Thus it was not at all strange for him to curse and write so poorly. Referring to the ancient oratorical battle between Corax and Tisias, Libavius refers to Guibert's essay as 'a bad egg from a bad crow.' Those who have praised Guibert in verse should properly sing a palinode [an ode or song recanting something written formerly] and will prefer to sing the praises of Cloacina [goddess of the sewer system] and Sterculus [god of manuring] than to adorn with music

---

[39] Niall Rudd, 'Horace,' *The Cambridge History of Classical Literature II, Latin Literature*, ed. E.J. Kenney and W.V. Clausen, Cambridge 1982, 370–404. William S. Anderson, 'The Roman Socrates: Horace and his Satires,' in Anderson, *Essays on Roman Satire*, Princeton 1982, 13–49. Cf. the role suggested by Robert Westman for Horace in the preface to Copernicus's *De Revolutionibus*; Robert S. Westman, 'Proof, poetics, and patronage: Copernicus's preface to *De Revolutionibus*,' in *Reappraisals of the Scientific Revolution*, 167–205.

[40] *Ars Poetica or Epistle to the Pisos* in *Horace: Satires, Epistles and Ars Poetica with an English Translation by H. Rushton Fairclough*, Cambridge, Mass. 1991 [first published, 1926], 442–488.

such a bad crow's worse offspring.[41] Yet, even these verses, if written by Paracelsians, would probably be found stylistically vulgar and
he notes that had he wished to give tit for tat, there would be any
number of boys at hand who could write disparaging verses with
equal talent.[42] The 'boys' referred to by Libavius were of course his
own pupils. For them, as well as for other boys being initiated into
the Latinate elite, the defense against Guibert was important for yet
another reason. It contained an important demonstration of academic masculinity.

Guibert had referred to his treatise as a manly attack on trans-
mutational alchemy.[43] There was, however, on Libavius's account,
nothing manly about it. Instead, Guibert had revealed himself to be
more like a child, or woman. In fact, the feminization, and thus
marginalization, of Guibert's arguments is one of the chief rhetorical devices in Libavius's response. Again, it is Horace who is most
present.

> Judging from your wicked, rabid, and diabolical apology, I willingly
> believe that without Peripatetic philosophy and the admonition of Philo
> you have been transformed into a dog, or rather into a living devil.
> But you have also sustained another metamorphosis. In the title of
> your *Alchymia impugnata* you declare yourself a MAN. But, when I con-
> sider your apology, I find that you have been transmuted into an ugly,
> little old woman and devilish old hag, worse than Canidia [i.e. a sor-
> ceress mentioned often in Horace] or any other, who, by violent insults,
> abuses, invectives and similar injuries, is in the habit of raving against
> those by whom she thinks herself offended, and, if possible, she even
> plots against their lives by the witchcraft of eyes and words, or by
> magical verses. Such is your transmutation... Your manhood having
> been taken away, you were changed into an altogether insane mae-
> nad [i.e. a priestess possessed by the god Dionysius].[44]

'Guibertus' becomes 'Guiberta' in Libavius's text, and Guiberta is
advised to 'stay home and shut up' [*Mane domini, et tace*].[45]

Libavius says he was expecting arguments, but found only sophis-
tic refutations, lies, and vanities. No brave man should be afraid of

---

[41] *Vita, Vigor et Veritas . . .*, 153.
[42] *Ibid.*
[43] *Alchymia Ratione et Experientia ita Demum Viriliter Impugnata et Expugnata unâ cum
suis Fallaciis et Deliramentis Quibus Homines Imbubinârat ut Numquam in Posterum se Erigere
Valeat*, Argentorati: Lazarus Zetzner, 1603.
[44] *Vita, Vigor et Veritas . . .*, 145.
[45] *Ibid.*, 159.

these sorts of things. In fact, a man who, through fear of being wronged, deserts his post, cannot earn the praise that is due a bold warrior. It is thus the warrior Libavius who seeks, in response to Guibert's feigned manly attack, Guibert's manly ruination.[46] The language is full of symbolic meaning at this point. In the title of his own work, Guibert had referred to alchemy as that which stained mankind with menstrual blood.[47] Libavius implies that it is just this impurity, mixed into Guibert's title,[48] with which he has in turn stained also reams of paper.[49]

In light of claims regarding Libavius's openness of chemical discourse, it is interesting to note that Guibert, like Graman, was precisely of the opposite view. For him, Libavius employed nothing but obscure and ambiguous language, full of double meanings. Libavius seemed everywhere to be saying something significant, although he spoke only of trifles. Six hundred words were used with other than there commonly accepted meaning. In fact, the worst accusation was that Libavius actually created words and phrases so as to manufacture a language completely distinct from common usage.[50] Can this be true? Can the figure that some have seen as the example *par excellence* in the early seventeenth century of clarity and openness in chemical language, of didactic utility, have been, from some points of view, intentionally obscure? What did it mean to Libavius to be open and clear? Libavius himself admits that because so much of what he has written has been of a polemical nature it has been sometimes necessary to exaggerate his opinions. 'In disputations,' he writes, 'when it comes to the point of opposing the arguments of our adversaries, it is unavoidable that we sometimes come rather close to one of the extreme positions . . .' He adds, 'this is how we destroy Paracelsian delusions, as we would like, meanwhile, for true chemistry to be safe.'[51] What was clear had to be didactically useful, but does that mean that it had also to be immediately intelligible to all? In constructing a language of openness, Libavius was not guided by anything like common or practical meaning. His use of

---

[46] *Ibid.*, 151.
[47] See note 43.
[48] *Vita, Vigor et Veritas* . . ., 177.
[49] *Ibid.*, 166.
[50] *Ibid.*, p. 170.
[51] *De Igne Naturae* . . ., 9.

words, just like his choice of grammar and his logic, gained legitimacy not through common clarity, but by means of classical origin
and the rhetorical requirements determined by academic convention.
Thus he argues that it is not uncommon for necessity to compel the
construction of a word, but this should not occur arbitrarily, but
should be derived from Greek, especially in any subject matter which
is devoid of Latin words. The more Guibert objects to Greek, and
opposes himself to that admirable custom, the more he demonstrates
his crudeness, inexperience, and stupidity.[52]

As the problem of language suggests, both Libavius and the
Paracelsians might claim, and be accused of, privileged knowing—
Libavius holding to the privilege of academic philosophy, Paracelsians
like Guibert, Scheunemann, and Johann Graman to the privilege of
revelation and personal inspiration based on the Paracelsian notion
of the 'light of nature.' Moreover, each form of privilege had its
own institutional foundation. For Libavius, the university must possess the power to legitimise learning. How else to protect the virtu-
ous, the elegant, the historically mediated from the irrationality of
private enthusiasm? But Paracelsians, although at times included
within university faculties, did not, as a rule, turn to the university
for institutional empowerment of their ideas. More often another
institution, the princely, royal, or imperial court, bolstered Paracelsian
claims to legitimate practice. The question was, which of these would
control medical and chemical language and learning?

Discrediting vulgar arcana involved also questioning the extent
of aristocratic and courtly powers of intellectual legitimation. The majority of Libavius's Paracelsian opponents had court connections. At
the same time, Libavius himself never advanced far within court circles. Whatever possibility there was for a position at the court of the
Holy Roman Emperor had been, he thought, sabotaged by Johannes
Hartmann who had so misrepresented his ideas to the imperial court
as to make, he believed, the *studia Libaviana* impossible there.[53] Hartmann, Croll, and Duchesne had well known aristocratic patrons, but
obscure Paracelsians too sometimes found places among less celebrated members of the aristocracy. Another of Libavius's Paracelsian
adversaries, Georg Amwald, replaced the prestige of court appointment with the claim of noble rank. In an emotional exchange with

---

[52] *Vita, Vigor et Veritas . . .*, 172 Also, *Neoparacelsica*, 694.
[53] See Moran, *Chemical Pharmacy Enters the University*, 22ff.

Amwald, much of it centered on exposing the true ingredients of Amwald's much touted universal medicine or panacea, Libavius underscored the meaninglessness of noble status in relation to virtue and learning. While accepting Amwald's claim of noble title he rhetorically demolished it as a title to truth by casting him into the ranks of dishonorable, vulgar, and, because of his secretiveness, unpatriotic men.[54]

The point is that, apart from differences about alchemical procedure and medical philosophy, the arguments between Libavius and Neoparacelsus also need to be viewed as arguments over linguistic expression and the power of institutions to define the conditions of linguistic authority. On what basis does one claim the power to name, and does that power not also include the right to the legitimate vision of the social world? Whether the vocabulary of medicine be Paracelsian or Galenic, its production depended upon the support of specific audiences from which it derived its particular worth. Libavius, in this regard, should be seen not as wasting the better part of his life in fruitless polemic, but, using terms derived from Pierre Bourdieu's model of cultural and symbolic capital, as investing an enormous portion of his cultural and intellectual estate in an endeavor of the greatest and most immediate importance to him—the defence of the academy's social legitimacy and its privilege of defining what was appropriate to learning and what was not. In that pursuit Libavius underscored the difference between those entitled to linguistic power as agents of legitimate institutions and those who, while claiming titles and court positions, professed a competency and linguistic authority resting upon irrelevant social footings. Students needed to learn the distinction, and in that effort Libavius forged from his polemics a didactic tool, transmuting apology into pedagogy and turning discussions of alchemy and medicine into moral, logical, and rhetorical lessons for those who would later need to speak for and to defend their inherited academic wealth.

* I wish to express my thanks to J. Mark Sugars and Michael McArthur for their translation assistance in the preparation of this study.

[54] *Gegenbericht von der Panacea Amwaldina ... autore Andrea Libavio ...* (Frankfurt: Johann Kollitz in verlegung Petri Kopffij, 1595), *An den Leser.*

CHAPTER SEVEN

'THEOPHRASTIA SANCTA' – PARACELSIANISM AS A RELIGION, IN CONFLICT WITH THE ESTABLISHED CHURCHES

Carlos Gilly

In 1569 an enthusiastic Paracelsian called Lambert Wacker wrote from Berlin that Theophrastus Paracelsus von Hohenheim had not only been a *'monarcha et princeps medicorum'*, a monarch and prince of physicians, but moreover, also a king amongst theologians and a chief of lawyers, or, as the author put it: 'I could also say: *Theologorum rex et Iurisconsultorum caput'*—as he had 'in everything shot nearer the mark than anyone before him'.[1]

Let us leave aside lawyers, as well as logicians and rhetoricians, for whom Paracelsus did not care much anyway.[2] But a king of theologians? Even Paracelsus himself, who was anything but modest, had never gone that far. It is true that in his book *Paragranum* of 1529–1530 he had challenged the entire medical world by proclaiming his proud 'according to me and not according to you' and his provocative 'Mine will be the monarchy', thus appointing himself *'monarcha medicorum'*. And when in the same book he took offence at the epithet 'the Luther of physicians', this was only because he felt that the title awarded him by his opponents was too slight:

> What is this mockery with which you insult me, that I am a *'Lutherus medicorum'*, meaning I am a heresiarch? I am Theophrastus and more than those with whom you compare me. I am the same, and moreover I

* An enlarged German version of this chapter has been published in *Analecta Paracelsica. Studien zum Nachleben Theophrast von Hohenheims im deutschen Kulturgebiet der frühen Neuzeit*, Heidelberger Studien zur Naturkunde der frühen Neuzeit, eds. W.-D. Müller-Jancke and J. Telle, Stuttgart, 1994, 425–88.

[1] Karl Sudhoff, *Versuch einer Kritik der Echtheit der Paracelsischen Schriften, II. Teil: Paracelsus-Handschriften*, Berlin 1899, 300; Paracelsus, *Sämtliche Werke*. 2. Abteilung, *Theologische und religionsphilosophische Schriften*, ed. Kurt Goldammer. Supplement: *Religiöse und sozialphilosophische Schriften in Kurzfassungen*, Wiesbaden 1973, 170–171.

[2] Paracelsus, *Sämtliche Werke*. 1. Abteilung, ed. Karl Sudhoff, Munich/Berlin 1922–1929, III, 95; Paracelsus, *Theologische und religions-philosophische Schriften*, Pt. 1, ed. Wilhelm Matthießen, Munich 1923, 103–104.

am the monarch of physicians ... I will let Luther defend his cause
and I will defend my cause, and I will defeat those of my colleagues
who turn against me'. And further on: 'Do you mean, I am only
Luther? I will give him and you some work to do!'[3]

The latter claim Paracelsus did indeed accomplish, but only decades
after his death. Generations of polemical theologians, Lutheran or
other, had to rack their brains over the writings of the Swiss physician, before they could even begin to attack the religious dissidents
and radical church critics of the late sixteenth and the entire seventeenth century.

While Paracelsus knew very well, that he had called into life a
new school of medicine with his works on medicine and natural philosophy—or, as he puts it, a 'Theophrastian sect, which will triumph,
so you will have to acknowledge my philosophy',[4] he had in his theological writings expressly refused to style himself the head of a new
religious movement.

And yet: in theology, too, Paracelsus had throughout remained
loyal to his famous motto: *'Alterius non sit, qui suus esse potest'*. There
is no need to doubt the statement circulated by his former medical
assistant Oporinus, 'When he began to write, he wanted to send
them [Luther and Zwingli], and the Pope all the more, back to
school'.[5] Already in his early work *De septem punctis idolatriae christianae*
of 1525 Paracelsus had turned away from the 'Mauerkirche' [the
stone church] of Rome, which he felt had absolutely nothing to do
with the 'catholic' church of the spirit, conscience and prophecy
which he so desired.[6] And in his book *De secretis secretorum theologiae*
six years later, Paracelsus exposed not only the Pope, but this time
also the reformers to bitter criticism:

> 'Anyone will say, I proclaim the gospel, I proclaim the basic truth, I
> proclaim the Word of God etc. do not believe this; [...] One man
> seeks the gospel amongst the Papists in Rome, another amongst the
> Zwinglians, a third one amongst the Lutherans, a fourth one amongst
> the Anabaptists etc'. 'Do not believe any of these, because it can never

---

[3] Paracelsus, *Sämtliche Werke*. 1. Abteilung, ed. Sudhoff, VIII, 62–63, 43.

[4] *Ibid.*, 56.

[5] 'Wann er [Paracelsus] anfieng zu schreiben, wollte [er] sy [Luther und Zwingli]
und auch den Bapst erst recht in die Schül füren', cf. Theodor Zwinger, *Theatrum
humanae vitae*, ed. Basel 1571, 1480; ed. Basel 1586, 2583; Carlos Gilly, 'Zwischen
Erfahrung und Spekulation. Theodor Zwinger und die religiöse und kulturelle Krise
seiner Zeit', Part I, *Basler Zeitschrift für Geschichte und Altertumskunde*, 77, 1977, 57–137;
Part II, *ibid.*, 79, 1979, 125–223 (I. 100).

[6] Paracelsus, *Sämtliche Werke*. 2. Abteilung, ed. Goldammer, III, XXVI–XXVII.

be found there. [. . .] It now follows, that they call each other impostors, and that is true; because that is what they are. That they call
each other liars, now that is true; because they lie. That they call each
other false Christians, now that is true; because on both sides they
are false Christians. That they call each other false prophets, is all
true: because God has not sent them to be prophets, but to be
destroyers of their own kingdom [. . .] The Pope and his party cry out
for blood: kill, hang, burn, drown etc. The others have killed many
thousands of men in a few years' time, and also scream: kill, drown
etc. Those are their fruits, which they offer, by which we shall recognize them [. . .] Against it all with the sword, with fire! This is what
the Pope does, as is apparent, and Luther, too, as is apparent, that
nobody is allowed to speak against them with impunity, but risks being
hanged!' [. . .] 'Christ did not send you Luther, Zwingli, Bucer, Lambert
etc.; because these, too, are [. . .] like monks and priests, who are
born liars'.[7]

What Paracelsus was aiming at with his theological writings was not
to establish a new sect, but on the contrary to try and deny all religious parties combating each other the very reason to exist, since
he strove for a church of the spirit, subject only to God and nature.[8]
Paracelsus himself knew best that such an attempt was hopeless, as
he prophetically wrote in his book *De imaginibus* on the subject of
religious schisms:

> Then soon after Luther appeared with his doctrine and one sect after
> the other under the guise of Lutheran doctrine, and still there is no

---

[7] *Ibid.*, 227, 175–176, 206–209. For Paracelsus's criticism of the Roman-Catholic
and the Reformed churches cf. Kurt Goldammer, *Paracelsus. Natur und Offenbarung*,
Hannover-Kirchrode 1953, 89–92; K. Goldammer, *Paracelsus in neuen Horizonten.
Gesammelte Aufsätze*, Salzburger Beiträge zur Paracelsusforschung, 24, Vienna 1986,
164–171 and *passim*; Hartmuth Rudolph, 'Einige Gesichtspunkte zum Thema 'Paracelsus und Luther', *Archiv für Reformationsgeschichte*, 78, 1981, 34–53; H. Rudolph,
Individuum und Obrigkeit bei Paracelsus, *Nova Acta Paracelsica*, NF 3, 1988, 69–76.

[8] *Theophrasti Paracelsi vonn Hohenhaimb Schreiben ahn einen glertten, von grundt des Alten
vnd Neüen Testaments vnnd vnserer Seeligkait* (the claim that this work is spurious is unsub-
stantiated) contains the words: 'Lieber N: daß du allein gegen alle Doctorn der
Romischen, oder (so es den Göttern gefelt) der Christlichen kirchen, die von der
Apostell zeit ahn biss auff dise heütige stundt einen grossen Rhuem gehabt, fülest
und glaubest vnd wolst lieber Allein gegen alle halten, dann mit allen oder mitt
dem Mehrern Thaill irren, Meines bedunckhens thuestu Recht daran, vnd Ich
zweifel nit, es soll dir solche Meinung ie lenger, ie mehr gefallen, vnd ich bitt auch
Gott, Er woll dich darin stercken. Dann [. . .] Ich gwißlich glaub, das die eüsser-
lich Kirch Christi mit sambt Ieren gaaben vnd Sacramenten durch einreissung vnd
verwüestung des Antichrists, ahn stund nach der Apostell Zeitt inn Himmell aufge-
fahren sej, vnd Ihm Geist vnnd Warheit verborgen lig, also das von tausend vier-
hundert Jahren kein eüsserliche versammelte kirchen, noch kein Sacrament gewest
seindt, Ich gantz sicher bin', cf. Sudhoff, *Paracelsus-Handschriften, loc. cit.*, 556–558.

end to this. Because there will be more sects, and each one wants to have the last word and be better and holier than the other with respect to its doctrine. And there will be no cohesion and peace in religion and in the churches, until the golden and last age.[9]

His solution, therefore, was not to get involved with the religious factions, but to maintain silence with regard to the outside world until the completion of his medical, philosophical and theological work, and to show only few people, what 'has been in my pen'. He wrote the following about the ruling churches in a late introduction to his entire theological work: 'I have kept my silence, so that thunder and storm would not strike my soil. I have managed to survive in this way until now and have not bothered about them'.[10]

Because of these prudent tactics in an age of growing intolerance, Paracelsus was spared denunciation and persecution by the ruling religious parties during his lifetime, unlike for instance Sebastian Franck, Schwenckfeld or Servetus. But because of this withdrawal he surrendered at the same time the immediate effect he could have had on his contemporaries. His explosive theological and natural philosophical manuscripts, which had been deposited in a safe place,[11] proved to be dangerously charged sleepers, which in the generations to come threatened to blow up the religious monopoly of the confessional churches and the epistemic rules of conservative scientists.

When Paracelsus died in Salzburg in 1541, silence enveloped him at first. Only very few people had any inkling of his vast written work. Conrad Gessner for instance, the city physician of Zürich and an authority on book matters, could in his *Bibliographia Universalis* of 1545 only make mention of the Basle broadsheet, the printed *Wundartznei*, a manuscript of the Basle lectures, together with 'I do not know what sort of theological works for the Abbot of St. Gallen, which I do not believe were published'.[12]

---

[9] Paracelsus, *Sämtliche Werke*. 1. Abteilung, ed. Sudhoff, XIII, 373.

[10] 'Mein mund hab ich zugehalten, darmit mir das wetter und der donder nit in acker schlüge, darmit hab ichs hindurch bracht bis auf die zeit und hab mich nit bekümmert umb sie', cf. Prologus totius operis christianae vitae (Preface to *De secretis secretorum theologiae christianae*), Paracelsus, *Sämtliche Werke*. 2. Abteilung, ed. Goldammer, III, 171.

[11] On the preservation of Paracelsian manuscripts in Neuburg an der Donau cf. Joachim Telle, 'Kurfürst Ottheinrich, Hans Kilian und Paracelsus. Zum pfälzischen Paracelsismus im 16. Jahrhundert', *Von Paracelsus zu Goethe und Wilhelm von Humboldt*, Salzburger Beiträge zur Paracelsusforschung, 22, Vienna 1981, 130–146.

[12] Konrad Gessner, *Bibliotheca Vniversalis, siue Catalogus omnium scriptorum locupletissimus, in tribus linguis, Latina, Graeca et Hebraica: extantium et non extantium, veterum ac recentiorum in hunc usque diem, doctorum et indoctorum, publicatorum et in Bibliothecis laten-*

It comes as no surprise therefore, that it was the same Conrad Gessner who sixteen years later publicly issued the first theological condemnation of his countryman, when he wrote in a letter in 1561: 'I am entirely convinced that Paracelsus was a follower of Arius'. With respect to the Paracelsian manuscript heritage, the famous bibliographer furthermore reported in the same letter that he neither possessed a catalogue of Paracelsian works, nor had he ever made the effort to obtain one, because Paracelsus 'must have been an irreligious man and a magus, who commerced with the devil, and so unworthy to be listed together with good and civilized writers, whether Christian or heathen'.[13]

Gessner's opinion of Paracelsus was shared by Johannes Crato von Crafftheim, to whom the letter had been addressed. He initiated the first public attack on Paracelsus and his followers in a long preface to a work by Johannes Baptista Montanus, printed in Basel in 1562. The fact that Paracelsus was not explicitly mentioned here, was not due to Crato, but to the highly dedicated Basle printer Peter Perna, who deliberately struck the name of Paracelsus from the preface. Yet it was obvious to any reader against whom Crato's insults, such as *'Magister Enthusiastarum'*, 'ignorant adventurer', or 'damned and criminal apostate' were directed.[14]

The by now unstoppable flood of editions of works by Paracelsus on medicine and natural philosophy issuing from the Basle, Cologne and Strasburg presses began to be increasingly opposed by the

---

tium, Zürich 1545, 614; cf. Robert Henri Blaser, *Paracelsus in Basel, Sieben Studien über Werk, Wirkung und Nachwirkung des Paracelsus in Basel* published by the Swiss Paracelsus Society, Muttenz/Basel 1979, 76; Edwin Rosner, 'Studien zum Leben und Wirken des Paracelsus in St. Gallen', *Nova Acta Paracelsica*, NF 3, 1988, 32–54, esp. 46.

[13] Conrad Gessner, *Epistolarum medicinalium libri tres*, Zürich 1577, ff. 1r–2v. Thus Milt's claims, according to which Gessner in his latter years was to have interested himself for no other person so much as for Paracelsus, prove to be very exaggerated, cf. Bernhart Milt, 'Conrad Gesner und Paracelsus', *Schweizerische Medizinische Wochenschrift*, 59, 1929, 486–488, 506–509.

[14] Joannes Baptista Montanus, *In nonum librum Rhasis ad R[egem] Almansorem lectiones restitutae a Ioanne Cratone*, Basel 1562, fols. a2v–b4r: 'Mirifica igitur quorundam fanaticorum, ex magistri sui [Paracelsi] falsa persuasione, est fatuitas, qui totam artem atque tam veteres quam nostri seculi summos artifices, propter errata quaedam et humanos in arte lapsus vituperant, ac more Enthusiastarum in Theologia omnia scripta vetustatis tanquam falsa atque erronea reiiciunt, sibique Deum firmamentum et nescio quae alia libros Medicinae esse fingunt, quos de suo lumine naturae interpretentur, et Alchymia, nova Astronomia rerumque universitatis Anatomia, cuius se investigatores atque abstrusissimarum rerum inquisitores esse somniant, confirment'; Gessner, *Epistolarum medicinalium, loc. cit.*, f. 15r. 'Legi tua quae in *Theophrasteious* scripseras in praefatione illa, quam Perna mutilavit'. On Crato's opposition to Paracelsism, cf. Gilly, *Zwischen Erfahrung und Spekulation*, Part I, 98s, 119s, 133s.

celebrities of orthodox medicine, although they used not so much the weapons of their own discipline, but rather arguments drawn from theology. They were the first to recognize the explosive theological force of these works and were furthermore convinced (as Rotondò has formulated it) that the most effective defence of a pattern of thought which the academic world then considered to be scientifically orthodox should have to begin with the defence of its theological framework.[15] Almost without exception they were men from the medical world, such as Gasser, Stenglin, Weyer, Solenander, Marstaller or Reussner, who in the first years of the so-called 'Paracelsian Revival' loudly proclaimed the charge of heresy with respect to Paracelsus and his followers.[16] This campaign reached a climax in 1571–1572 with the outpouring of malice and defamation in the first part of *Disputationes de medicina nova Paracelsi* of Thomas Erastus. Erastus was not beyond demanding capital punishment for the adherents of the magus Paracelsus, and he also tried to influence one of the most authoritative theologians of the Reformed party, the Zürich leader Heinrich Bullinger, in this sense: 'I swear to you by everything that is holy to me: neither Arius, Photin, nor Mohammed, nor any Turk or heretic were ever so heretical as this unholy magus'.[17]

---

[15] Antonio Rotondò, *Pietro Perna e la vita culturale e religiosa di Basilea fra il 1570 e il 1580*, Rotondò: *Studi e ricerche di storia ereticale italiana del Cinquecento*, Turin 1574, 273–392, quot. 389.

[16] Anonymous, *Thyrsus ὄναγου* [onagou] *In Tergum Georgii Fedronis*, s.l. 1565; Lucas Stenglin, *Apologia adversus Stibii spongiam a Michaële Toxite aeditam*, Augsburg 1569; Gervasius Marstaller, *Oratio de Theophrasto Paracelso*, 1570 (Erlangen, Universitätsbibliothek Erlangen-Nuremberg, Ms. 991, ff. 8v–26v); Bartholomäus Reussner, *Ein kurtze Erklerung und Christliche widerlegung, Der unerhörten Gotteslesterungen und Lügen, welche Paracelsus in den dreyen Büchern Philosophie ad Athenienses hat außgeschüttet*, Görlitz 1570; Bernardus Dessenius, *Medicinae veteris et rationalis adversus oberronis cuiusdam mendacissimi atque impudentissimi Georgii Fedronis, ac universae Sectae Paracelsicae imposturas, defensio*, Cologne 1573; Johannes Weyer, *De praestigiis Daemonum et incantationibus ac ueneficiis libri sex*, Basel 1566, 1568, 1577, 1583. In the first editions of Weyer's *De praestigiis*, Basel 1563 and 1564, the name Paracelsus does not occur, the first mention being the edition of 1566 (book 2, ch. 18 and bk. 5, 13); the criticism of Paracelsus and the Paracelsists is repeated in the edition of 1568 (196ss, 493), was partly mitigated in 1577 (219–220, 442), but reinforced in 1583 with new quotations. The new English translation (*Witches, Devils, and Doctors in the Renaissance. Johann Weyer, De praestigiis daemonum*, ed. George Mora, Benjamin Kohl, tr. John Shea (Medieval and Renaissance Texts and Studies, 75), Binghamton, New York 1991) is only based on the 1583 text, without indicating the important changes and additions made to the text of the earlier editions.

[17] Thomas Erastus, *Disputationum De Medicina Nova Philippi Paracelsi Pars Prima— Quarta*, Basel [1571]–1573; Rotondò, *Pietro Perna e la vita culturale e religiosa di Basilea*, loc. cit., 389; Gilly, *Zwischen Erfahrung und Spekulation*, Part 2, 182.

Neither Erastus nor any of those who shared his views had for that matter read a single word of the theological works of Paracelsus. Apparently they did not really consider this necessary, because, after all, they had all read Oporinus's notorious letter of 1565 with the anecdote relating to Paracelsus's religious way of life.[18] But even Oporinus's nephew, the cautious Theodor Zwinger, who a few years later came to acknowledge the greatness of Paracelsus as a result of his thorough study of Hippocrates, and publicized his findings to the horror of his academic colleagues, appears at first to have hardly occupied himself with the theological writings of Paracelsus. In 1564 he wrote in a letter often copied at the time:

> I do not wish to comment on the morals of Paracelsus, as I find this unnecessary; because whether good or bad, they have no impact on his scholarship. On the other hand, I can only testify concerning Paracelsus' piety and godliness, that he has written many works on religion, which are even today treasured by his followers as priceless jewels. But it is common knowledge, that Paracelsus was declared atheist.[19]

The first adherents and editors of Paracelsus found it difficult to oppose this wide-spread opinion, and found themselves on the horns of an uncomfortable dilemma. Either they left the theological accusations unanswered and confined the debate to the medical and nature philosophical field—a near-impossible task in an author like Paracelsus with his comprehensive cosmosophical ideas. Or else they had to decide, in order to elucidate matters, to publish the theological works of Paracelsus. In the light of the easily inflammable *'rabies theologica'* of the theologians of all confessions at that time this

---

[18] Udo Benzenhöfer, 'Zum Brief des Johannes Oporinus über Paracelsus. Die bislang älteste bekannte Briefüberlieferung in einer Oratio von Gervasius Marstaller', *Sudhoffs Archiv*, 75, 1989, 55–63 (also for the literature quoted so far). For the time it took to write the letter, cf. Gilly, *Zwischen Erfahrung und Spekulation*, Part 1, 93–94. To what has already been said here be added, that Oporinus's letter to Johann Weyer and to Reiner Solenander could not have been written on the date suggested by Petrus Foreest (26-11-1555). The date proposed by Johann Staricius ('Epistola anno 1565 ex Basilea de judicio admirandi medici Paracelsi') has now been confirmed as the result of the recent discovery of a MS at Wolfenbüttel (Cod. Guelf. 13.7 Aug. 4° 231r–232v: 'Ex Oporini Epistola 26 Nov. anno [15]65 Basilea ad D. Vierium scripta').

[19] Theodor Zwinger, Letter to Gervasius Marstaller of 7 January 1564 on the teachings of Paracelsus and the activities of the Paracelsists in Basel (contemporary manuscript copies in Paris, Bibliothèque Nationale, Fonds Dupuy 797, ff. 55–70, and Erlangen, Universitätsbibliothek Erlangen-Nürnberg, Ms. 991, fols. 15r–21v.)

might have impeded any further involvement with Paracelsus's medical works for decades.[20]

A number of Paracelsians, such as Bodenstein or Toxites, decided to dodge the specific theological issues in the prefaces to their editions of Paracelsus with the use of a few empty general phrases. Others, such as Quercetanus or Bovio, chose explicitly to distance themselves from the theological ideas of Paracelsus.[21] Gerard Dorn for his part attempted amongst others, to mitigate the force of the gnostic cosmogony presented in *Philosophia ad Athenienses* and to explain it in a more orthodox Platonic sense.[22]

Only a few of the better known early Paracelsians of the sixteenth century did not shun direct confrontation in the theological field. The Frenchman Bernard Penot, for instance, in a public letter addressed to the rabid antiparacelsist Andreas Libavius, pointed out not only that the charges of atheism levelled against Paracelsus lacked any ground, but in addition characterized the theological works of Paracelsus as directly inspired by God.[23] In a work written in 1584

---

[20] As a good example of this may serve the response of the Strassburg cathedral preacher Elias Schade, who was possibly the first orthodox theologian, in 1588, to have been requested to give a private 'Judicium' on 'certain theological writings' of Paracelsus. Schade's annihilating judgment concluded with the words: 'Derhalben ist mein Raht zuvorderst/ daß jhr [die Empfänger des *Judicium*] aller dings solcher Schrifften müßig gehet/ darinn weder leset/ noch darauß abschreibet: Darnach daß jhr die Bücher/ sie kosten gleich wenig oder viel/ auffs fürderlichst verbrennt/ oder in ein Profey werfft/ als deß Teuffels Dreck'. Cf. Ralf Georg Bogner, 'Das "Judicium" des Elias Schade (1589). Ein frühes Zeugnis der "Verketzerung" Theophrast von Hohenheims', in *Parerga Paracelsica*, ed. J. Telle, 122–139.

[21] Joseph Du Chesne (Quercetanus), *Ad Iacobi Auberti de ortu et causa metallorum Explicationem [. . .] Responsio*, Lyon 1575, fols. b1v–b2r: 'Ad Paracelsum vero quod attinet, equidem mihi nequaquam proposui ipsius Theologiae patrocinium suscipere, neque ipsi in omnibus astipulari unquam cogitavi, tanquam in eius verba iurassem'; on Du Chesne and the French Paracelsists cf. Hugh Trevor-Roper, *Renaissance Essays*, London 1985 (9. The Paracelsian Movement); on Tommasso Zefiriele Bovio cf. *Dizionario Biografico degli Italiani*, 13, 565–566.

[22] Gerhard Dorn, *De naturae luce physica ex Genesi desumpta iuxta sententiam Theophrasti Paracelsi Tractatus. Cui annexa est modesta quaedam admonitio ad Thomam Erastum*, Frankfurt 1583, 11, 32f., 370f.; *Theatrum Chemicum* I, *loc. cit.*, 327, 332ff. cf. Carlos Gilly, 'Das Bekenntnis zur Gnosis von Paracelsus bis auf die Schüler Jacob Böhmes', *De hermetische Gnosis in de loop der eeuwen*, ed. Gilles Quispel, Baarn 1992, 395–442, esp. 408–409.

[23] Bernardus Penotus a Portu S. Mariae Aquitanus, *Apologiae in duas partes divisa ad Iosephi Michelii Middelburgensis Medici scriptum [. . .] Adjuncta est [. . .] Epistola Bernardi Penoti ad D. Andream Libavium*, Frankfurt 1600, ff. +1r – + + 6v: 'Praeterea (D. Libavi) non tu solus, sed tui similes quoque nobis Paracelsi impietatem, atheitatem nobis obiicitis, quod vel quilibet facile proferre et effutire, probare autem sufficienter minime poterit. Longe aliud enim scripta Paracelsi Theologica, praesertim libri ipsius de Philosophia aeterna conscripti tractant. Nam si vel primam huius Philosophiae

the Englishman Thomas Moffet reproached Erastus for merely trying to discredit his medical competitors by means of his coarse theological arguments and his outrageous call for executions. For let us
assume, the commonsensical Englishman wrote, that Paracelsus's
views on the creation of the world and its divine rule really differed
from those expressed in the Mosaic books—what did that have anyway to do with medicine or in which respect did he then differ from
the arch-heathen Galen, whom Erastus and his colleagues almost
idolized?[24] Alexander von Suchten from Danzig simply mocked the
'Rag-books of Master Doctor Förtzle ["Fartling"!] of Heidelberg',
who, although he 'had read a great deal in Aristotle, Zwingli and
Arius', had as 'a good dialectician and rhetorician' not understood
the slightest thing about the books of Paracelsus and their 'stylo magico'.
This kind of magic was neither witchcraft nor the work of the devil,
as Erastus loudly proclaimed, 'but the very greatest wisdom of the
work of God and an acknowledgement of hidden nature'.[25] Or, as
Suchten expressed it even more radically in his De tribus Facultatibus:
'The wisdom of the old magical books of theology, of which only
the Old and New Testament had survived'.[26]

---

partem [. . .] legisses, non tantum omni ipsum impietatis suspicione liberares, sed
et peculiari spiritus sancti illuminatione instructum ipsum haec scripsisse affirmares
[. . .] O ter quaterque beatum felix regnum, cuius Paracelsus Dux eius. Porro regnum aureum merito dici poterit. Ibi etenim cunctorum hominum malorum finis et
terminus erit (huius aetatis respectu) Rabularum causidicorumve loquacitas, omnisque
denique iniustitia cessabit. Theologastrorum, sectarum haereses quoque termina-
buntur. Aristotelis Philosophia opinionibus suffulta pessum ibit'. That Penot in his
highly advanced years was to have distanced himself from his earlier enthusiasm
for Paracelsus, as Libavius and other have claimed repeatedly, is not correct. In
the fourth edition of his *Tractatus varii, de vera preparatione, et usu medicamentorum chymicorum*, Basel 1616, 7, the 97-year-old Penot addressed the traditional Galenists: 'O
laureati magistri, ab erroribus pedem retrahite et veritatem mendaciis sopprimere
desinite: Paracelsi Theodidacti scripta acri iudicio perlegite; ad rectam viam redite,
ne forte rerum opifex [. . .] irascatur'. On the antiparacelsist attitude of the arch-
conservative Libavius cf. Gilly, *Zwischen Erfahrung und Spekulation*. Part 1, 67–70;
Part 2, 175–176, 221.

[24] Thomas Moffet, *De iure et praestantia chymicorum medicamentorum Dialogus Apologeticus*,
Frankfurt 1584, 11 (also in *Theatrum Chemicum*, ed. 1659, I, 69). For Moffet see Allen
G. Debus, *The English Paracelsians*, London 1965, 71–76; Blaser, *Paracelsus in Basel*,
loc. cit., 200–209; Gilly, *Zwischen Erfahrung und Spekulation*, Part 1, 109–111.

[25] *Dialogus introducens duas personas interlocutrices, sc. Alexandrum et Bernhardum* [written
around 1575], Alexander von Suchten, *Chymische Schrifften*, Frankfurt 1680, 305–356,
esp. 337–339; cf. Wodzimierz Hubicki, 'Alexander von Suchten', *Sudhoffs Archiv für
Geschichte der Medizin und der Naturwissenschaften*, 44, 1960, 54–63.

[26] *De tribus Facultatibus*, A. von Suchten, *Chymische Schrifften*, *loc. cit.*, 357–382, esp.
370–374. From a theological viewpoint Suchten's work *De tribus Facultatibus* or *Kurtzer
Bericht von der Wahrheit und Sophisterei dreyer der furnembsten Faculteten, nemlich Theologiae,
Astronomiae et Medicinae* belongs to the most daring works of the entire Paracelsist

The Bible as a magical book! It is easy to imagine what sort of momentous consequences the publication of such a work at this early stage would have had for the beginning 'Paracelsian Revival'. This would also apply to the Paracelsian *Theologica*, which were passed on from hand to hand and copied with a frequency which makes up for the loss of the Paracelsian autographs.

As a result of this enforced clandestinity, theological Paracelsianism of necessity established contacts with other marginal religious movements such as the Osiandrists, Schwenckfeldians, Castellionists and other adherents of Tauler or the *Theologia Deutsch*. That this confrontation was an enrichment for Paracelsianism needs hardly be questioned. But it also caused a further radicalisation, as the common factors in these movements, the spiritual attitude regarding the established churches, the practice-oriented ethics and the prophetic-eschatological world view were now mutually reinforced.

An example of this is the famous *Cyclopaedia Paracelsica Christiana* of 1585, which as far as radical language is concerned outbids just about everything which Paracelsianism had until then produced. Mention may here be made first of all of the fact that the manuscript of the *Cyclopaedia* came from the library of a Schwenckfeldian, Marquard von Hattstein, who incidentally as Catholic Bishop of Speier was the formal representative of the Roman Catholic Church in his diocese. Secondly, the editor, too, was a well-known Schwenckfeldian, namely Samuel Eisenmenger alias Syderocrates, who was expelled from the orthodox-Lutheran university of Tübingen on account of his religious views. Finally, it must be noted that here, too, Eisenmenger did not fail to quote prominently from Sebastian Castellio's book against Calvin, *De calumnia*.[27]

---

movement. Here the reformers were for instance reproached for having thrown out the child with the bathwater when abolishing the rituals of the old church: 'Es haben ettliche Klüglinge wol gesehen/ das Meß hören/ Singen/ Orgeln/ Wachs/ Oel/ und Saltz uns nit seelig machen/ darum haben sie es verworffen' [. . .] Also haben sie solcher Magischen und Apostolischen Satzung viel verworffen/ [. . .] gedachten lang nicht/ daß es Magische Bücher waren/ die uns so viel/ ja auch besser lehreten/ dann die geschriebene Bücher/ zuverstehen das Geheimniß Gottes' [. . .] Dieweil ihre Bücher möchten verlohren werden [. . .] haben sie [die Magi] einer jeden [Facultät] solch Zeichen gegeben/ die nicht also vergehen können. Also daß die Bücher der Theologiae, von welchen uns die beyden Testament überblieben/ gaben sie auch der Theologiae ihr Zeichen/ auff das/ so wir die Bücher verlohren/ ander Bücher hätten die nicht also könten verlohren werden: Das sind die Zeichen/ und alles was sie in die Kirchen gegeben haben'; cf. Gilly, *Zwischen Erfahrung und Spekulation*, Part 1, 76–82.

[27] Sudhoff, *Bibliographia Paracelsica*, 352–355; Sudhoff, 'Gedanken eines unbekann-

Eisenmenger's favourite student, the Schwabian physician and astrologer Helisäus Röslin, was a Schwenckfeldian, Paracelsian and also a Chiliast of note, who is known in the history of science mainly for his prolonged controversy with Kepler. In his book *De opere Dei creationis seu de Mundo hypotheses* of 1597 Röslin explained a cosmology 'in harmony' with the biblical story of creation and the Paracelsian doctrine of the elements which was to play a significant role in the alchemy debate which ensued between Quercetanus and Jean Riolan in Paris in 1604.[28] His main work, however, was the *Speculum mundi* and the *Speculum Ecclesiae Harmonicum*, which appeared in print in 1604 in an incomplete and unauthorized edition. In this book Röslin attempted to explain the entire history of the world and the church on the basis of a prophetic system of coordinates, which was modelled on the prophecies of Daniel, the Apocalypse and mostly the fourth book of Esdras (*'vere propheticus liber'*).[29]

---

ten Anhängers des Theophrastus Paracelsus von Hohenheim aus der Mitte des 16. Jahrhunderts über deutschen Jugendunterricht', *Mitteilungen der Gesellschaft für deutsche Erziehungs- und Schulgeschichte*, 5, 1985, 83–90; Heinz-Peter Mielke, 'Schwenckfeldianer im Hofstaat Bischof Marquards von Speyer (1560–1581)', *Archiv für Mittelrheinische Kirchengeschichte*, 28, 1976, 77–83; Telle, 'Johann Huser in seinen Briefen', *Parerga Paracelsica*, 221–223, esp. note 109. On the basis of a few typographical characteristics I expressed in *Johannes Valentin Andreae (1586–1986). Katalog einer Ausstellung in der Bibliotheca Philosophica Hermetica*, Amsterdam 1986, 23–25, the view that the *Cyclopädia* was to have been published in Strassburg or Basel. The place of printing was in fact Strassburg, as Eisenmenger's pupil Helisäus Röslin explicitly confirmed in his *Prodromus Dissertationum Chronologicarum*, Frankfurt 1612, c2r: 'Hievon aber weitleufftig gehandelt ist in einem Buch Anno 1585 zu Straßburg bei Jobin getruckt/ außgangen/ Cyclopaedia Paracelsica Christiana intituliert'. Unfortunately Röslin did not also reveal the identity of the author, as a few pages later he again refers to the 'Cyclopaedia Paracelsica incerti authoris vor 20 Jahren zu Straßburg außgangen'.

[28] Helisaeus Röslin, *De opere Dei creationis seu de mundo Hypotheses orthodoxae quantumvis paradoxae: continentes summa summarum artium principia, Physices, Chymiae, Medicinae, Astronomiae, Astrologiae, Metaphysices: nec non praecipua fundamenta Philosophiae et veteris et novae*, Frankfurt 1597. On Röslin's readership of the texts of Paracelsus cf. also the same, *Historischer/ Politischer vnd Astronomischer Discurs Von heutiger zeit Beschaffenheit/ Wesen vnd Standt der Christenheit/ vnd wie es ins Künfftig in derselben ergehen werde*, Strassburg 1609, a3r–v; Röslin, *Prodromus Dissertationum Chronologicarum*, loc. cit., 3, 11. On Röslin as owner of autograph manuscripts of Paracelsus cf. J. Telle, 'Johann Huser in seinen Briefen', *Parerga Paracelsica*, 223f.

[29] [Röslin, Helisäus], *Speculum et Harmonia Mundi: Das ist/ Welt Spiegell Erster theil. Mit vergleichung der Monarchien vnnd Welt Regimenten durch die Vmbstende der Orter Zeitten vnd Personen auß Gottes Rathschlag mit denselbigen nach seinem Werck der Creation vnnd Schöpfung fürgenommen von anfang der Welt biß zu End gefürt. Darinnen vns zum rechten Verstand der Prophecey Danielis vnnd Offenbarung Johannis gute anleitung geben wird. Zuerkündigung dieser geferlichen letzten zeiten menniglich dienstlich/ sonderlich aber den Potentaten vnnd Regenten der Christenheit zu nutz Warnung vnd auffmuderung gestelt vnd geschrieben*. Getruckt zu Lich/ in der Graffschafft Solms/ durch Wolgangung (sic) Kezelium. Jm Jhar/ 1604; further

As an adherent of a general church of the spirit and in the firm
hope of an imminent and final reformation under the sign of the
'*Trigonus Igneus*', which had been ruling in the heavens since 1583,
Röslin had firmly rejected the four existing religious parties—whether
'Papist, Lutheran, Calvinist or Anabaptist'. At the same time, however,
in the majority of his works he put forward unlimited confessional
freedom (*'Libertas Religionis, Freyheit der Religion oder Freyheit des Glaubens'*)
as an unconditional claim for the restoration of religious peace, the
political balance and economic prosperity in the German-speaking
lands of the Holy Roman Empire. This call for religious tolerance,
strongly reminiscent in its wording of Sebastian Castellio and his
Conseil à la France désolée, was in Röslin based rather than on Paracelsus's
principle of tolerance, which in turn was rooted in cosmosophy,
astromancy, eschatology and apocalypticism. Thus Röslin did not
fail to include in his call for tolerance the postulate of free academic research: '*Das aber diese vnsere jetzige Zeit, die Zeit seye der Freyheit
der Religion*' [That these our present times are the times of religious
freedom], he wrote in *Prodromus Dissertationum Chronologicarum* of 1612,
dedicated to the newly-elected Emperor Matthias I, was proved not
only by the comets and the new stars of latter years or the biblical
prophecies from the fourth book of Esdras and the Apocalypse, but

---

title editions, with only the first gathering replaced, appeared in 1616 and 1617
'bei Johann Carl Unckel/ Buchhändlern zu Franckfurt am Mäyn'. These editions
were unknown to both Röslin's bibliographer Paul Diesner as well as Martha List,
cf. Paul Diesner, 'Der elsässische Arzt Dr. Helisaeus Röslin als Forscher und Publizist
am Vorabend des dreißigjährigen Krieges', *Jahrbuch der Elsaß-Lothringischen Wissenschaftlichen Gesellschaft zu Straßburg*, 11, 1938, 192–215; Martha List, 'Helisäus Röslin—
Arzt und Astrologe', *Schwäbische Lebensbilder*, ed. by Hermann Haering and Otto
Hohenstatt, Pt. 3, Stuttgart 1942, 468–480; The work is also omitted in the otherwise excellently documented work of Robin Bruce Barnes, *Prophecy and Gnosis in the
wake of the Lutheran Reformation*, Stanford, 1988. Manuscripts of the first part of the
Welt Spiegel can be found in Stuttgart (Württembergische Landesbibliothek, cod.
Theol. 2° 72), in Stockholm (Riksarkivet, Skoklostersaml. Fol. 16) and in the Halle
university library (Ms. 23 B 3). Karl Widemann's collection furthermore contained
two other unprinted chapters of the *Welt-Spiegel* as well as the complete *Kirchen-
Spiegel* under Röslin's pseudonym 'Lampertus Floridus', cf. Kassel, Landes- und
Murhardsche Bibliothek, Ms. chem. Fol. 7, ff. 59–123; of Röslin's 'Geheime Ausle-
gung in das vierdtte Buech Esdrae Prophetae auf das gaist[liche] vnd Weltliche
Regiment' Widemann produced in 1619 an (abbreviated?) Latin translation 'Inter-
praetatio Mystica et Vera in Quartum librum Esdrae Prophetae', which he sent to
King James I of England, cf. London, British Library, Ms. Royal 2D XX, 1r–53v.
On the meaning of the 4th book of Esdras in heterodox literature cf. Alastair
Hamilton, 'The Book of "vaine fables": the reception of 2 Esdras from the fifteenth
to the eighteenth century' in *Kerkhistorische opstellen aangeboden aan Prof. dr. J. van den
Berg*, Kampen 1987, 45–61.

also by the latest achievements in science, and therefore, according to Röslin, should *'allen Gelehrten, beydes in Religions Sachen vnnd andern Künsten, der freyhe Lauff gelassen werden'* [all scholars, both in religious matters as well as in the other arts, be given free rein].[30]

When Röslin died in 1616, his unpublished astrological, theological and kabbalistic works were absorbed in the manuscript collection of Karl Widemann.[31] The name of the Augsburg city physician Widemann is a household name for every Paracelsus researcher, because for more than thirty years he untiringly copied and collected works of Paracelsus and so succeeded in preserving many unprinted works by Paracelsus for posterity. Few people on the other hand know that as a leading Schwenckfeldian, he also possessed and similarly rescued a large part of Schwenckfeld's manuscripts as well as virtually the entire estate of his closest collaborators, Valentin Krautwald and Adam Reissner.[32] After completing his medical studies

---

[30] Helisäus Röslin, *Mitternächtige Schiffarth/ Von den Herrn Staden inn Niderlanden vor XV Jaren vergebenlich fürgenommen [. . .] Ein künstlicher Philosophischer Tractat*, Oppenheim 1611, 103–114; Röslin, *Prodromus Dissertationum Chronologicarum*, loc. cit., a3r–a4r. On Paracelsus's eschatology and views on tolerance cf. Kurt Goldammer, *Paracelsus in neuen Horizonten. Gesammelte Aufsätze*, Salzburger Beiträge zur Paracelsusforschung, 24, Vienna 1986, esp. 87–176, 250–262; on Castellio cf. Hans R. Guggisberg, 'Castellio und der Ausbruch der Religionskriege in Frankreich. Einige Betrachtungen zum Conseil à la France désolée', *Archiv für Reformationsgeschichte*, 68, 1977, 253–267; Guggisberg, 'The Defence of Religious Toleration and Religious Liberty in Early Modern Europe: Arguments, Pressures, and some Consequences', *History of European Ideas*, 4, 1983, 35–50; Guggisberg, 'Sebastian Castellio and the German Reformation', *Archive for Reformation History*, Special Volume: *The Reformation in Germany and Europe: Interpretations and Issues*, Gütersloh 1993, 325–343. That the spiritualist and rationalist Castellio was sometimes moved by chiliastic motives in his writings, is demonstrated in his preface to the Latin Bible edition addressed to King Edward VI (cf. *Religiöse Toleranz. Dokumente zur Geschichte einer Forderung*, ed. Hans R. Guggisberg Stuttgart-Bad Cannstadt 1984, 99–102), which induced Christoph Besold to quote large passages from Castellio immediately after quotations from Paracelsus and Brocardo in a *Dissertatio Historica de veteribus novisque Chiliastis*, cf. Besold, *Discursus Politici, I. De Monarchia*, Strassburg 1623, 245–248.

[31] In the manuscript catalogues mentioned above (Kassel, Landes- und Murhardsche Bibliothek, Ms. chem. Fol. 7, ff. 59–123) Widemann extensively described various manuscripts of Röslin under the name 'Lampertus Floridus' with precise indications of format and length. A number of them were also included as entries 213–215, 217–219, 221–223 in the printed catalogue of Joachim Morsius' *Nuncius Olympicus Von etzlichen geheimen Bücheren vnd Schrifften*, Philadelphia [Amsterdam] 1626. In the last volume of the bibliography of the early Rosicrucians planned by the Bibliotheca Philosophica Hermetica, Amsterdam, I shall attempt to give for the edition of Widemann's catalogues bibliographical records of Röslin's manuscripts which are generally believed to be lost.

[32] Irena Backus, 'Valentin Crautwald, Bibliotheca Dissidentium', in *Répertoire des non-conformistes religieux des seizième et dix-septième siècles*, ed. A. Séguenny, VI, Baden-Baden 1985, 9–70. For the manuscripts by Adam Reissner, Schwenckfeld and

Widemann, as secretary to the English alchemist Edward Kelley, worked in Prague at the court of Emperor Rudolph II in the years 1587–1588 and in Třeboň with the Rožmberks, which enormously facilitated his contacts with most contemporary Paracelsists. Amongst his relations were in any case the earliest propagandists of the Rosicrucian Manifestos and the first publishers of the Paracelsian *Theologica* and the Weigelian and pseudo-Weigelian writings.[33]

A discussion of Valentin Weigel's writings nowadays is no easy matter, as recently the number of works definitively to be attributed to Weigel has been drastically reduced.[34] For the evolution of Paracelsism into a religion, however, the distinction between genuine and spurious works by Weigel plays a secondary role, as first of all the entire corpus of 'Weigelian' works had a simultaneous and integral effect, and secondly both Weigel as well as his collaborators, continuators and/or forgers were all enthusiastic readers of the theological and natural philosophical works of Paracelsus. Whether Weigel's collaborators also meddled with the works of Paracelsus cannot be ruled out entirely. Had they done so, however, they merely continued an already existing tradition of both impatient radicals and able propagandists, who used Paracelsus as a stepping stone to finally rid themselves of the double yoke of the Roman Antichrist and the apoc-

---

Paracelsus which were sold to Wolfenbüttel cf. Widemann's letters in Wolfenbüttel, Herzog August Bibliothek, Bibliotheksarchiv, 44–47. For Widemann see the *Andreae-Katalog der Bibliotheca Philosophica Hermetica*, 46–51, 94–98.

[33] The Třeboň state archive, Archivium Schwarzenbergicum, Rožmberk family, section 25, holds the autograph farewell letter to Vilém Ursinus Rožmberk [autumn 1588]. For Widemann cf. Robert J.W. Evans, *Rudolf II and his World. A Study in Intellectual History 1576–1612*, Oxford 1973, 216. Manuscript DD V 34 from the Strahov library in Prague quoted by Evans (*loc. cit.*, 226) ('Alia purificatio... Vom Engelender aus Wittgenaw H. Edu. Keleo 1588', which is also listed in Kristeller, *Iter Italicum* III, 168, as *Paracelsi Testamentum*) is incidentally an autograph recipe book by Karl Widemann, in which are also copied letters from Kelley's assistant Johann Grueber. For Widemann's circle of friends see C. Gilly, *'Iter rosicrucianum. Auf der Suche nach unbekannten Quellen der frühen Rosenkreuzer'*, Das Erbe des Christian Rosenkreuz. *Vorträge gehalten anlässlich des Amsterdames Andreae-Symposiums*, Amsterdam 1988, 62–89, esp. 73–82; Julian Paulus, 'Alchemie und Paracelsismus um 1600. Das Verzeichnis spagyrischer Mediziner des Augsburger Stadtarztes Karl Widemann. Kritische Edition und Kommentar', *Frühneuzeit-Info*, 1992, 3, Vol. 2, 48–72.

[34] Cf. Horst Pfefferl, *Die Überlieferung der Schriften Valentin Weigels* (doctoral dissertation, partly published), Marburg/Lahn 1991. The author has drastically reduced the number of works attributed to Weigel to a minimum, so that a full appreciation of Weigel's works can not be made until Pfefferl's evidence has been published in its entirety. Pfefferl, however, goes too far, when he absolves Weigel of all 'heresy' or classes Weigel's relentless battle against church and dogmas (for instance in the *Dialogus de Christianismus*) merely as a 'limited' and 'moderately presented' 'theological and church-critical attitude'.

alyptic beast (this is how the old Paracelsist Johannes Montanus used to characterize the Augsburg confession).[35] But these pseudepigraphic products, too, are amongst the historical witnesses of Paracelsianism and therefore deserve to be taken into account.

Around the year 1600 the corpus of medical and natural philosophical works of Paracelsus was already available in print. The collected edition by the Catholic Johann Huser and his Protestant collaborator Paul Linck, which remains authoritative to this day, appeared in Basle from 1589 with the financial support of the Archbishop of Cologne. As was to be expected, the theological works were left aside as unreclaimed territory—to some extent even to this day. The last one who had access to the theological autographs of Paracelsus and who excerpted them profusely was the earlier-mentioned co-editor Paul Linck in an unpublished chiliastic work *Rechter Bericht von den dreyen Seculis und Judiciis divinis post diluvium* of 1599–1602, in which Paracelsus (in addition to Joachim of Fiore, Brigitta of Sweden, Johann Tauler and Guillaume Postel) is presented as the proclaimer of an imminent Golden Age (*'einer Guldenen Welt'*).[36]

Paracelsus had now been promoted to the status of seer. It is therefore no surprise to find that the majority of the works by Paracelsus which were published separately between 1605 and 1635 consist of prophecies.[37]

---

[35] August von Anhalt, letter to Widemann, Plötzkau 1. September 1614 (Staatsarchiv Oranienbaum, Abteilung Köthen, A 17a Nr. 100, f. 94v): '[. . .] ersuch des [Daniel] Sudermanns büchlein mir etwa zukommen zu laßen, praesertim des C[aspar] S[chwenckfeld] bedencken vber die A[gustana] confess[io], welche der alte Montanus pflegte, die bestiam zu nehnnen, so vom meer aufsteigt, will ich damitt göttliche gnaden zu aller wolfart befohlen haben'.

[36] *Rechter Bericht Von den Dreyen Seculis vnd Judiciis Divinis post Diluvium, Als nemblich: 1: Von der Zerstörung Jerusalem vnd Untergang der gantzen Jrrdischen Policey. 2: Von der grossen Trübsal über den gantzen Erdtkreis vnd Vntergang aller Ständ der Welt. 3: Vom Jungsten Gerichte oder Letzten Tag der gantzen welt, welcher in der H. Schrifft* τό τελος [to telos] *finis vnd* Συντελεια το αιωνος [synteleia tou aionos] *Consumatio Seculi genennet wird. Geschrieben durch Paul Lincken Med. Doctore[m] anno 1599, Mense Januario vnd Volgends, Anno 1602 vermehret vnd Vollendet* (Hamburg, Staats- und Universitätsbibliothek, Cod. Theol. 1914, 1–615; Rostock, Universitätsbibliothek, Ms. Theol. Fol. 72, unfoliated; Wolfenbüttel HAB, 981 Helmst., Bl. 1–241). For Linck cf. Joachim Telle, 'Johann Huser in seinen Briefen', in *Parerga Paracelsica*, 215–216. Paul Linck's *Bericht* is not mentioned by neither Barnes, *Prophecy and Gnosis* or Enrico de Mas, *L'Attesa del secolo aureo (1603–1625)*, Florence 1982. The same applies to the work of the Paracelsist Julius Sperber, written in 1597, *Von dreyerley Seculis oder Hauptzeiten, Tröstlicher Prophecey vnd Weissagung. Von der zunahenden güldenen als der Dritten vnd Letzten Zeit vnd dem gantzen zustande derselben* (Mss. in Wolfenbüttel, 772 Helmst., ff. 173–287, and in the Heimatmuseum Köthen, printed in Amsterdam in 1663).

[37] Karl Sudhoff, *Bibliographica Paracelsica*, nos. 288, 296, 316, 317, 318, 322, 330, 338–354. A friend of Libavius characterized Paracelsus as a 'Guckguck Grossvater'

What is more, he became posthumously the founder of a new religion: the religion of two lights (the light of grace and the light of nature), in which, as the Paracelsian Oswald Croll enthusiastically put it in the famous preface to *Basilica Chymica*, 'the *summum* of theological and philosophical truth and the foundation of perfect religiousness from the book of grace and the book of nature are joined together'.[38]

And this religion also soon obtained a name: she was called '*Theophrastia Sancta*', Holy Theophrastia.

The first to mention '*Theophrastia Sancta*' in print was the widely-travelled Paracelsist Benedictus Figulus, who in the preface to *Pandora magnalium naturalium aurea et benedicta* of 1608 did not only announce his plan, to 'promote' in print the 'Cabbalistic and theological books' 'of our dear highly-gifted leader and teacher Ph. Theophrastus of blessed memory' to the 'eternal benefit and salvation of all Christendom', but also for the first time publicly called himself a student of the 'Sacrosancta Theophrastia and immortal philosophy of Christ'.[39]

However, Figulus himself had not coined this phrase. His attention had been drawn to it as a result of his acquaintance with Adam Haslmayr, a Tyrolean schoolmaster, musician and alchemist who had read the theological books of Paracelsus so intensively and had internalized them to such a degree, that he spoke only of the holy Theophrastia.[40] Adam Haslmayr or Haselmeier is known to all who

---

of the 'newen ungeweyheten und unberufenen Weissager, die vielleicht Eulenspiegels Prophetenbeer gekostet', cf. Melior [!] Rudolph Janicola, *Strena [. . .] Was von den newen Paracelsischen Propheten/ vnd Thurneuserischen Warsagern zu halten*, Hamburg 1601; Nicolaus Hunnius in his *Gründtlicher Beweiss wie Theophrastus Paracelsus, Weigel, Felgenhauer, Teting ud andere [. . .] mit falschen Weissagungen umbgehen*, s.l. 1634, 33, also wrote about Paracelsus as the source and beginning of 'so viel wunderbarlicher seltzamer Propheceyunge', who 'in diesen jetzigen sehr Trübseligen zeiten an das Licht der Welt, mündlich und schriftlich, herrfür komen'.

[38] Oswald Croll, *Basilica Chymica continens Philosophicam propria laborum experientia confirmatam descriptionem et usum Remediorum Chymicorum Selectissimorum e Lumine GRATIAE et NATURAE desumptorum*, Frankfurt [1611], 69. For Croll see Telle, 'Johann Huser in seinen Briefen', in *Parerga Paracelsica*, 204–205; Wilhelm Kühlmann, 'Oswald Crollius und seine Signaturenlehre. Zum Profil hermetischer Naturphilosophie in der Ära Rudolphs II', *Die okkulten Wissenschaften in der Renaissance*, ed. by August Buck, *Wolfenbütteler Abhandlungen zur Renaissanceforschung*, 12, Wiesbaden 1992, 103–124; Gilly, *Zwischen Erfahrung und Spekulation*, Part 2, 174–175, 220–221.

[39] Benedictus Figulus, *Pandora Magnalium Naturalium aurea et Benedicta. De Benedicto Lapidis Philosoph[orum] Mysterio*, Strassburg 1608, ff. rv 8r: cf. Joachim Telle, *Benedictus Figulus*, 323–324.

[40] For the relations between Figulus and Haslmayr see C. Gilly, *Adam Haslmayr, Der erste Verkünder der Manifeste der Rosenkreuzer*, Amsterdam 1994.

are interested in the history of the Rosicrucians, because he was the first to respond in public to the then as yet unprinted Rosicrucian Manifestos, for which reason (as can be read on the title-page of the first edition of the *Fama Fraternitatis* of 1614) he 'was imprisoned by the Jesuits and bound in chains on a galley'. I have only recently managed to locate the long looked-for original edition of Haslmayr's response, dated 1612, the full title of which will now be communicated as a 'scoop': *Antwort An die lobwürdige Brüderschafft der Theosophen von RosenCreutz N.N. vom Adam Haselmayr Archiducalem Alumnum, Notarium seu Iudicem ordinarium Caesareum, der zeyten zum heiligen Creutz Dörflem bey Hall in Tyroll wohnende. Ad Famam Fraternitatis Einfeltigist geantwortet. Anno 1612.*[41]

In this response Haslmayr had thanked the Rosicrucians, who were otherwise unknown to him, for their 'Theophrastiam and divine gift', because he saw in them 'those, who are now chosen by God, to spread the eternal Theophrastiam and divine truth, which has been miraculously preserved until now'. Haslmayr felt that Rosencreutz and Paracelsus had aimed at the same goal and he accordingly appealed to the members of the invisible brotherhood, finally to come forward, to help realize the hoped-for breakthrough of the new religion of the '*evangelical freedom*, which Theophrastus and Christian Rosencreutz promised this latter world'.

In a letter of December 1611 Haslmayr also called upon his closest friends to respond to the Rosicrucians: 'Respond you lords and doctors, especially those whom God exhorts, to the Fama Fraternitatis C.R., so that one time we will be worthy to have these men as

---

[41] It was for that matter the very first mention of the word 'Rosenkreuz' in a printed book. The title-page has already been reproduced in the exhibition catalogue *Paracelsus in der Bibliotheca Philosophica Hermetica*, Amsterdam, In de Pelikaan, 1993, 84. The complete facsimile edition has meanwhile been published in Gilly, *Haslmayr*. The text is furthermore reprinted in the first edition of the *Fama fraternitatis*, cf. *Allgemeine vnd General REFORMATION, der gantzen weiten Welt. Beneben der FAMA FRATERNITATIS, Deß Löblichen Ordens des Rosenkreutzes/ an alle Gelehrte vnd Häupter Europae geschrieben: Auch einer kurtzen RESPONSION, von dem Herrn Haselmeyer gestellet/ welcher deßwegen von den Jesuitern ist gefänglich eingezogen/ vnd auff eine Galleren geschmiedet: Jtzo öffentlich in Druck verfertiget/ vnd allen trewen Hertzen communiciret worden.* Gedruckt zu Cassel/ durch Wilhelm Wessell/ Anno M. DC. XIV. English translation F.N. Pryce, *The Fame and Confession of the Fraternity of R.C., commonly of the Rosie Cross. With [. . .] a Translation of the letter of Adam Haselmeyer*, Margate 1923, 57–64. For Haslmayr cf. Walter Senn, 'Adam Haslmayr. Musiker, Philosoph und "Ketzer"', Festschrift Leonhard C. Franz, *Innsbrucker Beiträge zur Kulturwissenschaft*, 11, Innsbruck, 1965, 379–400; *Andreae-Katalog der Bibliotheca Philosophica Hermetica*, 45, 50, 55, 94–98; Gilly, *Iter rosicrucianum*, 63–89, esp. 73–75.

teachers, and the disagreeable bad world will recognize the magnalia and will be converted, causing our good old pious Lorentz Lutz,
too, to heave a heart-felt sigh, because of these Rosicrucian people,
who revealed the Theophrastiam'.[42]

This Lorentz Lutz of Meran was not only Haslmayr's teacher, but
notably also the last living medical assistant of Paracelsus.[43] Whether
Lutz had recommended this idea to Haslmayr, or whether the latter had thought of it himself while reading the Paracelsian manuscripts kept by his teacher, is not clear. The main thing is, that
Haslmayr acted as the proclaimer or defender of the newly founded
religion, the *'Theophrastia Sancta'*, in the majority of the 200 works
which he wrote between 1605 and 1630. Some of the titles are:

—'Theophrastia vom Geist und Leben ad Augustum von Anhalt'.

—'Eu Angelica Philosophia, darinn verfasst ist die gantze Thëophrastia. Warumb der Mensch erschaffen und was sein Ambt ist hie
auf erden'.

—'Thëophrastia in iter Iesu, das ist die Teütsche Theologiam gründtlich zue versteen, das ist der warhaftige Weg Iesu Christi den Alle
geen müessen welche seligkeit begehren, per Theophrastum'.

—'Von falscher gewalt vnnd vbermuth/auch verführung des Volckes/
ein Göttliche offenbarung. Von falscher Gewalt und Übermut.
Theophrastia Revelationis'.

—'Sacro-Sancta Thëophrastia Von der Wahren seligmachenden Religion und von Krefften des Glaubens ahn die Fursten und Potentaten
Europae und an die Ersten rätd der Reichstätte'.

---

[42] Haslmayr, Letter to K. Widemann dated 24 Dezember 1611, copied Karl
Widemann, *Sylva Scientiarum* (Hannover, Niedersächsische Landesbibliothek, Ms. IV
341), 356.
    [43] 'Lorentz Lutz. burger vnd Bader im Algundt 1/4 Meil von Meron im Etschland.
Obiit. Diser hatt Theophrastum selber kenndt und ist [. . .] Gabriel von Marwisen
bei Ime doselbsten zur herberg glegen, auch [. . .] Adam Haslmayr mitt Ime geraisst.
Hat vill scripta Theophrastica so noch nit gmein', cf. *Andreae-Katalog der Bibliotheca
Philosophica Hermetica, loc. cit.*, 48; Paulus, *Alchemie und Paracelsismus um 1600. Das
Verzeichnis spagyrischer Mediziner, loc. cit.*, 50. Lutz is furthermore mentioned in
Widemann's *Sylva scientiarum, loc. cit.*, 274: 'De mercurio praeparando: [Dieses] braucht
der Lorentz Lutz, Theophrastischer alhie noch lebender diener, zu seinem feüren',
retulit oretenus Adam Haslmayr'; cf. also Wolfgang Irtenkauf, 'Abraham Schnitzer,
der "gelehrte Scharlatan". Leben und Werk eines Bergmeisters im 16. Jahrhundert'. *Veröffentlichungen des Tiroler Landesmuseum Ferdinandeum*, 64, 1984, 9–56, esp. 23
and 41.

—'Sacro-Sancta Thëophrastia von der Ordnung Gottes und Weltlichen Regiment als ewiger Religion Iesu Nazareni Regis Iudeorum an das gantze R[ömische] R[eich] Europae und sonderlich der zerstörtesten lesten Christenheitt Teütscher Nation, anno 1624'.

—'Thëophrastia Paracelsi christiana Vom Langen gsunden Leben der werden christen'.

—'Prophecei ex S.S. Thëophrastia über das Vatter Unser, doraus Alle vernufft sehen und erkennen kan, ob ein Glaub in der Weldtt sëy an Alle Gelerte und Ungelerte Christen auf dise leste Zeitt zuer Warnung und Ermanung gesteldt, anno 1626, von einem verworffenen Menschen'.

—'Thëophrastia de Partu Virginis, Darinn auf dise leste Zeit geoffenbaret wirt Wahin man verfüert hat das gantze Menschliche Geschlecht durch die selbslauffende unnutze und ohnmächtige Lerer, dorauff die Mechtigen, die Reichen diser Weldt wohl achtung geben mögen. Höher kan die verfüerung nicht mehr kommen durch Alle ständ der christenheitt'.

—'Thëophrastia Sacro-Sancta de Anfractu christianorum a Seculo 1600 annorum usque ad 1660 Christi, Darinnen gefunden Aller christen Irrtumb, Übermuet, falscher gwalt und verfüerung des Volckhes per Theophrastum Paracelsum magnum'.

—'Schuel der Geheimnussen [. . .] Theophrastia alma an die alte Reichstadt Augspurg / vnd an die Praedicanten zu Nürnberg / sonderlich die Theophrastum in den erleuchten Mann Gottes M. Valentino VVigelio verwerffen'.

—'Sacro-Sancta Thëophrastia, oder Thëologia Paracelsica Intacta. Von der Narren oder falschen kirchen zuer offentlichen Apologia wider die 99 gantz Nerrische Puncten D. Matthiae Hoÿe [. . .] zue Dresden wider die Reformiertten oder calvinisten erdacht'.

—'Thëophrastia luminosa sive lux oriens Mortalium de perpetua religione seu Evangelica Philosophia, darinn das gantze Leben und Ordnung, Mandat, Recht undgerechtigkeit Iesu Christi unsers ainigen gesetzgebers und Erlösers, Wie es seit der geburt und Himmelfart Christi hette sollen jederzeit in Aller Welt gehaldten sein worden, wolten wir kaine feind und Plagen Jemalen im christentumb gehabt haben, begriffen wirdt, auf dise leste Römische Monarchei ann Tag gegeben durch Thëophrastum Paracelsum magnum

secretarium Christi vor 80 Jaren beschriben, ietzt gefunden, an
das R[ömische] R[eich] und sein haubt de anno 1623'.

—'Thëophrastia sancta von Recht und gerechtigkeit Iesu Christi,
Wie es seider des Lesten Abendmals einsetzung gehaldten soll sein
worden bis zue ende der Weldtt, wolte Man nicht Im fluech und
Maledeiung sein gefallen vor Gott. Also daß der Türckh dië chris-
ten solte meistern, durch Thëophrastum magnum Eremitam ad
Ferdinandum II. Imperatorem'.

—'Thëophrastia de Verbo Dei vivo und vom langen Leben In gmei-
nen auf diser Lesten Zeitt Völcker gesteltt von einer verurteidtten
Person, 1622. Wider Alle selbs lauffende Propheten und Apostel
dobei auch Cura Lunaticorum, id est, die sich das gstirn regiern
lassen Inn und under Allen Ständen'.

—'Thëophrastia de Vita longa Principum, und Ursachen, warumb
den Potentaten und Fursten Ir Leben abgekürtztt wirtt, und wie
disem fürzuekommen sei, ex Thëophrasto'.

—'Theophrastiae Cabalisticae Isagoge'.

Those interested in these and many other titles by Haslmayr only
have to consult the final pages of the second volume of Karl Sudhoff's *Bibliographica Paracelsica*, where they are reproduced in full by
Sudhoff, who did not know who the author of these books was.[44]
The titles can also, and even better, be read in Joachim Morsius's
Nuncius Olympicus, printed in 1626, because this work is the sale catalogue of 228 manuscripts in the fields of theology, Kabbala, magic,
chemistry, medicine and philology, which were written by an 'ancient
and famous philosopher and physician'.[45] That the author was
Haslmayr can be learnt from the catalogues of the library of Karl
Widemann, who marked a large part of the titles listed in the *Nuncius*
with the abbreviation 'A.H.', that is, Adam Haslmayr. In his catalogues, Widemann also mentioned the total number of manuscripts

---

[44] Sudhoff, *Paracelsus-Handschriften*, 755–764.
[45] Anastasius Philareta Cosmopolita [Joachim Morsius], *Nuncius Olympicus Von
etzlichen geheimen Bücheren vnd Schrifften/ so ein fürnehmer Gottesgelehrter vnd hocherleuchter
berümbter Theosophus vnd Medicus, in Theosophia, Cabala, Magia, Chemia, Medicina vnd
Philologia, durch viel beschwerliche Reisen vnnd grosse Vnkostung/ Ecclesiae vnd Reip[ublicae]
literariae commodo zusammen gebracht/ darin die gröste Himlische vnnd Jrrdische Weißheit begriffen
ist* [. . .] Gedruckt PHILADELPHIAE [Amsterdam] 1626. This book lists 227
Manuscripts with their full titles. Facsimile edition in Gilly, *Haslmayr*.

by Haslmayr deposited in his Augsburg home: '*Adam Haselmarii Manuscripta*: In Folio 66, in Quarto 94, together 160'.[46] Of these 160 manuscripts some 40 have been located during my research for the Rosicrucian bibliography. The manuscripts are either in Haslmayr's own hand, or in Widemann's. In addition, the libraries of Florence, Hannover, Gotha, Innsbruck, Kassel, Copenhagen, London, Weimar and Wolfenbüttel contain a further 50 autographs by Haslmayr unrecorded in either the *Nuncius* or in Widemann's own catalogues. This is discussed in greater detail in my study on Haslmayr. Here it may be noted that some of Haslmayr's works even appeared in print, and under Paracelsus's name. These are the *Astronomia Olympi Novi* or the *Theologia Cabalistica von dem volkommenen Menschen*, which were included in the Paracelsian-Weigelian compilation *Philosophia Mystica* of 1618.[47] The pseudonymous publisher Huldrich Bachmeister of Regenbrunn, alias Johannes Siebmacher of Nuremberg, obviously took these two works for works by Paracelsus. Only in the case of the added *'Particulae'* did Siebmacher express doubts as to its Paracelsian authorship, because he could not decide, whether this was only the work of a 'disciple of the holy Theophrastia'.[48]

---

[46] Kassel, Landes- und Murhardsche Bibliothek, Ms. chem. Fol. 7, f. 53v: 'Adamj Haselmarij Manuscripta: In Folio 66, *in Quarto 94, Zsammen 160*. Plurima hic tractantur secretissima in naturalj et supernaturalj lumine. Diser fromme Mann ist 4 1/2 Jar vf der galeeen gfangen ghalten worden. Durch die Jesuwider in Tirol dahin deputirt, well er Ieren bedrug vnd Abgötterej gestrafft'. Both Sudhoff, *Paracelsus-Handschriften*, 748 as well as Will-Erich Peuckert, *Das Rosenkreutz*, Berlin 1973², 71, have failed to notice the italicized words.

[47] [Adam Haslmayr] *ASTRONOMIA OLYMPI NOVI, Das ist: Die gestirnkunst deß newen Himmels/ welche allein auß dem Glauben entspringet/ darauß der Mensch alle Magnalia Gottes vnd der Natur/ die den glaubigen seynd zuwissen/ sehen vnd erlernen mag. Authore Paracelso ab Hohenheim* and *THEOLOGIA CABALISTICA De perfecto homine in Christo Iesu, et contra de perdito animali homine in Adam, qui Lunaticus dicitur. Das ist: Von dem vollkommenen Menschen in Christo Jesu/ vnd hergegen von dem verdorbenen thierischen Menschen in Adam/ welcher ein Mondsüchtiger genennet wird. Authore Theophrasto Paracelsi ab Hohenheim,* both published in: *PHILOSOPHIA MYSTICA, Darinn begriffen Eilff vnterschidene Theologico-Philosophische/ doch teutsche Tractätlein/ zum theil auß Theophrasti Paracelsi, zum theil auch M. Valentini Weigelii, gewesenen Pfarrherrn zu Jscopaw/ bißhero verborgenen manuscriptis der Theosophischen Warheit liebhabern. An jtzo in zweien Theilen zum Christlichen Vorschub/ beyde Liechter/ der Gnaden vnd der Natur/ in vns zuerwecken/ in offenen Truck gegeben. Deren Titul vnd Nahmen/ wie ein jedes insonderheit von den Authoribus selbst genennet/ die nachfolgende seite zeigen wirdt. Gedruckt zur Newstadt [Frankfurt]/ vnd zu finden bey Lucas Jenes/ Buchhändler,* 1618, 33–39 and 40–53; cf. Sudhoff, *Bibliographia Paracelsica*, 514–516.

[48] The first of the appended *Particulae* concerns a letter of Haslmayr to his sovereign the Archduke Maximilian of Tyrol. For the identification of 'Huldrich Bachsmaier' as Johannes Siebmacher cf. Johann Valentin Andreae, *Ein geistliches Gemälde. Entworfen und aufgezeichnet von Huldrich StarkMann, Diener des Evangeliums. Nach dem wiedergefundenen*

What Haslmayr actually understood by this concept 'Theophrastia', repeated not only in titles, but also in almost every one of his discourses, can be gauged from an oration (*Oratio reuelatoria*), which Haslmayr sent to his sovereign, the Archduke Maximilian of Tyrol, immediately before being sentenced to the galleys in August 1612.

In this *Oratio reuelatoria* Haslmayr reported how he, 'while so many writers and high prophets these latter days' manifested themselves, also got up to speak and as 'a simple Tyrolean' had to make a stand against such 'prophets', who 'hold themselves in such esteem, that heaven should depend on them, or nothing is right, but what they teach, imagine and write'. In reality, however, they are as theologians as good 'as the jugglers and charlatans are good poets or Cicero a preacher of Christ'. These theologians now upbraid him that it does not become him, Haslmayr, to write *'Revelationes theologicas'*, as he is merely 'a common layman', and has not completed the Aristotelian *'cursum philosophicum'* at any university, as if 'Narristoteles' [the fool Aristotle] 'ever completed, or even came near, our Christian curriculum'. 'What, then, should we care about the heathen's curriculum?', Haslmayr adds.

> May the spirit of God not go where it wants, or must he first consult the universities and bishops? All men may fully share in the grace of God and the school of the holy Apostle is as open as it was during Pentecost, only now it is lodged in the mind and in the truth, in asking, seeking and appealing, and not in the annointment of humans or the tonsure [. . .] as Doctor Paracelsus Magnus explains, the mighty Cabalista.

The *'Sancta Theophrastia'*, according to Haslmayr, 'is not based (God be praised) on the elements of the common world, but on Christianity,

---

Urdruck, Tübingen 1615, ed. by Reinhard Breymayer, Tübingen 1991 [1992], XX–XXII. As in the case of Andreae, Huldrich here stands for Johannes, while Bachsmeier and Regenbrunn are anagrams for Siebmacher and Nürnberg. It is the same man, whom Widemann in his list of Spagyric physicians called 'Johann Sibmacher. Philosophus vnd chymicus zue Nörnberg'. Whether this Siebmacher was indeed also the author of the anonymous *Wasserstein der Weisen* (first edition Frankfurt 1619), as Breymayer assures us, requires further investigation. Everything depends on the genuineness or spuriousness of the preface and poems, which in the later editions of the *Wasserstein der Weisen* were either inserted at the beginning or else appended with the new titles *Das Goldene Vlieβ* (Leipzig 1736 und 1737) or *Das allerhöchste, edelste, kunstreichste Kleinod* (Frankfurt and Leipzig 1755). In the 18th century Wolfgang Siebmacher, minister of St. Leonhard's in Nuremberg, who in 1622 was suspected of Weigelianism, was also named as author of *Wasserstein der Weisen*.

and proves that all arts and faculties are to be slighted, which do not have their feet or foundation and cornerstone in theology'. And this is actually the case, according to Haslmayr, with the 'eternal Sophia sancta', which, 'in particular under this new monarchy and century from 1600 onwards', 'calls us all and invites us to learn from her all the sciences, art and wisdom, which wisdom is nobody or nothing else, but Christ'. Not surprisingly, Haslmayr concludes his discourse with a plea for the Rosicrucians and with a passage from the *Fama Fraternitatis*:

> Do we then need Narristoteles [that fool Aristotle] or Galen or Cicero in Christian schools? Now under the Reign of the Holy Spirit? We do not need them at all. Blessed the country, which lets us learn only the 12 lights of God, because these teach us nothing else, but Jesus, who is above all wisdom, wherefore also we have from the Holy Spirit of the Ancients the wonderful adage: JESUS NOBIS OMNIA.[49]

Haslmayr understood the *'Theophrastia Sancta'* to be a sort of perpetual religion, which since the days of the apostles had been practised in concealment until the time when the 'German Trismegistus, Philippus Theophrastus', began publicly to expound its meaning. The basis for this true Theophrastia (and at the same time the way and the method for a true progress in all arts and sciences) were the *'Tria cabalistica prima'* for Haslmayr. The three cabbalistic principles, which Paracelsus, following Matthew 7:7 had already described in the *Philosophia Sagax* as the road to all research as it is ordained by God and nature: 'As all things to be studied are based in three principles, in *"Bitten, Suchen und Anklopfen"* [asking, seeking and appealing]'.[50] Haslmayr added to these three cabbalistic principles the 'four rules of our Christendom' and 'eight virtues of holiness' based on the Sermon on the Mount, which he described as follows in many

---

[49] Innsbruck, Tyroler Staatsarchiv, Pestarchiv VIIa, 18, ff. 13r–17v: *Ad Reuerendissimum et Serenissimum Principem meum, Maximilianum Austriae, Teutonici Ordinis Magistrum vigilantissimum, Oratio Reuelatoria* (Subscript: 'Vnderthenigister Clyens et Alumnus Adamus Haslmaÿr, N[otarius] C[aesareus] von Hall'). For the Innsbruck documentation on Haslmayr cf. Walter Senn, *Adam Haslmayr. Musiker, Philosoph und 'Ketzer'*, 1965, 379–400, and Gilly, *Haslmayr*, 32–67.

[50] [Adam Haslmayr], *Extractus et Theophrastiae cabalisticae Isagogen, Das ist, Die einlaittung der Heilligen gehaimen Khunst vnd Weißheit der Propheten. Ohn welche Khunst vnnd gnaden kheiner die heilig Schrifft verstehen noch gründtlich erkleren khan* (Weimar, Herzogin Anna Amalia Bibliothek, Ms. Q. 286/20, 1r–5r, here 2r); cf. also Paracelsus, *Sämtliche Werke*. 1. Abteilung, ed. Sudhoff, XII, 185.

of his works, including the *Verweisung* to Hippolytus Guarinoni of 1611 and the *Theologia Cabalistica* printed in 1618: 'I. To love our enemies; II. To abandon selfhood; III. Patiently suffer slander inflicted on us; IV. To refuse to accept all honour bestowed'. Haslmayr considered these four rules to be the 'key to the holy secret science and the *magnalia* of God' and at the same time the 'law, order and policy' of the true Christian, whose lives are based on the Sermon on the Mount or, as Haslmayr formulated it again and again, are concerned to excel in 'the eight virtues of blessedness'. Through the principle of *'Nosce teipsum'*, that is through the observation of the three spirits lodged in man (animal, astral or syderial, and divine) he can penetrate the sacrament of the element and the word.[51]

In order to clarify this *'elementi verbique sacramentum'*, Haslmayr had developed his own hieroglyphic sign in 1612 (in imitation of John Dee's *Monas Hieroglyphica*). In many of his works he called this sign *'Trimonas'* (threefold one), *'Monarchia Stellae signatae'*, or simply as the 'Signatstern' ('sign star') of Paracelsus. Through this sign, which he often explained in philosophical, medical or alchemical terms, but often also expounded in a purely theological or chiliastic sense, Haslmayr wished to visualize the close relationship between the 'Mystery of theology', the 'Secret of philosophy' and the 'purpose of medicine'.[52] By means of this *'stella signata'* Haslmayr symbolized at the same time the relation between *'ergon'* and *'parergon'* of the Rosicrucians,

---

[51] Adam Haslmayr, *Verweisung vnd Vnderweisung, wie Guarinonius, Statt phÿsicus zu Hall in Tÿrol halt den volgenden Text, Matth. 24, [15] von whuest vnd Greul soil außgelegt haben, vnd die Christenheit nicht in verrere Ihrsallen gefhiert, als biß her beschehen ist durch Europa* (1611), Wolfenbüttel, HAB, Ms. 17.30 Aug. 4°, ff. 165v–173; Paracelsus [Adam Haslmayr], *Theologia Cabalistica de perfecto homine, Philosophia Mystica, loc. cit.*, 42. I have found the first enumeration of these four main points in the introduction to the *Thesaurinella Alchimiae* of Benedictus Figulus of 1609 (Kassel, Landes- und Murhardsche Bibliothek, 8° Ms. Chem. 25, f. 1): 'TRIA CABALISTICA prima Ex ore Spagÿri Trismegisti I[esu] Christi Domini et Redemptoris nostri prolata: PETERE, QUAERERE, PULSARE. Die 4 Haupt Puncten Des Wahren Christenthumbs alß der vnvberwindlichen CABALAE: 1) Unsere Feindt alle lieben, 2) Aygens verlassen, 3) Angethane Schmach gedultig leyden. 4) Anerbottene Ehr allenthalben verniechten'.

[52] The first work of Haslmayr in which I have found this sign, is the *Philosophia Sagax* addressed to the Arch Duke Maximilian, which Widemann received for Christmas from Genua in 1612 (Hannover, Niedersächsische Landesbibliothek, Ms. IV, 341, 501–508, 'Ex Autographo Adami Haslmayr Senioris'). Haslmayr then adapted this work a year later for the *Astronomia terrestris vonn der Sphaera oder Himmell Saturni (loc. cit.*, 521–528; *Nuncius Olympicus* no. 48); the sign reappears in a new guise on the title-page of *Novum Lumen Physico-Chymicum, Das ist: Ein Newes Liecht der Chimischen Phÿsica, welches vor Aller Zeiten die hohen Philosophi vnd König gehabt, vnd sich dardurch zum Langen Leben, gerechten Reichtumb vnd ewigen Weißheit, gebracht haben* (Florence, BN, Ms. Magliab. XVI, 104, ff. 32–41, Haslmayr's autograph), dedicated to the Grand Duke

that is, the close connection of the higher religion and sciences obtained as a result of the *'theosophico oratorio'* (through imitation of God's works) and the *'chymico laboratorio'* (through the personal study of nature).[53]

Following the Rosicrucians (*Confessio Fraternitatis*, ch. 10) Haslmayr, too, reiterates that it is possible to glean 'all sciences and faculties from the Bible'. But at the same time Haslmayr depreciates the value of the 'external' biblical text, as did Thomas Müntzer, Ludwig Hätzer, Sebastian Franck, Servetūs or Castellio, but also Paracelsus:[54]

> The books of the Christians are the living creatures. The books written on paper by the prophets are no more than memorials and witnesses, so that we men are reminded of what is in us, because the sense is not in the book, but in the spirit, now the spirit houses in

---

of Tuscany and signed by 'Adam Haslmaÿr von Bozen auß Tÿrol etc. der Freÿen vnd geheimen Kunsten der Philosophei vnd Medicin Requisitor, der Zeit Gfangner in das 4t. Jar, daselbsten auff S. Georgen Galeen in Genoa. 16 Aprilis 1616'. This work was translated into Latin by Haslmayr under the title *Novum Lumen Physicae intactae* and dedicated to the Genoese Andrea Grimaldi (Florence, BN, Ms. Magliab. XVI 104, ff. 42r–49r, Haslmayr's autograph); the Italian translation was based on this version: *Lume nuovo de la phisica mai tocata. La quale é el solo desiderio Christiano. De Lapide philosophico* (Florence, BN, Ms. Magliab. XVI, 104, ff. 50r–57r): All three versions contain cryptic quotations from the *Fama Fraternitatis*, but only the first one contains Haslmayr's sign. The sign appears again *AHT Sermo ad Filios. Gmeine philosophei Paracelsi Magni. An meine Kinder* (Hannover, NSLB, Ms. IV, 370, 1–16, Haslmayr's autograph). Haslmayr's sign with the accompanying text appeared in print in Liberius Benedictus's German and Latin edition, *Nucleus Sophicus, oder Außlegung in Tincturam Physicorum Theophrasti Paracelsi* and *Nucleus Sophicus seu Explanatio in Tincturam Physicorum Theophrasti Paracelsi*, both published by Lucas Jennis in Frankfurt in 1623, 76–78 resp. 62–64. Haslmayr's most detailed report on the sign appeared in a tract in 1629: *Amphitheatrum Chimicum Sacrum Wider die Sophistischen Spötter vnd vnuerstendigen Mercatänter, welche ihnen traumt laßen, die Alt Spagyrische Scienz sei nur ein gedicht der Betrüger, vnd derhalben sei nichts recht, als was sie thun, handlen, lehren, vnd üben, widerlegt von einem Armen Schüler Theophrastischer Disciplin*, (Kassel, Landesbibliothek und Murhardsche Bibliothek, 2° Ms. Chem 15, ff. 206r–212v and 260v, Haslmayr's autograph).

[53] [Adam Haslmayr], *Consideratio Figurae Ergon et Parergon* (Kassel, Landesbibliothek und Murhardsche Bibliothek, 2° Ms. Chem. 19, 115r–119r, Widemann's hand, 'Ex autographo, octobri anno 1626'); Lübeck, Stadtbibliothek, Ms. Hist. 4° 25, ff. 820r–830r, Joachim Morsius's hand). The 'ERGON et PARERGON Fratrum R.C. Cabalistica deductio de Olÿmpo Terrae' already appeared without the illustration in Michael Maier, *Tractatus Posthumus sive Ulisses . . . Una cum annexis Tractatibus de Fraternitate Roseae Crucis*, Frankfurt, Lucas Jennis, 1624, 183–186.

[54] For the attitude of these and other spiritualists to the 'äußeren Buchstaben' of the Bible, cf. Carlos Gilly, *Das Sprichwort 'Die Gelehrten die Verkehrten' oder der Verrat der Intellektuellen im Zeitalter der Glaubensspaltung, Forme e destinazione del messaggio religioso. Aspetti della propaganda religiosa nel Cinquecento*, ed. by Antonio Rotondò, Florence 1991, 229–375, esp. 273–275, 284–289, 325–327. For Paracelsus cf. *Labyrinthus Medicorum errantium*, in Paracelsus, *Die Kärntner Schriften*, ed. by Kurt Goldammer, Klagenfurt, 1955, 108.

men, which we must allow to work in us freely, and listen, to what
God tells us inside of us.[55]

The living word of God, therefore, was for Haslmayr not to be found
in the 'external characters' of the Bible, but in the inner being of
Man. And at the same time also in all creatures in the world, since,
as he wrote in other places, 'all creatures' are 'the living incarnate
word FIAT of God' and 'all men have impressed in their hands the
signs with which to recognize the works of God'.[56]

Through practical, 'hands-on' experience, that is through the individual and immediate experience of things and not as a result of
mere speculation or an appeal to 'paper' authorities Haslmayr felt
the 'textus libri Naturae' could be deciphered and the 'Mysterium of
the word and the elements' could be solved. For just as the 'true'
followers of Christ were recognized, 'not for rhetorical discourse',
not for 'talking and preaching of God', 'not for making the sign of
the Cross', but for 'carrying the Cross' and for fulfilling the 'works
of Christ', so must he who wishes to be 'the follower of God and
Nature' prove himself through his own works.[57]

It was only deeds which mattered in this entire debate, as Haslmayr
demonstrated so explicitly by means of a quotation drawn from
Paracelsus: 'Note, therefore, dear reader, that he who is not tried
and proved in theology and in medicine through his works, has lost
his case and wins even less in arguing'.[58]

This caution applied to those physicians and philosophers whose
knowledge did not evolve from practical experience and experimental
discovery, but was only founded on the authorities of Antiquity; those
who with unbelievable arrogance and self-confidence declared the
sciences to be already complete and rounded off, and who cried out
for the henchman, if anyone but dared to question the sacrosanct

---

[55] [Adam Haslmayr], *Pansophia illuminati cuiusdam Viri, doraus die falschen Propheten,
Apostel vnd Schreiber vnserer lessen vnd gferlichen Zeitt, Im gaist- vnd welttlichem Statu gantz
aigentlich mögen erkanndt werden* (Wolfenbüttel, HAB, Ms. 60.1 Aug. 2°, ff. 256–290,
in Widemann's hand), 271f.

[56] [Adam Haslmayr], *Amphitheatrum Chimicum Sacrum, loc. cit.*, f. 211r; [Haslmayr],
Theologia Cabalistica de perfecto homine, in Paracelsus, *Philosophia Mystica*, Newstadt 1618,
loc. cit., 45; Haslmayr, *Philosophia Sagax von Heylung allerley Kranckheiten*, (Hannover,
Niedersächsische Landesbibliothek, Ms. IV, 341), 508.

[57] Haslmayr, *Oratio reuelatoria, loc. cit.*, 40r; [Haslmayr], *Pansophia*, 277.

[58] [Haslmayr], *Pansophia*, 273. Cf. also H. Rudolph, 'Einige Gesichtspunkte zum
Thema "Paracelsus und Luther"', 24, note 30.

authority of an Aristotle or a Galen. The caution also extended to the theologians of the several churches, who, priding themselves on their dogmatic confessions, engaged in bitter mutual controversies, persecuted dissidents, always seeking the patronage of the powerful or placing themselves at the helm of power.

The solution of the adherents of Paracelsus regarding theory and practice was quite different: Whether it concerned religion or science, for them counted 'the recognition of each thing from experience/ from action and feeling/ from the works of truth [. . .] because knowledge and learning flows forth from experience', as Johannes Arndt formulated it in the first of his *Vier Bücher vom Wahren Christentum*.[59] Thus many Paracelsists did not concern themselves overmuch with the dogmatic tenets and orthodox confessions of the theologians and in this sense belonged to those who surpassed not only the confessional confines of the existing churches, but also rejected and combatted the churches, pronouncing them to belong to 'external Christendom'.

This radical rejection of the 'churches of stone' and the advocacy of a church of the spirit, tied neither to 'external ceremonies' or certain 'places, cities or people' ('pure man is the temple', as Haslmayr put it once),[60] was something which not only Paracelsus, but also

---

[59] Johann Arndt, *Vier Bücher von wahrem Christenthumb [. . .] Das erste Buch*, Jena, Tobias Steinmann, 1907, 388 (book I, cap. 37). For Arndt and Paracelsus cf. Edmund Weber, *Johann Arndts Vier Bücher vom wahren Christentum als Beitrag zur protestantischen Irenik des 17. Jahrhunderts. Eine Quellenkritische Untersuchung*, Studia Irenica 2, Hildesheim, 1978; Gilly, *Zwischen Erfahrung und Spekulation*, Part 1, 97, 112–113; Gilly, *Iter Rosicrucianum*, 80; Hans Schneider, 'Johann Arndts Studienzeit', *Jahrbuch der Gesellschaft für Niedersächsische Kirchengeschichte*, 89, 1991, 133–176; Schneider, 'Johann Arndt als Lutheraner?', *Die lutherische Konfessionalisierung in Deutschland*, Schriften des Vereins für Reformationsgeschichte, 197, Gütersloh 1993, 274–298.

[60] *Ex Manuscripto eiusdem Viri illuminati* [Haslmayr] *de Baptismo Optime propter falsos Prophetas at Pseudoapostolos Vltimi Temporis notanda, qui salutem in externis ponunt et collocant contra Christum vnicam Veritatem.* (Wolfenbüttel, HAB, Ms. 60.1 Aug. 2°, ff. 290–302, in Widemann's hand): '[. . .] im armen Geist, alß der teütsche Edle Philosophus Christi Primus D.D. Theophrastus Eremita vnd andern ein Exempel ist, deme nun alle Nationen nach müessen wandlen vnd er aber nitt Inen nach, dorauff sich nuhn die wahre Theosophische Turba Fratrum R.C. (zue diser Lesten Römischen Monarchia herfürgeben dise ware Kirchen Christi wider einzuesetzen, wie sie zue der Apostelln Zeitten war) [. . .] Dise H[eilige] Kirche ist nicht gebunden (sagen sie) an eüsserlichen ceremonien, Ortt, stött oder Menschen, dann Christus da allain Haubt ist vnd bleibett inn Ewigkeitt; Pura mens ist der Tempel [. . .] die falschen Kirchen (1) ist ain sichtbare versamlung der Menschen (Weltmenschen) (2) Nicht auß Gott, (3) sonder auß der gailen Natur gebornen, (4) gebunden an gwisse Örter, Personen, Ceremonien inn (5) villfachen Secten, Rotteň zerrissen vnd zertailt (6) da Christus nicht das Haubt ist, sonder ettliche aufgeworffene Lehrer vnd

Weigel had stood for, and therefore it is logical, that Haslmayr in his *Pansophia* also promoted the minister of Zschopau to one of the chief teachers of the *'Theophrastia Sancta'* with the following words:

> Now you Romish and Protestant and you mercenary sectarians and all you factions, look at this complete *Büechlein vom gebett* by Weigel and *Informatorium* also (to lead you to the narrow path to Christ) and all other books of the 2 men most enlightened by the spirit of God, D[ominus] D[octor] Theophrastus Eremita Germanus et primus philosophus Christianorum and then M[agister] Valentin Weigel.

Both had aimed at one thing only, namely the divine word, which is hidden in all creatures and which forms the centre and life of all things. This in contrast to the 'so-called holy temple-lords', who of old have, in their 'bricked-up temples', 'extinguished and obscured' self-knowledge or 'holy Gnothi Seauton'.[61] For, 'if the Theophrastian works had been taught in the faculties of the universities in Christendom for the past 100 years instead of the pagan writings', Haslmayr fulminated in his anonymous 1619 *Pansophia illuminati cuiusdam Viri, doraus die falschen Propheten erkannt werden*, 'Magi or Theosophists' would now have been available, who would long since have managed to overcome the 'false teachers', namely 'the Pope, Luther, Calvin and their ilk', 'but when the haughty get up to rule and teach, the humble theosophers and the pious true Christians hide themselves'.[62]

Yet soon, or so Haslmayr hoped, referring to the *Fama Fraternitatis*, the era of the *'Gloria Dei intacta'* and the *'Evangelion Libertet'* would dawn, in which 'all classes and religions, factions and sects will meet', in order publicly to seek out these 'concealed theosophers'. And then the adherents of the Pope will have to confess: 'We, poor confused and far too clever Papists have trusted far too much in the alleged saints, who have abandoned the road of truth'. The Protestants, too, 'with all their followers' will confess publicly: 'And we, Lutherans of all sorts, have taken everything to be good and just and true, which the lascivious women's theologian Luther or Calvin or Zwingli or Flacius Illyricus, Hus, or the Anabaptists told us [. . .] and also fed ourselves with lies, no less than the Papists.[63]

Menschen alß Babst, Luther, Caluin, Zwingl, Flaccius, Tauffer vnd dergleichen etc. deren (7) was aigen nutz suecht (8) vnd das ewige Liecht nicht versteen auß dem Natürlichen Liecht'.

[61] [Haslmayr], *Pansophia*, 256, 272.
[62] *Ibid.*, 287.
[63] *Ibid.*, 287–88.

For Haslmayr at any rate the following was clear: not until the acknowledged and unacknowledged churches saw the errors of their ways and turned away from the false teachers, would the true Christian church of the prophets and apostles be established, being a church founded not 'on the rich Simon Magus, but on the poor holy Peter', not with walls of brick, but only 'built in the spirit'. Then 'the school of the Pentecost and the Olympian languages of all wise believers in Christ will stand open', so that the 'Latinists' and other 'cacosophists and world-learned Doctors' will not even 'be worthy to serve as stokers for the wise'. Then only 'the Theophrastia Sancta and the eternal Sophia will flourish and be made public'.[64]

---

[64] [Adam Haslmayr], *Theosophia Decretalis. Vom Weltlichen Regiment zue den stoltzen Fursten und Landen Vermanung vnd Prophecey inn 7 Reglen verfasst Auff die 7 Bitt des heiligen Vatter Vnser, Ahn die gantze Christenhait, sonderlich aber ahn die stoltze Fürsten vnd Landt, so sich halber nit kennen, auch nit bessern wollen*, [written in 1612, revised in 1627]. (Halle, Universitätsbibliothek, Ms. 22 E 7, 350–368, in Widemann's hand): 'In sollichem christlichen Leben befinden wir noch keinen Salomonem oder Hermetem, das ist keinen Kaiser oder König der Christenheit, die Iere vermeindtte Reichthumb oder zergenkhliche güetter nicht mitt Schaden wider die Lieb des Ne[ch]stens eroberett hetten, alß eben der groß Monarcha Paracelsus, stella signata christicolarum Sophorum, alß in seinen Büechern vber die Propheten vnd über die Büecher der Weißheit, vnd des Neüen testaments, sonderlich über die Psalmen Dauids vnd in den Secretis secretorum Theologiae, vnder andern vill 1000 seiner Monarchischen Büechern zue ersehen, Diser hatt gesehen, was der Neüe Willen Gottes vnd das *'nequaquam uacuum legis Iugum'* seÿ, wie auch die verborgenen Fratres Thëosophi vom Rosen Creütz werden tempore predestinato offenbaren' [. . .] 'Das ist das Studium Sapientiae aeternae Theophrastiae, darzue vns dann durch die Gnaden Gottes kaine Büecher manglen' [. . .] 'Was im Brott vnd inn allen creaturen sey, dise Arcana machen ine, Theophrastum, zum Monarcham der Smaragdischen Taffell vnd Neüen guldenen Ierusalem' . . . 'Eure vermaindtten Hoche Schuelen der 7 Secten oder freyen Künsten sollen dem Vulturno, ia dem nechsten lufft zuegeweichet vnd inn Rauch gehengkht werden vor allen Weisen Christi solt Ir ein Namenkappen sein [. . .] Eure edle Lateiner sollen wissen, die auch dardurch den Himmel versprochen vnd Ir inen Schuelen vnd Collegia gebauen vnd aufgerichtet, daß die Olympischen linguae, ia die Sprachen der Schuel des Pfingsttages, die Lehrer des h. Geistes, die Theophrastia, die ewige Sophia müesse floriern vnd offenbar werden, vnd sie eure Latiner sollen nicht wertth sein, calefactores der Weisen zue sein'; cf. also Adam Haslmayr, *Theologia intacta Mysteriarchae Theophrasti Eremitae germani, Darinn alle Irthumb, falsch, Lugen vnd Betrug der falschen selbst erwehlten, vngeschickhten, vnkundigten, Söldnerischen Apostel vnd betrüglich listigen Lehrer begriffen vnd angezeigt werden. Zur Fursehung auf dise gefehrlichste Letzte Zeit an Tag gegeben. 1622 etc. Mit wahren, gwaltigen, vnpartheÿschen, grundtlichen vnderricht, wie man die falschen Apostl, vnd Allen Betrug versehen vnd erkenen soll, auß Christi vnsers Erlösers Mundt selbsten. Jtem wie man seider seiner Himelforth biß hero solte gelebt haben, das wir vns der seeligen hoffnung in Glauben zu getrosten hetten zur gwißen Seelikeit. Auch wie man dan iezt, nach Reformation der ganzen Welt hinfort an wirt leben in Aller Welt Nationen, Sprachen vnd Völckern Mit kurzen, doch gruntlichen Argumenten niemant weiters von der Seelikeit verfhiert werde aufs einfeltigist furgestelt. V[on] einem Theophilo.* (Hannover Niedersächsische Landesbibliothek, Ms. I, 69 [alt 24], 1–16, Haslmayr's autograph).

Unfortunately there is no room to discuss the intensive religious contacts between the 'Catholic' Adam Haslmayr in Tyrol, the 'Lutheran' Karl Widemann in Augsburg and the 'Calvinist' Prince August von Anhalt in Plötzkau between 1611 and 1631. But it may be said of their mutual strategy for the propagation of the *'Sancta Theophrastia'*, that Haslmayr had been appointed to lead the secret printing press of August von Anhalt from the summer of 1611 onwards, in order to allow publication of the theological works of Paracelsus and also the works of Weigel. Because of Haslmayr's arrest and other adverse circumstances, only few works were actually produced by this secret printing press. Most of the works intended for publication had to be given to other publishers such as Cristoph Bismarck in Halle, Johann Francke in Magdeburg or Lucas Jennis in Frankfurt, who for a full decade supplied the German-speaking market even in the remotest corners with the books of the *'Theophrastia Sancta'*, that is with the editions of Weigel and Paracelsus, but also Lautensack, Egidius Gutmann, and, of course, Haslmayr himself. Widemann or August von Anhalt supplied the manuscripts for many of these editions, while Anhalt often also provided the funds for these undertakings.[65]

When August von Anhalt abandoned these hazardous activities in 1621 after having assumed responsibilty for affairs of state, Widemann and Haslmayr, who had returned from the galleys, attempted to win Duke August in Wolfenbüttel for the plan to publish further theological works of Paracelsus, 'Taulerian and Eckhardian books' and other 'Theological manuscripts ... against the errors and mistakes of the Papists, Lutherans, Calvinists' through the presses of the Stern brothers in Lüneburg. 'After all', Widemann wrote to Duke August, 'the works of Weigel and Arndt, too, have managed to evade the censorship of the theologians'.[66] However, the Duke immediately put a halt to this plan. He informed Widemann 'that the Theophrastian and Weigelian books are not allowed to be printed in these domains; as they would cause great confusion in our theology'.[67]

The theologians had already seen to it that the feared confusion

---

[65] More of this in Gilly, *Haslmayr*, 110ff. and 125ff.

[66] Widemann, Letter to Duke August, Augsburg, 29 and 17 June 1621: Wolfenbüttel HAB, Bibliotheksarchiv, letter by Widemann, [4r–5r].

[67] Duke August, letter to Hainhofer, Hitzacker, 16 June 1621, *Der Briefwechsel zwischen Philipp Hainhofer und Herzog August d.J. von Braunschweig-Lüneburg*, ed. by Roland Gobiet, München 1984, 334.

had been halted. The great number of Weigelian and Paracelsian editions had soon provoked a true avalanche of works by the orthodox theologians from the Lutheran and Reformed camps (the Catholics did not get involved, because to them this controversy was one between enemies and heretics anyway).[68]

The guardians of Lutheran orthodoxy in the German lands were the most vehement in their reactions. Because of the reading-public and market aimed at by these German-language works, they were justified in believing themselves the immediate target of the Theophrastic and Weigelian 'rubbish'. Furthermore, the majority of these 'seditious' books were by and by printed in Lutheran cities, without the theologians managing to prevent the publication of these works. All that was left for them to do, was to warn against the danger of this 'new and fanatical theology' in increasingly strong terms, and then to try to combat the damage already done with a plethora of rabid polemics. The Wittenberg minister Nicolas Hunnius, for instance, responded at first in Latin in his *Principia Theologiae Fanaticae, quae Paracelsus genuit atque Weigelius interpolavit* (1618), later in German in the *Christlicher Betrachtung der neuen Paracelsischen und Weigelianischen Theologie* (1622). The Halle minister Andreas Merck in the *Treuherzige Warnung vor dem Weigelianismo* (1620), the Hamburg theologian Johannes Schellhammer in the *Widerlegung der vermeinten Postill Weigelii* (1621), the Tübingen Professor Theodor Thumm in his *Impietas Weigeliana* (1622) and many others responded in similar fashion.[69]

As far as the response of the German Calvinists is concerned, it took them rather longer to refute the 'Weigelian errors', but they were more thorough in return, as is evident above all from the *Exercitationes Theologicae* by the Anhaltian Christian Beckmann, published

---

[68] Paracelsus himself had long since been placed on the index of prohibited books. Only during the inquisitorial trials against Johann Baptista van Helmont in Brussels in 1634 did Roman-Catholic theologians make a concerted effort to subject the teachings of Paracelsus to detailed censorship, cf. C. Broeckx, *Notice sur le manuscript Causa J.B. Helmontii, déposé aux Archives Archiépiscopales de Malines*, Annales de l'Académie Royale d'Archéologie de Belgique, 9, 1852, 277–327, 341–347; Robert Halleux, 'Helmontiana', *Academiae Analecta. Mededelingen van de Koninklijke Academie voor Wetenschappen, Letteren en Schone Kunsten van België*, 45, 1983, No. 3, 33–63, esp. 35–36 and 53–54.

[69] Julius Otto Opel, *Valentin Weigel. Ein Beitrag zur Literatur- und Kulturgeschichte Deutschlands im 17. Jahrhundert*, Leipzig 1864, esp. 70–120; Winfried Zeller, *Theologie und Frömmigkeit. Gesammelte Aufsätze*, ed. by Bernd Jaspert, Vol. 1 (Marburger Theologische Studien, 8), Marburg 1971, 51–84; Siegfried Wollgast, *Philosophie in Deutschland zwischen Reformation und Aufklärung 1550–1650*, Berlin 1988, 522–534.

in Amsterdam in 1641,[70] or the *Antiweigelius* of Johannes Crocius, printed in Kassel in 1652. However, there cannot have existed an initial sympathy, or even political complicity on the part of the Calvinists with the Rosicrucian and Weigelian movement (which many Lutheran theologians were only too happy to believe at the time, a fact which some historians even today cite as evidence).[71] Because it was precisely at the Reformed university of Marburg and at the

---

[70] Christian Beckmann, *Exercitationes Theologicae. In quibus De argumentis pro vera deitate Christi Servatoris nostri Contra Fausti Socini, Valentini Smalcii, Christophori Ostorodi, Ioannis Crellii Franci, et similium recentissimas molitiones: Ut et De argumentis pro vera humana Natura Christi ejusdem, Contra Mennonem Simonis, Theophrastum Paracelsum, Valentinum Weigelium, Paulum Felgenhauerum et alios huius notae*, Amsterdam 1642, 343–488. His great knowledge of then as yet unprinted theosophical works and his familiarity with dissident circles makes the Anhaltian theologian one of the best sources for the study of contemporary heterodox movements in Germany.

[71] This thesis, already put forward by Johann Salomo Semler, *Unparteiische Sammlungen zur Historie der Rosenkreuzer*, I, Leipzig 1786, 112, was recently presented by Frances A. Yates, *The Rosicrucian Enlightenment*, London 1972, as her own discovery and subsequently it obtained wide acceptance. In order to supplement the rather flimsy documentation adduced by Yates to underpin her thesis, I could mention numerous political pamphlets, prophecies and songs or works by participants in the Rosicrucian debate (Johannes Plaustrarius, Paul Nagel, Paul Felgenhauer, Philipp Ziegler, Isaac Habrecht, 'Johannes Germanus', Johannes von Röhrig, Wilhelm Eo, Irenäus Heiland, Simon Partlicius, Gottfried von Schwanbach and even Widemann or Haslmayr), in which from 1618 onwards the cause of the Elector Palatine and King of Bohemia Frederick V is advanced and which have been completely ignored by Yates. Most of these men would have supported any other prince who would have opposed the growing power of the Habsburgs and the Jesuits in Central Europe. However, this late spate of publicity, which made propagandistic capital out of the 'prophecy of the lion from the north', and even the *Fama* of the Rosicrucians, in support of the policy of Frederick V of the Palatinate or the glory of Gustav Adolph of Sweden, did not play any role in the origin of the Rosicrucian movement. On the contrary: in 1605 Tobias Hess for instance saw in Duke Frederick of Wurttemberg the political promotor of the future world reformation, while Haslmayr did all he could to persuade his protector Prince August von Anhalt to take on this part. The latter declined in a letter dated 5 June 1612 with the words: 'Wenn ich der leo [der Löwe aus Mitternacht] sein solt, so würde die liebe posteritet ubel versogt sein'. The court at Heidelberg was hardly interested in the Rosicrucians; if at all, it condemned them, as did for instance the influential Palatine theologian Abraham Scultetus under the pseudonym Matthias Ehinger 1623: *Iudicium De fundamentis, quibus in praedictionibus suis utuntur NOVI PROPHETAE in Germania, Nagelius, Zieglerus, Geigerus, Plaustrarius, Praetorius, Stifelius, Faulhaberus, Wilhelmus Eo, alij, Coloniae* [Berlin] 1623, or in German: *Bedencken vnd Vrtheil MATTHIAE EHENGERI, Von den fürnehmen gründen/ derer sich in Jhren weissagungen dick vnd offt gebrauchen Die NEWE PROPHETEN Jn Deudschland/ Nagelius, Ziegler, Geiger, Felgenhawer/ Praetorius, Stifel, Faulhaber/ Wilhelm Eo, vnd andre Fladder vnd Wirgeistere.* Erstlich Gedruckt im Latein zu Cöln [Berlin] Anno M. DC. XXIV. For the identification of 'M. Ehinger' with A. Scultetus cf. Caspar Landorpius, *Acta Publica*, Second Part, Frankfurt 1630, 292–295.

command of the Calvinist Landgrave Moritz von Hessen-Kassel that the first, and also normative, inquisitorial trials in Germany against the Rosicrucian, Weigelian and other errors of 'the Theophrastic sort' were conducted in the years 1619–1620.[72]

In Marburg, for instance, the son-in-law of the printer of the Rosicrucian Manifestos, Philipp Homagius, was sentenced to life imprisonment in a fortress town on the charge of having recommended and propagated the works of the 'excellent and enlightened essential theologians Weigel and Theophrastus' as the keys to the understanding of Holy Scripture; he also praised the Rosicrucians as 'true and highly enlightened perfect Christians' and 'had held them in a higher esteem than he could express in words'; and had thus shown himself to be one of their faithful adherents: 'the Brothers of the Rosicrucian Fraternity', Homagius declared, 'and the followers of Theophrastus and Weigel agree in the fundamental articles of faith, although one reached a higher degree of faith than the other'.[73]

---

[72] Karl W.H. Hochhut, 'Mittheilungen aus der protestantischen Secten-Geschichte in der Hessischen Kirche, Vierte Abtheilung: Die Weigelianer und Rosenkreuzer', *Zeitschrift für die Historische Theologie*, NF 26, 1862, 86–159; NF 27, 1863, 169–262; NF 28, 1864, 301–315. The original documents of Homagius's trial are deposited in Marburg, Hessisches Hauptstaatsarchiv, 4i N 235 (402 leaves); contemporary copies of the interrogations of Homagius and his co-defendant Georg Zimmermann are also available in Darmstadt, Gießen, Lüneburg, Schleswig and Wolfenbüttel. Three years after this Marburg trial an 'Inquisition über Rosenkreuzerei und weigelianische Schwärmerei' was also instituted at the Lutheran university of Gießen against Heinrich Nollius because of his Rosicrucian work *Parergi Philosophici Speculum*, Gießen 1623, because whatever was right for the alchemy enthusiast Landgrave Moritz von Hessen-Kassel, was certainly proper for Landgrave Ludwig von Hessen-Darmstadt, who was hostile to alchemy, cf. Heinrich Klenk, 'Ein sogenannter Inquisitionsprozess in Gießen anno 1623', *Mitteilungen des Oberhessischen Geschichtsvereins*, NF 49/50, 1965, 39–60. The relevant original documents are partly deposited in Gießen, Universitätsbibliothek, Universitätsarchiv, Allg. B15, Allg. 98 and 99 (1183 leaves), partly in Darmstadt, Hessisches Hauptstaatsarchiv, Abteilung 6 1, Gießen, Konv. 19, Fasc. 7; Abt. 5 A1, Konv. 41, Fasc. 9. Both trials will be dealt with at length in my forthcoming bibliography of the early Rosicrucians.

[73] The outcome of the Marburg trial is well-known. Zimmermann, who made a show of remorse, was banished. Homagius on the other hand, who insisted in his advocacy of Paracelsus, Weigel and the Rosicrucians, was sentenced to 'eternal imprisonment' on the express order of Landgrave Moritz. Quite misleading in this context is Bruce T. Moran, *The alchemical world of the German court. Occult philosophy and chemical medicine in the circle of Moritz of Hessen (1572–1632)* Sudhoffs Archiv, Beiheft 29, Stuttgart 1991, 128ff. Moran incomprehensibly placed the Marburg trial against Homagius in Rostock ('one Philipp Homagius who had already been condemned in Rostock as a seditious hereticus') and concentrated solely on the Gießen trial against Nollius, in order to polish up the brilliance of the 'hermetical patronage' of Moritz of Hessen: 'How different were the intellectual sympathies of the Kassel court! There, what was condemned at Giessen reigned as official

The orthodox theologians knew very well who had been responsible for the errors for which Weigel was being denounced: it was Paracelsus. Each, after his own strength, was concerned to reiterate and, where possible, to surpass in separate chapters the slanders and taunts against Paracelsus which had been collected since the days of Oporinus and Erastus. As scholars steeped in theology they were, however, wise enough not to get involved in the medical and natural philosophical arena, and so they fulminated in particular against their apostate colleague Weigel, whose theological terminology was probably more easily accessible to them.

That is why these opponents all liked to speak of Weigelianism rather than Theophrastia or Paracelsism, which could have led to misunderstandings amongst the medical profession and other professional groups, because the merits of Paracelsus 'in physics, in chemistry and in the medical art', as Christian Beckmann conceded, could not but be acknowledged even by the theologians.

Thus 'Weigelianism' was an invention of the theologians, who styled it the chief-heresy of the seventeenth century in Germany ('unde factum est, ut Religionem Fanaticam nostra aetas vocare coeperit VVeigelianam'),[74] although from a historical viewpoint—and this in contrast to the fol-

---

philosophy. In Moritz's circle, Noll's Rosicrucian essays amounted to standard fare in the court's hermetic-alchemical diet. Neither were his Paracelsian interpretations, at least as they related to medicine and alchemy, in any way eccentric to the court's intellectual and religious views. Rather, as we shall see next, they took a place beside other uses of Paracelsian natural philosophy that served diverse alchemical, magical, and religious court interests'.

[74] Balthasar Meisner, *In Systematis theologici partem primam generalem De Religione et ejus articulis [. . .] Disputatio XVI. De Religione Fanatica [. . .]* [respondit] Johann Spleiß, Wittenberg 1626, a2v: 'Hinc quoque est, quod Religio haec a Paracelso *Paracelsica* inscribitur [. . .] 'Non ausus vero fuit Paracelsus dum esset in vivis, bellum suum foetum quem parturiebat, in Ecclesiae sinum promere, quamvis non raro dicere solitus feratur, se aliquando Lutherum et Melanthonem in Theologia non aliter reformaturum, atque fecerit in Medicina Galeno et Hippocrati. Itaque praeceptoris sui Theophrasti opera usus M. Valentinus VVeigelius, hyperaspistes illius acerrimus, in homiliis suis super Evangelis Dominicalia, in Dialogo de Christianismo, in Gnothi seauton et hujus furfuris libellis aliis hoc mysterium iniquitatis abunde nobis revelavit. Unde factum est, ut Religionem Fanaticam nostra aetas vocare coeperit VVeigelianam'. For the central role awarded to Weigelianism by the orthodox historiographers, cf. Johann Georg Walch, *Historische und Theologische Einleitung in die Religions-Streitigkeiten außer der Evangelisch-Lutherischen Kirche*, Jena 1733–1736 (Facsimile reprint Stuttgart-Bad Canstatt 1985), IV.2, 1024–1090. Walch, who bibliographically recorded a great number of Weigelian and anti-Weigelian books, did not hesitate to begin the relevant chapter with the words: 'Unter den Fanaticis, welche sonderlich in Deutschland bekannt worden, sind die Weigelianer als die Vornehmsten mit anzusehen'.

lowers of Schwenckfeld, Paracelsus, Jacob Böhme or even Johannes Arndt—hardly anybody in the baroque era considered or called himself a Weigelian.

Abraham von Franckenberg hit the mark when in 1637 he gave his epochal work on the correspondences between the teachings of the ancient gnosis and the views of his co-religionists the significant title *Theophrastia Valentiniana*. The adjective 'Valentiniana' here stands for the gnostic heretic Valentinus from the first century after Christ, while the substantive noun 'Theophrastia' was meant to denote the newly founded spiritual and theosophical movements of the late sixteenth and early seventeenth centuries, which with this designation were led back to their real origin, to Paracelsus.

Paracelsus, therefore, was very prescient, when he wrote a hundred years earlier in his book *Paragranum*: 'I will give Luther and you some work to do!'[75]

---

* Translated from German by Cis van Heertum, Bibliotheca Philosophica Hermetica, Amsterdam.

[75] [Abraham von Frankenberg], *Theophrastia Valentiniana. Das ist: Ein unpartheyischer Schrifft- und Naturmässiger Bericht Über ein Fragmentum Von der Lehre Valentini, genommen aus einem Büchlein, Welches durch Gerhardum Lorichium Anno 1540 zu Cölln ediret, Und Vallum Religionis Catholicae intituliret*, Im Jahre Christi 1703, Gottfried Arnold, *Supplementa der Kirchen-Historie*, Frankfurt 1703, 10–48; also printed in the later editions of Arnold's *Unpartheiischer Kirchen- und Ketzer-Historie*. Cf. Gilly, *Das Bekenntnis zur Gnosis von Paracelsus bis auf die Schüler Jacob Böhmes* 425–32.

CHAPTER EIGHT

HOHENHEIM'S ANTHROPOLOGY IN THE LIGHT OF HIS WRITINGS ON THE EUCHARIST*

Hartmut Rudolph

Hohenheim set down or expressed his conceptions of the Eucharist (the Last Supper)[1] in over twenty separate (in part exegetical) texts; some of these belong to his extensive commentaries on Scripture; but others are in fact included in the first division of the Sudhoff edition among the works designated there as *'naturphilosophische Schriften'* ('writings on natural philosophy').[2] In view of the significance of this theme within the works as a whole it is no wonder that modern scholarship on Paracelsus has shown considerable interest (relatively speaking) in the texts on the Eucharist—some already printed as a group (in Magdeburg) by 1618[3]—and has given them, their fair share of critical analysis. Heinrich Bornkamm went into the subject as early as 1932.[4] Stefan Török took up, as one topic, Hohenheim's conception of this sacrament in his dissertation of 1946—a piece of work which has unfortunately attracted far too little notice.[5] Neither of these scholars, to be sure, had recourse to the relevant writings of

---

[1] I dedicate this essay to Dr. Marijn de Kroon, for many years my colleague at the Bucer Research Centre in Münster (Westphalia); I am grateful to him for the productive work we shared, in friendship, while dealing with Martin Bucer's German writings. His Eucharistic texts (1534–37) made up a large part of our common endeavour, which bore the stamp of de Kroon's wealth of experience and sublime knowledge of the theology of the Strasbourg Reformer.

[2] Theophrast von Hohenheim gen. Paracelsus, *Sämtliche Werke. 1. Abteilung. Medizinische, naturwissenschaftliche und philosophische Schriften,* ed. Karl Sudhoff, 14 volumes, Munich and Berlin 1922–33. Further references to this edition will be identified by the Arabic numeral 1, followed by a virgule, the Roman numeral of the volume cited, and the page number(s). Analogous hereto: Theophrast von Hohenheim genannt Paracelsus, *Sämtliche Werke. 2. Abteilung. Theologische und religionsphilosophische Schriften,* ed. Kurt Goldammer, Wiesbaden 1955–.

[3] Paracelsus, *Philosophia de limbo aeterno perpetuoque homine novo secundae creationis ex Iesu Christo Dei filio,* ed. Johannes Stariz, [Magdeburg] 1618.

[4] Heinrich Bornkamm, 'Äußerer und innerer Mensch bei Luther und den Spiritualisten', in *Imago Dei, Festschrift für Gustav Krüger,* Gießen, 1932, 85–109.

[5] Stephan Török, *Die Religionsphilosophie des Paracelsus und ihr zeitgeschichtlicher Hintergrund,* Theol. diss., Vienna 1946.

Paracelsus still unpublished at the time. Then Kurt Goldammer, with the entire Paracelsian corpus at his disposal, turned his attention to Hohenheim's sacramental conception and wrote on it repeatedly.[6] Michael Bunners's dissertation for the Humboldt University (published in East Berlin in 1961) was the first to be devoted exclusively to the topic in question.[7] He himself saw—though without realizing the full implications of the matter—that the designation 'writings on the Eucharist', taken as it is from theology, does not necessarily do justice to the substance of the texts it is used to denote.[8] Witness Paracelsus's own term for a group of these writings as announced in the so-called *'Prologus et initium voluminis limbi aeterni'*: *'volumen von der untötlichen philosophei'* ('volume on immortal philosophy').[9] The above mentioned collection of eucharistic texts from 1618 employs the general heading *'Philosophia de limbo aeterno perpetuoque homine novo secundae creationis ex Iesu Christo Dei Filio'*. This points up for the interpreter the connection with Hohenheim's 'philosophy', i.e., the *Philosophia sagax der großen und kleinen Welt* ('Philosophia sagax of the Macro- and the Microcosm'; 1/XII)—to borrow the title of his philosophical magnum opus; this link may serve as a pathway to an understanding of the so-called eucharistic writings.

It is my intention to take a few steps along this pathway. First, however, a few remarks are in order to determine the position of Paracelsian theology in the theological spectrum of his day; it is generally known, after all, that, when it comes to placing a writer of the Reformation period, his understanding of the sacrament of the Eucharist is a particularly useful gauge.

It can be safely assumed that the greater part of the texts dealing with the Eucharist go back to the early 1530's. In the case of the extensive piece on the Lord's Supper, *'De coena Domini ad Clementem VII'*,[10] the death of this pope (1532) gives us the terminus *post quem*

---

[6] Cf. in particular Kurt Goldammer, 'Paracelsische Eschatologie I: Die Grundlagen (1948)', in: Kurt Goldammer, *Paracelsus in neuen Horizonten: Gesammelte Aufsätze* [hereafter: *Horizonte*], Vienna: Verband der wissenschaftlichen Gesellschaften Österreichs, 1986), 87–122; *idem*, 'Das Menschenbild des Paracelsus zwischen theologischer Tradition, Mythologie und Naturwissenschaft (1967)', in: *Horizonte*, 209–28.

[7] Michael Bunners, *Die Abendmahlsschriften und das medizinisch-naturphilosophische Werk des Paracelsus*, Theol. diss., Berlin/DDR, 1961.

[8] Bunners, *Abendmahlsschriften* 15f. and 64.

[9] Leiden University Library, Codex Vossianus Chymicus in F° 24 [cited hereafter as L₁], fol. 7ʳ.

[10] L₁, 162ᵛ–193ʳ. This text is dated 1530 in the dedication; on this cf. Karl Sudhoff, *Versuch einer Kritik der Echtheid der Paracelsischen Schriften*. Part II, Berlin 1899, 331f.

non. At this time—especially in the wake of the Speyer Diet of 1529, the formation of the Schmalkaldic League, and the Diet of Augsburg of 1530—the controversy over the proper understanding of the sacrament, in particular the question of the real presence of Christ in the bread and wine, went far beyond the internal interests of the Church to the point of shaping discussion of political alliances in the German-speaking world. (I refer to the debates on the Eucharist, starting around 1525, which were conducted with increasing acrimony between Luther and his followers on the one hand and Oecolampadius, Zwingli, and theologians in South Germany, especially Bucer, on the other.)

In the attempt to determine Hohenheim's place in the denominational spectrum at the time, one can find clues not only in the still largely unpublished theological writings from the beginning of the 1530's but also in early drafts (from the same period) of *'Die Bücher von den unsichtbaren Krankheiten'* ('The Books on Invisible Diseases'), a work with immense significance for Paracelsian theology. (The specific text in question is called *'Fragmentum libri de morbis ex incantationibus et impressionibus inferioribus, das ist von den unsichtbaren krankheiten'*.) Here, initially in the context of a discussion of superstition, Paracelsus takes up the Last Supper (*'nachtmal Christi'*), expressly rejecting the elevation of the Host. This is, he says (perhaps recalling his own early childhood in Einsiedeln), 'lovelier, prettier, more delightful, and finer' (*'schöner, hüpscher, lieblicher und feiner'*) than simply sitting down at a table as Christ did; but given such a 'pretty arrangement' (*'hüpsche ordnung'*), magic, witchcraft, and prognostication by augury can creep in (1/IX, 355). Paracelsus then quotes a version of the proverb on the perversity of the learned (it can also be found in Sebastian Franck's *Paradoxa*), *'je gelerter, je verkerter'* ('the more learned, the more mixed up').[11] It may be that this proverb is not just meant as a jibe against scholastic sophistry: it could also be aimed at the theological controversies within Protestantism in those years—interpreting Paracelsus's comments on the proverb as saying, 'faith does not need learning or wisdom, only simplicity, in which it is to go on its way quite undeterred' (*'dan der glaube [be]darf keiner gelerten, weisheit; nur einfalt und in derselbigen straks onverrukt wandlen'*) (1/IX, 355). Somewhat later Paracelsus discusses the phenomenon that a mummy (i.e., a

---

[11] On this cf. Carlos Gilly, Adam Haslmayr. *Der erste Verkünder der Manifeste der Rosenkreuzer*, Amsterdam 1994.

corpse buried in the earth) can attract the sick like a magnet and produce miracles of healing with them. In such cases people think they are dealing with a saint, and precisely this belief alone is what cures them. For Paracelsus this, on the one hand, is a natural process, explicable, in his words, by the 'philosophy of the corpse' (*'philosophei der toten leichnam'*) (1/IX, 363f., with reference to Matthew 10:1); in this connection on the other hand he sees himself obliged, however reluctantly (*'wiewol es gar heftig eindringt uber mein furnemen'*, 1/IX, 364), to launch into an excursus on the Last Supper. He starts—once more the opponent of the Roman Catholic idea of Transubstantiation—with an allusion (so typical for the times) to cockroaches gobbling up the leftovers of the priest's consecration. But Paracelsus moves on to his concern to differentiate the remains of deceased saints, or relics regarded, say, as a target for pilgrimage, from the body and blood of Christ offered in the Eucharist. Saints' relics, as accords with their effectiveness, are natural phenomena; they pertain to and involve natural man. To differentiate these phenomena from the Eucharist viewed as a supernatural event Paracelsus employs in an unmistakable way the arguments and terminology used by the South Germans and the Swiss (Bucer, Oecolampadius, and Zwingli), in their disputes with Luther noting that God gave his body and blood (insert: exclusively) to *his disciples*. There is no transformation, no 'show' (*'nichts wird furgemacht'*); what is eaten (that is to say the elemental bread and wine) is enclosed by the mouth and digested in a natural way. The body and blood of Christ on the other hand are relished in faith (Latinized that would be Augustine's *frui*), a formulation much in favour for use against the Wittenberg theologians. This is also true of making the presence of the body and blood of Christ depend on faith (Paracelsus speaks of the 'body in/through faith'—*'glaubisch leip'*, 1/IX, 365); similarly with the aligning with the soul here. The soul, and not the body, of the Christian, is the recipient of the body and blood of Christ. Further indications of this kind can be found in *'De coena domini ad Clementem VII'*; thus when Paracelsus writes that the food of Christ is 'no fill for the belly'—*'kein bauchfülle'* (L₁, 170ᵛ–171ʳ; on 179ᵛ his word for the Eucharist is 'a congregation's memorial meal, not fill for the belly'; one is reminded of Bucer's standing formula in this regard, likewise negated: *'Bauchspeise'* or *'Pastete'* ('food for the stomach'/'pâté'). Another parallel found in the argument derives from the frequent reference to John 6; in fact, when it comes to the Eucharist, Paracelsus is capable of giving

John 6, which the Lutherans viewed as irrelevant to an understanding of the Last Supper, preference over the Synoptic Gospels in its role as 'elucidator of the other Gospels' (*'erklärer der andern evangelien'*) (L₁, 170ʳ). In the same text he speaks out against the idea of sacrifice basic to a mass; this is nothing but an 'idolatrous operation' (*'Götzen-arbeit'*, L₁, 178ᵛ). He inveighs against organ music and singing, as well as against the altar ('let the heart alone be our table', L₁, 179ʳ). In a later passage Paracelsus employs the expression *'tropi und figuren'*; these are brought in by Oecolampadius and Zwingli in interpreting the words of institution (*'hoc est corpus meum'*, Matthew 26:26); however, Paracelsus's usage is uniquely characteristic, which is to say that it is directed at differentiating the natural understanding at the disposal of all men from the faith required for comprehending properly the secret of the Last Supper; that is, in another Paracelsian formulation, the light of the eternal and of the spirit (L₁, 186). But with this it is clear where the line is to be drawn in such a textual anatomy, in a quest of this kind for parallels to positions in controversies of the day. And Paracelsus himself, at least in regard to the 'ordnung' of the Eucharist, expressly rejects a sectarian stand: *'darin bin ich unparteiisch'* ('in this I am not a partisan', 167ᵛ). His reservations vis-à-vis the liturgical conduct of the Roman mass are nonetheless indisputable; yet he also appears to want to detach himself from spiritualizing and rationalizing modes of argument (the reasons for this will be touched on in a later place), as when, in what is called his 'First' *Matthäus-Kommentar*, he elucidates Matthew 26:26 by adding, *'das ich in der Hand habe'* ('which I have in my hand')[12]— surely a remark that can only be directed against Karlstadt's 'hoc'-interpretation.

The above attempts at positioning Paracelsus among the denominations must certainly not be given undue importance or be extended as a generalization. For me, they simply permit me to conclude that, in a certain phase of his development, Paracelsus drew close to the position taken by Reformed theology in Switzerland; this we know, incidentally, from other witnesses as well, above all the dedication (dated 26 August 1531) of the tract on a recent comet (1/IX, 373). This seeming proximity to the Swiss Reformation was but an episode; it is not characteristic of Hohenheim's theology as a whole. Other writings on the Eucharist also contain statements that enable us to

---

[12] Leiden University Library, Codex Vossianus Chymicus in F° 25, fol. 104v.

define Paracelsus's denominational place (e.g., '*Modus misse summa dei sacramentorum*', L₁, 72ff.). Different things are at stake here—if only for the reason that the '*nachtmal*', Paracelsus notes, is not to be celebrated every day or week or month, but rather once a year (on Maundy Thursday?) as a memorial meal: '*dann es ligt nit am fressen alle tag, es ligt an der frucht [. . .] dieselbig frucht sol für und für das ganze jar bleiben und bis in tod nit von uns weichen*' (L₁, 77^{r-v}) ('for what is of concern is not feasting day after day, but rather the fruit [. . .] this selfsame fruit is meant to remain on and on through the whole year, and not depart from us till death'). To sort out such statements in accordance with discussions carried on at the time by theologians of the various church groups and to match them denominationally makes little sense; indeed, putting it more trenchantly, such a procedure is, methodologically, extremely dubious. With his '*philosophia de limbo aeterno*' Paracelsus pursues an interest which is not replicated in these disputatory exchanges; it is, rather, one which aims at an image of Man also identifiable from his writings on medicine and natural philosophy; and it finds its correspondence, or certain definite parallels, in Renaissance philosophers far more readily than in the theologies of Zwingli or Bucer, or Luther or Eck. Two successive steps may now serve to sketch in this point. The first entails an explanation of the basic characteristics of Hohenheim's picture of the Eucharist, with attention to its relationship to his natural philosophy (special consideration being given here to his concept of the limbus); this will be followed by an attempt to place the Eucharistic writings in the Paracelsian oeuvre as a whole.

I

Paracelsus's reflections have two essential guidelines (which are mentioned repeatedly): 1) Nothing goes to heaven which is not from heaven. 2) Man is to go to heaven bodily. The first statement leads to the theory of the two bodies; the second concerns the continuity of the person on earth and in heaven. The body of natural man, born from the seed of Adam or—to take up the central concept still to be explained later—born from the limbus of Adam, is mortal; for Paracelsus this means, without flinching from the cold facts, that the body will become a feast for worms and be totally metamorphosed back into what it came from. By contrast, the eternal body, born from the spirit of God, the limbus of Abraham, of Christ, or of Maria, is immortal and, 'clarified' as a transfigured (*'clarifizirter'*) body, will repair to its place of origin, heaven. This process alone answers to the anthropological targeting which God had set in creating man. According to the plan, Man, as a being born from the spirit of God (Genesis 2:7), was meant to remain forever in the unity resulting from God's marrying body and soul.[13] But with the Fall this marriage was smashed to pieces, so that a new marriage was required through the agency of the Son of God, who gives the soul an immortal body. This is born out of the heavenly limbus. Paracelsus's terminology, the new birth, the new creature, is biblical. This process is completed in baptism, which thus becomes the indispensable precondition of immortal life. Just as the Adamic-earthly man metabolizes the fruits of the earth by digestion into mortal flesh and blood and in this fashion grows, so, too, the heavenly body grows by its being nourished from the heavenly manna, the body and blood of Christ, which sometimes can be called the spirit of God or the word of Christ. It is precisely here, from this analogy, that Paracelsus interprets the Last Supper and derives its essentiality for salvation. The fullness and complexity of the forms of his argumentation (this is, incidentally, not integrated) grows out of the tension which consists on the one hand in the spiritual origin of this heavenly birth and its nourishment (that is to say, its origin in the spirit of God) and, on the other hand, in the attempt nonetheless to elucidate the mysterious happening of the birth and the growth of the new creature from the *limbus aeternus* as a *bodily* process, indeed, to explain it as a *comprehensible* process by forming an analogy with natural reason, with natural-Adamic corporeality. Paracelsus sees himself quite expressly as a successor to the Apostle Thomas, who, so to speak, puts the heavenly-clarified body of Christ which has appeared to him to the test (John 20:24ff.); *'ein greiflich prob'* ('a tactile test'), i.e. proving by sensory experience, is possible and necessary.[14] For Paracelsus this represents, as does all cognition in the light of nature in general, an essential element of faith.

Several observations on the term *limbus* are necessary here, as this concept could offer a key to elucidate the question at hand. Up till now I have not succeeded in proving that the term limbus was in

---

[13] *'De coena Domini ad Clementem VII'*, L₁, 164ᵛ.
[14] *'Von den miraculen und zeichen'* ('On miracles and signs'), L₁, 142ᵛ.

use before Paracelsus in his sense; such a proof would naturally call
for a re-examination of Goldammer's thesis that the concept was
created by Paracelsus.[15] The dictionaries are no help, since the ancient
meanings of limbus, for example Varro's use of the word to mean
the Zodiacal circle, are too remote in their applications.[16] The pre-
dominant meaning of 'limbus' is 'border', 'fringe', 'hem', which
led to its use in the sense of (the English) limbo, 'Vorhölle' ('vesti-
bule of hell'), first recorded in topographical writings on the Hereafter from scholastic theology: 'limbus patrum' stands for the place
where the patriarchs of the Old Testament are gathered until the
general resurrection in expectation of eternal bliss; 'limbus infantium'
is similar: the place for unbaptized infants who have died without
any actual sin.[17] This usage is not found in Paracelsus, not even
when he is addressing this very matter (e.g., 1/XII, 311). The attempt

---

[15] Cf. Kurt Goldammer, 'Die Paracelsische Kosmologie und Materietheorie in
ihrer wissenschaftlichen Stellung und Eigenart', 1971, *Horizonte*, 288–320 (here 299):
'Wort und Idee [scil. "limbus" as term and concept] sind eine Neubildung und
Eigengut Hohenheims.' Similarly in 'Paracelsische Eschatologie I: Die Grundlagen,
1948', *Horizonte*, 120, n. 116, Goldammer, adducing Genesis 2:7 ('limus terrae'),
takes the concept of limbus as being derived from the word 'limus' (Latin for
'Schlamm' ['mud']), thus 'related to the German Lehm, Leim'; he holds any connection with the Latin 'limbus' in the sense of 'edge' or 'border' to be 'scarcely
probable' at best.

[16] Cf. *Thesavrvs lingvae latinae*, vol. VII,2,2: 170–79, col. 1402f.—M. Terentius
Varro, *Rerum rusticarum libri tres* (lib. II,III,7), is certainly not a putative source for
Hohenheim's limbus concept despite the basic proximity of Varro's world view,
namely a (macrocosmic) correspondence between astrology and cattle breeding: '[. . .]
harum [scil. caprarum] enim dentes inimici sationi[s], quas extra lembum duodecim
signorum excluserint; sunt duo haedi et capra non longe a tauro', ed. G. Goetz,
Leipzig, 1912, 83.—Likewise, Jerome's use of the concept of limbus—*Commentariorvm
in Matthevm liber IV* (on Matthew 27:27) (Corpus Christianorum ser. lat. LXXVII
[Turnhout, 1969], 268)—must be ruled out as a possible source, regrettably so,
since Paracelsus must have known biblical exegeses by the Church Father; one can
instance the fact that, according to the *Inventarium* drawn up by the notary Kalbsohr,
the scanty effects left by Paracelsus at his death in Salzburg included 'Interpretationes
Hieronymi super Euang. in duobus libellis [. . .]' (Will-Erich Peuckert, *Theophrastus
Paracelsus*, Stuttgart and Berlin 1941, 469).

[17] Cf. J. de Mahuet, article 'Limbes', *Catholicisme*, 7, cols. 792–800; M. Laarmann,
article 'Limbus patrum/L. puerorum', *Lexikon des Mittelalters*, V, Munich and Zurich
1991, col. 1990f.—H.M. Nobis, article 'Limbus', *Historisches Wörterbuch der Philosophie*,
col. 328f., refers, on the one hand, to Paracelsus, in whose 'doctrine of an analogy
between the micro- and the macrocosm' limbus becomes 'a central concept', and,
on the other, to Jacob Boehme, with whom the concept has 'taken on' a 'particular theological and philosophical significance'. For the analysis of the reception of
the ideas of Paracelsus by the Upper Lusatian philosopher (the connection has been
known for some time) much could be gained from a corresponding investigation
into each thinker's ideas of 'limbus'.

to derive his usage from this semantic complex[18] is unconvincing. The medieval concept is also present in Dante's *Commedia* (it may be noted in passing that several important motifs in the *Commedia* recur in Hohenheim's theology).[19] As well, there seem to be indications in the *Commedia* that the concept has acquired an anthropological-ethical import going beyond its associations with the history of salvation and with topography (as known from Thomas Aquinas).[20] In Paracelsus the term seems close to *'lehm'*, the Low and Middle German equivalents to the High German *'leimen'*, *'leim'*, whose root Paracelsus himself possibly derives from 'limus' (Genesis 2:7: *formavit deus hominem de limo terrae'*); or it is a synonym of 'seed' (*'Samen'*).[21]

If one follows the chronology established by Sudhoff, the first use of the term limbus is in *'Liber de podagricis'*, from the early 1520's. The context is one of theory of knowledge. Paracelsus is discussing the prerequisites for the proper art of the physician. Academic medicine (especially the teachings of Avicenna, Galen, and Hippocrates), innate facility, and experiences do not make a perfect physician. The requirement for achieving this is, rather, the 'things which deal with the philosophy and the astronomy of both worlds' (*'ding, so philosophia*

---

[18] Cf. Kurt Goldammer, 'Bemerkungen zur Struktur des Kosmos und der Materie bei Paracelsus', (1971), *Horizonte*, 263–87 (here 282f., n. 34).

[19] At the very least the two figures meet in their radical criticism of the official church of their respective times, a critical position indebted to views passed on by the spiritual Franciscans: the demand for complete poverty and the renunciation of claims to secular power. As with Paracelsus, so with Dante the high officials of the church can become 'ravening wolves'. Over and above that one could look into a possible parallelism between Dante's *nobilità* and Hohenheim's *'adelikeit der zweifüßigen'* ('nobility of the bipeds'), attributable to Christ's having 'been of our sect' (*'unserer secten gewesen'*) and having 'taken on our form' (*'unser form angenommen'*; 1/I, 248f.); and one might investigate a possible correspondence in the concept of *liberalitas*, to which Paracelsus devoted a treatise of his own (*'De felici liberalitate'*). It is striking that Hohenheim, in *'De cena domini prologus et initium'* (L₁, 3f.), refers quite positively to Virgil. Perhaps correspondences could also be established in the concept of 'monarchia', so important for both men. Granted, in all of this it is still a question of very vague observations. What is unquestioned, of course, is that both writers draw, at least in part, on the same traditions. On Dante cf. R. Imbach and J.D. North, article 'Dante Alighieri V. und VI.', *Lexikon des Mittelalters*, III, cols. 553–59.

[20] Cf. the reference in Fausto Montanari, article 'Limbo', *Enciclopedia Dantesca*, 3, 651–54 (here 653), to the *'esaltazione della natura umana in generale, dove l'individualità viene a essere assorbita dalla categoria'*.

[21] As early as in his article on Paracelsian eschatology, 1948 (see n. 6, above) Goldammer advanced such a derivation for 'limbus' (*Horizonte*, 120, n. 116).—Cf., further, the reference to Job 10:9: *'das du mich aus leimen gemacht hast, und wirst mich wider zu erden machen'* ('thou hast made me as the clay, and wilt thou bring me into dust again?'); *Deutsches Wörterbuch*, vol. 6, Leipzig 1885, col. 697.

und astronomia beider globul tractiren', 1/I, 316). These 'teachers' ('*ler-meister*') bring about everything which Man and hence the physician can do. They are the teachers in Man that put at his disposal the light of nature and that are to be understood, not as an immanent part of Man, but as 'that which grows in him and comes down from above' ('*was von oben herab in im wachst und kompt*', 1/I, 325). Now, that which comes from above has left its '*vestigia*' and its '*philosophia*', which can be traced by, say, '*chiromantia*' or '*physionomia*', and which teach the physician how to find the correct medicine(s). In this context Paracelsus says of the limbus: '*Alle ding sind gewesen unsichtbar bei gott, die so jezund sichtbar sind, die selbigen all, wie sie gewesen sind, sind gefaßt in ein limbum, das ist in ein sichtig corpus*' ('All things have been invisible with God; those which are now visible, all of them just as they were, are comprised by a limbus, that is a visible body'). From this limbus the macrocosm was created, from which, in turn, Man was made as microcosm (1/I, 316). In this passage the term limbus already denotes the means or material with which spiritual, divine things become visibly, tangibly concrete.

By a kind of self-seduction on the part of the 'fathers of the first limbus' ('*veter des ersten limbi*', 317) created beings were split into the good angels and the bad (fallen) angels or, simply, devils. Corresponding to this split, Man has at his disposal two 'teachers' ('*lermeister*'), two paths to knowledge, the 'angelic' ('*englisch*') and the 'mortal' or 'deathly' ('*tötlich*'). The 'mortal schoolmaster' ('*tötlich schulmeister*') signifies one's persistence in oneself, one's own phantasies and experiences, one's cleaving to the errors of mortal (deathly), earthly wisdom of this or that sort. However, the 'angelic' teacher searches for and finds knowledge, not in himself, but by being 'born down from above' ('*von oben herab geborn*'); 'man in his birth down from above' ('*[der] mensch in der geburt von oben herab*') is a disciple of the right 'schoolmaster' (318). In this early text Paracelsus can still apply to this schoolmaster directly the name 'light of nature' ('*Licht der Natur*') (*ibid.*); it is 'an eternal light, for it comes from the angels and remains in those souls in which there is no death; but the mortal (deathly) light, *that* dies, that is the mortal (deathly) schoolmaster' ('*ein ewigs liecht, dan es kompt aus den engeln und bleibt in den seelen, dorin kein tot ist. das tötlich liecht aber, das sterbt, das ist der tötliche schulmeister*', 319).

What we have here is undoubtedly a very early formulation, and still extremely uncertain terminologically, of what Paracelsus will later express with greater clarity and terminological precision in the *Astro-*

nomia Magna but also in other writings on many topics, making then a distinction between the light of Nature and the light of the eternal or the spirit. In Part Two of his main work, the *Astronomia Magna,* '*von der ubernatürlichen wirkung der himlischen astronomei*' ('on the supernatural operations of heavenly astronomy', 1/XII, 275) there is mention of 'two schools on earth' ('*zwo schulen auf erden*'); the school 'from the earth' has its schoolmaster 'from nature, in nature and is nature' ('*von der natur, in der natur und ist die natur*'); that is to say, it is no longer conceived as the mediator of errors; the other 'school down from above [. . .] teaches heavenly wisdom in the newborn man through him who is from heaven' ('*[die andere] schul von oben herab [. . .] leret im neugebornen menschen die himlische weisheit durch den, der vom himel ist*', 316f.). Such teachers or schoolmasters also appear in the writings on the Eucharist in the same context. Clearly the dualism of mortal (transitory) and immortal (eternal) in the form in which it gives a basic stamp to Hohenheim's speculations on the Eucharist is found in these early passages just as in the later ones. This neoplatonic background is no more questionable in the early writings of Paracelsus than it is in his later works.

One finds nearly all these terminological constituents which are contained in the so-called writings on the Last Supper in the above mentioned writings on natural philosophy as well: limbus, the opposition mortal-eternal, and above all the connection with ethics, with the conduct of social life, even accompanied by biblical citations, particularly the parables of the sower (and the tares) (Matthew 13), the topos of the 'false prophets' of Matthew 24, the '*Verführer*' ('seducers'), as Paracelsus will later cite them in his biblical exegeses and polemical writings. The term limbus is used most extensively in the period Sudhoff called the '"Para"-Zeit', that is at the beginning of the 1530's when Hohenheim turned to the 'immortal philosophy' ('*untötliche philosophei*')[22] of his writings on the Last Supper. In the first elaborated draft of the *Buch Paragranum* Paracelsus discusses— once again in a context of medical epistemology—the origination of Man. Man cannot have been 'born of man' ('*aus dem menschen geboren*'); Adam cannot have been the father, and Eve not the mother, of human beings; 'for in the first man was no prior man but rather the creature [i.e., the totality of creation apart from man], and out of the created beings the limbus came into being, and the limbus became

---

[22] See above, n. 9.

man, and man has remained the limbus' ('*dan im ersten Menschen ist kein vormensch gewesen sonder die creatur, und aus den creatis ist der limbus und der limbus ist der mensch worden und der mensch ist der limbus bliben*'). The close of this sentence strikes one as a description or paraphrase of Hohenheim's anthropology of the microcosm. This limbus, that of the macrocosm, is enclosed in man's skin ('*mit der haut beschlossen*') and 'taken over from the father' ('*aus dem vatter fürgenomen*'); but that means with respect to illnesses and hence with respect to the art of the physician that the point of departure has to be, on the one hand, the corporeality of man as such, the one limbus—'all men [regard-less, say, of their national distinctions] one limbus' ('*alle menschen ein limbus*'); on the other hand, healing must begin with a person's indi-viduality; Paracelsus speaks of the heaven which each person has specially (1/VIII, 100). In the *Opus Paramirum* itself (1531, in St. Gallen) the idea of the limbus is further developed in this direction in detail. The limbus is so to speak the creator's means of being able to pre-sent the macrocosm in Man in such a way that he carries and pos-sesses everything that is good and bad in it (1/IX, 54ff.). In the context of the concept of the 'Mothers' as part of the theory of mat-ter and the elements Walter Pagel calls the limbus 'the sum total of the semina [platonically speaking] of created objects'; it is the lim-bus 'in which the upper-celestial and the lower-physical elementary principles are still conjoined'.[23] The limbus out of which Man was made is 'the whole world' ('*die ganze welt*'); the body of Man takes on the world's body; this is 'one blood and one body' ('*ein blut und ein leib*'), 'distinct or separated only in regard to the soul' ('*geschiden mit der sel alein*')—since the soul by definition is not earthly and tran-sitory but rather spiritual, divine, imperishable—'but in scientia undi-vided' ('*in der scientia aber ongescheiden*', 94). Thus scientia, as Pagel shows,[24] is a concept which is not limited to the cognitive faculty and hence to man's subjectivity, but rather—a purely neoplatonic view—the operative force residing in the world and the things of the world and shaping them in the spirit, the spiritual principle that operates in things and in Man as microcosm. And the idea of Man as the centre of the macrocosm, present in this connection in Ficino,[25]

---

[23] W. Pagel, *Paracelsus. An Introduction to Philosophical Medicine in the Era of the Renais-sance*, 2nd rev. edition, Basel 1982, 356.

[24] *Ibid.*, 59f.

[25] Cf., e.g., P.O. Kristeller, *Studies in Renaissance Thought and Letters*, Rome 1956; offset reprint Rome 1969, 268 and the citation there on the *soul as 'centrum naturae,*

reappears in Paracelsian cosmology. Knowing (cognition) is thus not subjective but, rather, *compositio*, a union with and *in* this operative force or power. Man alone is able to take on that *compositio*, because he extends beyond animal (*'viehisch'*) nature and participates in the *'mens* of heavenly beings',[26] the angels for instance (Paracelsus occasionally uses Ficino's term 'dei'—'gods').[27]

The progression (crossing over) found in the fairly late major work, the *Astronomia Magna*, from a natural philosophical viewpoint à la paganism to one that is theological in a Christian sense—in the language of Hohenheim, celestially philosophic (*himlisch philosophisch*)— this progression, spelled out in detail, is already fundamental to the early oeuvre of Paracelsus and to his *Opus Paramirum*. What this signifies in terms of Paracelsian anthropology is the attachment of the 'invisible' (*'unsichtbar'*), 'incomprehensible' or 'ungraspable' (*'un[be]-greiflich'*) body to the visible, natural body (1/IX,117ff.). Only the latter is from the limbus of the macrocosm, whilst the invisible body is 'from the breath of God' (*'aus dem atem gottes'; 'spiraculum vitae'*, as in Genesis 2:7). The *Opus Paramirum* speaks of two bodies, that from the limbus and that from the breath of God. But Paracelsus stresses that despite this two-bodiedness there is only one flesh, 'not two' ('nit zwei'), and this flesh is from the limbus (118, above). This flesh

---

universorum medium, mundi series, vultus omnium nodusque et copula mundi'. What Ficino usually attributes to the soul or, occasionally, to the *'complexio humana'* as well is applied in Paracelsian cosmological anthropology to the whole man: *'das medium [scil. für die himmlischen Kräfte] ist der [!] centrum, der centrum ist der mensch'* (1/XII, 122) ('the middle [for the heavenly powers] is the centre, the centre is man'; man as the 'centrum' of the entire world: 1/XII, 455). On this cf. Goldammer, *'Menschenbild'*, as well as his investigation *'Die Paracelsische Kosmologie'*, which is essentially intended to show the 'independence of the Paracelsian world view' (305) and is hence at least partially directed against the analyses of Walter Pagel; Pagel is unable to see anything decisely original in regard to this point in Hohenheim's cosmological anthropology ([. . .] the unification of 'Nature' and 'Spirit', of natural philosophy and religion, which Paracelsus achieved in his grand vista of man as a microcosm, had been accepted Neoplatonic and Renaissance teaching. In this [. . .] no original principle was introduced by Paracelsus; cf. Pagel, *Paracelsus*, 347); still, 'Paracelsus should be found original in his thinking in analogies which in his case afforded a strong synthesis of medicine, alchemy, chemistry, religion and cosmology—a synthesis that is entirely his own' (*ibid.*, 348).

[26] Cf. Michael J.B. Allen, Marsilio Ficino on Plato, the Neoplatonists and the Christian Doctrine of the Trinity, *Renaissance Quarterly*, 37, 1985, 555–84 (here 560).

[27] 'Dei' is characteristic of the phraseology of the treatise 'De praedestinatione et libera voluntate'; 2/II, 111–18. In *De vita libri tres* Ficino defines 'dei' as *'spiritus aliqu[i] super homines'*, Venice 1498, reprint Hildesheim and New York 1978, fol. y [3^r].

will be transfigured and will resurrect; all the same it is the flesh that also continues to be 'subiectum medicorum' (*ibid.*). Here we reach the heart of Paracelsian anthropology and therewith the fundamental motif of his idea of the Last Supper as set forth in numerous places, e.g., the *'Liber de usu cenae domini'* (L_1, 156ᵛ). Man shares his divine origin with the angels, he is, like them, a spiritual being, born from above, etc. Still, man differs from the angels through his corporeality in flesh and blood; this defines him, determines his being *'imago dei'*. Since, then, Paracelsus says, *human beings* are meant to go to heaven, they must go to heaven bodily too. Since, as noted at the start, only that goes to heaven which is from heaven, heavenly corporeality is needed, but precisely in flesh and blood! Therefore, as he says for example in 'On miracles and signs' (*'Von miraculen und zeichen'*) (L_1, 142ᵛ), the wine of the Eucharist becomes blood, not 'wineblood' (*'weinblut'*) (that would be in scholastic terminology consubstantiation) but rather 'quite warm, red, wet, coloured [. . .]' (*'recht warm rot, feucht, färbig'*).

Thus there exists an objective continuity, an inextricable connection, between the earthly and the heavenly body and thereby between natural philosophy and theology, between medicine and soteriology in the thought of a fleshly—or, expressed in modern language, personal—identity that embraces both bodies, the mortal natural one no less than the eternal one. This identity is made possible (in accordance with neoplatonic thinking) by the dynamic realism or spiritual materialism of the world of the spirit, of the divine and the eternal. The guarantor of this is the Paracelsian concept of the limbus as an instrument of mediation between spiritual and bodily.

Paracelsus stresses repeatedly that even after the Transfiguration Christ, when he passed through the wall, was 'no spirit but rather a body' (*'kein geist, sonder ein leib'*).[28] In *'Quod sanguis et caro Christi sit in pane et vino'* (L_1, 148ʳ) an analogy from natural philosophy is worked out very lucidly with the same idea of the Last Supper as is discernible in all the treatises; in this text, though, there appears a particular feature (one that seems especially revealing) at the outset of the argumentation: a certain lingering proximity to Swiss criticism of a magical real presence: Paracelsus opposes (remarkably enough right in his exegesis of Luke 24:39, which is concerned with the bod-

---

[28] *'Caena Domini nostri Jhesu Christi Declaratio'*, L_1, 28ᵛ.

ily '*ipse ego*') the erroneous idea that we eat Christ's flesh and bones bodily: 'it is not that, but rather that we relish his *word* in bread and wine, which word is the *spirit* that does not have flesh and bones' ('*das ist nit, sonder wir nießen sein wort in brot und wein, welches wort der geist ist, der nit fleisch und bein hat*'). Thus far the text could be said to show a spiritualistic understanding of the sacrament. But: that is contrary to his intention, for he continues as follows: Just as a child is not engendered from the blood and flesh of his parents, but rather 'through the semen, which is neither flesh nor blood, neither bone nor blood vessel' ('*durch den samen, der weder fleisch noch blut, weder bein noch geäder ist*')—and as earthly natural man is not Adam either but 'from Adam, that is: from his body and blood [. . .] that is caused by the semen alone, from which we are all born and which is not cut out of the body itself [. . .] but comes from the semen which, in turn, is the father himself' ('*von Adam, das ist: aus seinem leib und blut [. . .] das ursachet alles der samen, aus dem wir alle geporen werden, und nit aus dem leib selbs geschnitten, [. . .] sonder aus dem samen, der dann der vatter selbst ist*') (a form of argument, as shown above, found in his early writings on natural philosophy)—'so also Christ's word is our semen. The semen is the spirit. The spirit is life. Now we are from *his* body and blood, we eat and drink thus, which is possible for us to do' ('*also ist Christi wort unser samen. der samen ist der geist. der geist ist das leben. iezt seindt wir aus seinem leib und blut, also essen und trinken wir, das uns müglich zue tun ist*', L_1, 148ᵛ). At death the flesh of Adam ('*das leiblich aus Adam*') and that of Christ ('*das leiblich aus Christo*') separate; 'Adam is flesh from the earth like an animal, Christ flesh from heaven like a spirit; but both are bodily' ('*Adam ist ein fleisch von der erden wie ein vich, Christus ein fleisch aus dem himmel wie ein geist; aber beide leiblich*'). The flesh of Christ is also 'palpable' ('*greiflich*') (one is to think of Thomas in John 20:24ff.), but spiritual in its essence, 'visible and invisible, passing through walls and doors; *that* is impossible for someone on the level of an animal ('*sichtpar und unsichtpar, durch mauren und türen gangen. das vermag der vichisch nit*'). We are confronted here with something quite different from a theology of the Word of God as known from the Reformers (a relevant catchword of theirs: *fides ex auditu*); for what Paracelsus calls 'word' comes by its meaning on the basis of the creation of the new body from a spiritual semen tantamount to a *prima materia*, a creation conceived in analogy to the neoplatonic idea of the limbus. The analogy even extends to viewing the digestion of the flesh and blood of Christ as a digesting of the spiritual semen for the new creature, the heavenly, and seeing the immortal corporeality as no less necessary than the process of metabolizing earthly materiality (e.g., grain, fruit) into earthly Adamic corporeality of flesh and blood. It is this which propels him to write one new tract on the Last Supper after another. But this impulse does not stand alone, as the second step in our presentation will bring out.

II

This conception of the Last Supper is matched in many respects in the content Hohenheim's other theological writings and—this point seems the most important one—corresponds to what Paracelsus himself often mentioned as his motive in writing theology. The initial theological writings were treatises and/or biblical exegeses on Mariology, the doctrine of the Trinity, and Christology, all of which show signs of the author's difficulty in bringing customary doctrinal statements— in their correspondence to symbols of the medieval church or to the basic material of the catechism—into line with his interest in heavenly corporeality vs. earthly, mortal corporeality, and in interpreting these doctrinal statements accordingly. As with his readings of the Last Supper, he interprets the process of the unfolding of the Trinity, the origin and birth of Christ, as well as the figure of Mary by analogy with statements he makes on medicine and natural philosophy. Indeed, the analogies with Mary strike one as setting the very direction in which one's understanding has to go. Concepts already mentioned can be taken as supporting this thesis; but additional reference may be made to the position of Mary in Hohenheim's theology. As is well known (on this one may compare works by Arlene Miller Guinsburg[29] and Katharina Biegger[30]), Paracelsus's early writings describe Mary as God's spouse, i.e., as a preexistent figure within the Godhead, within the Trinity. Much of this is reminiscent of the ardent Marianism which we find among the radical Franciscans;

---

[29] Arlene Miller Guinsburg, 'Von Paracelsus zu Böhme: Auf dem Wege zu neuen Bestandsaufnahmen in der Beeinflussung Böhmes durch Paracelsus,' *Paracelsus in der Tradition, Vorträge/Paracelsustag 1978, Salzburger Beiträge zur Paracelsusforschung*, 21, Vienna 1980, 96–118.

[30] Katharina Biegger, *'De Invocatione Beatae Mariae Virginis'. Paracelsus und die Marienverehrung*. Kosmosophie, VI, Stuttgart 1990.

however, this allusion does not yield a sufficient explanation in terms of historical tradition of the uniqueness of Paracelsian Mariology. The key to understanding it is to be found instead, once more, in Hohenheim's anthropology. *'Das Buch von der Gebärung der empfindlichen Dinge in der Vernunft'* ('The Book on the Generation of Things with Sensation in Reason') argues that unlike insensible things, say, a nut-tree, the birth of Man as a sensitive being requires the semen of two persons, since the semen of a single person is not complete by itself. Individuality derives from the mixture of the semen of the man and of the woman, with the result that no one person is like another (1/I, 262f.). Something similar is said in the *'Liber de generatione hominis'*: 'For God created the birth of the human being in such a way that it resides in *two* people, and in each case the one is impressed on the other, the man on the woman et econtra' (*'dan also hat got die geburt des menschen erschaffen, das sie stehet in beiden menschen und ist ie eine dem andern eingebildet, der man der frauen et econtra'*, 1/I, 294). It is in virtually the same terms that Paracelsus describes the birth of Christ within the Trinity in the *'Liber de s. trinitate'*: this birth of the Son required the dividing of God into *two* persons, God the *man* and God the *woman* as his spouse. From these two was born the Son (2/III, 244–46). Paracelsus himself points out the analogy with the creation of the 'mortal (deathly)' (*'tötlich'*) Adamic man, and develops the content of the analogy as well (264f.).

As regards Hohenheim's motivation in writing on theology, we have several statements by the author himself; one of them should be singled out here. At the start of the above-mentioned tract *'Prologus et initium voluminis limbi aeterni'* he describes his way to theology as follows: The thorough study of nature, its natural processes, all its works, forces, and virtues—in other words, everything Paracelsus calls 'philosophy'—has led him, the philosopher, to the frightening recognition of the mortality of Man in particular, but also that of other things. This recognition is unbearable; death appears to him as an inappropriate determination: 'thus it worsens the philosopher's heart and mind [*"gemüet"*] and displaces him from love; for death, and not only in man, is so terrifying [. . .] and thereupon death produces in the philosopher another way of feeling, another mental disposition [. . .], thinking about the deathlessness which [. . .] has overcome death' (*'so entschlecht es dem philosopho sein gemüet und entsetzt ihn von der liebe dann so erschröckenlich ist der tod nit allein im menschen [. . .] und uf das bringt der tod dem philosopho ein ander gemüet [. . .] nachzu-*

denken dem untötlichen das [. . .] den tod überwunden hat', L₁, 3ʳ). The language here shows traces of the neoplatonic teachings about epistemology. The other 'mental disposition' (*'gemüet'*) is the 'mens' of the angelic or divine beings—the *'dei'* which Ficino defines as *'spiritus aliqu[i] super homines'*,[31] a *'mens'* in which man participates.[32] And the 'love' (*'liebe'*) surely points us to that *'amor'*, that power of affinity which 'everywhere' attracts 'similar things to similar' (*'überall das Ähnliche zum Ähnlichen [hinzieht]'*), which penetrates the macrocosm at all of its levels, the very power which Ficino cites as the basis of our knowledge.[33] This passage in Paracelsus makes clear a close connection between the profession of physician, which gave Hohenheim the incentive to take up philosophy in the light of (mortal) nature, and the motive he had for turning to 'heavenly philosophy' and thus doing theology. In its motive and its goal this theology corresponds as a whole, despite undeniable differences in particulars, to Renaissance philosophers such as Ficino, whose *'Theologia platonica'* in general is avowedly indebted to the teaching of the immortality of the soul.[34]

The final and clearest demonstration that Hohenheim's body of writings on the Eucharist, too, has to be seen against this background is provided by his discussion of 'heavenly philosophy' in the second (*'anderen'*) part of the *Astronomia Magna*, which a number of times comes in contact with or even matches completely passages in his theological oeuvre, especially concerning the Last Supper, but also, for example, the various exegeses of Matthew. In his new, heavenly body man can exercise the capacity to do divine works (1/XII, 315). In accordance with the 'two schools on earth' (*'zwo schulen auf erden'*) a change of 'schoolmaster' takes place, more precisely, there is a gradual transition, a progression to a higher school. Instruction in the wisdom of heaven (*'himlische weisheit'*, ibid.) is no longer given in the school of nature but is given in the newborn body 'down from above' (*'von oben herab'*). As heavenly magus, born through baptism, his growth achieved by means of the Eucharist, man now rules over the heavenly *'magnalia'*. This is attested to many times over in the

---

[31] See n. 27, above.

[32] See n. 26, above. Cf. also Marsilio Ficino, *Three Books on Life: A Critical Edition and Translation with Introduction and Notes* by Carol V. Kaske and John A. Clark, Binghamton, New York 1989, III, chaps. 18 and 26.

[33] Cf. P.O. Kristeller, *Philosophie des Marsilio Ficino*, Frankfurt/M. 1972, 92ff.; idem, *Eight Philosophers of the Italian Renaissance*, London 1965, 43f.

[34] Cf. Kristeller, *Studies in Renaissance*, 269.

Old Testament (by prefiguration) and in the New. Such a celestial magus can perform miracles: he can survive in the fiery furnace like Daniel, walk on water like Christ, pass through walls, heal the sick like the Apostles, indeed bring the very dead back to life (329). Christ himself is in this respect merely an example, albeit an outstanding one, but not unique ('nit allein in Christum'); in exactly the same way he is not singular in his role of bearer of heavenly corporeality; the 'limbus' of Christ is, rather, identical with the limbus of Mary, that of Abraham, etc.

Paracelsus views and describes sacramental doctrine, biblical soteriology and eschatology from the same horizon of expectation as that which had governed the anthropology of a Pico or a Ficino. It cannot be denied that he shares with these figures the concept of natural magic as set forth, for example, in the Picatrix, in De dignitate hominis, in De vita libri tres, where it constitutes the 'pars practica scientiae naturalis'; with this concept, man, being the centre of the macrocosm, is enabled to 'coelo maritare mundum': 'nulla est virtus in coelo aut in terra seminaliter et separata, quam et actuare et unire magus non possit', Pico says (Conclusiones, 3, 10ff.).[35] But it is also undeniable that Hohenheim's theological anthropology, his 'philosophia de limbo aeterno', pursued the same goal as that which was held by the neoplatonists to be man's final and actual determining; to speak with Plato's Theaetetus (176b).[36] Like Paracelsus, Ficino also has an awareness of the 'magus coelestis', the adept of the heavenly light and immortal life, as a being gifted with heavenly powers.[37]

What guides Hohenheim's interest in epistemology in general and his interpretation of the Eucharist as well might be given the name magical dynamism. His understanding of the Last Supper dovetails with what, in his very earliest writings, he had shown to be a precondition of hermeneutics and the goal of the physician, and developed against a Platonic background. Hence, it no longer makes sense to contemplate his theology as a discrete unity divorced from and opposed to his natural philosophy, on the assumption that this natural

---

[35] Cited from Eugenio Garin, ed., Giovanni Pico della Mirandola, De dignitate hominis, Bad Homburg [etc.] 1968, Introduction, 17.

[36] Cf. Raymond Marcel, ed., Marsile Ficin. Théologie platonicienne de l'immortalité des âmes, Paris 1964–70, I, 12 (introduction).

[37] See n. 32, above.

philosophy is essentially free from neoplatonic elements (as is still occasionally maintained). It is rather the case that magical dynamism constitutes the *leitmotif* of his writings on the Last Supper as also of the other truly essential theological pieces; and it represents a kind of bond between the beginnings of his theologizing in the 1520's and the tremendous vision in the 'second' (*'andern'*) part of his main work from 1537–38, the *Astronomia Magna*. In the end, it binds the theological and the medical or natural philosophical parts of his whole oeuvre together into an indissoluble unity; this unity is what Paracelsus strove for so impressively in his Eucharistic writings in particular by his firm retention of the personal individuality of the Adamic *and* the heavenly body alike.

* My sincere thanks to Dr. Joseph B. Dallett (Adjunct Research Professor, Carleton University, Ottawa) for translating this essay from German.

CHAPTER NINE

ON PARACELSUS'S EPISTEMOLOGY IN HIS EARLY THEOLOGICAL WRITINGS AND IN HIS *ASTRONOMIA MAGNA*

Ute Gause

This topic, constitutes a difficult and controversial area of research. Even the term epistemology does not completely apply here, because at no point in his works does Paracelsus present a systematically formulated outline, nor does he develop an epistemological theory in the strictest sense. His primary concern is with the question of what means of gaining knowledge offer themselves to Man in this world— by which he means the possibility of knowing God—and of what instruments of cognition human beings have at their disposal.

When dealing with this question, it is important to consider the difference of opinion in the scholarly literature: on the one hand, Paracelsus is described as a 'Christian Magus', who supposedly represented the conviction that knowing of God or at least a recognition of 'heavenly' works was possible with the help of knowledge gained through nature. On the other hand, Paracelsus is characterised not only as a natural philosopher, but also classified as a bible-oriented lay theologian[1] who viewed his primary epistemological interests—knowledge of nature from nature itself, and knowledge of God from Scripture—as two differentiated and not necessarily mutually exclusive possibilities, but simultaneously dismisses any possibility of knowing Christ through nature.

Arlene Miller-Guinsburg is the primary advocate of the first opinion mentioned above: through analysis of the *Astronomia Magna* and other writings of the later period, she proves that Paracelsus thought it possible for Man to gain knowledge of the 'heavenly' or even the

---

[1] Compare with Hartmut Rudolph: 'Kosmosspekulation und Trinitätslehre. Ein Beitrag zur Bezichung zwischen Weltbild und Theologie bei Paracelus', *Salzburger Beiträge Zur Paracelsusforschung*, 21, 1980, 32–47. esp. 33. *Ibid.* Rudolph mentions the 'gnostic-neoplatonic Magician' and the 'natural philosopher functioning as a biblical-christian apologist'—the problems which have resulted from these different evaluations remain unsolved to this day.

'divine'. She does not confine her explorations solely to his philosophical writings, but includes the theological works in her investi-
gations as well. She reaches the conclusion that such a manner of
thinking also plays a considerable role in Paracelsus's' theological
writings and that it generates a clear change primarily in the concept of belief:

> Paracelsus invested the concept of belief with power; belief was not a
> static or passive condition in which the Christian acknowledged only
> his understanding of and relationship to Christ but an *active, dynamic
> state*. It was founded on the Christian's bond with Christ and its end
> was no less than the power to accomplish seemingly supernatural effects
> on earth.[2]

Magic is—according to Arlene Miller-Guinsburg—not just another
differently oriented means of gaining knowledge from nature, but for
the Christian magician, it is simultaneously a possibility for coming
to know God. The Christian magician can search for divine revelation in the heavens. In addition, since he is possessed of the Holy
Spirit, he is also capable of reaching a higher plane of knowledge
than other human beings.[3] His faith affects the world beyond him,
in that it is capable of producing miracles. Arlene Miller-Guinsburg
comes to the conclusion that for Paracelsus, the knowledge gained
through nature was of the highest priority, even if the knowing of
God had more value to him. This means that for Paracelsus, faith
and the knowing of God indeed are the priority in theory, but it is
demanded of him repeatedly—and this not only in the *Astronomia
Magna* but also in the *Theologica*—to embrace the world and to achieve
mastery of it by inquiry into nature through the medium of magic.
He demands both, as the fulfilment of a God-given task that leads
to Christ.[4]

The debated question around which this chapter shall focus, is as
follows: Which paths to the knowing of God are there according to

---

[2] Arlene Miller-Guinsburg: Paracelsian Magic and Theology. A Case Study of
the Matthew Commentaries, *Kreatur und Kosmos. Internationale Beiträge zur Paracelsusforschung*,
(ed.) Rosmarie Dilg-Frank, Stuttgart-New York 1981, 125–139, here 135.

[3] Compare to Arlene Miller-Guinsburg, 'Die Ideenwelt des Paracelsus und seiner
Anhänger in Hinsicht auf das Thema des Christlichen Magus und dessen Wirken',
Salzburger Beiträge zur Paracelsusforschung, 22, 1981, 27–54, here 44.

[4] Compare to Arlene Miller-Guinsburg *'Ideenwelt'*, 44: 'One would not be mis-
taken by concluding that Paracelsus assumed that the exercise of natural magic
would lead man to Christ'.

Paracelsus, and what role does the knowledge of nature play in this context? The concept of a Christian magic should be investigated through this, as should the elucidation of the knowledge of God through faith as it appears in his theological writings.[5] It is quite possible that a disparate picture will emerge.

I

I shall begin with a portrayal of the assertions of the *Theologica* of the '20s regarding the knowing of God and of nature—if Arlene Miller-Guinsburg's thesis is to be proved true, then there must already be some statements to be found here that emphasise the undeniability of natural knowledge and that favour Christian magic.

For Paracelsus, the starting point for human means of understanding is always God. The Holy Spirit, then, as a person of the Trinity, mediates various ways of knowing God for humans:

> *Zwei liecht seind, menschlich und geistlich und komben beide von gott, nemblich das liecht der weisheit und das liecht des menschlichen lebens und das liecht des glaubens und des geistlichen lebens [. . .] dieser heilig geist, der also aus gott dem schöpfer dem menschen geben, hat nichts [aus] genomben aus der person des suns, [. . .] und ist da ein geist gewesen, der allein aus dem vatter ist ausgangen bis auf Christum. und alle vernuft, weisheit und anders dergleichen, so der mensch gebraucht hat, ist komben vom heiligen geist aus gott dem schöpfer.[6]*

There are two lights which emanate from God: the *lumen naturale*, depicted here as the light of wisdom, and the *lumen supranaturale*, which Paracelsus speaks of here as the light of faith. The *lumen naturale* is attributed to God the Creator; the *lumen supranaturale* emanates from Christ. The light of wisdom and of human life allows Man to recognise God the Creator. Christ the Saviour is not, however, incorporated into this knowledge. Human reason must always be conscious of its incompleteness, its limitations and its need of salvation. The light of nature offers only limited possibilities for knowledge, and Paracelsus even characterises it here as 'subtle temptation'.[7] The

---

[5] I will restrict myself, as already indicated by the title, to the *Theologica* of the '20s. For the early Theological writings compare as well to Ute Gause: *Paracelsus, Genese und Entfaltung seiner frühen Theologie*, Tuebingen, 1993.

[6] Paracelsus, *Sämtliche Werke. 2. Abteilung. Theologische und religionsphilosophische Schriften*, ed. Kurt Goldammer, Wiesbaden, 1955, vol. 3, 259f.

[7] *Ibid.*, 259.

certainty of the reality of God does not present itself as such through the arguments of human thought. The light of faith is much more a gift of God mediated through the Holy Spirit, a gift that indeed— in contrast to the light of wisdom—not every human being possesses. Paracelsus does not emphasise the cognitive possibilities of the human being and their relevance. He raises in their place the need of salvation of the human creature. Faith and with it complete knowledge of God come only through Christ, the Saviour. Any human powers which might be used to seek the grace of God are denied. One can establish a similarity to conceptions of the Reformation here, because Christology and Soteriology are very closely connected with one another. Nevertheless, the human relation to God is only partially defined by this Christology. It remains indeterminate for the most part.

Although the quotation describes the human capability for knowledge, this capacity is not only devalued but also unrelated to any power of Man. According to this, one can determine that both means of cognition are made evident, but remain abstract. It is nevertheless clear that the world as God's creation and the potential for rational knowledge at least allow for the recognition of God the Creator. A striving for knowledge of the Creator-God is possible through the knowledge gained from nature.[8] This approach places Paracelsus thoroughly in line with the scholastic theology of the Middle Ages, in which the doctrine finds its expression in a two-fold source for the knowledge of God. This teaching differentiates between the knowledge of God which can be attained by reason, and the saving revelation, which is mediated through the authority of Holy Scripture and can only be made known by faith.

At another point, Paracelsus makes it clear to which means of knowing should be accorded the greater relevance. Human beings must seek their refuge in Christ, the Saviour, because the wisdom which God the Creator allows to be known through the light of nature is transitory:

---

[8] Compare this with Dietlinde Goltz, 'Naturmystik und Naturwissenschaft in der Medizin um 1600', *Sudhoffs Archiv*, 60, 1976, 45–65, which establishes that a 'struggle against the Ratio and the scholars method of science' began in the Renaissance, which led, among other things, to a 'new religious feeling [. . .] no longer oriented directly towards God as in medieval mysticism [. . .] but rather so to speak, via nature to God'.

das ein ist zugenglich, [. . .] als in ein schöpfer zu fliehen, das ander ist ewig, als in christum, als in einen erlöser zu fliehen, dann der glaub gehet aus ihm.[9]

With this attribution, a contradiction between knowledge and belief emerges. The singular power of the Creator-God culminates precisely in God's mercy on humanity[10] through Jesus Christ, 'in whom life is to be sought'.[11] Accordingly, this is constitutive of the relationship of God to humanity, in that God perceived the necessity of offering salvation to humans and of freeing them of the burden of their limitations as creatures.

Paracelsus' conceptions become more concrete in his early commentary on the Gospel of Matthew. Here, Paracelsus shows himself to be a theologian of the Reformation by making the Bible the basis for his assertions. He is not concerned with producing an interpretation that exactly captures the literal sense of the words, but with expressing the urgent and existence-changing meaning of the biblical messages. Furthermore, declarations regarding the perceptive possibilities of Man are put forward. In his interpretation of Matthew 2 Paracelsus comments on the magicians and their capabilities: Magicians are understood as people, who through their knowledge of the light of nature have come to the conclusion that there is still something greater than this light,

> *demselbigen haben sie nachgestellt, und ihr vernunft und weisheit für ein abweg der seligkeit geacht und ein volkomne irrung. und haben verstanden: nach diesem leben ein anders leben uns bereit, also dass die natur nit das höchste gut sei.*[12]

At this point it becomes clear that human wisdom and knowledge of Christ are not at all complementary! Quite the contrary: the light of nature, human reason and wisdom are diversions. Knowledge of God through them is not even part of the picture; instead it is made clear that knowledge of God is something which lies beyond the grasp of human reason. It is impossible to even suggest a correspondence of the two ways: in view of the knowledge of Christ, all other knowledge is worthless; that necessarily means even the knowledge of the Creator-God through the light of nature.

---

[9] Paracelsus, *Sämtliche Werke. 2. Abteilung*, 3, 248.
[10] Compare with *ibid.*, 249.
[11] *Ibid.*, 250.
[12] 'Frühe Ausarbeitungen zum Matthäuskommentar' (1525), the quote is from the transcript of the Hs.G (83) 209 (65), 180.

Another part of Paracelsus's commentary on the Gospel of Matthew should serve as an additional illustration; here the effect of the penitential sermon of John the Baptist is discussed.

> *und hoereten von Johannes die erklerung der poenitenz, dass sie solten abstehen von allen den satzung, die der mensch erdacht hat und dass in des menschen vernunft ganz klein steble [Buchstabe] wer, das zu der selikeit dienen moecht, sondern allein, dass der weg in den himel durch das widerspil derselbigen beschehen sol. auf das erkanten sie ihr suend und bekanten sich selbst, dass alle ihr vernunft nichts wer.*[13]

True penitence originates from the sinfulness of every person and acknowledges the worthlessness of human reason. Understanding and sense, thought, cunning and intelligence should die off in the human being, for only when this part of Man is silent can the spirit live. This intellectual deadening should be accompanied by a physical equivalent. The desires of the flesh must also be eliminated, in order that a state of contemplation may be entered into that will then lead to knowledge of God:

> *darumb zu merken ist auf den weg der seelikeit, dass mit nichte in uns grueen oder leb, als allein die schreiend stimm unsers geists und dass das ander alles verdorr und faule. das ist die rechte wueeste, darin wir wonen sollen, woellen wir das reich der himmel gewinnen.*[14]

Here, a clearly mystical and ascetic access to God is described: The way to salvation is cleared when the spirit dominates over the body. The deadening of the flesh and of the intellect leads to proper knowledge of God. The inner distancing from the world—not the investigation of nature—furthers the closeness to God. Christ destroys all human truth: 'Christ, he will be the dearest, for he is everything and man is just filth, which has neither strength nor forms'.[15]

This knowledge leads to the demand that human beings should melt into Christ: '. . . because we find all our shelter in him, sit with him in grace and go through him and in him and with him'.[16] One must take Christ in, and through his flesh and blood[17] follow the way to the Kingdom of Heaven. Here, by the way, the Paracelsian doctrine on the Eucharist becomes evident. The amalgamation of

---

[13] *Ibid.*, 208. Compare with *ibid.*, 185.
[14] *Ibid.*, 198.
[15] 'Anhang zum frühen Matthäuskommentar', 39a. The transcript of the manuscript K4 (120) was used.
[16] *Ibid.*, 37b.
[17] Compare with *ibid.*

the human being with the flesh and blood of Christ leads to the giving up of the individual identity, so that the human takes on the form of Christ. By this, Christ then reveals the true path to those who seek him. This also means that any person who wants to follow this path must turn away from worldly life in order to follow the narrow path according to the example of Christ.[18] Christ's shedding of blood represents the link between God and humanity. Knowledge of the father, the Creator-God, comes only through the son. Christ is the mediator of grace, on whose intercession with God humans may place their trust. Paracelsus expresses this in the following manner: 'out of what love he pleads for us, that for us his shedding of blood came to stand for his intercession to his heavenly father'.[19]

Up to this point, the facts have worked together straightforwardly: the type of knowledge of God that comes through nature is beside the point. Belief in Christ has the power to change one's existence, but not in a way that leads to supernatural knowledge. The Christian proves himself much more through his everyday life, in which he must choose the path of poverty and suffering. The ethical transformation is continually demanded: the acceptance of a sinner through Christ without an accompanying change of life is unthinkable for Paracelsus. The verifiability of belief is called into question, meaning that belief must continually be realised in one's life.

The picture becomes quite different and far less straightforward when one turns to the statements regarding the Holy Spirit in the commentary on the Gospel of Matthew. It is the Holy Spirit alone who can impart the truth of Christ. The truth does not depend on the mediation of the church, and it changes people in many ways:

> er [Gott] will uns in seiner warheit nach seinem willen manigfaltig haben in mancherlei des verstandes und des grundes, nicht eine leiren oder ein liedle nicht ein stim oder ein maul sondern viel und mancherlei.[20]

Paracelsus here no longer exclusively has the path of suffering and poverty in mind, but rather the paths prescribed by God, which demand the use of reason, and which can be highly varied. At this

---

[18] Compare with *ibid.*, 28b the commentaries to Matth. 7, 13 (*'Introite per arctam portam'*). See also Chapter 8 above.

[19] *Ibid.*, 43b.

[20] *Ibid.*, 35b.

point he warns emphatically against following the ways of Peter or
Paul—there are other and apparently equal callings.[21]

Even if this idea is not taken to its conclusion there are further
statements which demonstrate that Paracelsus did not proceed from a
Christocentric belief. This is the case in the commentary on Matthew
16:13, namely, that from the knowledge of Christ, belief arises inde-
pendently of the clerical authorities which twist and falsify the teaching of Christ. Paracelsus concludes that the gospel must be mediated,
because it reports of the birth, death and teaching of Christ:

> *darumb schau ein jeglicher, dass das evangelium wol betrachtet werde, denn da
> hilft kein entschuldigung. Ursachen: Christus ist geboren, ist gemartert, hat lehre
> angezeiget . . .*[22]

The 'sola scriptura' is relativised, however, since Paracelsus comes
to speak of the possibility that human beings who, if they thirst for
justice, are also nourished by God—even those who have never heard
of Christ. In contrast to his previous call to the Gospel, Paracelsus
suddenly declares here that direct spiritual inspiration through Christ
also exists and that any human mediation through sermon, teaching and instruction is superfluous. This spirit, which he characterises
as the thirst for justice, is in everyone, regardless of whether man
or women, Moslem or Christian.[23] In other words, this means: in principle, true believers do not differ from one another. They are distinguished by their thirst for true knowledge. This leads in the end
to the pouring out of the Holy Spirit. Paracelsus thus differentiates
implicitly between a *revelatio generalis*, imparted through the spirit
of God, to which man opens himself through his thirst for knowledge, and the *revelatio specialis* in Christ, which is imparted through
Holy Scripture. At this point, both *revelationes* stand as equals beside
one another.

In spite of this, such an interpretation does not do justice to the
main tendency of the early Paracelsian *Theologica*. The other conceptions which I showed earlier are much more prevalent, and they
dominate in the early *Theologica*. Even if there is a *revelatio generalis*,
the possibility of knowing Christ through it in any form is excluded.
I would like to demonstrate this finally with a quotation from the
early commentary on the Gospel of Matthew:

---

[21] Compare with *ibid.*, 35b.
[22] *Ibid.*, 48b.
[23] Compare with *ibid.*, 49a.

merkent, dass vil ist, dass wir menschen auf erden kein gesicht mit uns auf die
welt bringen betreffent das ewige liecht. so wir nun das nit mit uns bringen,
sondern wir mueessens von dem son gottes haben, das ist durch sein wort. So
folget auf das, dass wir Christum oder seine apostel oder sein wort hoeren und
haben sollen.[24]

II

I shall now focus on the epistemological interests of the *Astronomia
Magna*, which came into being between 1537 and 1538. Paracelsus
realised an ambitious project with this work, since he aimed to do
nothing less than to portray 'the entire *Philosophia sagax* of the great
and small world, including that which accompanies it', meaning that
he wants to show which possible means of gaining knowledge present themselves above all to the astronomer. In the preface, he already
describes himself as compelled to defend this intention, since he
begins with the premise that God has prescribed for Man to turn
to the light of nature, since it springs from God the Father, by whom
humanity was created.[25] Precisely as in the early text quoted at the
beginning, Paracelsus differentiates between a wisdom which comes
from the Creator-God and a wisdom from the Saviour-God. While
in his early *Theologica* he only concerned himself with the latter, he
now embraces the knowledge gained through the light of nature,
which he regards as sensible and necessary. This is already a distinction to the early theological writings, where the *lumen naturale*
hints at this, but little attention is paid to its significance. Now he
allows for a significant role for knowledge acquired through nature
and places it on an equal level with the knowing of Christ:

> *der erste, als der vater, hat geschaffen den menschen von unden herauf. der ander,*
> *als der son, von oben herab. iezo wie die zwein geschoepf seien, ist das erste durch*
> *got den vater in kraft des heiligen geistes gesezt zum natuerlichen liecht. darumb*
> *so sie aus dem natuerlichen liecht lernen und leben, aus dem heiligen geist das sel-*
> *bige empfahen [. . .] ob ich nun schreib von dem natuerlichen liecht des vaters,*
> *warumb wolt mich der son hassen oder neiden.*[26]

---

[24] *Ibid.*, 286a.
[25] Compare Paracelsus, *Sämtliche Werke. 1. Abteilung, Medizinische, naturwissenschaftliche
und philosophische Schriften*, ed. Karl Sudhoff, 14 vols., Munich and Berlin 1922–33,
vol. 12, 4.
[26] *Ibid.*, 9.

As an astronomer Paracelsus wants to describe how the stars rule the body,[27] and he is of the opinion that this must be defended, since it is a type of knowledge which yields no knowledge of Christ. Acting within the natural light is required by God, however, even if the knowledge gained through it is transitory.[28] The astronomer knows nothing of Christ and can also learn nothing of him through his art.[29] This is, in any case, the basic orientation of his argumentation. From case to case he deviates from it, though. Paracelsus thus relativises the knowledge gained through nature, on the one hand, but on the other hand, he can also contend that it is to be viewed as a necessary instrument for coming to know Christ:

> ... dieweil leib und sel bei einander stehen und hie auf erden keins one das ander sein mag, von wegen der neuen creaturen, so durch Christum geschaffen ist. also mag die natuerliche vernunft und die ewige weisheit wol sein in eim, aber die natuerliche vernunft mag wol on die ewige weisheit sein die nach dem heidnischen handelt und nicht nach dem ewigen achtet. die ewige vernunft aber mag on die natuerliche weisheit nicht sein, in dem das der mensch aus dem natuerlichen das ewig erkennen sol.[30]

At this point, the step from knowledge gained through nature to knowledge of God is made complete.[31] Both lights must be realised in man, whereby 'the wisdom of the natural light [. . .] is a fleck of dust',[32] namely fleeting. Nevertheless—and here his position is quite different from that in the early theological works—travelling in the light of nature, meaning the search for understanding of natural contexts, is designated by Paracelsus as the way of the Lord, which keeps the mortal body from going astray.[33] He of course specifies directly after this that Christ must naturally be sought first, but quite clearly the foreground for this is the affirmation of knowledge gained through nature as a form of knowledge of the Creator-God, which blends harmoniously with the knowing of Christ and thus simultaneously brings about this knowledge of Christ and knowledge of God. Likewise related to this is the call to investigate nature, which is

---

[27] *Ibid.*, 19.
[28] *Ibid.*, 26.
[29] Compare with *ibid.*, 30.
[30] *Ibid.*, 29.
[31] Compare likewise with *ibid.*, 136: 'Because God wants that we should spend our short time in this valley of sorrows in that natural magnalibus, so that we know how to recognise our creator in his works. And as we go, so do we go in the Lord'.
[32] *Ibid.*, 30.
[33] Compare with *ibid.*, 30.

regarded only under the aspect of its unlimited availability for mankind: 'if things in nature are so, it is for the sake of humanity'.[34] There are no boundaries placed upon this investigative activity; Man is entrusted to reveal everything which lies hidden in nature.[35] To this corresponds the conviction, that humanity constitutes the centre of the universe.[36]

The mastery of the world, which is possible through the knowledge of the heavens and the investigation of nature, does not, however, lead to a repression of the spirit of imitation of Christ. This is emphatically made clear at another point:

> das ist unser kreuz, das wir die gaben gottes tragen und suchen und dieselbigen nicht zu gebrauchen zum argen, sonder Christo damit nachfolgen, das ist, im herrn sterben und leben und wanteln.[37]

The active love of one's neighbour is realised when Man becomes master of the heavens and then places the knowledge thus gained in the service of his neighbour. Christ is mentioned explicitly by Paracelsus as the example that human beings should follow in their actions.[38] Belief in Christ and likewise in his relevance for human life is thus tacitly assumed. Even if Paracelsus repeatedly talks about 'eternal wisdom' and its meaning for every human being, the means by which this type of understanding are to be gained are not developed as a theme. This surely can be explained by Paracelsus' insistence on restricting himself to philosophical facts. He creates the impression, though, that a mixture of *revelatio generalis* and *revelatio specialis* takes place, inasmuch as the *revelatio specialis* is relativised by the knowing of God through creation. If knowledge of nature is necessary for following the example of Christ, but knowledge of Christ and belief in him do not become problematic, then the impression begins to arise that this knowledge and its accompanying belief are not at all necessary. Such a 'Christology of example,' which reduces Christ to his miracles, which are then to serve as an example for humanity, leads to simple ethicism. Paracelsus then logically formulates it as a decreed obligation that humans realise the gifts of God within themselves, and thus praise God, their Creator. Knowledge

---

[34] *Ibid.*, 149.
[35] Compare with *ibid.*, likewise with 157.
[36] Compare with *ibid.*, 164f.
[37] *Ibid.*, 62.
[38] Compare with *ibid.*, 60.

of nature therefore appears as the way recommended by Christ to knowing the Creator. For Paracelsus this means:

> ... das wir erfarn und ergruent sollen sein in allen gewechsen der natur, und die kunst, so uns got geben hat, zu volendung der selbigen damit begabet, das wir im selbigen wantlen und unser zeit auf erden nach dem natuerlichen liecht im natuerliechen leib verzeren, damit wir nicht muessig gefunden werden, schlafend, sondern in arbeit, gleich so wol im leiblichen, als im ewigen, damit kein teil feire. dan solche arbeit unsers schweiss vertreibt den teufel und sein rott von uns, das keiner bleibe wo die arbeit ist.[39]

This work is propagated as the path to salvation.[40] Although this conception does not include a Christology which explains the significance of Christs death and resurrection to the sinful human, it nevertheless corresponds to the point in the early commentary on the Gospel of Matthew where Paracelsus formulates the significance of work for the human being. There, the necessity of physical work is also emphasised as something which brings salvation to the body.[41] A similar conception seems to predominate through the *Astronomia magna*, definitely according the light of the world a far reaching potential for producing knowledge, but never explicitly drawing the conclusion that through this knowledge one could come to know Christ.[42] It has already been demonstrated that this attitude shines through. That Paracelsus also assumes this partially with respect to the knowing of God of the Christian magician (as described in the *Astronomia magna*) shall be explained briefly in the last part of this chapter.

In the second part of the *Astronomia magna*, Paracelsus embraces the philosophy that comes out of heavenly and supernatural effects. Man, because he has a soul, possesses an organ for the recognition of heavenly interventions.[43] Though this organ, it is also possible to come to know God: 'the flesh of Adam'—according to Paracelsus— 'does not see God, but the flesh of the new birth through Christ: this sees God'.[44] This knowledge of Christ through the soul allows Man to work miraculously from it:

---

[39] *Ibid.*, 241.
[40] Compare with *ibid.*, 242.
[41] Compare with '*Anhang zum frühhen Matthaeuskommentar*', 21a(f).
[42] Compare with the closing statement of part 1, *Paracelsus, Sämtliche Werke. 1. Abteilung*, vol. 12, 273: 'of this, regardless of what is begun in nature, do not follow that which shall stop there in nature to remain in it, but seek further and end in the eternal, that is in God's being and going'.
[43] Compare with *ibid.*, 296.
[44] *Ibid.*, 296.

nun bedenkt die wesen der menschen, das der mensch gemacht ist, hie auf erden zu sein ein kurze zeit, und was er in der zeit erlangt, das folget im ewig nach. so er nun wil ein gut erlangen tun, so muss er in diser composition erfaren sein, und sich in die himlische wirkung richten, auf das er ein magus coelestis sei, ein apostolus coelestis . . .[45].

Here, the knowing of Christ becomes the key to a new form of mastery of the world, because the 'new birth' through baptism makes him capable of using supernatural powers. Prior to this, of course, the Gospel must be heard and assimilated.[46] There is neither a knowing of God possible from nature—the *lumen naturale* is transitory and therefore to be neglected—nor does the knowing of Christ lead to being like Christ, meaning the ethical behaviour of the imitation of Christ. Heavenly knowledge instead leads to Man becoming capable of an even more powerful mastery of the world, since he possesses heavenly powers, than is possible with the help of nature.[47] The *magia coelestis* encourages the domination of the world in even greater measure than the *magia naturalis*. Thus, Paracelsus can categorise the 'coelestis magia' as a 'potestas divina'.[48]

Now it must be questioned how this 'heavenly magic' is to be evaluated. I would like to define natural magic—like Kurt Goldammer—as a 'power of knowing which comes primarily from God, and penetrates and masters nature and the structure of the world'[49] while simultaneously I view its Paracelsian development—likewise in the same sense as Goldammer—as a stylising of this power of knowing. Heavenly magic then deals with the employment of those powers which are not—or not yet—rationally explainable.[50] This magic is then certainly not concerned with coming to know God, in this way, as it may appear upon casual investigation. Otherwise it would be completely impossible to explain why Paracelsus accords so much significance to the investigation of creation in the first part of the *Astronomia magna*. This means that 'heavenly magic' is not a specifically *Christian* form of magic. In the *Astronomia magna*, the expression 'Christian magic' is never used, but rather, the discussion always focuses on *magia coelestis*.

---

[45] *Ibid.*, 315.

[46] Compare with *ibid.*, 313.

[47] *Ibid.*, 334: 'what nature does through its powers, that is natural magica, what the heavenly powers do in us and through us, is heavenly magica, and what comes out of nature, is natural, and what is from god, is divine'.

[48] *Ibid.*, 369.

[49] Kurt Goldammer, *Der göttliche Magier und die Magierin Natur*, Stuttgart 1991, 16.

[50] Compare with *ibid.*, 49.

III

To conclude, I would like to summarise what I have stated in the two previous sections. Namely, that comparison between the commentary of the early theological writings and the *Astronomia magna* shows an astounding concurrence between Paracelsus's leading epistemological interests and the means of knowing God which he portrays. Above all this concurrence becomes clear in the following three points:

1. For Paracelsus, knowing of God, the Creator, is possible through nature. This means that there is a *revelatio generalis*. Its description in the *Astronomia magna* encompasses a broad space, while it is only formulated as a possibility in the early *Theologica*.

2. As a consequence of this interpretation, a relativisation of the *revelatio specialis* takes place, in favour of the *revelatio generalis*, in other words, in favour of the knowledge of God which is produced by the *lumen naturale*. This concept is once again more broadly explained in the *Astronomia magna* than in the early *Theologica*. It culminates in the declaration that Man can recognise the eternal through the natural. Despite this, it is posited over and over again that the knowledge gained through the Creator-God is transitory.

3. The concept of imitation of Christ remains present throughout the works discussed here. Work in the light of nature is viewed as God-given. Knowledge of God always involves active emulation.

The following two points must likewise be considered as significant differences between the *Astronomia magna* and the early *Theologica*:

a. In the early *Theologica*, exact declarations are made as to which ways Man can come to know Christ: Only intellectual and physical deadening makes one ready to receive the spirit. A shunning of worldly life is demanded; this goes along with hearing the Word. The light of faith is a gift. Knowledge of nature is unimportant for such realisation. The knowing of Christ comes through contemplation and asceticism.

b. The acquisition of 'heavenly magic', as it is described in the *Astronomia magna*, does not lead to a knowing of Christ, but to an extensive mastery of the world, as it is to be reached through the exploration of the light of nature. It is therefore misleading to label this 'heavenly magic' as 'Christian magic', because its dependence on Christ in particular is not made evident. This also does not correspond to the knowing of Christ as it is formulated in the early *Theologica*.

It can therefore be established that Paracelsus follows two leading epistemological interests in these texts: in the one case he is concerned with knowing the Creator-God from nature, among other things with the help of magic. Understandably, this concept plays a major role in the *Astronomia magna*. This knowledge, though, theoretically remains clearly separated from the knowing of Christ. In the other case, he attributes important relevance to the knowing of Christ through the Gospel; this alone allows Man to act in emulation of Christ.

If I were now to answer my original question—the question of whether Paracelsus represents the idea of a 'Christian Magus' or whether as a bible-oriented lay theologian he held the knowing of God as possible only through the *revelatio specialis*—I cannot provide a straightforward answer. It must remain an unsatisfying 'as much the one as the other'.

Nevertheless, the importance of 'heavenly magic' for Paracelsus as a means of gaining knowledge appears to me to have been overrated in the past. By comparing these texts, I hope to have made it evident that Paracelsus formulates the different possibilities for coming to know God repeatedly, but that 'heavenly magic' is to be seen much more as a form of mastery of the world than as a means of coming to know God.

(Translated by David Holsinger)

PART THREE

THE PHILOSOPHICAL AND MEDICAL PARACELSUS

CHAPTER TEN

PARACELSIANISM AND THE DIFFUSION OF THE CHEMICAL PHILOSOPHY IN EARLY MODERN EUROPE

Allen G. Debus

The history of science has traditionally emphasized astronomy and the physics of motion. The Scientific Revolution of the sixteenth and seventeenth centuries has been—and remains for the most part—a story of progress leading us from Copernicus to Tycho and Kepler, and then on to Galileo and Isaac Newton whose work presents us with classical mechanics, the basis of modern science. This is the way in which historians of the Enlightenment viewed the intellectual progress leading to their 'century of light'. It is an approach that appealed to August Comte and William Whewell in the nineteenth century, and it is the way in which George Sarton developed the history of science in the first half of the present century. I think that this remains the standard treatment.[1] More recently there has developed a special interest in the societal relations of science, but because the rise of modern science has been interpreted largely in terms of the mathematically based physical sciences, the emphasis has remained on those figures who contributed to that development.

Of course we are interested in the steps that have led to modern science, but I believe that history can be a dry subject if it is only the relation of progress. Indeed, the historian of any field—be it politics, art, economics or literature—should be concerned more with the rich context of his sources than with their 'correctness' measured by the standards of today. And if we look at the spectrum of scientific and medical works of the sixteenth and seventeenth centuries we find quickly that the debates that occurred relate perhaps less to Copernican thought than they do to chemistry and medicine. The application of chemistry to medicine presented a major problem, not

---

[1] There is an increasing interest in the historiography of the history of science. I have discussed this subject in a series of lectures presented at the University of Coimbra in 1983 and published as *Science and History: A Chemist's Appraisal*, Coimbra: Edição do Serviçi de Documentação e Publicaçãoes da Universidade de Coimbra Subsidiado pela Fundação Calouste Gulbenkian, 1984.

only to traditional physicians, but also to the learned in other areas—especially in fields related to religion and the study of the ancient classics. Here I would like to touch on the problem briefly and indicate the manner in which chemical thought spread throughout Europe in the sixteenth and early seventeenth centuries.

If we are to say anything about the intellectual turmoil resulting from the introduction of chemistry into medicine in the Renaissance we must pause for a moment to explain the points of tension that occurred then. The humanistic search for ancient texts affected medicine in the late fifteenth and early sixteenth centuries. The result was the glorification of Galen who became the 'Prince of Physicians'. Almost without exception the medical scholars of Europe sought new texts and more accurate translations of ancient texts, and especially the works of Galen.

But at the same time the recovery of the *Corpus Hermeticum* and a revived neo-Platonism encouraged a more mystical approach to Man and nature through its reliance on the macrocosm and the microcosm. Whatever was to be found in the great world would also be found in Man. The Creator had offered great wonders to mankind, but these had been lost at the time of the Fall. The natural magicians, however, encouraged by the Hermetic texts, hoped to discover these secrets in nature since they had been 'signed' in such a way that we might recognize their true worth and inner virtue. Moreover, by recovering these long lost treasures—many of which would preserve our health—we would also learn more of our Creator. Thus, the call for new observations in nature was coupled with a religious quest.

Influenced by both the Aristotelian-Galenic revival and the Hermetic recovery was Paracelsus (1493–1541) who was to be known as the 'Luther of Medicine'.[2] Little need be said here of his life other than to underscore the fact that he was almost constantly on the move and that he had an argumentative and difficult nature. As a youth he picked up interests and skills that were to stay with him. He surely learned some medicine and alchemy from his father, who practiced in the mining communities of southern Germany and the

---

[2] Although the literature on Paracelsus is voluminous, perhaps no twentieth-century scholar has been more influential in discussing this work and its sources than Walter Pagel whose *Paracelsus. An Introduction to Philosophical Medicine in the Era of the Renaissance*, Basel, 1958; Second edition, Basel et al. 1982, is a landmark study, one that influenced many scholars both in Europe and the United States.

Swiss Cantons. At the same time he observed the metallurgical and mining practices of the area.

Leaving home at the age of fourteen, he travelled widely visiting numerous universities and picking up much traditional learning which he grew to hate. He also added to his medical knowledge through observing local practices and serving as a surgeon in mercenary armies. In 1527 he was called to Basel where he held a position as city physician, but he antagonized the medical faculty at the University by giving lectures in German and burning the revered *Canon* of Avicenna, a fundamental text for medical students. He left Basle after a disastrous legal battle and spent the remainder of his life moving from one town to another in Switzerland and Germany, finally dying in Salzburg in 1541 at the early age of 48.

We should also mention that relatively few of his voluminous writings had been published at the time of his death in 1541. Surely the most important of these was his *Greater Surgery*. It took ten years before the fame of his cures began to spread and physicians began to search for the manuscripts he had left behind as he moved from town to town. In fact, it was not until the 1560s and 1570s that the work of Paracelsus became widely known.[3] Gradually his work and that of his followers were developed into a system of the macrocosm and Man that represented at the same time a call for a new science and a new medicine.

The word 'system' may be rather strong, but sixteenth-century Paracelsians did hold many beliefs that characterize them as a group. Here my comments will be general in nature, and may not all apply to each figure referred to. Although the Paracelsians may have borrowed much from Aristotle and Galen, they were united in their attack on the ancients and the educational establishment. And, like Paracelsus, they called for new observations of nature. Their world—at least for most of them—was based on the analogies of the macrocosm and the microcosm. Whatever is in one will be found in the other.

The ancients, they felt, were deceived in making mathematics the basis of their philosophy. Here they most frequently meant the logical reasoning of geometry.[4] They argued that mathematics had

---

[3] I have discussed the Paracelsians and their work in a number of papers and books, particularly in *The Chemical Philosophy: Paracelsian Science and Medicine in the Sixteenth and Seventeenth Centuries*, 2 vols., New York 1977.

[4] The distrust of mathematics by the Paracelsians is a significant difference between

flawed the work of Aristotle and that Galen's medicine was just as bad because he had applied Aristotle's mathematical approach to medicine, a field in which it had no value.

But what, then, was the proper key to the study of nature? Here they turned to chemistry. After attacking the use of mathematical abstraction in the study of nature, Jean Baptiste van Helmont wrote that

> I praise my bountiful God who hath called me into the Art of the fire, out of the dregs of other professions. For truly, Chymistry, hath its principles not gotten by discourses, but those which are known by nature, and evident by the fire; and it prepares the understanding to pierce the secrets of nature, and causeth a further searching out in nature, then all other sciences being put together: and it pierceth even unto the utmost depths of real truth: Because it sends or lets in the Operator unto the first roots of those things, with a pointing out the operations of nature, and powers of Art: together also, with the ripening of seminal virtues. For the thrice glorious Highest, is also to be praised, who hath freely given this knowledge unto little ones.[5]

A Paracelsian natural philosopher should go abroad, collect samples, and then return to his laboratory—a chemical laboratory—where he will subject those samples to analysis.[6] He will then find not the Aristotelian elements, Earth, Water, Air and Fire, but three fundamental principles, Salt, Sulphur and Mercury.[7]

Confirmation of laboratory results seemed to be found in the cre-

---

them and the mechanists. I have discussed their views in detail in 'Mathematics and Nature in the Chemical Texts of the Renaissance,' *Ambix, 15*, 1968, 1–28, 211.

[5] Jean Baptiste van Helmont, *Ortus medicinae. Id est, initia physicae inaudita. Progressus medicinae novus, in morborum ultionen ad vitam logam*, Amsterdam, 1648; reprinted Brussels: Culture et Civilisation, 1966, 463; *Oriatrike or Physick Refined. The Common Errors therein Refuted. And the whole Art Reformed & Rectified. Being a New Rise and Progress of Phylosophy and Medicine, for the destruction of Diseases and Prolongation of Life*, translated by J(ohn) C(handler), London 1662, 462.

[6] The call to travel for medical knowledge recurs frequently in the works of the Paracelsians. For examples see Peter Severinus, *Idea medicinae philosophicae. Continens Fundamenta totius doctrinae Paracelsicae, Hippocraticae & Galenicae*, Hagae-Comitis 1660; 1st ed., 1571, 39.

[7] 'I say, every *Paracelsian*, which doth but onely carry coals unto the work, can shew you by eye three principles of *Theophrastus* Physick.' Bernard G. Londrada A. Portu Aquitans (Penotus), 'An Apologeticall Preface' to the *One Hundred and Fourteen Experiments and Cures of the Famous Physitian Theophrastus Paracelsus*, in Leonard Phioravant (Fioravanti), *Three Exact Pieces of Leonard Phioravant Knight and Doctor in Physick ... Whereunto is Annexed Paracelsus his One hundred and fourteen Experiments: With certain Excellent Works of B.G. à Portu Aquitans. Also Isaac Hollandus his Secrets concerning his Vegetall and Animall Work With Quercetanus his Spagerick Antidotary for Gunshot* (London: G. Dawson for William Nealand, 1652), sig. Ddd 1r. This collected edition is a reprint of John Hester's sixteenth-century translations.

ation account in Genesis. Here there is no reference to the creation of fire and therefore fire must be rejected as an element. There are no 'four elements' and for this reason van Helmont wrote that 'the fourfold kinde of Elements, Qualities, Temperaments or Complexions, and also the foundations of Diseases, falls to the ground.'[8] In short, the whole of ancient philosophy and medicine is based on the four elements, and if even one of them is not a true element, then the entire superstructure falls.

Van Helmont was a late figure but he maintained an interest in a new chemically oriented world view and in this he differed little from other Paracelsians. Ancient medicine had been built on the four humors: blood, phlegm and yellow and black bile. Health resulted from a proper balance of these within the body while disease resulted from an imbalance. The task of the physician was to restore a humoral balance to his patients. On the other hand, Paracelsus spoke of seeds of disease entering the body through the process of respiration or through food. These seeds would then become lodged in specific organs where they might grow and cause illness or death.[9] The process was similar to their explanation of metallic seeds entering a proper earthly matrix and then maturing to metals. This similarity of disease theory and metallic growth is hardly surprising in light of the Paracelsian conviction of the essential connection and similarity of the macrocosm and the microcosm.

For the Paracelsians part of a physician's training was travel. In this way he learned of diseases that were not known to Galen: the sweating sickness in England, the scurvy of Germany, plica—a hair and scalp disease endemic to Poland, the colic common to Alsatia, and the new venereal diseases afflicting all areas of the continent.[10] For these new diseases new remedies were required since the herbal mixtures of the traditional *materia medica* seemed useless. But more, these chemical physicians broke with Galenic theory in rejecting their belief that 'contraries cure.'[11] A disease characterized as hot and of a certain degree of intensity would be cured by a cold medicine of

---

[8] Van Helmont, 'Elementa' (Sects. 9–10), *Ortus*, 53: *Oriatrike*, 48.

[9] On humoral pathology and Galenic medical philosophy see Owsei Temkin, *Galenism: Rise and Decline of a Medical Philosophy* (Ithaca and London 1973), 10–50. For Paracelsian disease theory see Walter Pagel, *Paracelsus*, 134–44.

[10] Joseph Duchesne (Quercetanus), *Le Povrtraict de la Santé...*, S. Omer 1618, 134–44.

[11] Pagel, *Paracelsus*, 144–49.

the same intensity. Paracelsus and his followers were influenced by folk medicine which affirmed that like cures like. Thus, if a disease is thought to be a poison, the physician might cure it with a poison. Instead of prescribing often bland herbal mixtures, physicians were now encouraged to give their patients strong and often dangerous chemicals. And why not? they argued. Since the body operated chemically surely the proper chemicals would maintain its health. The Galenists reacted with alarm, calling the chemists poisoners and murderers. In his 'Ignatius, His Conclave' (1611), John Donne has Satan name Paracelsus the 'Prince of Homicide Physicians.'[12] And if the Paracelsians replied that they paid careful attention to dosage,[13] it is true, nevertheless, that their remedies included preparations compounded from mercury, arsenic, antimony, and numerous other metals and minerals.

There was then good reason for the confrontation that developed. The medical establishment had raised the work of Galen to a new level of authority while Paracelsus sought to overturn his work and that of Aristotle as well. They rejected the four elements and their attendant humors. With the latter went the traditional theory of disease while chemistry—practically unknown to ancient medical theory— was to become the basis of a new cosmology and human physiology. Above all, this new emphasis on chemistry introduced new chemically-prepared remedies to medical practice—remedies that often had violent effects on the body.

In the third quarter of the sixteenth century a large number of Paracelsian texts were printed. The result was the growth of an enthusiastic group of chemical physicians—and an equally enthusiastically opposed group of Galenists who sought to halt the advance of these medical heretics. With the increased number of Paracelsian texts there was an attempt to synthesize the Paracelsian system. One of the first of these works was the *Idea medicinae philosophicae* of Peter Severinus (1542–1602), physician to Frederick II of Denmark. This work of Severinus appeared in 1571 and was considered to be author-

---

[12] John Donne, 'Ignatius His Conclave' (1610) in *Complete Poetry and Selected Prose*, London/New York 1936, 357–409. On Paracelsus, see 366–69.

[13] R.B. Esquire [R. Bostocke]. *The difference betwene the auncient Phisicke, first taught by the godly forefathers, consisting in vnitie peace and concord: and the latter Phisicke proceeding from Idolaters, Ethnikes, and Heathen: as Gallen, and such other consisting in dualitie, discorde, and contrarietie . . .*, London 1585 sig. Ev[v].

itative for a century. A year after the publication of the *Idea*, Thomas Erastus (1524–1583), professor of medicine at Heidelberg, published the first part of his Galenic refutation of the new medicine, the *Disputationes de medicina nova Paracelsi* (4 parts, 1572–1574).[14]

And yet, as in most disputes, there was a middle ground. The renowned Johannes Guinter of Andernach (ca. 1497–1574), who had been professor of medicine in Paris in the 1530s and the teacher of both Andreas Vesalius and Michael Servetus, began to read the new works on chemical medicine in his later years.[15] Originally one of the most prominent of the medical humanists—he had translated much of the work of Galen as well as many other ancient medical authorities—Guinter prepared an enormous work on the new and the old medicine which was published at Munich in 1571. Here he held to much of the traditional medical teaching, but in his lengthy discussion of the *materia medica*, he strongly supported the new chemical medicines. Elsewhere he argued that the chemical principles were not too different from the ancient elements, and he felt that chemical procedures might so alter dangerous substances that their poisons could be made wholesome to the body. In other words, the apparently sharp differences between the Paracelsians' cure by similitude and the Galenists' cure by contraries did not really exist or at least were far less than had been argued.

It is safe to say that the Paracelsian medico-chemical sect originated in Central Europe. This is where Paracelsus himself worked and this is where his 'first generation' followers found and published his manuscripts. But there was a rapid diffusion of chemistry and chemical medicine throughout Europe—a diffusion that was affected by local conditions—and this is the subject of our main interest.

Interest in the work of Paracelsus appeared first in France[16] as a result of the famous commentary on Dioscorides by Pierre Mattioli. Published first in Latin in 1544, this work appeared in French translation in 1561.[17] Although Dioscorides dealt primarily with plants

---

[14] For a comparison of Severinus and Erastus see Debus, *Chemical Philosophy*, 1, 128–34.

[15] On Guinter von Andernach, see *ibid.*, 135–45.

[16] On French Paracelsism see my work on *The French Paracelsians: The Chemical Challenge to Medical and Scientific Tradition in Early Modern France*, Cambridge 1991.

[17] M. Pierre Andre Mattioli, Medecin Senoys, *Les Commentaires . . . sur les six liures des Simples de Pedacius Disocoride Anazarbeen*, Lyon 1561. In the 1556 edition the chapter on antimony is on 444–45.

and their medicinal properties, the fifth book is on stones, minerals and metals. Here a chapter on antimony includes a long commentary on its medicinal use for a variety of ills including the plague, melancholy, persistent fevers, asthma, spasms, and paralysis. In short, it was presented as a cure-all. Above all, it was noted that only one author, Paracelsus, had described its internal use as a purgative. Antimony had long been known for its ability to remove impurities from gold in the process of refining. But man is perfect among living creatures as gold is perfect among metals and it seemed reasonable that antimony would remove impurities—that is, disease—in a form of medical purification.

The actual debate began over this issue, the internal use of antimony. A physician from Montpellier, Louis de Launay (fl. 1557–1566), prepared a tract on the medicinal qualities of antimony in 1564.[18] He was answered two years later by a member of the Parisian Medical Faculty, Jacques Grévin (1538–1570), who branded antimony as a poison and then took his case to the Faculty, where it was officially declared a poison on 3 August 1566. This decree was not to be rescinded for a full century.

The initial exchange related to antimony alone, but within a year the entire Paracelsian cosmology became an issue. Grévin translated Jean Wier's work on magic in 1567 and here he included a damning attack on Paracelsus. In the same year Pierre Hassard translated Paracelsus' *Greater Surgery* while Jacques Gohory produced a short compendium of Paracelsian philosophy. From this time on works on chemical medicine found a steady readership in France.

The Medical Faculty became involved once more in 1578 in the case of Roch le Baillif (fl. 1578–1580), a Paracelsian from Brittany who had been appointed physician in ordinary to Henry III.[19] Le Baillif had extended his activities to practice in the City and to give public lectures. Here he was vulnerable since the Faculty asserted its historic right to control medical practice in the area surrounding Paris. Le Baillif was ordered to halt his practice as well as his public lectures. He was then brought to trial and expelled from Paris.

---

[18] On the debate between de Launay and Grévin see Debus, *French Paracelsians*, 21–26.

[19] Prior to his move to Paris, le Baillif had written *Le Demosterion... Auquel sont contenuz Trois cens Aphorismes Latins & François. Sommaire veritable de la Medecine Paracelsique, extraicte de luy en la plus part, par le diet Baillif*, Renne 1578. His trial and expulsion from Paris is summarized by Debus, *French Paracelsians*, 38–40.

Still, halting the activities of this one individual certainly did not end the flow of Paracelsian publications.

There were religious overtones to this debate. For the most part, physicians interested in the new medicine were Protestants, and this held throughout Europe. The Galenists, however, were Roman Catholic. Indeed, medical students in Paris were required to be orthodox Roman Catholics, a restriction that was not required at the rival medical school in Montpellier.[20] This became a matter of importance in the final decade of the century. Henry of Navarre took Paris in 1593. Although he converted to Roman Catholicism, he had been a Protestant, and he brought with him physicians who favored the chemical medicine of the Paracelsians. Many of these came from families that had left France at the time of the St. Bartholomew's Day Massacre in 1572.

Prominent among the chemical physicians at the court were the First Physician to the King, Jean Ribit (ca. 1571–1605), and two physicians in ordinary, Joseph Duchesne (ca. 1544–1609) and Theodore Turquet de Mayerne (1573–1655).[21] The latter two were to have the most lasting influence. Duchesne was a Calvinist who had taken his degree at Basel. From 1575 he had engaged in debates supporting the new medicine. The parents of Turquet de Mayerne had fled France in 1572 and the boy had been raised in Switzerland, but returned to France to take his medical degree at Montpellier in 1597 where the Faculty had long favored chemistry as an aid to medicine. When the young graduate arrived in Paris he was a fervent convert to the new system.

Both Duchesne and Mayerne fostered the teaching of pharmaceutical chemistry in Paris to the alarm of the Medical Faculty, but the debate was truly ignited by a work on the *Matter of the True Medicine of the Early Philosophers* published by Joseph Duchesne in 1603.[22] Here, and in a work on the *True Hermetic Medicine* published

---

[20] Howard M. Solomon, *Public Welfare, Science and Propaganda in Seventeenth Century France: The Innovations of Théophraste Renaudot*, Princeton 1972, 5.

[21] I have discussed the work of Duchesne in *The Chemical Philosophy, 1*, 148–67 with additional points in *The French Paracelsians*, 50–53. On Turquet de Mayerne's relation to Jean Ribit and the Court physicians, see Hugh Trevor Roper, 'The Sieur de la Rivière, Paracelsian physician of Henry IV' in *Science, Medicine and Society in the Renaissance. Essays to Honor Walter Pagel*, edited by Allen G. Debus, 2 vols., New York 1972, 2, 227–50.

[22] The debate in the period 1603–1615 is discussed by Debus, *French Paracelsians*, 53–65.

the following year, Duchesne defended chemistry theoretically and practically, both as a key to nature and as the font of the new chemical medicines. He rejected the traditional humors and called for the adoption of the three Paracelsian principles. These two books by Duchesne were considered extremely dangerous by the Medical Faculty and their members engaged in polemic warfare against the chemists that lasted long after Duchesne's death in 1609. The literature on the Parisian debate was so extensive—and considered so important—that Andreas Libavius (1540–1616) wrote two discussions of the conflict (1606, 1607). By 1615 the Medical Faculty issued a decree forbidding the sale of chemical remedies in the Kingdom of France,[23] but this attempt to halt the activities of the chemists was no more successful than their earlier efforts.

Marin Mersenne, also active in the call for a new science, was deeply concerned with the demands of some chemists that a mystical cosmology be established as the basis of a new philosophy. Instead, in 1625, he called for a new science based on mathematics and said that chemists must be policed by an academy that would keep them from discussing religious, philosophical, and theological questions. For him chemistry was useful only for the preparation of some new medicines.[24] It is clear in the debates between Fludd and Mersenne, Pierre Gassendi and Johannes Kepler that the mystical chemistry and cosmology described by some authors could be viewed as a basis of a new philosophy.[25] Surely Mersenne and Gassendi looked upon this interpretation of nature as a great danger to their own dream of a new science based on mathematics, observation and the mechanics of motion. For them the grandiose claims of these chemists were as dangerous as they seemed to be for the Galenists, but for a different reason.

Although the Medical Faculty remained resolutely opposed both to the internal use of chemicals in medical practice and to all other applications of chemistry to medicine, they never seemed to be able to end the activities of their adversaries. Chemists had offered private courses in Paris from the early years of the century, and their

---

[23] Discussed with the text of the document in Pascal Pilpoul, *La Querelle de l'Antimoine (Essai historique)*. Thèse pour l'Doctoral en Médecine, Paris 1928, 38–39.

[24] Marin Merenne, *La verite des sciences. Contre les septiques vo Pyrhonniens*, Paris 1625; Reprint, Stuttgart/Bad Cannstaat 1969. Presented in dialog form, the first section offers a defence of the alchemical position in opposition to the mechanists and sceptics. See Debus, *Chemical Philosophy, 1*, 156–67.

[25] On the various debates with Robert Fludd see *ibid.*, 153–90.

many textbooks sold in quantity and went through numerous editions. Guy de la Brosse (ca. 1586–1641) drew up plans for a botanical garden which was formally opened in 1640.[26] Included was a teaching program, and the first professor of chemistry was the Scot, William Davisson (ca. 1593–1669), who was appointed in 1648. It need hardly be said that the plan of la Brosse was opposed at every step by the Parisian Medical Faculty.

The French chemical physicians found an ally in Cardinal Richelieu who supported them in his attempt to break the monopoly of the medical establishment. To this end he fostered the activities of Théophraste Renaudot, a Montpellier physician who established a Bureau for the benefit of the poor.[27] Along with an employment agency and a banking service offering low interest loans, this Bureau offered free medical consultations and weekly conferences on every conceivable subject. Renaudot favoured the new chemical medicines, and he was viewed as a threat by the members of the Medical Faculty who began legal proceedings against him. With the death of Richelieu and Louis XIII Renaudot lost his protection. He lost the case and was stripped of his honors and privileges. Once again the Galenists seemed to have won a decisive victory, but by mid-century the use of antimony and other chemicals was becoming more fashionable; and with the deaths of the older members of the Medical Faculty, the traditional opposition declined. In 1658 an antimony purge cured Louis XIV in the field and at a full session of the Medical Faculty in 1666, antimony—in the form of emetic wine— was approved as a purgative.[28] It was exactly one hundred years after the Faculty had first damned antimony as a poison.

The acceptance of chemical medicines in England was far less stormy than in France.[29] To be sure, the London College of Physicians

---

[26] The important role of Guy de la Brosse was discussed by Henry Guerlac in 'Guy de la Brosse and the French Paracelsians' in *Science, Medicine and Society in the Renaissance, 1*, 177–99. His work has been continued by Rio Howard in 'Guy de La Brosse: Botanique et chimie au début de la révolution scientifique,' *Revue d'Histoire des Sciences, 31*, 1978, 301–26 and 'Guy de La Brosse and the Jardin des Plantes in Paris' in *The Analytic Spirit: Essays in the History of Science in Honor of Henry Guerlac*, edited by Harry Woolf, Ithaca 1981, 195–224.

[27] The most recent discussion of the life and activities of Renaudot is to be found in Solomon, *Public Welfare*.

[28] Pilpoul, *Querelle de l'antimoine public welfare*, 84–87; Debus, *French Paracelsians*, 95–99.

[29] On chemistry and chemical medicine in sixteenth- and seventeenth-century England, see Allen G. Debus, *The English Paracelsians*, London 1954.

at first demanded that Fellows adhere strictly to Galenic teaching, but from an early date there was a willingness to accept chemically-prepared remedies. As in France, the first references to Paracelsus appear in books printed in the 1560s.[30] Some Marian exiles learned of the Paracelsian innovations while in Switzerland in the 1550s. However, relatively few details of medicinal chemicals appeared until the following decades when influential surgeons such as George Baker (1540–1600) in 1574 and John Banister (1540–1610) in 1589 praised some of the new chemicals—for the most part when they were used as salves for external use.[31] The only extensive defence of the Paracelsian system in English in the sixteenth century was that of R. Bostocke (fl. 1585) whose *Difference betwene the auncient Phisicke . . . and the latter Phisicke* (1585) discussed the chemical Creation, the Paracelsian principles and the macrocosm-microcosm universe as well as the medical aspects of the new philosophy.[32] However, for Bostocke, Paracelsus was not an innovator. Rather, he had revived ancient truths that could be connected with the knowledge known to Adam before the Fall. For him acceptance of the chemical medicine had religious overtones and the work of Paracelsus could be compared with that of Luther and other Protestant reformers in religion.[33]

London practitioners of the closing decades of the sixteenth century were able to choose from a wide variety of chemically prepared remedies available from John Hester (d. ca. 1593) who also translated into English some of the more practical tracts of the Italian, Leonardo Fioravanti (d. 1588), the German, Philip Herman (fl. 3rd quarter 16th century) and the French authority, Joseph Duchesne.[34]

---

[30] The references to Paracelsus by William Turner (1557), William Bullein (1562) and John Jones are discussed in *ibid.*, 55–56.

[31] Paracelsian remedies in the works of sixteenth-century English surgeons are discussed in *ibid.*, 56–57, 69–70.

[32] Bostocke's *Difference* (1585) is discussed in *ibid.*, 57–65.

[33] Paracelsus 'was not the author and inventour of this arte as the followers of the Ethnickes phisicke doe imagine, as by the former writers may appeare, no more than Wicklife, Luther, Oecolãpadius, Swinglius, Calvin &c. were the Author and inventors of the Gospell and religion in Christes Church . . . And no more than Nicholaus Copernicus which lived at the time of this Paracelsus, and restored to us the place of the starres according to the truth, as experience and true observation doth teach is to be called the author and inventor of the motions of the stars, which long before were taught by Ptolemeus Rules Astronomicall . . .' Bostocke, Chapter 19. sig. Hvii^v to Hviii^r.

[34] Paul H. Kocher, 'John Hester, Paracelsian (fl. 1576–93)' in *Joseph Quincy Adams Memorial Studies*, edited by James G. McManaway, Giles E. Dawson, Edwin E. Willoughby, Washington 1948, 621–38. Debus, *English Paracelsians*, 66–69.

Few were willing to condemn all of the chemists, and the renowned English surgeon, William Clowes (ca. 1540–1604) argued that there were both true and quack Paracelsians.[35] Physicians should be willing to borrow valuable remedies from any source, whether Galenic or Paracelsian.

Nor were the members of the London College of Physicians as inflexible as their counterparts in Paris. Thomas Moffett (1553–1604), a prominent Fellow of the College, was a friend of the Danish Paracelsian, Peter Severinus, and had received his degree at Basel in 1584 where Paracelsus had taught. His defence of chemical medicines appeared in 1584 and was dedicated to Severinus.[36] It was to be reprinted three times in the various editions of Zetzner's *Theatrum Chemicum* in the course of the seventeenth century. It is little wonder that when the College planned the publication of an official pharmacopoeia Moffett was placed in charge of the committee on chemical medicines (1589).

The English connection with Continental Paracelsism was not limited to Moffett's friendship with Severinus. Far more important was the French connection. John Hester had translated Duchesne's early works on gunshot wounds and on the use of chemical medicines, while a minister, Thomas Tymme (d. 1620) translated large sections of Duchesne's theoretical discussions of Paracelsian cosmology and medicine, which were published in 1603 and 1604 as *The Practise of Chymicall, and Hermeticall Physicke* (1605).[37] Like Bostocke, Tymme saw in the Paracelsian system an approach to the study of nature and Man that avoided the issue of the 'heathnish' texts of antiquity.

But knowledge of the French debate was not limited to hearsay or the translations of Hester and Tymme. Duchesne's colleague and ally in Paris in 1603 had been Theodore Turquet de Mayerne (1573–1655) whose *Apologia* for Duchesne had earned him the hatred of the Medical Faculty. Mayerne moved to London in 1606 where he was appointed physician to the Queen.[38] After a brief return to Paris, he left his homeland permanently for England at the death of

[35] William Clowes, *A Right Frutefull and Approoved Treatise for the Artificiall Cure of that Malady called in Latin Struma*, London 1602, 'Epistle to the Reader.'

[36] Debus, *English Paracelsians*, 71–76. Moffett's *De Ivre et Praestantia Chymicorum Medicamentorum Dialogus apologeticus*, Frankfurt 1584, has a special significance because of the author's position in the London medical establishment. See also below Chapter 11.

[37] Tymme's *Practise* is discussed in Debus, *English Paracelsians*, 87–96.

[38] The life and works of Turquet de Mayerne are currently being studied by Hugh Trevor-Roper. There are few older studies and the one most frequently cited

Henri IV in 1610. He was then appointed Chief Physician to James I and made a Fellow of the College of Physicians. Deeply interested in all aspects of chemical medicine, Mayerne joined a College that was by this time open to the consideration of all aspects of the subject.

The earlier plan to issue a pharmacopoeia had by this time been shelved, but it was of great interest to Mayerne who was instrumental in reactivating the project. The *Pharmacopoeia Londinensis* did, in fact, appear in two editions in 1618, and in addition to the traditional Galenic preparations there were sections on salts, metals, minerals, on chemical oils and on what were termed 'more useful chemical preparations.'[39] The preface, probably written by Mayerne, referred to the Fellows' veneration of traditional medical learning, and also of their willingness to use the newer chemical remedies.

In short, although influenced by the work of French authors, the English reaction to the chemical innovations of the sixteenth century was quite different from the developments in Paris. There the Medical Faculty tried to halt the advance of chemistry which was looked on as a threat to tradition. In contrast, in England there were proponents of the new medicine present in the College of Physicians at an early date and there was relatively little resistance to the election of chemists during those same years which witnessed the most vicious battles between the Medical Faculty and the Court Physicians in France. However, England did not boast two historically eminent medical schools of the level of Montpellier and Paris, nor was there the same level of underlying religious tension associated with the new medicine that caused friction in France. But in London as in Paris, the medical establishment sought to extend its control over the profession. Here they watched unaffiliated chemists with care. The 1617 Charter to the Apothecaries permitted them to dispense but not prescribe medicines, and the 1618 *Pharmacopoeia* may be viewed as a guide to the preparation of medicines. Twenty years later the Fellows of the College were instrumental in establishing the City Company of Distillers. This, too, may be seen as an extension

---

is Thomas Gibson's 'A Sketch of the Career of Theodore Turquet de Mayerne,' *Ann. Med. Hist.*, New Series, 5, 1933, 315–26.

[39] The historical background to the 1618 editions of the *Pharmacopoeia Londinensis* was examined by George Urdang in *Pharmacopoeia Londinensis of 1618 Reproduced in Facsimile with a Historical Introduction by George Urdang*, Hollister Pharmaceutical Library, Number Two, Madison, 1944, 1–81.

of their own rights of control. Indeed, by mid-century the College had appointed its own chemist and set up its own laboratory so that chemical medicines could be obtained directly from them.[40]

The difficulties encountered by chemists in France differed considerably from the relatively easy acceptance of these remedies in England. But the situation in Spain and Portugal was unique due to local conditions and religious restrictions.[41] Fear of the Protestant Reformation had led Philip II to attempt to separate Spain from foreign influences as early as 1557–1558, a date prior to the widespread dissemination of Paracelsian ideas. Both the Council of Castile and the Spanish Inquisition were charged with the licensing of books and those who published or circulated unlicensed books were subject to death and confiscation of goods. In a similar fashion higher education was closed to foreign influences. As part of the same draconian measures Spanish students were ordered to return home from all outside universities within four months with the exception of Bologna, Rome, Naples and Coimbra. Needless to say, in the century from 1560 to 1660 the Spanish universities did not keep pace with others in Europe. This is particularly true of the sciences at a time that was crucial in the development of the Scientific Revolution. The cost of preserving religious orthodoxy was high.

But again we are concerned primarily with the pace of chemistry in the larger fields of science and medicine. In 1585 the Spanish *Index* took note of Paracelsus by expurgating several passages to be found in his lesser work on surgery. The edition of 1632 classified him as a Lutheran and forbade the reading of most of his work. Indeed, he was placed in the 'first class of authors of damned memory.'[42] Indeed, the only work that may be called Paracelsian in this period is a short text on practical chemical remedies published in

---

[40] Cecil Wall, H. Charles Cameron and E. Ashworth Underwood, *A History of the Worshipful Society of Apothecaries of London*, London et al., 1963, *1*, 93.

[41] I have discussed the Portuguese and Spanish development in 'Chemistry and Iatrochemistry in Early Eighteenth-Century Portugal: A Spanish Connection' in *História e Desenvolvimento da Ciência em Portugal*, Secretary-General of the Colloquium, Prof. Doutor António Vasconcellos Marques, 2 vols., Lisboa: Academia das Ciências de Lisboa, 1986, *2*, 1245–62. A summary of recent Spanish research in this field will be found in J.M. López Piñero, 'La Ciencia en la España de los Siglos XVI y XVII' in vol. 5, *La Frustración de un Imperio (1476–1714)* of Manuel Tuñon de Lara, *Historia de España*, Barcelona 1981, 357–427.

[42] The problem of Paracelsus and the Spanish *Index* is discussed in anon., 'La Historia de la Ciencia en España como Realidad Marginal en su Organización y Contexto Social,' *Anthropos*, no. 20, 1982, 2–15, (4).

1589 that exists as a single copy.[43] In the Iberian peninsula medical instruction remained uncompromisingly Galenic throughout this period which, as we have noted, was characterized by debate and open discussion in other parts of Europe.

A new interest in the sciences occurred only in the 1660s due to Don Juan of Austria who acted as Regent during the minority of Charles II. He relaxed the censorship laws and personally cultivated the sciences. As a result, along with references to William Harvey, Nicholas Copernicus and corpuscularian philosophy we find a sudden interest in chemistry and the chemical medicine of Paracelsus, Thomas Willis (1621–1675) and Franciscus de la Böe Sylvius (1614–1672) as part of the new philosophy.

By 1679 Juan Bautista Juanini (1636–1691) was proposing iatrochemistry as the basis for a new medicine, while in 1687 Juan de Cabriada commented on the backwardness of Spanish science and called for the adoption of the 'new' chemical medicine and the establishment of a Royal Academy of Science.[44] For these authors—and others well into the eighteenth century—chemistry rather than physics was to be the key to a new science and medicine. Indicative of this is the fact that Cabriada's call for an academy of science bore fruit in the founding of the Regia Sociedade de Medicina y otras Ciencias in Seville in 1697.

This delayed Paracelsian influence resulted in a number of works that reflected the concerns of the sixteenth rather than the eighteenth century. A Jesuit, Hernando Castrillo, had written a *History of Occult Philosophy and Natural Magic* which had first appeared in 1643, but was reprinted in 1693 and 1723. The author was careful to point out that his object was to 'propagate the faith', but at the same time he was convinced that the 'Magical Art is an absolute science' which was first communicated to Adam and whose object is the discovery of the secrets implanted on earth by the Creator.[45]

---

[43] This unique copy has been reprinted with an introduction by J.M. López Piñero as El 'Dioalogus' (1589) del paracelsista Llorenç Coçar y la cátedra de medicamentos químicos de la Universidad de Valenica (1591) in the Cuadernos Valencianos de Historia de la Medicina y de la Ciencia XX (Serie B—Textos Clásicos), Valencia 1977.

[44] J.M. López Piñero, 'La Carta Filosofica-Medico-Chymica (1687) de Juan de Cabriada, Punto de Partida de la Medicina Moderna en España,' Asclepio, 17, 1965, 207–12.

[45] Padre Hernando Castrillo, Historia, y Magia Natural, o Ciencia de Filosofia Oculta, Con noticias de los mas profundas mysterios, y secretos del Universo visible, en que se trata de Animales, Pezes, Aves, Plantas, Flores, Yervos, Metales, Piedros Águas, Semillas, Parayso, Montes, y Valles . . . Donde trata de los Secretos que pertenecen à las partes de la tierra, Madrid 1723, 53.

No less interesting is Francisco Suarez de Rivera (ca. 1680–1753) who published some forty books between 1718 and 1751.[46] Having taken his M.D. in Salamanca in 1711, he later practiced in Seville and eventually became physician to the Bourbons in Madrid. Suarez was widely read in all fields of medicine and wrote a number of books on chemical medicine. Again we have here a figure who reflects the late sixteenth century rather than the period of the Enlightenment. His books emphasize the three Paracelsian principles and natural magic which he calls 'the most subtil science of physics and consists of the investigation of the phenomena which are observed in diverse natural bodies.' Suarez wrote also of the universal solvent, the alkahest, the powder of sympathy and potable gold. He informed his readers that he had personally read the work of Paracelsus and he recommended this author to others stating that he personally had no interest in religious orthodoxy, only in the health of the public.[47]

In the case of Spain, I have gone well beyond the chronological limit I set for myself. Still, the consequences of the policies of Philip II were so unexpected that I thought it of some interest to note why we find there a science typical of the Renaissance as late as the eighteenth century. Indeed, there is little doubt that the introduction of chemistry to medicine in France, England and Spain indicates the effect of local conditions. I am sure that studies of Paracelsism in other areas of Europe would yield similar results.

I will pass over studies that relate to Scandinavian and Eastern European Paracelsism. Dr. Grell's chapter will enlighten us about the Danish scene, and Jole Shackelford has also completed a dissertation on this subject in the United States.[48] Even the Italian scene has not been examined with the detail I would like to see.[49] Rather,

---

[46] Debus, 'Chemistry and Iatrochemistry in Portugal,' 1254–57. See also Luis S. Granjel, *Francisco Suarez de Rivera: Médico salamantino del siglo XVIII*, Salamanca, 1967, and José-Luis Valverde, *La Farmacia y las Ciencias Farmaceuticas en la Obra de Suarez de Rivera*, Salamanca, XIII, 1970.

[47] Francisco Suarez de Ribera, *Anatomica Chymica, Inviolable, y Memorable*, Madrid 1743, 21–22.

[48] See below Chapter 11 and Jole Shackelford, 'Paracelsianism in Denmark and Norway in the 16th and 17th Centuries (Ph.D. dissertation, University of Wisconsin-Madison, 1989). See also O.P. Grell 'The reception of Paracelsianism in early modern Lutheran Denmark: from Peter Severinus, the Dane to Ole Worm', *Medical History*, 1995, 39, 78–94.

[49] Giancarlo Zanier has published 'La Medicina Paracelsiana in Italia: Aspetti di un'accoglienza Particolare,' *Rivista di storia della filosofia*, n. 4, 1985, 627–53 and Massimo Luigi Bianchi has published 'Occulto e manifesto nella medicina del

let me take as a final example the Ottoman Empire, an area where we would not expect to find much evidence of western science. Again we have only a limited number of studies to refer to, but what we have is of considerable interest. We know that a physician from Aleppo, Salih ibn Sallum (d. 1669–1670), completed a work on medicine in Istanbul no later than 1640.[50] It was there while employed as a physician to the Sultan that he learned Latin and studied the works of Paracelsus and his followers, many of whom he refers to by name. The fourth section of ibn Sallum's text is titled the 'New Chemical Medicine Invented by Paracelsus.' Here Galenic humoral theory is rejected and reliance is placed rather on the three principles. He accepted the concept of a universal medicine and then went on to describe the occult properties of plants and minerals as well as their connection with the planets and parts of the human body. And here also is to be found the doctrine of signatures along with laboratory procedures and specific preparations of medical value.

Ibn Sallum's knowledge of Paracelsian sources is further evidenced by an appendix which is ostensibly a translation of one of the classic texts of Paracelsian medicine, the *Basilica chymica* (1609) of Oswald Croll (1560–1609). His version, probably incomplete, is divided into a treatise on general diseases and another on diseases of specific organs. Once again emphasis is placed on mineral and metallic remedies and it is significant that he added to the text a discussion of the principles of health prepared by Hunain ibn Ishaq in the ninth century. Clearly, Ibn Sallum saw the work of Paracelsus as being compatible with traditional Islamic medicine.

Manuscript copies of Ibn Sallum's work on Paracelsian medicine are not rare and they seem to have been influential. Hosam Elkadem has noted the work of another Turkish physician, Omar Sifai, who wrote a text on chemical medicine in 1704[51] while Julio Samso has

---

Rinascimento Jean Fernel e Pietro Severino' in the *Atti e Memorie dell'Accademia Toscana di Scienza e Lettere: La Colombaria, 47*, (Nuova Serie-33), 185–248. Two other works of special interest are Ferdinando Abbri, *Elementi, Principi e Particelle: la teorie chimiche da Paracelso a Stahl*, Turin, 1980, and Paolo Galluzzi, 'Motivi paracelsiani nella Toscana de Cosimo II e di Don Antonio dei Medici: alchimia, medicina "chimica" e riforma del sapere' in *Scienza, credenza occulte, livelli di cultura*, Firenze 1982, 31–62.

[50] Manfred Ullman, *Die Medizin im Islam*, Leiden 1970, 182–184; Allen G. Debus, 'Mysticism and the Rise of Modern Science and Medicine,' *Studies in History of Medicine*, 4, 1980, 199–213 [reprinted in *Journal of Central Asia*, 3, 198, 46–61].

[51] Hosam Elkhadem, 'Du Latin a l'Arabe: Introduction de la Doctrine Medico-Chemique de Paracelse en Orient au XVIIIe Siècle,' *Civilisations, 38*, no. 1, 53–73.

referred to other Arabic translations of Paracelsian texts existing in Tunisian libraries.[52] This material is important in the diffusion of scientific and medical thought in the seventeenth century, but it is also of importance for our knowledge of the interaction of such thought between Western Europe and Islam in the period of the Scientific Revolution.

The Paracelsian text of ibn Sallum is normally presented as evidence of the introduction of modern medicine to Islam in the seventeenth century. This is quite true, but it is of interest also to observe his work in the broader context of the Scientific Revolution. The numerous copies of the *New Chemical Medicine Invented by Paracelsus* stand in stark contrast to the much rarer references to Copernicus and the mechanical philosophers in Arabic texts. But the debate between the Paracelsian chemical philosophers and the mechanical philosophers in Europe involved one system based upon a unified cosmos consciously allied with religion in opposition to a second system that emphasized mathematical abstraction and the examination of phenomena in isolation from other factors in nature. It was the latter science that was to triumph in Europe and the result was the separation of nature and religion by the philosophes of the period of the Enlightenment. But the philosophical and religious climate of Islam had little in common with this approach. Normally the great period of Islamic science may be said to have ended prior to the Western Scientific Revolution. A key to this may well be found in religion. Surely the influential work of Al-Ghazzli (eleventh century A.D.) pointed away from the sciences. He questioned the value of mathematics, complained that logic was overestimated, and said that the natural sciences were not to be rejected, but that they were peripheral subjects for the true believer. With this turn toward the more religious climate it is not too surprising that of the two major innovating philosophies seeking a new science to replace the works of Aristotle and Galen in the West, it should have been the work of the Paracelsians that proved to be more interesting to Islamic physicians and scientists.

Let me close by saying again that I do not believe that the Scientific Revolution should be presented simply as a battle between 'ancients' and 'moderns' since these words are nearly impossible to

---

[52] Julio Samso, 'A proposito de dos libros recientes sobre las relaciones culturales entre España y Tunez,' *Ethica* (Barcelona), 9, 1975, 243–54, 252.

define satisfactorily. Nor do I think that it should be discussed only in terms that led to the Newtonian Triumph since the more we learn of the eighteenth century the less triumphal this achievement seems to have been. Here I have discussed chemistry as a third approach ... an approach calling for new observations that would lead to a chemical philosophy of Man and nature. These philosophers differed from contemporary mechanists in their deeply held religious convictions that shaped their concept of the cosmos and in their openly expressed distrust of mathematics as a key to the understanding of natural phenomena. The widespread interest in this Chemical Philosophy shows that it was able to compete strongly for more than a century not only with the Aristotelians and Galenists, but also with the mechanists. By the late seventeenth century the persistence of the chemists had led to a general acceptance of chemically-prepared medicines and to the academic acceptance of chemistry as a valid subject on most of the medical faculties of Europe.

However, my main theme has been less to define the Chemical Philosophy, than it has been to indicate that as we study its acceptance that we see that this story reflects areas of general interest and concern to historians in general, not only historians of science. As we move from France to England to Spain we see that religious and political events played a part in the acceptance or rejection of this system. And surely the study of the acceptance of the new science is as important as the purely technical developments we read of most often in texts devoted to the history of science. I believe that we need a broader understanding of the rise of modern science. Even today there are too many traditional historians of science who would argue only for technical and internalist studies related to specific sciences. On the other hand, there are those who reject the internal history and call exclusively for research on the relation of science to society. In this volume we have a group aware of the significance of mystical thought in the development of modern science. In reality all of these approaches are needed. I believe that even this brief overview of the work of the Paracelsians indicates that any technical approach to this field of study should be combined with a broader historical and contextual approach. The historian of science should be grounded not only in the sciences, but in the intellectual, the social, the political and the religious history of his chronological period.

CHAPTER ELEVEN

THE ACCEPTABLE FACE OF PARACELSIANISM: THE LEGACY OF *IDEA MEDICINÆ* AND THE INTRODUCTION OF PARACELSIANISM INTO EARLY MODERN DENMARK

Ole Peter Grell

The importance of Peter Severinus, the Dane, and his book, *Idea medicinæ philosophicæ* (Basle 1571) for spreading Paracelsian medical doctrines in the late 16th century while simultaneously making them respectable and internationally acceptable for the first time, has already been emphasized by many of the leading scholars working in this field, such as Hugh Trevor-Roper, Allen Debus and Charles Webster.[1] However, it still remains to be properly explained how and why Severinus was so successful in achieving what had so far eluded Paracelsus and his followers: Paracelsianism had, after all, been considered both socially and medically unacceptable by the establishment for a generation after Paracelsus's death.

As always timing was of the essence. Peter Severinus and his Paracelsian fellow-student from Denmark, Johannes Pratensis, commenced their *perigrinatio academica* in the mid-1560s. This turned out to be a most fortunate moment in Paracelsian terms. It coincided with the re-discovery of Paracelsus's manuscripts in Basle by Adam von Bodenstein who had then recently, joined the medical faculty at the University in the city. Not surprisingly, considering Von Bodenstein's family roots in radical Protestantism—his father was Luther's estranged collaborator, Andreas (von Bodenstein) Karlstadt— he became an ardent Paracelsian. Having grown up in a climate of Protestant radicalism the step towards an equivalent medical radicalism signified a natural move for Adam von Bodenstein. His attempt to introduce Paracelsian teachings at the medical faculty of the University of Basle turned out to be premature, however, and led to his

---

[1] See H. Trevor-Roper, 'The Paracelsian Movement', in idem, *Renaissance Essays*, London 1986, 149–99; A.G. Debus, *The French Paracelsians: The chemical Challenge to medical and scientific Tradition*, Cambridge 1991, 18–19 and C. Webster, 'Essay Review', *Isis*, 1979, 70, 591.

expulsion in 1564. This experience probably caused him to set off on a publishing career which saw him publish more than forty works of Paracelsus. In other words, Peter Severinus and Johannes Pratensis commenced their post-graduate studies in medicine at a time when the most significant of Paracelsus's works became available in print for the first time.[2]

Undoubtedly, this explosion of Paracelsian literature coming from Basle and Strasburg in particular, proved of the greatest significance. It created what can best be described as the Paracelsian moment and it inspired Peter Severinus to write his *Idea medicinæ*. But did Severinus really, as claimed by Walter Pagel become 'the most genuine and reliable expositor of Paracelsus'?[3] Rather than similarities between Severinus and his works and those of Paracelsus it is the differences between the two men and their writings which spring to mind when compared. Some of these differences have already been noted by Hugh Trevor-Roper who considers Severinus to have been an 'urbane and civilized' character who purged Paracelsianism of its 'grossness' and inconsistency.[4] Further and immediate differences can be inferred from the fact that Paracelsus wrote and published his works in vernacular German while Severinus published his in polished Latin. Severinus's works were in other words aimed at the scholarly world whereas Paracelsus's appealed to a much broader and more popular market.

Furthermore, if we compare the background and careers of Paracelsus and Severinus, it is again the differences rather than the similarities which dominate. Paracelsus was the son of an emigrant physician who had settled in Switzerland, while Severinus was born into a settled and influential burgher-family in the town of Ribe in southern Jutland. Severinus received his secondary schooling in the town's Latin school which educated a fair number of the leading figures of this period's Danish intelligentsia.[5] He then followed the traditional pattern of talented, Danish students of the early modern period, continuing his studies at the University of Copenhagen. Here

---

[2] W. Pagel, *Paracelsus. An Introduction to Philosophical Medicine in the era of the Renaissance*, Basle 1958, reprint London 1982, 31 and Trevor-Roper, 'Paracelsian Movement', 152–53.

[3] W. Pagel, *Joan Baptista van Helmont*, Cambridge 1982, 139.

[4] Trevor-Roper, 'Paracelsian Movement', 161.

[5] See B. Kornerup, *Ribe Katedralskoles Historie*, 2 vols., Copenhagen 1947 & 1952.

he received his MA in 1564, before he set out on his *perigrinatio* with the view of acquiring his MD.

Paracelsus, on the other hand, demonstrated his restlessness from the outset. Little is known about his schooling, but the fact that his Latin was fairly basic may well indicate that his secondary schooling was lacking in some respects. Nor, does he appear to have followed a traditional pattern with regard to his tertiary education. He may well have studied at a number of European universities among them those of Vienna, and Ferrara in Italy, but he is not likely to have acquired any formal qualifications and certainly never received the MD.[6] Paracelsus was, in other words, a natural outsider, radical and aggressively critical, and constantly running into conflict with the authorities where ever he went. As has recently been demonstrated by Charles Webster his critique of learned medicine constituted only part of his wider social and religious radicalism.[7] He led a peripatetic life unable to settle in any one place for long, constantly falling out with the political, religious and academic authorities in the places where he attempted to establish himself.

Peter Severinus, on the other hand, was very much an establishment character despite his attraction to Paracelsianism.[8] A glance at the title page of his *Idea Medicinæ* is very informative. The full title of the work: *The idea of philosophical medicine which constitutes the foundation for all the doctrines of Paracelsus, Hippocrates and Galen*, indicates that his work, even if innovative, seeks to place itself within the scholarly tradition of learned medicine. Furthermore, its author clearly considered himself to be part of this learned medical tradition, so despised by Paracelsus. This is emphasized by Severinus's use of the titles natural philosopher and physician. That the work was dedicated to the Danish King, Frederik II, is further proof of Severinus's social and intellectual ambition to be part of the establishment.[9]

---

[6] For the life of Paracelsus, see Pagel, *Paracelsus*, 7–29. For Severinus, see O.P. Grell, 'The Reception of Paracelsianism in Early Modern Denmark: from Peter Severinus, The Dane, to Ole Worm', *Medical History*, 1995, 39, 78–94. See also H.F. Rørdam, *Kjøbenhavns Universitets Historie fra 1531 til 1621*, vol. 2, Copenhagen 1872, 572–84 and *Dansk Biografisk Leksikon*, 3rd edition, henceforth *DBL*.

[7] C. Webster, 'Paracelsus: medicine as popular protest', in O.P. Grell & A. Cunningham (eds.), *Medicine and the Reformation*, London 1993, 57–77.

[8] See Grell, 'Reception of Paracelsianism'.

[9] See titlepage, P. Severinus, *Idea Medicinæ Philophicae fundamenta continens totius doctrinæ Paracelsicæ, Hippocraticæ, & Galenicæ*, Basle 1571.

248 OLE PETER GRELL

Apart from his *pegrinatio academica* Severinus remained in Denmark as
Royal physician until his death in 1602, at a time when he had just
been appointed professor of medicine at the University of Copenhagen. In other words, Peter Severinus pursued a successful if un-
eventful carreer.

The differences between Paracelsus and Peter Severinus could
hardly have been greater. Paracelsus was and remained an outsider,
radical, unsettled and single, whereas Severinus quickly established
himself in the world of learned medicine. Having been appointed
Royal Physician to Frederik II he later married into one of the
wealthiest burgher-families in the country and became a family man.
Thus, Severinus was and remained part of the establishment both
socially and academically.[10]

No wonder Severinus and his *Idea medicinæ* were widely admired
among the scholarly community in early modern Europe, by pro-
tagonists, as well as antagonists, of Paracelsianism. Here, for the first
time, was a purified and systematized version of some of Paracelsus's ideas, de-radicalized and neatly incorporated into learned medicine. Even the leading anti-Paracelsian, the physician and theologian
Thomas Erastus, recommended Severinus's book as the most palat-
able face of Paracelsianism as early as 1579.[11] Later critics, such as
the Wittenberg professor of medicine, Daniel Sennert, acknowledged
Severinus's importance for the dissemination of Paracesian ideas in
a purified and organized form. Sennert considered Severinus to have
been of such significance that he saw him as having given rise to a
particular and dominant school of Paracelsianism which he labelled
Severinian.[12]

Naturally, Severinus was widely praised by those who, like him,
were attracted to an eclectic, neo-Platonic variety of Paracelsianism,
such as the Basle professor of medicine, Theodore Zwinger and the
English physician, Thomas Moffett. Zwinger, who had been instru-

[10] For Severinus's marriage, see E. Bastholm, *Petrus Severinus og hans Idea medicinæ philosophicæ*, Odense 1979, 8. Severinus and Johannes Pratensis are supposed to have promised each other never to marry, but to devote themselves fully to natural phi-losophy, see Rørdam, *Kjøbenhavns Universitet*, 2, 579.

[11] See J.R. Shackelford, 'Paracelsianism in Denmark and Norway in the 16th and 17th centuries', dissertation, University of Wisconsin 1989, 129 and Debus, *The French Paracelsians*, 18–19.

[12] D. Sennert, *De chymicorum cum Aristotelicis et Galenicis consensu ac dissensu Liber*, Wittenberg 1619, 57. See also Shackleford, 'Paracelsianism', 163 and A.G. Debus, 'Peter Severinus' in *Dictionary of Scientific Biography*, 14 vols., New York 1970–80.

mental in the expulsion of Adam von Bodenstein in 1564, seems to have come to share Severinus's eclectic, 'Hippocratized' Paracelsianism during the 1570s and a close friendship grew up between the two men.[13]

Severinus also struck up a friendship with Thomas Moffett, whom he met when Moffett visited Copenhagen as part of an English embassy in 1582. Moffett had undoubtedly already read Severinus's *Idea medicinæ* while a student in Basle in the late 1570s and probably heard the Dane mentioned positively by his professor, Theodore Zwinger. Two years later Moffett dedicated his defense of Paracelsus and iatrochemistry to Severinus. Entitled, *De Jure Præsantia Chymicorum* (1584), this book went through several editions on the continent and served to enhance Severinus's reputation as the period's leading exponent of Paracelsiansism.

However, even if the *Idea medicinæ* was widely praised by learned physicians, it is evident that Severinus's work had also been widely attacked by a considerable number of traditional, Galenist physicians across Europe. In his dedicatory letter to Severinus in *De Jure* Moffett pointed out that he would have published his book sooner had he not expected Severinus to be about to deliver a 'golden reply' to his anti-Paracelsian antagonists. Similarly, in a letter of 5 May 1584 Moffett urged Severinus to respond to

> the outrageous, insolent and arrogant vehemence of the anti-Paracelsians, and to consider that it is not you, but iatrochemistry which is in danger, and, if I am not mistaken, you will not be able to keep it free of attack before you have deprived these anti-Paracelsian writings of all authority and vehemence.[14]

That this was not only Moffett's opinion can be seen from the letter Severinus wrote to Theodore Zwinger in Basle in February 1583.

---

[13] For Theodore Zwinger, see C. Gilly, 'Zwischen Erfahrung und Spekulation. Theodor Zwinger und die religiöse und kulturelle Krise seiner Zeit', *Basler Zeitschrift für Geschichte* 1977, 77, 57–137 & 1979, 79, 125–223. See also Trevor-Roper, 'Paracelsian Movement', 163–64. For Thomas Moffett, see *Dictionary of National Biography*. For the friendship between Zwinger and Peter Severinus, see Grell, 'Reception of Paracelsianism', 81. For early modern Danish medicine and its close contacts with Basle, see O.P. Grell, 'Caspar Bartholin and the Education of the Pious Physician', in O.P. Grell & A. Cunningham (eds.), *Medicine and the Reformation*, London 1993, 78–100.

[14] For the dedication, see Shackelford, 'Paracelsianism', 135–36. For Moffett's letter to Severinus of 5 May 1584, see Rørdam, *Kjøbenhavns Universitet*, vol. 4, Copenhagen 1874, 320–21 (my translation).

Here Severinus emphasized that 'most people knew how certain critics had received his works with severity and unfair criticism. That
is why I have opted for silence: I abhor polemics and abuse'.[15]

Theodore Zwinger and others of Peter Severinus's friends continued to encourage him to answer his critics, especially by publishing
his short description of natural philosophy. As early as August 1583
Severinus had promised Zwinger to publish this work in the immediate future; but he was clearly worried about the possible consequences, adding that 'it would probably generate hostility among
contemporaries which is the common destiny of all scholarly works,
which remove themselves some way from the beaten track.[16]

Zwinger kept prodding Severinus to add the finishing touches to
his work on natural philosophy and get it published. But Severinus
still prevaricated, pointing out:

> Those things, which were self-evident and supported by Holy Scripture
> I considered sufficient to be presented for the appraisal of other schol-
> ars. But warned and instructed by the unfortunate and unexpected
> result which the publication of my Idea generated, I have realized that
> I have not yet been able to satisfy everybody, since what I have adduced
> based on the revealed evidence of nature, without considering the
> Aristotelian philosophy in the least—which I do not recognize as my
> authority—has been assessed, condemned and rejected by my oppo-
> nents on the basis of the physical laws and doctrines of Aristotle.[17]

Severinus's work on natural philosophy clearly offered a similar neo-
Platonic interpretation, co-ordinating natural philosophy, the Book
of Nature, with the Word of God, as found in the Bible. He was
still working on this book five years later, when the learned Josias
Mercer arrived in Copenhagen as secretary to the English ambas-
sador, Daniel Rogers. Mercer, who took the opportunity to visit Peter
Severinus, noted in his diary that Severinus was about to publish a
book 'on the whole of natural philosophy, based on those principles
which can be drawn from Holy Scripture with which the Platonists
generally tally, but with which the doctrines of Aristotle are at odds.'[18]

---

[15] For this letter of 23 February 1583, see Bastholm, *Petrus Severinus*, 45–9, especially 46 (my translation).
[16] For this letter of 12 August 1583, see *Ibid.*, 49–51, especially 50.
[17] For this letter, dated 16 August 1587, see *Ibid.*, 54–58, especially 54 & 58.
[18] Mercer's diary is published by C. Behrend, 'En dagbog fra en rejse i Danmark
i året 1588', *Fra Arkiv og Museum*, vol. 5, 1912–1915, 294–310, see especially 298.
For the Latin text, see *Danske Magazin*, Series 6, vol. 1, 1913, 334–44. Severinus

Thus, in spite of having done his utmost to place his neo-Platonic and eclectic version of Paracelsianism, emphasizing its Hippocratic roots, within the parameters of traditional, learned medicine, Severinus nevertheless failed to achieve what he had hoped for: acceptance, if not necessarily agreement, by the majority of his learned collegues in natural philosophy and medicine. Being a naturally cautious and irenic man, he was disinclined to confront the 'conservative' scholars who had attacked him. Severinus had no ambition to be associated with radicalism of any sort and accordingly opted for silence. He never published another book, not even his much anticipated work on natural philosophy. The reasons for this, may not solely be found in the hostility with which the *Idea medicinæ* had been received by traditional Galenists, but may also be explained by the dangers which the growing doctrinal conflict within German Lutheranism, from the mid-1570s onwards presented even for innovators in natural philosophy, such as Severinus.

However, before turning to the Danish political and religious context into which Severinus's version of Paracelsianism was introduced in 1571, it will be useful to take a closer look at the particular Paracelsian message delivered by the *Idea medicinæ*. Writing to Theodor Zwinger in 1583 Severinus described how he had come to write his book:

> But because practice and experiences appeared to contradict theories and methods, I started to work with greater care and diligence, to look more thoroughly at the doctrines of Plato and Hippocrates, and often to consider the theories and practice of the Ancient iatrochemists. Through such nightly studies I was introduced to the true and secret progress of the creation processes, while realizing the firm and eternal principles of the bodies and nature.

Severinus added that he had written his book 'not in order to declare war on the older generation, but only in the hope that his efforts may receive the gratitude from the younger generation they deserved.[19]

In the introduction to *Idea medicinæ* Severinus provided further information about this undertaking, claiming that it was while practising as a physician that he had come to realise that Galen's theories were inadequate, and that the drugs recommended by Galen

---

had circulated a manuscript version of his work among his friends, see Jacques Bongars letter to Severinus, 1 June 1596, printed Bastholm, *Petrus Severinus*, 40.
  [19] Letter in Bastholm, *Petrus Severinus*, 46.

often proved useless. While staying in Germany Severinus had for
the first time heard positive reports about the drugs produced by
Paracelsus. Accordingly, he had begun to study Paracelsus's writings
which had recently become available in print. Initially he had encountered serious difficulties in understanding Paracelsus's works which
he found full of contradictions and incomprehensible definitions.
Eventually, however, through the study of the writings of the Ancient
Greeks, Hippocrates in particular, who had written on 'natural history, the properties of the elements, the 'semina', agriculture, and
observations on the origin of the stars, plants, minerals and animals', these authors had helped Severinus to understand Paracelsus's
classifications and interpretations and the method of 'vitalistic astrology' which Paracelsus used in all his natural philosophy and medicine.[20] According to Severinus most of Paracelsus's ideas had in fact
already been launched by Hippocrates and other ancient authors
and only been forgotten because of Galen's unfortunate tendency to
theoretize. Where, according to Severinus, Paracelsus had been able
to add to the teaching of Hippocrates it had only been possible because new diseases unknown to Hippocrates had developed. Hippocrates had after all lived in a more fortunate age which had not
been darkened by the appearance of new diseases which were difficult
to cure.[21]

By placing his version of Paracelsianism firmly within the Hippocratic tradition Severinus was able to make a more convincing case
for Paracelsian ideas within learned medicine.[22] The eclectic Paracelsianism he advocated was, however, highly critical of scholastic
medicine and Galenic pathology. It fitted into the Paracelsian rhetoric
of reform, but only just, having been cleansed of all popular and
radical elements. It was a compromise between traditional learned
medicine and Paracelsianism, as can be seen from the conclusion of
the *Idea medicinæ* where Severinus admitted that he did not want to
see traditional medicine abolished, but only gradually changed in a
dialectical confrontation with the eclectic Paracelsianism advocated
by him.[23] This evolutionary approach is also in evidence in the drug
therapy recommended by Severinus. According to him, herbal med-

---

[20] Severinus, *Idea medicinæ*, fols. A4v–Br.
[21] *Ibid.*, 374–75.
[22] Shackelford, 'Paracelsianism', 76–78.
[23] Severinus, *Idea medicinæ*, 406–07.

icines should remain in use by the physicians, even if certain improvements could be achieved in their preparation, while the more potent mineral preparations were to be given greater attention by the medical practitioners.[24]

Having seen his *Idea medicinæ* through to publication in Basle, Severinus returned to Denmark together with his friend and fellow-Paracelsian Johannes Pratensis. Both men had recently received their MDs abroad and were now returning home to take up the prominent positions they had been groomed for through royal patronage.[25] They could hardly have chosen a more opportune moment. The Seven Years' War with Sweden (1563–1570) had finished only the previous year and as a result more money had become available for education in general and the University of Copenhagen in particular, in what proved an economically expansive phase for the country.

The Paracelsian orientation of Severinus and Pratensis may actually have benefited them rather than causing them problems with their royal benefactors, Frederik II and Queen Sophie, who were both actively interested in iatrochemistry and Paracelsianism.[26] Not surprisingly, the most prominent of the two, Severinus, was immediately offered the lucrative position of royal physician to Frederik II.[27] The *Idea medicinæ* and its dedication had evidently been noted by the king.

Pratensis, however, had to wait a couple of weeks before he was appointed to the vacant, second chair in medicine at the University. Evidently there was some opposition to Pratensis's appointment within the University. It was, however, on the suggestion of the Vice-Chancellor and the country's leading theologian, Niels Hemmingsen, that Pratensis was offered the second chair. Hemmingsen may well have been prodded by his friend, the influential court preacher,

---

[24] For this point, see Shackelford, 'Paracelsianism', 119. Thus, Severinus does not appear to have used iatrochemical or mineral drugs in his treatment of Frederik II during the king's last illness in 1588, see A. Lübbbers, *De Oldenborgske Kongers Sygdomme og Død*, Copenhagen 1906, 56–58.

[25] See Grell, 'Reception of Paracelsianism', 80–81.

[26] *Ibid.*, 81–82 and Bastholm, *Petrus Severinus*, 13.

[27] The basic salary Severinus received for his position as royal physician appears to have been equivalent to that drawn by the leading professors at the University of Copenhagen, but the considerable emoluments which went with the post of royal physician were not matched by those of the professorships, compare Bastholm, *Petrus Severinus*, 7 with V. Helk, *Dansk-Norske Studierejser fra Reformationen til Enevælden* 1536–1660, Odense 1987, 15.

Niels Nielsen Kolding, who was the inspiration behind many of Frederik II's educational initiatives.[28] But the fact that Hemmingsen made the suggestion is far more significant than the restrictions imposed on Pratensis's teaching: He had to promise to teach fully in accordance with the Hippocratic and Galenic medicine taught at the Lutheran Universities of Wittenberg and Leipzig. If Hemmingsen and his theological colleagues had nurtured any religious reservations about the eclectic Paracelsianism expressed by Pratensis and Severinus, Hemmingsen would hardly have suggested Pratensis for the job. The limitations imposed on Pratensis's teaching should, in other words, rather be seen as a politic and prudent move which made it difficult for those within the University who opposed his appointment to put up continued resistance to his promotion, than a serious attempt to prevent the teaching of Paracelsianism at the University. Even if the restrictions had been seriously meant by Hemmingsen they appear to have failed in their objective. In a letter to Severinus Pratensis joked about the promises he had been forced to make at his appointment to the chair, pointing out that he had been 'obliged to honour the teaching of Galen as an oracle and to spurn the poor and incomprehensible inventions by others who attempt to demonstrate, through a wonderful and hitherto unknown anatomy, new phenomena and exceptional changes in nature'. He appears to have disregarded these restrictions on his teaching from the outset and introduced an eclectic Paracelsianism through the back door when criticizing Galen in his lectures. That this was so is confirmed by the University of Copenhagen when, at his death in 1576, it praised him for his teaching of both medical systems, 'the Galenic and the Paracelsian'.[29]

More or less simultaneously with Severinus's and Pratensis's return to Copenhagen another neo-Platonist and eclectic Paracelsian, who was to acquire European fame in astronomy, Tycho Brahe, arrived in the capital after extensive studies abroad. His private research academy, Uraniborg, on the island of Hven in the Sound, where

---

[28] Pratensis's appointment was discussed by the governing body of the University on 3 July 1571, see J.D. Herholdt & F.V. Mansa (eds.), *Samlinger til den danske medicinal-Historie*, vol. 1, Copenhagen 1833–35, 148–49. For Niels Nielsen Kolding, see *DBL*. The close connection between Hemmingsen and Kolding can be seen from one of Kolding's edifying books, *De besynderligste Historier . . .*, Copenhagen 1567, to which Niels Hemmingsen wrote the introduction.

[29] For Pratensis's letter to Severinus, see Bastholm, *Petrus Severinus*, 41–44. For the praise of the University, see *Ibid.*, 6–7.

Brahe seems to have been preoccupied with alchemical work rather than astronomy during the 1570s,[30] became the third cornerstone in a neo-Platonist/Paracelsian triangle which was anchored within the Court and its royal physician, Peter Severinus, and included the University and Johannes Pratensis. This group of eclectic Paracelsians to a large extent owed their promotion to two of the University's leading professors, Hans Frandsen in medicine and Niels Hemmingsen in theology. Hans Frandsen, like Severinus born and educated in the town of Ribe, appears despite his Galenist orientation to have been keen on promoting young students with new, neo-Platonist/Paracelsian ideas. His friend, the theologian Niels Hemmingsen, who dedicated his famous book, *Syntagma Institutionum Christianarum*, Basle 1574, to Frandsen—a work, which by the way caused Hemmingsen to be suspended from his professorship in 1579, accused of crypto-Calvinism—held similar 'liberal' views. Thus, like his mentor, Philip Melanchthon, Hemmingsen considered astrology to be important. In a letter to the nobleman, Henrik Rantzau, from 1593, he admitted that he knew little of astrology personally, but he believed 'that all events had their causes, necessary or accidental, and that the exceptionally skilled could read future occurrences from the Book of Nature unto which God had written like a tablet'.[31] When Tycho Brahe gave his lectures on astronomy at the University of Copenhagen in 1574–75, which promoted a neo-Platonist natural philosophy and eclectic Paracelsianism, Niels Hemmingsen attended the lectures and publicly demonstrated his approval of them.[32] Furthermore, it was Niels Hemmingsen, who in 1577 made the unusual suggestion that Tycho Brahe who was not a member of the University, be appointed Vice-Chancellor.[33]

It is worth bearing in mind, that Hemmingsen was by far the

---

[30] For Tycho Brahe's interest in alchemy, see Shackelford, 'Paracelsianism', 203–10; see also J.R. Shackelford, 'Paracelsianism and patronage in early modern Denmark', in B.T. Moran (ed.), *Patronage and Institutions: Science, Technology and Medicine at the European Court*, Suffolk 1991, 95–105.

[31] Cited in J. Glebe-Møller, 'Socialetiske Aspekter af Niels Hemmingsen's Forfatterskab', *Kirkehistoriske Samlinger*, 1979, 7–56; see 24 (my translation). See also S. Kusukawa, 'Aspectio divinorum operum. Melanchton and astrology for Lutheran medics', in O.P. Grell & A. Cunningham (eds.), *Medicine and the Reformation*, Routledge 1993, 33–56.

[32] See V.E. Thoren, *The Lord of Uraniborg: a biography of Tycho Brahe*, Cambridge 1990, 79–85.

[33] Grell, 'Caspar Bartholin', 87. See also Grell, 'Reception of Paracelsianism', 84–85.

most influential member of the University of Copenhagen during most of this significant decade for the University. Undoubtedly the irenic and non-confrontational approach favoured by many of its leading members, including Pratensis and Severinus, owed much to the views of Hemmingsen. This irenicism was constantly emphasized by Hemmingsen as can be seen from the introduction to his, *Historia Domini Jhesu*, Copenhagen 1562, where he requested ministers and teachers to do their utmost to preserve unity in faith and teaching, pointing out that peace edifies while strife destroys![34]

Undoubtedly the strength and influence of the neo-Platonist/Paracelsian camp was somewhat weakened by Philip Pratensis's sudden and unexpected death in 1576 while lecturing to his students. However, the employment of other prominent eclectic Paracelsians such as Anders Krag—yet another scholar from Ribe—served to fill the gap. Krag, who had received his medical training in Basle and Montpellier where he was awarded his MD, came to serve the University in various professorial capacities from 1586 until his death in 1600. He was a fervent defender of Peter Ramus's natural philosophy and an active iatrochemist. His Paracelsianism was of the moderate Severinian variety which characterized the other Danish neo-Platonists of the age. Writing to his friend the Bamberg physician, Sigismund Schnitzer, Krag expressed how pleased he was that Schnitzer appreciated iatrochemical drugs as useful for many therapies. Krag added that he personally rated iatrochemical medicine highly, since he daily experienced its usefulness. He pointed out, however, that it was to be used only with caution and that Paracelsian drugs in general ought to be toned down while the Galenist approach should not be totally abandoned.[35]

By the beginning of the 17th century most, if not all, of the first generation of eclectic, Danish Paracelsians had died, including Tycho Brahe, Anders Krag and Peter Severinus. Only Tycho Brahe's former assistant, Cort Aslaksen, who eventually became professor of theology in 1607, was still actively promoting the Severinian version of Paracelsianism within the university.[36] At the court of Christian IV

---

[34] See Rørdam, *Kjøbenhavns Universitet*, 2, 24.

[35] For this letter, see T. Bartholin, *Cista Medica Hafniensis*, Copenhagen 1662, 109–12 and S. Veibel, *Kemien i Danmark*, Copenhagen 1937, 30. See also Rørdam, *Kjøbenhavns Universitet*, 3, 508–21.

[36] See Rørdam, *Kjøbenhavns Universitet*, 3, 585–99 and O. Garstein, *Cort Aslakssøn*, Oslo 1953.

the tradition begun by his father, Frederik II, of employing a Paracelsian physician/iatrochemist, was continued. In 1609 Christian IV built a distilation house in the garden of Rosenborg Castle and employed the Paracelsian physician, Peter Payngk, who had recently returned from the court of Emperor Rudolph II in Prague, as royal chemist. Payngk became busily engaged in providing chemical preparations for the King, the court and the nobility until his retirement in the 1640s. Evidently, he shared the ecletic Paracelsianism of his predecessor, Peter Severinus.[37]

Far more significant, however, were the changes which had taken place in the religious and political domain in Denmark by the beginning of the 17th century. Gone were the days when a 'liberal' Melanchthonian Lutheranism had dominated church and state which had coincided with the return of Severinus, Brahe and Pratensis. The first warning that this positive environment for a renewal in theology, as well as natural philosophy, was under threat can be seen from the case of Niels Hemmingsen. Due to the theological confrontation in Wittenberg in particular, between hardline, orthodox Lutherans-Gnesiolutherans—and 'liberal' Philippists, Niels Hemmingsen suddenly found himself in the firing line in the mid-1570s. Some of the Phillipists in Saxony had referred to Hemmingsen's recently published *Syntagma Institutionum Christianarum* (Basle 1574) in order to prove their orthodoxy. Rather than saving the embattled Wittenberg Phillipists, it served to draw the Duke of Saxony's attention to Hemmingsen and his theology. The Duke immediately accused Hemmingsen of crypto-Calvinism in letters to his brother-in-law, Frederik II. Niels Hemmingsen, who was undoubtedly positively inclined towards Calvinism, especially its interpretation of the Eucharist, was eventually suspended from his professorship in Copenhagen, not least because of the possible negative implications of his theology for Danish foreign policy in the period.[38]

This episode affected Severinus and many of his Philippist friends seriously, such as the minister, Johannes Pistorius. Severinus spoke for them all when he ended a letter to Pistorius, stating how sorry

---

[37] For Payngk, see A. Fjeldstrup, *Dr. Peter Payngk: Kong Christian IV's Hofkemiker*, Copenhagen 1911; see also Shackelford, 'Patronage', 106–08.

[38] See T. Lyby & O.P. Grell, 'The consolidation of Lutheranism in Denmark and Norway', in O.P. Grell (ed.) *The Scandinavian Reformation. From evangelical movement to institutionalisation of reform*, Cambridge 1994, 120–22.

he felt for the theologians and adding that 'to live in peace and quiet is the safest'.[39] This was a maxim which Severinus followed closely; undoubtedly the Hemmingsen-affair served to confirm him in his inclination not to publish any more of his works. Apart from the hostility he had already encountered from conservative, Galenist colleagues within the university-world, Hemmingsen's fate had emphasized the risks involved in publishing heterodox views.

Hemmingsen's fall was only a sign of what was to follow around the turn of the century. By then the political and religious climate had begun to change in Denmark. Christian IV had come of age in 1596 and the regency which had followed the death of Frederik II in 1588 had come to an end. By then the men who had dominated the government of the Kingdom since the end of the Seven Years War with Sweden, Peder Oxe and Chancellor Niels Kaas, who had both actively supported Niels Hemmingsen, Tycho Brahe and Peter Severinus, were all dead. Under the leadership of the new Chancellor, Christian Friis of Borreby (1596–1616), the power of the state was considerably enhanced. These developments eventually led to the introduction of a fully fledged absolutism in 1660. The desire to create a stronger and more centralized state also involved the Lutheran Church, where the recently appointed professor of theology, Hans Poulsen Resen (1597), in close collaboration with Christian Friis of Borreby, took steps to create a more uniform Church. Such moves were made particularly urgent by the growing impact of Counter-Reformation Catholicism and Calvinism in Scandinavia. Resen's campaign for uniformity within the Church led to a number of prominent, 'liberal' Philippists or crypto-Calvinists of the Hemmingsen ilk loosing their jobs within University and Church in the second decade of the 17th century. Resen and Friis, however, cannot be described as orthodox gnesio-Lutherans—the *Book of Concord* which had been anathema in Denmark since the reign of Frederik II continued to be rejected—instead, they wanted a uniform Church for political and ecclesiastical reasons. In ecclesiastical terms, Resen was a Danish equivalent to Archbishop William Laud in England. Accordingly, he cannot be seen to have nurtured any animosity towards the 'moderate' Paracelsianism and Ramism which continued to exist within

---

[39] For this letter, see Bastholm, *Petrus Severinus*, 39–40. For Pistorius, see introduction to A. Andersen (ed.), *Quattuor Centuriæ Epistolarum*, Historisk Samfund for Sønderjylland 1971, v–vii.

the University. If anything, Resen's inclination towards mysticism and a neo-Platonic natural philosophy would have made him positively inclined towards such views, while his participation in the reform of the Latin schools in 1604 demonstrate his Ramist leanings. Thus it was not the Paracelsian leanings of his co-professor of theology, Cort Aslaksen, which worried him in the years 1611–14, but Aslaksen's perceived crypto-Calvinism.[40] Furthermore, Resen did not remain unaffected by the pre-Pietist Lutheranism of his noble friend, Holger Rosenkrantz, whose theology was inspired by the German theologian, Johan Arndt. Rosenkrantz, like Arndt, wanted to complete, with a reformation of life, the Reformation which Luther had begun in teaching. The government's prohibition of 1623 against swearing and disregard of holidays and the penitential ordinance of 1629, which were geared towards improving piety among the people, all demonstrate the pre-Pietist influence on Resen's ecclesiology.[41]

Furthermore, the neo-Platonic and speculative aspects of Resen's theology are strongly in evidence in his writings leading up to his confrontation with the crypto-Calvinists in the Danish church in 1614, a year prior to his promotion to the bishopric of Zealand. There are, for example, considerable overlaps between important aspects of Resen's theology and that of the spiritualist Sebastian Franck whose ideas were close to those of Paracelsus.[42] Resen, who owned and heavily annotated a copy of Franck's *Paradoxa*, advocated similar ideas about Christ's eternal omni-presence in Nature. Likewise, Resen's teaching about 'unio mystica', concerning Christ's innate presence in the re-born Christian, is likely to have been inspired by his reading of Johan Arndt's *Vier Bücher von wahrem Christenthumb*. Thus further aspects of Resen's theology appear to have been influenced by another German, Protestant theologian who was positively inclined towards Paracelsianism.[43]

---

[40] For Peder Oxe, Niels Kaas, Christian Friis of Boreby and Hans Poulsen Resen see *DBL*; for Resen, see also B. Kornerup, *Hans Poulsen Resen*, 2 vols., Copenhagen 1928 & 1968. For the Counter-Reformation, see V. Helk, *Laurentius Nicolai Norvegus S.J.*, Copenhagen 1966.

[41] H.F. Rørdam (ed.), *Danske Kirkelove*, 3 vols., Copenhagen 1883–89, vol. 3, 98–102 and 140–69. For Resen's friendship with Rosenkrantz, see J.O. Andersen, *Holger Rosenkrantz den Lærde*, Copenhagen 1896, 133–38.

[42] For Sebastian Franck and Paracelsus, see Pagel, *Paracelsus*, 40–42.

[43] For the influence of Sebastian Franck on Resen's theology, see Kornerup, *Resen*, 1, 354, 391, 430 and 458. Resen owned a heavily annotated copy of Arndt's *Vier Bücher von wahrem Christenthumb*, Jena 1607, see Kornerup, *Resen*, 1, 372.

Even if Resen won the theological confrontation with the crypto-Calvinists in 1614 he did not come out of the debacle totally unscathed: he was forced to promise to refrain from publishing theological tracts similar to his recent neo-Platonic, Christological disputations. He does not, however, appear to have changed his views. In fact, Resen's subsequent writings demonstrate that he did not fully adhere to his promise. At most, it resulted in the mystic elements in his theology becoming less conspicuous. Thus Resen never disowned neo-Platonism, even if he made a point of dismissing Rosicrucianism as dangerous religious fanaticism.[44]

Thus, it was most fitting, despite his later drive for confessional uniformity, that it was Hans Paulsen Resen, who delivered the funeral sermon for Peter Severinus in 1602. Resen, after all, while a mature student had befriended a number of neo-Platonists and heterodox characters, such as John Dee and Giordano Bruno.[45]

However, in spite of the drive for uniformity within state and church pursued by Chancellor Christian Friis of Borreby and Hans Paulsen Resen, especially in the second decade of the 17th century, the uniformists did not have it all their own way. This is after all the period when the influential nobleman, Holger Rosenkrantz, became the leading exponent of a pre-Pietist variety of Lutheranism in Denmark, which advocated a return to a purely Scripture-based theology with an emphasis on double justification through faith and acts. Not only did Rosenkrantz influence a number of prominent theologians within the Danish Church, but also a whole generation of leading scholars in a variety of fields. The school he established on Rosenholm, his estate in Jutland, provided teaching in a number of subjects, such as Greek, Hebrew, Mathematics and Astronomy, and Rosenkrantz's advocacy of reform was not restricted to theology. In many areas the influence of his private academy matched that of Tycho Brahe's private research-centre on Uraniborg in the late 16th century. Furthermore, Rosenkrantz had befriended Tycho Brahe in 1592 and occasionally assisted him in his research. John Dury, the well-travelled advocate of Protestant unity in the early 17th century,

---

[44] See Kornerup, *Resen*, 2, 32 and 124.

[45] For Resen's friendship with John Dee and Giordana Bruno, see his *Album Amicorum*, Thott MS 572, 8, fols. 55r and 139v in the Royal Library, Copenhagen. A MS-copy of Resen's funeral sermon for Peter Severinus is inserted in the copy of Severinus's *Idea medicinæ* held by the Library of the University of Copenhagen, Universitetsbibliotekets 2. afdeling, Pat. 17560. See also *Christian IV og Europa*, Catalogue from the 19th Exhibition of the Council of Europe, Denmark 1988, 437.

considered Rosenkrantz to be the most learned and pious man in the whole of Germany.[46]

Like his German inspirer, Johann Arndt, who had studied medicine under Theodor Zwinger in Basle, Rosenkrantz was undoubtedly a supporter of some form of eclectic Paracelsianism.[47] Thus Rosenkrantz's wife, Sophie Brahe, Tycho Brahe's niece, regularly bought chemical preparations from Peter Payngk in Copenhagen, while he himself, according to Samuel Hartlib, the great Protestant intelligencer who himself was interested in Paracelsianism and iatrochemistry, was 'very intimate' with the itinerant, German, Paracelsian physician, Nicolaus Teting.[48]

However, more significantly in this context Rosenkrantz exercised considerable influence over two of the most influential professors of medicine at the University of Copenhagen in the early 17th century, Caspar Bartholin and Ole Worm. Already while studying abroad Bartholin had recognized the importance of Rosenkrantz's patronage for an ambitious scholar and in December he dedicated his famous anatomical textbook, *Institutiones Anatomicae* (1611) to him. Bartholin took the opportunity to praise not only Rosenkrantz's well-known piety and learning, but also his extensive medical library, his herbarium, and his substantial knowledge of pharmacy.[49]

Caspar Bartholin succeeded Tycho Brahe's assistant, Gellius Sascerides, as professor of medicine in Copenhagen in 1613. Undoubtedly Severinus's legacy of eclectic Paracelsianism was continued by Sascerides, and from his appointment Caspar Bartholin demonstrated a keen, if critical, interest in Paracelsianism.[50] Throughout his life, even after he had left the medical faculty to become professor of theology, Bartholin continued to promote a 'moderate' Paracelsianism close, if not identical, to that introduced in Copenhagen forty years

---

[46] Andersen, *Holger Rosenkrantz*, 90 & 112–14 and G.H. Turnbull, *Hartlib, Dury and Comenius*, London 1947, 159.

[47] See S. Lindroth, *Paracelsismen i Sverige till 1600-talets mitt*, Uppsala 1943, 432–37.

[48] Sheffield University Library, Hartlib Papers MSS, 'Ephemerides' 1635, 29/3115A; for Hartlib, see C. Webster. *The Great Instauration. Science Medicine and reform 1626–1660*, London 1975, 303–04. Rosenkrantz had been among the recipients of copies of Johann Valentin Andreae's works, *Societatis Christianæ Imagio* and *Christiani Amoris Dextera* which the Rosicrucian Joachim Morsius had distributed during his visit to Denmark in 1617, see J. Young, *Faith, Medical Alchemy and Natural Philosophy in the 17th century: Johann Moriaen and the Hartlib circle*, to be published by Ashgate in 1998.

[49] Grell, 'Caspar Bartholin', 78–100.

[50] See the medical disputations he presided over in 1613 & 1614: C. Bartholin, *De Philosophiae in Medicina Usu et Necessitate*, 17 Nov. 1613, fols. A2r–A3r; and C. Bartholin, *Exercitatio Disputationis Secundæ Ordinariæ & Anniversariæ in Academia Regia Hafniensi*, 7 Nov. 1614, fols. A4r and Br.

earlier by Severinus and Pratensis. Thus, in 1626 he wrote a manual for the study of medicine dedicated to a relation, Peder Charisius, who was also the grandson of Peter Severinus. In the introduction to *De Studio Medico* (published 1628) Bartholin referred to Severinus as 'of blessed memory, the unrivalled physician and spagyrist of his age, whose fame was celebrated everywhere'. In the manual he warmly recommended iatrochemistry as essential to the aspiring physician. It was a subject which should be studied day and night and the student should not only rely on the works and chemical arcana of such leading lights as Joseph du Chesne and Oswald Croll, but they should seek information everywhere possible. He considered the arcana of Peter Severinus, Tycho Brahe, John Banister, Johannes Hartmann and even King Christian IV particularly useful, while referring students to his own extensive alchemical library. Bartholin acknowledged the negative attitude among traditional, Galenic, physicians to alchemical medicine, but stressed that 'while the one should be pursued the other should not be neglected'. In this connection, Bartholin emphasised the need for personal and practical experience in the field, underlining the importance of experimenting with alchemy and 'its charcoal and glass flasks'. He added that no-one should be ashamed to seek information from old wives and barbers about their remedies, nor to use them as long as they had proven effect.[51]

The significance of eclectic Paracelsiansim or Severinianism for Bartholin's approach to the study of medicine is evident when compared with a slightly later manual written by another Danish physician, Johannes Rhodius, *De Artis Medicæ exercitatione, Consilia tria, Amicis intimæ tantum admissionis hactenus communicata.*[52] Rhodius, who like most of his Danish colleagues of this period, had studied at a number of European universities, settled in Padua in 1622, where he continued his studies and practiced medicine until his death in 1659. He was an active and highly esteemed member of the international republic of letters and was offered professorships in both Padua and Copenhagen.[53] As opposed to Caspar Bartholin's insistence on the need for the aspiring physician to study the writings of iatrochemists

---

[51] C. Bartholin, *De Studio Medico*, Copenhagen 1628, fols., 1r, 7v–8r; see also C. Bartholin, *Opuscula Qvatuor Singularia*, Copenhagen 1628, where Bartholin includes Paracelsus among the authors consulted and quoted.

[52] Printed in Bartholin, *Cista Medica*, 616–29.

[53] For Johannes Rhodius, see *DBL* and E. Snorrason, *Danskeren Johan Rhode i det 17. århundredes Padua*, Copenhagen 1965.

and Paracelsians in depth, Johannes Rhodius considered the study of such authors a waste of time. He only advised his readers to work with chemical preparations when occasionally given the opportunity, but always to use them with great care. Peter Severinus and his arcana, praised by Bartholin, were not mentioned at all by Rhodius. The difference between the two manuals could hardly have been greater with regard to their appreciation of alchemical and Paracelsian medicine: for Bartholin it was an essential part of natural philosophy, as well as practical medicine, for Rhodius only the occasional and careful application of chemical medicine was to be contemplated.[54]

When Bartholin became professor of theology in 1624 he was succeeded in the medical faculty by his brother-in-law, Ole Worm, who like him was strongly influenced by Holger Rosenkrantz's pre-Pietist Lutheranism.[55] Ole Worm remained close to Rosenkrantz even after the latter was censured for religious heterodoxy in 1636, composing a Latin poem for Rosenkrantz's funeral in 1642.[56] From his student days, when he had travelled widely in Europe and studied primarily under Jacob Zwinger in Basle, Ole Worm had been deeply interested in Paracelsianism. In 1609 he intended to study iatrochemistry under Joseph du Chesne and Theodore de Mayerne in Paris and in 1611 he studied under Johannes Hartmann in Marburg. During his stay in England in 1612, he befriended Theodore de Mayerne, who had by then become royal physician to James I.[57]

Worm's interest in Paracelsianism is also demonstrated by the eagerness with which he tried to obtain information about the Rosicrucians. In 1611, some years before the publication of the so-called 'Rosicrucian manifestos', the *Fama*, the *Confessio* and the *Chemical Wedding of Christian Rosencreutz*, Ole Worm had been shown a manuscript copy of the *Fama* by a German iatrochemist. Worm had initially considered Rosicrucianism to be pure fantasy and enigma, 'which was hiding something mysterious'. At the time, however, his German intelligencer had managed to convince him of the value of

---

[54] See Bartholin, *Cista Medica*, 624–25.

[55] Andersen, *Rosenkrantz*, 237–40.

[56] See H.F. Rørdam, 'Breve til og fra Holger Rosenkrands', *Kirkehistoriske Samlinger*, Series 3, vol. 6, 1887–89, 35–36.

[57] See Schepelern, *Worm*, vol., 1, nos. 8, 13 and 14, and H.D. Schepelern, *Museum Wormianum*, Odense 1971, 74–85 and 98. As opposed to Schepelern, I am convinced that Worm retained his interest in Paracelsianism after he became professor of medicine in 1624, see below.

Rosicrucianism through his weighty arguments.[58] Consequently, during most of the second decade of the 17th century Worm appears
to have been deeply interested in and positively inclined towards the
phenomenon. He even forwarded Rosicrucian material to colleagues
and friends, such as the professor of theology, Jesper Brochmand,
who later became a forceful advocate of Lutheran uniformity. Thus
in February 1618 Brochmand thanked him: 'The requested pamphlets about the Rosicrucian Society, which you have lent me for
personal use for a considerable time, I return with gratitude'.[59] Gradually, however, during 1618 Worm's doubts were growing and by
1620 he had come to reject Rosicrucianism. He now realized that
the Rosicrucians were nothing but an amalgamation of different sects
whose claim to Lutheranism was spurious. Instead, he considered
the Rosicrucians to represent a dangerous mixture of fanaticism and
Anabaptism combined with Paracelsianism.[60]

Evidently, Worm was worried about the speculative, non-empirical
nature of Rosicrucianism, but his main concern was the religious heterodoxy it implied. In place of the Severinian version of Paracelsianism, which had de-mystified and de-radicalized Paracelsianism,
in the religious, as well as the social and intellectual domain, Rosicrucianism threatened to re-introduce all these elements and re-associate
Paracelsianism with dangerous religious radicalism. As such, it evidently had serious implications in Denmark, at a time when doctrinal and ecclesiastical uniformity was the goal of the government.

Worm's rejection of Rosicrucianism proved very timely and served
to disassociate 'moderate' and eclectic Paracelsianism from the danger
of being connected with religious heterodoxy. As already mentioned
Rosicrucianism was later denounced by the leader of the Lutheran
Church in Denmark, Bishop Hans Poulsen Resen, as dangerous
heterodoxy. More significantly, however, in 1622 Holger Rosenkrantz found himself accused of being a Rosicrucian by his former
teacher, the Stettin professor of theology, Daniel Cramer. According
to him, Rosenkrantz, whose influence was not limited to the king-

---

[58] For Worm's early interest in Rosicrucianism, see introduction to his *Oratio
Inauguralis de Fratrum R, C. Philosophiam Reformandi Conatu*, 10. May 1619; cited in
Schepelern, *Museum Wormianum*, 115–16. For Rosicrucianism, see F.A. Yates, *The
Rosicrucian Enlightenment*, London 1972.
[59] Schepelern, *Worm*, vol. 1, no. 41 (my translation); for Brochmand, see *DBL*.
[60] *Ibid.*, no. 78; see also nos. 20, 25, 38, 44, and 48–9.

dom of Denmark, but stretched far into Germany, had become the
mouthpiece of Spiritualists and Rosicrucians. Considering how difficult
it proved for Rosenkrantz to disassociate himself from these accusations,[61] one realizes how politically sound and timely the rejection
of Rosicrucianism by Ole Worm turned out to be. Not only did it
serve to protect Worm's own career, but it also guaranteed the survival of a 'moderate' and eclectic Paracelsianism within the University
of Copenhagen.

Having disassociated himself from the dangers of heterodoxy Worm
continued to demonstrate his adherence to some form of eclectic
Paracelsianism. Thus in June 1620, Worm acting on behalf of the
Chancellor, Christen Friis of Kragerup, requested Peter Severinus's
son to publish his father's manuscripts. Worm politely indicated that,
if Frederik Sørensen consented, he himself was willing to undertake
the editing and publication of his father's manuscripts. Furthermore,
the Chancellor wanted to borrow some of the manuscripts for personal use. Apparently, Christen Friis, who was also Chancellor of
the University, admired Severinus greatly and wanted to spread his
fame.[62] Like his master, Christian IV, Christian Friis appears to have
been keenly interested in alchemy and Paracelsianism. Thus during
the summer of 1622 the Danish agent in Stockholm forwarded a
'prognosticum fratum rosæ crucis' to Christen Friis, who had already shown
considerable interest in the Rosicrucian, Joachim Morius, during the
latter's visit to Copenhagen in 1617.[63] Thus support for an eclectic
Paracelsianism in the Severinian mould continued to find strong
support within court and government circles and within the medical
faculty, through professors such as Caspar Bartholin and Ole Worm.

Ole Worm continued the empirical tradition begun by Peter Severinus.[64] Like Severinus he was attracted to Paracelsianism and alchemy, but not uncritically. He held reservations, even concerning
Severinus's particular natural philosophy and type of Paracelsianism. In principle, however, he remained an advocate of a Severinian
type of Paracelsianism, as can be seen from a number of the annual
disputations he presided over as professor of medicine. Here he not

---

[61] See Andersen, *Rosenkrantz*, 254–71.

[62] Schepelern, *Worm*, vol. 1. nos. 73–4.

[63] For Christian Friis of Kragerup, see *DBL*. For Friis's interest in Rosicrucianism
and Jaochim Morsius, see Lindroth, *Paracelsismen i Sverige* 173 & 425. For Morsius,
see also Schepelern, *Museum Wormianum*, 316–17.

[64] See Grell, 'Reception of Paracelsianism', 93–94.

only praised Severinus as the leading iatrochemist of the age, but he
also expressed support for Severinus's neo-Platonist doctrine of semina.[65]

Furthermore, Worm continued to prescribe Paracelsian drugs
throughout his life: He kept a manuscript book, which contained
extracts from Paracelsian writings and more importantly his own
commentaries which demonstrates his extensive knowledge of the
Paracelsian literature. Similarly, he continued to encourage his students to study iatrochemistry on their *perigrinatio academica*, more often
than not recommending eclectic Paracelsians as teachers, such as
Guy de la Brosse in Paris.[66]

Finally, Worm may well have taken over Peter Severinus's arcanum,
which the latter had described to Theodor Zwinger in a letter of
February 1584:

> And even if it seems incredible, I have experienced barren women
> become pregnant through the power and force of this remedy, which
> has happened in several cases, so that no possibilities for doubts about
> the causes of the unexpected results remained, especially concerning
> those women for whom conception was prevented by too much and
> thick mucus generated by the uterus and who occasionally failed to
> menstruate.[67]

It is highly likely that this was the same drug/arcanum Ole Worm
forwarded to Jens Dinesen Jersin, the later Bishop of Ribe, in 1624,
whose first wife Anne died childless a year later. In his letter Worm
referred to some pills he had included which would cure Jersin's
wife of her complaint of the uterus. These pills, he added, had been
chemically produced by him personally.[68]

It can be concluded that the Paracelsian legacy of the *Idea medicinæ* survived in Denmark well into the 17th century. Whether or
not it survived intact in the hands of Caspar Bartholin and Ole
Worm may be open to debate; but to try to measure to what extent
an already elastic and accommodating type of Paracelsianism became
even more flexible is, in my opinion, a futile undertaking. Let me

---

[65] See O. Worm, *Controversiarum medicarum exercitatio II*, Copenhagen 1626; *Exercitatio
IV*, Copenhagen 1630; *Exercitatio XII*, Copenhagen 1644; see also E. Hovesen, *Lægen
Ole Worm*, Århus 1987, 161, 165, and 185.

[66] For the prescription of Paracelsian drugs, see Shackelford, 'Paracelsianism',
302; for the manuscript book, see MS Rostgaard 33, 8, the Royal Library, Copenhagen and Shackelford, 'Paracelsianism', 266–67.

[67] The letter is printed in Bastholm, *Petrus Severinus*, 51–53.

[68] Schepelern, *Worm*, 1, no. 166; for Jersin, see *DBL*.

conclude by saying that I find it difficult to accept the above mentioned claim by Walter Pagel that Severinus was a 'reliable and genuine expositor of Paracelsus'. In so far as most of the ideas in Severinus's *Idea medicinæ* are of Paracelsian origin Pagel is correct, but the way these ideas were dressed and systematized served to remove mystical elements from them, and furthermore to deradicalize them religiously, as well as socially. Paracelsus would, in my opinion, have had considerable difficulties in recognizing his radical ideas for change in their Severinian form. The success of *Idea medicinæ* owed as much to its anodyne and polite character, as to its willingness to compromise, when need be, with Galenic, learned medicine. It also gave an acceptable face to Paracelsianism something it had hitherto lacked.

CHAPTER TWELVE

THE PARACELSIAN BODY

J.R.R. Christie

For historians of chemistry taking the long view of chemistry's development in history, Paracelsus and the phenomenon of Paracelsianism remains obligatory passage points for an intelligible narration of chemistry's early modern growth.[1] This has been the case for as long as academic histories of chemistry have been written. Paracelsus was the pre-eminent figure in Herman Boerhaave's history of chemistry, and, in the next generation, William Cullen also accorded Paracelsus considerable significance.[2] Cullen, teaching latterly in Edinburgh, but firstly at the University of Glasgow, location of the Colloquium from which this present volume is drawn, would each November expound the significance of Paracelsus for chemical historiography, as part of an introductory series of lectures on history of chemistry, with which he annually began his chemistry courses. Although Cullen's own forms of chemical understanding were relatively remote from those of the Paracelsians, and although his own project for chemistry can be thought of as a reversal of the Paracelsian project, insofar as it aimed substantially to detach chemistry from medicine, rather than unite them, nonetheless Cullen's evaluation of Paracelsus was by no means negative. He thought Paracelsus 'the author of so considerable a revolution in the affairs of pharmacy and medicine', and 'clear of all prejudices in favour of the system then prevailing'.[3] Cullen then proceeded to ascribe to Paracelsus the discovery and employment of a large number of pharmaceutical remedies and, just as important, a mode of life and career which, arousing intense controversy, had the greatly beneficial effect of generating considerable renewed interest and activity in chemistry and natural science—

---

[1] See W.H. Brock, *The Fontana history of chemistry*, London 1992, 43–48; and B. Bensaude and I. Stengers, *Histoire de la chimie*, Paris 1993, 35–37.

[2] Herman Boerhaave, *A new method of chemistry*, trans. P. Shaw and E. Chambers, London 1727, 21–28; William Cullen, 'History of Chemistry', Royal College of Physicians of Edinburgh, Cullen MS C11, 65, then new pagination, 1–10.

[3] Cullen, 'History of Chemistry', 65.

generally.[4] Further, he analysed the success of the later Paracelsian movement in its anti-Galenical campaigns in directly political terms, noting the crucial strategy of obtaining princely patronage.[5] Thus, although Paracelsus sought to subjoin medicine to chemistry, where Cullen felt obliged, perhaps even as a response to the long-run and now institutionalized success of the Paracelsian project, to free chemistry from its curricular dependence upon medicine and establish an independent philosophical chemistry, and although Cullen's general attitude toward alchemy was an Enlightened scepticism, he nevertheless remained capable of appreciating both the practical and political arts of Paracelsus and his followers, attributing to them a revolutionary impact.

Cullen was not uncommon in conceding to Paracelsus considerable practical knowledge of the chemical arts. It is this notion of alchemical practice, taken from a certain restricted viewpoint, together with, from the same restricted viewpoint, a Cullenian emphasis upon the ideological and political dimensions of this practice, which this essay seeks to renew. The viewpoint in question is one focused upon the body of the early modern man of science, and its agency in natural scientific practice. This is an obviously difficult but, if successful, correspondingly rewarding topic to pursue. It is difficult, because in much natural philosophical and chemical discourse in this, and indeed all other historical periods, nothing is more swiftly and thoroughly erased of its presence than the effectivity of bodily agency. It is as if, much of the time, scientific practitioners were disembodied intellects; and of course they were not. It does not require much reflection to propose instead the necessary existence of a very large array of highly active and skilled observational strategies and techniques reliant upon specifically focused and at times well-trained sets of human senses, and equally, of a considerable range of manual, manipulative and constructive skills, both skills and senses adapted to the necessities of disciplinary practice, and in principle at least, capable of analysis at the level of the historical individual. One might think here, for instance, of the apparently extraordinary limits to which Isaac Newton was willing to push his own senses in pursuit

---

[4] *Ibid.*, new pagination, 3.
[5] *Ibid.*, 8. For further analysis and information see J.R.R. Christie, 'Historiography of chemistry in the eighteenth century: Herman Boerhaave and William Cullen', *Ambix*, 41, 1994, 4–19.

of optical data, and equally of the moments when those senses failed him, leaving him reliant upon other eyes.[6]

Acquaintance with other, less individualized material, allows focus at the level of disciplinary practice. Some eighteenth century natural history works, particularly mineralogical texts which functioned partly as mineral identification guides and manuals, offer relevant illustration. For the non-mineralogist, they list a numerous and often baffling set of visual distinctions, and further, use the sensory cues of taste, sound and touch as well.[7] From such texts it is possible to construct sensory maps or graphs for mineralogy which can be compared and differentiated from sister-disciplines in natural history such as botany, and, *a fortiori*, from comparably constructed maps for chemistry, natural philosophy, and so forth. This is to project the basis for a regular, corporeal history of the sciences, able to recognize and evidence the acute and necessary differential agency of the man of science's body, certainly at a disciplinary level, and where evidence allows, at the level of the individual.

Once sensitized to the possibility of such evidence, it can then be seen in some unexpected places. What specific sensation, for example, was instrumental with respect to the pursuit of some of Faraday's researches? He noticed that 'several of the metals, when rubbed, emit a peculiar smell and more particularly tin. Now smells are generally supposed to be caused by particles of the body that are given off. But I suspect their electric states are concerned'.[8] The chemist's nose, the manipulative rubbing and the metallic tin, together invoke an integrated set, of substance, action and sensation which, one might claim, Paracelsus himself could have recognized as familiar in kind, and in some detail, to the experience of the Paracelsian laboratory. Insofar as historians and philosophers of science have noticed or commented on such knowledge-productive sets, they have been labelled and largely marginalized as 'craft' or even 'tacit' knowledge, perhaps appearing from time to time in some manuals of practice, but most often relegated to the status of the oral and ostensive dimensions of scientific life: those things acquired or learned quite informally, simply by being there, say in a laboratory, listening, watching, imitating,

---

[6] Isaac Newton, *Certain philosophical questions: Newton's Trinity Notebook*, eds. J.E. McGuire and M. Tamny, Cambridge 1983, 438; and *Opticks*, 4th ed., London 1730, republished Dover 1952, 126.

[7] E.g. John Walker, *Lectures on geology*, ed. H. Scott, Chicago 1966, 26–29.

[8] Cited in J.G. Crowther, *British scientists of the nineteenth century*, London 1935, 95.

having one's attention drawn to this or that. Fundamental as they might be, such elements of practice have often failed to acquire evidential status, that is failed of translation to written word or print, or else, should they attain such status, lie disregarded by the historian.

The term agency is used repeatedly in this chapter, partly to stress that the bodily, sensory dimensions of practice which are hereby drawn attention to, are not indeed passive recordings or receptions of sensory input from external phenomena—that Lockean model is inadequate for this purpose. They are instead the result of active, trained, focused and purposeful sets of human senses. 'Agency' is also used to distinguish in some measure the historiography envisioned here from that of Michel Foucault's corporeal histories. The interest and relevance of these is not denied, and indeed this chapter's opening consideration of some kinds of Paracelsian body will be obviously indebted to his methods. But whether in Foucault's earlier formulations, where the body tends to be produced by purely discursive formations, or in his later formulations, where the body is seen as subjected to and incited by the combined forces of institutional and discursive régimes which focus their power upon the human body, there is most often a kind and level of passivity which attaches to the Foucauldian body, and which does not serve well the intention of this chapter. The closest approximation by Foucault to the kind of analysis proposed here is his discussion of what he called the 'medical gaze', the experimental eye of the new clinically-based physician of the late eighteenth century, whose objective, studious regard also and thereby began to define and control the patient in newly intensified ways.[9]

Paracelsus and his followers make an inviting starting-point for the initiation of a corporeal history of science and medicine. Simply as writing, Paracelsus's own discourse is saturated in corporeal reference, and not only because of its medical intent. To track all the range of bodily terminology in one for whom cosmos and body were in some quite strict terms in a relation of identity, is a major task in itself—but the historian cannot complain that there is little material with which to work. Additionally, and in ways particularly rel-

---

[9] M. Foucault, *Discipline and punish: the birth of the prison*, London 1979, and *The birth of the clinic*, London 1973. For a partly Foucauldian corporeal analysis of seventeenth century literary, philosophical, artistic and scientific material, see F. Barker, *The tremulous private body: essays on subjection*, London 1984, and for its methodological limitations, see my review, 'Bad news for the body', *Art history*, 9, 1986, 263–71.

evant for corporeal analysis, the Paracelsian project required kinds
of writing which had the potential to overcome just that barrier
already complained of, namely the often scarce ability of the craft
or tacit knowledge to attain written form. The oft-repeated aim of
Paracelsus was precisely to give to hitherto taciturn, sometimes secre-
tive craft-based practices and the knowledge they produced voice
and visibility, together with medically valuable elements of oral,
popular practice and belief. It is at just this historical conjuncture,
the intersection of craft and popular knowledge with an expanding
and commercializing print-culture, that some emphatic notation of
the tacit might be expected.[10] Further, the consistent challenge and
rallying-cry of Paracelsianism, across a century or more of adversarial writing, the appeal to 'experience', the trial of 'ocular demonstration', might equally be expected to leave substantial traces and
exemplifications in Paracelsian texts. These expectations can often be
fulfilled, in sometimes surprising ways, and sometimes in ways which
support and dovetail with the findings of Paracelsian scholars.

Finally by way of introduction, Paracelsian texts, notoriously those
of Paracelsus himself, are prone more than most to produce those
salutary *aporia* of scholarly understanding, those pauses in analytical
reading which, in the case of Paracelsus mark the scholar's inward
question: not so much 'what does he mean?', but more something
akin to 'what on earth could he possibly have meant?'. Does corporeal analysis offer any aid in such circumstances? Two well-known
examples can serve to give some positive indication, as well as to
broach in detail the Paracelsian body.

> Let me tell you this: every little hair on my neck knows more than
> all your scribes, and my shoe-buckles are more learned than your
> Galen and Avicenna, and my beard has more experience than all your
> high colleges.[11]

As Allen Debus has remarked, such characteristic anti-Galenical pro-
nouncements become eponymous, 'bombastic'. But they are not
uncommon in tone in agonistic writing of the sixteenth and seventeenth century, and thus the history of our own rhetorical termi-

---

[10] For further exploration of this conjunction, see William Eamon, *Science and the secrets of nature. Books of Secrets in medieval and early modern culture*, Princeton 1994, especially chaps. 3–6.

[11] Paracelsus, *Sämtliche Werke*. I Abteilung Medizinische, Naturwissenschaftliche und Philosophische Schriften ed. K. Sudhoff, 14 vols. Munich and Berlin 1922–33, vol. 8 (Paragranum), 65.

nology combines with an early modern preference for a broader and more muscular scholarly invective than ours, to produce an explanation of such language which suffices often enough. One may nonetheless remain struck by the specificities of this particular passage, and attempt to read it as having more to offer than a designation of 'Paracelsian rhetoric' can allow. Paracelsus did *not* write 'My hair, beard and shoe-buckles know more than you and the Galenical scribblings of your Colleges.' He wrote that his little neck-hairs *know* more than is contained in the physicians script-based knowledge; that his shoe-buckles possess more *learning* than Galen and Avicenna; and that his beard has more *experience* than the medical colleges. There are therefore three terms of cognition involved, knowledge, learning and experience, and each is referred separately to three distinct objects, two items of body hair and one of clothing. Hair knowledge is contrasted with book knowledge, the knowledge of the orthodox medical scholar-theoretician in Paracelsus's connotation. Beard experience is contrasted with the colleges, governors of current medical education and practice. The learning of the shoe-buckle, product of the contemporary and humble small-metal artisan, stands against the elder sages of medicine, Galen and Avicenna. There may even have been a further twist to the insult of beard experience. Paracelsus is traditionally and conventionally pictured as beardless. If this traditional representation is correct, then the insult of the beard may be understood as saying that the medical experience of the colleges is less than nothing.[12] These points will be returned to; for the moment the foregoing remarks are made only to demonstrate the methodological point that further analysis of the specific semantics and syntax of such corporeal passages is indeed possible, and possibly productive.

The second example is briefer. Regarding the qualifications of a good surgeon, Paracelsus wrote 'He must not have a red beard'.[13]

---

[12] The accretion of scandalous rumour concerning Paracelsus in the later sixteenth and seventeenth century was often focused upon his bodily habits, as drunken, unwashed and so on. One of the worst rumours concerned his early castration by a pig, see Boerhaave, *New Method*, p. 26, from Oporinus. If true, this scandal would tend to confirm Paracelsus's beardlessness. Much more recently, and more to the point, I recently received a verbal report of an exhumation of Paracelsus's tomb in Salzburg, and an analysis of the organic remains. I have not seen this analysis, but by verbal report, the remains of Paracelsus lack the male-differentiating Y-chromosome.

[13] Paracelsus, *Sämtliche Werke*. I Abteilung vol. 5, *Antimedicus*, 476.

A common first reaction to this is, 'why not?'. And how does one seek an explanation? The following has some plausibility. Think first of colouring, a fundamental issue for Paracelsian astral alchemy, and from redness, proceed to Mars, who astrologically oversees all things to do with munitions and war. From this, the conclusion is that red beards would sign a strong, war-like *astrum*, which would indeed incline against the possessors of red beards being good surgeons, that is healers. Equally, however, an account based on the procedures of Paracelsus's astral alchemy could demonstrate to the contrary that red-bearded men make the best surgeons. War-like or aggressive, hence drawn to military engagements, they will gain the necessary experience of wounds. Inwardly, that is astrally, and according to the doctrine of similitudes central to Paracelsian astrological under-standing and alchemical therapy, it could be held that like was treat-ing like. Wounds would often be the result of iron or steel weaponry, by both substance and occasion operative under the sign of Mars. Such correspondences could indicate against Paracelsus that red-bearded men are eminently suited to the occupation of surgery. This example makes another essentially methodological point, that so far as the astral body of Paracelsian therapeutics is concerned, however one may attempt formally to systematize astral medicine there are strict limits to its deductive form, and especially so far as the pre-cise similitudes which are in play, both for the kinds of persons who should or should not be drawn to chemiatric practice, and the alchem-ical specifics they should or should not use in therapy. Astronomy may be one of the four pillars of medicine, but its right application, especially with reference to selection of the correct vector of simili-tude, was rather than a deductive inference, much more a matter of practice, both experientially learned, and also ineffably or imag-inatively discerned from the innate and inward stars constituting the practitioner's astral body. If further elucidation is sought from Para-celsus, this point is obliquely endorsed in his own doctrine of sig-natures, where he considered the variety of signs which exist, how they may be considered, and the extent of what they determine.[14] It was in the course of this doctrine of signatures that he announced his opinion concerning the indeterminacy of celestial star signs for the characters and lives of men: 'the stars are subject to the wise man', not *vice versa*, it is only the 'animal' body which is compelled

---

[14] *Ibid.*, vol. 11 (*Die 9 Bücher de Natura rerum*), 375ff.

by the stars.[15] Shortly afterwards, there follows a section on physiognomic signs. He limited his treatment of these to a consideration
of those signs possessed by the individual *qua* individual, excluding
consideration of the important signs which accompany hereditary
semina, signs derived from parents. Remarkably, red beards are again
briefly considered, but only in the following general and finally dis-
appointing fashion.

> Concerning the hair of the head or of the beard, the signs are not very
> plain, since experience teaches us that this can be marvellously varied
> according as it is black, yellow, red, or white, or hoary or curled.[16]

Even Paracelsus, therefore, despite the blunt assertiveness of 'He
must not have a red beard', in general conceded the uncertainty of
hair-colour signs. The historian's uncertainty must therefore match
his. What follows now is perhaps most basically an attempt to negotiate
and decrease such uncertainties in the understanding of Paracelsian
practice by more detailed consideration of its corporeal dimensions.

Even in the preceding, attenuated discussion of the limited topic
of hair, beard, their signs and stars, it has nonetheless become apparent that there is no singular Paracelsian body. This indeed is
the general point of the discussion. Already in play are an astral-
chemical body, a medical agent's body, a physiognomic body, and
the animal body, which is perhaps as close as Paracelsus came to
naming the appetitive, physical body we might recognize as such.
Others may be discerned. From the theological point of view, there
is also the luminous or 'sacramental' body:

> Man has a body which does not spring from matter and consequently
> is not subject to any physician; for it was breathed into man by God,
> and like every breath, is intangible to our hands, and invisible to our
> eyes. . . . According to Holy Writ we shall be resurrected in the flesh
> on the Day of Judgement and called to account for our misdeeds. . . .
> For we shall not give an account of the health and sickness of our
> visible bodies . . . but of the things that proceed from the heart, because
> only these actually concern Man, and they belong to a body which
> does not consist of matter, but comes from the breath of God. But
> since one day, clothed in the flesh, we shall see our Lord and Saviour,
> it follows that the body which derives from the *limbus*, and is mate-
> rial will also be present at that moment. Who can be ignorant of this

---

[15] *Ibid.*, 378.
[16] *Ibid.*, 381.

transfiguration, which is accomplished through the mouth of God, and by virtue of which both bodies will be present? For we shall rise again in the flesh, and we only know one flesh not two; two bodies, and one flesh. . . .[17]

Paracelsus's complex resurrection theology posits a uniting of the earthy, or limbic body with the eternal or sacramental body at the Day of Judgement.[18] From the viewpoint of corporeal history, it further extends the range of the Paracelsian body, in the following senses. Firstly, at the end of mundane time, and into eternity, it is the body which will persist; and secondly, in a conceptual dimension, it has become quite clear that the Paracelsian body is a far broader entity than the notion of matter itself, it is not a subset of matter. Even the breath of God in man, the 'soul', was for Paracelsus a body.

Finally in this bodily proliferation, and given the highly gendered potentials of corporeal history, it should be noted that Paracelsus insisted upon a strong differentiation of the female from the male body, and not only in anatomical or physiological terms.

> Man is the Little World, but woman . . . is the Littlest World, and hence she is different from man. She has a different anatomy, a different theory, different effects and causes, different divisions and cares. . . . Thus the cosmos is the greatest world, the world of man the next greatest, and that of woman the smallest and least. And each world—the cosmos, man, and woman—has its own philosophy and art.[19]

The gendering of the Paracelsian body was thereby not only a question of anatomy and disease, but at its largest, became reinscribed within the cosmological framework, the female now as the lowest level of the ontology of 'Worlds', the microcosm now split and re-ordered according to a male over female hierarchy.

As a discursive entity, therefore, the Paracelsian body requires extensive pluralization, or else, if it remains singular, it needs to be conceived of as a manifold, turning now this aspect, now that, to the historian's analytical attention, according to which element of Paracelsian practice is being examined. It is nonetheless of some

---

[17] *Ibid.*, vol. 9 (*Opus Paramirum*), 117–19.
[18] For further, more refined and expert consideration of these theological elements, see above chapters 8 and 9.
[19] Paracelsus, *Sämtliche Werke*. I Abteilung, vol. 9 (*Opus Paramirum*), 178–9.

partial and temporary heuristic benefit to try and focus some central elements of this manifold. Most helpful here proves to be adaptation of a term used by Owen Hannaway, in turn derived from Foucault's characterization of the pre-Classical 'episteme', in terms of more conventional periodization the late mediaeval and Renaissance centuries, the era of 'Resemblance'. This term is 'semiotic', that is, pertaining to the science of signs.[20] The reason for focusing upon the Paracelsian body as an arena of signs is that it accords with two basic positions of the Paracelsian physician, the diagnostic, confronted with a diseased body, and the alchemical-preparative, required to select and prepare appropriate remedies. The first task was one of identification, which could require long periods of time spent with the patient. In principle at least, this time should be spent maximizing sources of information bearing upon the patient, including local environmental and subsistence factors.

> The physician must give heed to the region in which the patient lives, that is to say, to its type and peculiarities. For one country is different from another; its earth is different, as are its stones, wines, bread, meat.... This means that each country, in addition to the general properties common to the whole world, also has its own specific properties. The physician should take this into account and know it, and accordingly he should also be a cosmographer and geographer, well versed in the disciplines.[21]

Such knowledge would however at length be focused upon the occurrence of the disease as a particular kind of *event*, which was the visible manifestation of the disease, thought of as the dysfunctional eruption of the healthy astral body, normally invisible, into visibility under the influence of the *entia* responsible for disease. Diagnostic art was then identification of the type of *entia*, and with reference to which particular internal star of the body which was being caused to act abnormally. The human body in Paracelsian discourse, whether male or female, and however differentiated natally by parentage, environmentally by locality, economically by occupation, individualistically by temperament (and all such differentiations were medically significant for Paracelsus), was as a patient, first of all semiotic.

---

[20] O. Hannaway, *The Chemists and the Word: the Didactic Origins of Chemistry*, Baltimore and London 1975, especially 'The semiology of experience', 62–27. M. Foucault, *The order of things*, New York 1970, chap. 2.

[21] Paracelsus, *Sämtliche Werke*. I Abteilung, vol. 4 (*Anatomie und Physiologie*), 501–2.

This semiosis carried over into the selection and preparation of remedies. Here the Paracelsian reading of signs is again unintelligible unless regarded in the light of the doctrine of signs and the associated learning of similitudes, which in turn derived their overall coherence from the macrocosm-microcosm framework, understood by Paracelsus himself not as a system of analogy, but as an identity—a point well-made, albeit in critical vein, by Sennert.[22] Remedies would therefore be selected upon some principle of *similarity* (as opposed to Galenical treatment by contraries), but this, as emphasized earlier, was a matter of learning and experience. Similitude vectors could be various, and corresponded along numerous perceptual axes. Here is a list from Paracelsus and it includes shape, internal sensation, topology, pattern, motion and time:

> Behold the *Satyrion* root, is it not formed like the male privy parts? No one can deny this. Accordingly magic discovered and revealed that it can restore a man's virility and passion. And then we have the thistle; do not its leaves prickle like needles? Thanks to this sign the art of magic discovered that there is no better herb against internal prickling. The *Siegwurz* root is wrapped in an envelope like armour; and this is a magic sign showing that like armour it gives protection against weapons and the *Syderica* bears the image and form of a snake on each of its leaves, and thus, according to magic, it gives protection against any kind of poisoning. The chicory stands under special influence of the sun; this is seen in its leaves, which always bend towards the sun as though they wanted to show gratitude. Hence it is most effective while the sun is shining, while the sun is in the sky. As soon as the sun sets, the power of chicory decreases.[23]

Other examples, drawn by Hannaway from Croll, operated upon touch, and smell, taste and colour.[24] And this is surely to evoke not simply a 'conceptual' world, but an arena and form of practice, which demanded numerous, complex and sophisticated sensory labours from its Paracelsian practitioners. Some of it may remain irrecoverable for modern historians; but equally, much of it is recoverable, and it requires emphasis, for without it, much of what Paracelsus and followers such as Croll were actually *doing* will continue to escape us.

---

[22] D. Sennert, *De chymicorum cum Aristotelicis et Galenicis consensu ac dissensu*, Wittenberg 1633, 63.

[23] Paracelsus, *Sämtliche Werke*. I Abteilung, vol. 13 (*Liber de imaginibus*), 377.

[24] Hannaway, *The Chemists and the Word*, 67, 71.

The other central aspect of the Paracelsian body which most help-
fully focuses some of its key features may be approached through
the work of Walter Pagel, who laid stress upon the significance of
'time' for Paracelsus. Pagel summarized his views thus: 'various aspects
of time can thus be discerned, astronomical, numerical and physical time in the orthodox and ancient sense, time as determined by
the object and situation, biological time and finally theological time.'[25]
Some of these must bear very directly upon correct representation
of the Paracelsian body, for it was an acutely temporalized body,
which a static conception cannot well capture. Internal *astra*, for
instance, were dynamic, with their own astrologically correspondent
sets of rising, ascendancy and setting. According to Paracelsus, 'The
Astra give the time', and that astral temporality had relevance to the
state of the body, for it could 'give, take, make whole or break by
means of natural forces.'[26] It is possible to give more emphasis to
theological time than did Pagel, who describe the Paracelsian notion
of theological time as perfect, an 'eternal now', justifying this with
reference to Paracelsus on repentance, which takes but a moment's
accomplishment but which stands in eternity.[27] But the theological
material cited earlier, together with more recent work by Charles
Webster on Paracelsian prophecy, might indicate a more complex
theological temporality, and especially when the corporeal elements
are kept in focus.[28] Paracelsus evidently registered and expressed
some contemporary conceptions of Providential, prophetic and eschatological time, and these are of immediate relevance to consideration of the Paracelsian body. Firstly, that body is as it is, subject to
disease and capable of finding remedies, as a consequence of the
narrative time of Christian history, from Creation and Fall through
to redemption, salvation, resurrection and judgement. The complexity
of that body at the latter stages of the sequence has already been
referred to, and there is a comparable complexity at the first stages.
For Paracelsus, the astral body was itself *created* at the Fall; 'it is the
ethereal body, which Adam and Eve acquired in Paradise through
eating the apple; it was only by acquiring this body that Man became

---

[25] W. Pagel, *Paracelsus: an introduction to philosophical medicine in the era of the Renaissance*,
Basel and New York 1958, 81–2.
[26] *Ibid.*, 80. Paracelsus, *Sämtliche Werke*. I Abteilung, vol. 4 (*Kommentore zu den Aphorismen
des Hippokrates*), 501.
[27] Pagel, *Paracelsus*, 80.
[28] C. Webster, *From Paracelsus to Newton: magic and the making of modern science*,
Cambridge 1982, 15–27.

completely human, with knowledge of good and evil.'[29] Moreover, the astral body is itself mortal: 'the sidereal, subtile body dissolves gradually and goes back to its source'.[30] Compensatingly, at the Fall knowledge was received from the Angel, and the inward stars of the body are considered as engraven with 'arts', which can be supplemented with more conscious learning.[31] Again, the coming together of practitioner and patient was seen by Paracelsus as a matter of Providential time.

> If providence has decided otherwise than you physicians intend, you will not be able to cure the patient by any remedy. But if the hour of Providence has struck you will succeed in curing him. . . . Only when the hour of recovery strikes for the patient does God send him to the physician, not before.[32]

It is therefore possible to demonstrate a profound, theologically temporal dynamism for the Paracelsian body, and reinforce the conclusion that static representation would thereby fail to register some of its most essential features.

The semiotic and temporalized natures of the Paracelsian body serve to centre and explore some of the most fundamental and significant features of Paracelsus's own discourse, and the medical practices inscribed therein. Certain of its aspects and properties are directly relevant to the topic next under examination, the bodily agency of Paracelsian alchemy. Alchemy, in its Paracelsian formulation the perfecting of natural bodies by the separation of their essences, their stars or *arcana*, was also, as is generally well-known, a matter of time. The alchemist performed the work of time insofar as he induced and intensified processes which are themselves mimetic of nature. These processes, most often in Paracelsus processes of distillation, produced the severally refined chemical fractions with which he sought to cast out Galenical therapeutics, and the filthy broths prepared by some apothecaries. Hence alchemy as the Third Pillar of medicine, in its Paracelsian form inducing a novel, and according to some historians, productive and progressive concentration on mineral and, more particularly, metallic chemistry. What of its bodily dimensions?

---

[29] Paracelsus, *Sämtliche Werke*. I Abteilung, vol. 9 (*Opus Paramirum*), 119.
[30] *Ibid.*, vol. 12 (*Astronomia Magna*), 18.
[31] *Ibid.*, vol. 8, 290–92.
[32] *Ibid.*, vol. 1 (*Das Buch von der Gebärung der empfindlichen Dinge*), 227.

Firstly, Paracelsus characterized it in acutely corporeal terms. The nature of which it was most directly mimetic was that of the human body itself. Just as the *archeus* of the stomach (its shaping, directive power), which separated and purified nutrition from poison, was called the 'inner Vulcan' or the 'alchemist within', so alchemical process and apparatus mimicked that archeal action and setting. The inner Vulcan sublimates, distils and reverberates: 'All the arts are prefigured and practised within the body of man, no less than without, in Alchemy.'[33] In this conception, the triad of alchemist, stomach and Paracelsian 'kitchen' are an obviously connected set, linked by functional correspondence. There was strict correspondence also between planets, metals and organs.

> Everything relating to the brain is Luna, by means of Luna. What relates to the spleen flows thither by means of Saturn; all that refers to the heart is carried thither by means of Sol. So too the kidneys are governed by Venus, the liver by Jupiter, the bile by Mars.[34]

The planets, sun and moon have in turn their correspondent metals: gold for Sol, silver for Luna, copper for Venus, and so on. These fundamental astral correspondences linked astrology to an organology, and projected the basis for a metalline therapy. Astrologically, Paracelsus further advised that the timing of the remedy's preparation be dictated by the relevant astrological period: '. . . take care so to regulate your preparation in this case also that it shall duly be directed by the stars'.[35] In these senses, then, the correspondences between stars, metals and organs could recommend precise preparative and therapeutic practices.

It has already been seen how, with respect to herbal selection, certain kinds of visual discrimination were a part of Paracelsian practice. But what analogous discriminations were to operate in the alchemist's laboratory? Paracelsus's chemical sensorium, his sensory labour, involved especially sight, odour and taste:

> Besides this, he must be a skilled and practised alchemist, to know what is or is not combustible, what is fixed and what volatile, what does or does not pass into flux, and what thing is heavier than another.

---

[33] Paracelsus, *Hermetic and alchemical writings of Aureolus Phillippus Theophrastus Bombast, of Hohenheim called Paracelsus the Great*, 2 vols., London 1894, vol. 2 (*Liber Paragramum*), 166–67.

[34] *Ibid.*, 150.

[35] *Ibid.*, 148.

> He must also have investigated in every object its natural colour, odour, acidity, austerity, acridity, bitterness, sweetness, its grade, complexion and quality.[36]

Among all these, the most significant sensory concentration was upon colour. This points towards two roots for Paracelsian alchemy. In traditional terms, and particularly its old Greek form, alchemy had anciently been a practice to do with colour and coloration. This sensory focus was however renewed and strengthened in Paracelsus, and most probably because of his early metallurgical experience in the Függer mines at Schwatz. He wrote knowledgeably concerning the signs indicative of mineral ores, and did so in terms of the colours of clays, the colours of certain 'coruscations' seen at night in mines, and how particular coruscations indicated the presence of specific ores. Nor were these simply gross distinctions. Metallurgical practice enjoined more precise sensation: 'Add to this that a slight and subtle coruscation constitutes the best sign'.[37]

Subtle colour discrimination was most likely built into the Paracelsian sensorium as an effect of this early metallurgical training. Translated into the laboratory, it became even more intensely focused and discriminating, because colour was the primary sensory test not just or simply of the presence of one substance or another. Instead, colour was indexed both to and *within* particular substances, and also to the gradation, or particular stage of preparation. And all this required discriminating notation, because colour, so indexed, was also the perception of the particular virtue of the substance.

> Now the alchemy of colours is so to separate Art and Nature, that this separation shall extend not only to the colours, but to the virtues. As often as a transmutation of colours takes place, so often occurs a transformation of virtues also. In sulphur, there is yellowness, whiteness, redness, darkness and blackness. In each colour there is a special power and virtue; and other substances which possess these same colours, have not the same, but different virtues lying hid in the colours. And there is latent knowledge of colours just as there are latent colours.[38]

The same emphasis is found in more specifically practical passages, for example in the testing of vitriol, in practice one of Paracelsus's most often used substances.

---

[36] *Ibid.*, vol. 1 (*Nature of Things*), 162–63.
[37] *Ibid.*, 184.
[38] *Ibid.*, vol. 2 (*Liber Paragranum*), 157.

First, if it tinges an iron plate to the colour of copper, the more deeply it does so, the better is it considered. . . . We must not omit to speak of its colours. That which is altogether cerulean is not so strong in medicine as that which under the same colour has red and yellow spots mixed together. That which is of a pale sky blue colour should be selected before all others for the preparation of the green and white oil. . . . The last test is when with oil it makes a very black and dark ink. . . . The species, therefore, are reckoned to the tests.[39]

These and other comparable passages in Paracelsus make it clear that colour perception was no simple set of identification cues, employed as tests for presence. The characterization of colours has to be thorough, requiring the shade in addition to the colour, colour mixture, and sometimes (notably with gem stones and metallic stars) qualities of sparkling, glow, transparency, and the like.[40] With respect to some metals, notably natural gold, its shades and colours are indicative of the inequality of proportions of the *tria prima* (the Paracelsian principles of Salt, Sulphur and Mercury) in its composition.[41] With respect to other metallic preparations, the optical quality of what happens in the furnace could take an acute practical relevance: 'Iron, which is completely fused in the furnace, sends forth limpid, clear sparks, which rise to a height. As soon as these appear, unless the iron be at once removed from the fire, it will be burnt up like straw.'[42] Finally, the Paracelsian alchemist was himself an active colourer. The seventh and last preparative stage of alchemy was Tincture, and this did not mean the simple tingeing of a substance to alter its colour. It 'makes all imperfect things perfect, transmutes them into their noblest essence. . . . For a Tincture colours all things according to its own nature and its own colour.'[43] Here, coloration constituted a final augmentation of astral virtue for the most efficacious form of the medicine.

Given the emphatic proliferation of colour-based cues, tests and processes throughout Paracelsus's alchemy, this allows the conclusion that the palette of Paracelsian colour was therefore the principle mode of sensory labour as regards alchemical embodiment and agency. Further study along these lines might recommend the following

---

[39] *Ibid.*, (*Economy of Minerals*), 102.
[40] *Ibid.*, vol. 1 (*Nature of Things*), 291.
[41] *Ibid.*, vol. 2 (*Economy of Minerals*), 111.
[42] *Ibid.*, vol. 1 (*Nature of Things*), 188.
[43] *Ibid.*, 155.

enquiries. As Paracelsian alchemy developed over the century following his death, there was a noticeable shift in its attention. Whereas Paracelsus's own separative techniques were focused upon the distilled, often volatile chemical fractions produced by separation, some of his successors became equally interested in the properties of the chemical residues, which could be studied in several ways, but most significantly by solution analysis. The significant point here is not the abandonment of the colour vector, but its survival and reorientation, such that colour changes in certain reagents were increasingly used as identification tests.[44] What were the implications of such procedures for the original Paracelsian colour cues, in terms of addition, or replacement? How far did the partial externalization of colour cues in an altered practical setting lead to a recomposition of the original Paracelsian assemblage of skill and sense? And did the later Helmontian focus on gases and the category of 'odour' bring the sense of smell into prominence?[45] Answers to those and comparable questions will be relevant for understanding the later history of the alchemical body, from the 1570s onward, but they must await further investigation.

Meanwhile, there are two further significant features of the Paracelsian body to explore as a conclusion to this initial investigation. 'Action' is itself a term of Paracelsian emphasis, opposed to orthodox medical book-learning and prescription. True medicine and alchemy consisted in deeds, rather than words, and useable knowledge came from active, practical experience. The Paracelsian body, the agent of alchemical and medical practice, was active in ways which not only lead the historian into the practical detail of alchemical preparation, but which also pertain to the political and ideological history of Paracelsus and Paracelsianism.

Howsoever Paracelsianism developed technically in medicine and chemistry, there was considerable consistency in the self-characterization of certain of its features. Time and again, in Paracelsus himself, in Croll or Penotus, Severinus or van Helmont, the same kinds of emphasis occurred. The first is the necessity of travel. Paracelsus's

---

[44] See R. Multhauf, *The origins of Chemistry*, London 1966, 222–25. Allen Debus, 'Sir Thomas Browne and the study of colour indicators', *Ambix*, 10, 1962, 29–36, and 'Solution analysis prior to Robert Boyle', *Chymia*, 8, 1962, 41–62.

[45] For Helmontian 'odour', see Pagel, *Joan Baptista van Helmont: reformer of science and medicine*, Cambridge 1982, 70–78.

own insistence that the physician be also a 'geographer' has already been noted. He further emphasized:

> He who would explore nature must tread her books with his feet. Holy Scripture is explored through its letters, but nature is explored from country to country; it has as many pages as there are countries. This is the code of nature, and thus must her leaves be turned.[46]

Penotus 'judged it to be necessary to travell, and to go to farre places to seek out learning and knowledge', and as a result 'learned those things which for Christian love sake I can no longer keep silent.'[47] Croll mentioned his 'many troubles and painfull peregrinations of various fortune', and remembered his adoption of 'that common Chymicall Custome, *Give something, and take something*'.[48] Severinus's invocation is perhaps most famous:

> sell your lands, your houses, your clothes and your jewelry; burn up your books. Contrarily, buy yourselves stout shoes, travel to the mountains, search the valleys, the deserts, the shores of the sea, and the deepest hollows of the earth; note with care the distinctions between animals, the differences of plants, the various kinds of minerals, the properties and mode of origin of everything that exists. Be not ashamed to study diligently the astronomy and terrestrial philosophy of the peasantry. Lastly, purchase coal, build furnaces, watch and operate the fire without wearying. In this way and no other, you will arrive at a knowledge of things and their properties.[49]

Severinus struck a number of authentically Paracelsian notes: the book-burning, the valorization of popular knowledge and practical alchemy, the knowledge which travel will bring, are all Paracelsian reflexes. Equally, the possible Biblical allusion ('Sell all that thou hast.') and the hints of *imitatio Christi* and a voluntary poverty were echoes of themes in Paracelsus.[50]

The Paracelsian body was itinerant, and to such an extent that the utility of a space-time map of Paracelsian travel would be a considerable adjunct to scholarship. This bodily motion could take diverse

---

[46] Paracelsus, *Sämtliche Werke*. I Abteilung, vol. 11 (*Sieben Defensiones*), 145–46.

[47] B.G. Penotus, 'An Apologeticall preface', in L. Phioravant, *Three exact pieces of Leonard Phioravant Knight*, London 1652, 2.

[48] O. Croll 'Admonitory Preface', in *Philosophy reformed and improved in four profound tractates*, trans. H. Pinnell, London 1657, 3–4.

[49] Peter Severinus, *Idea Medicinae Philosophica*, [1571], The Hague 1660, 39.

[50] Paracelsus, *Sämtliche Werke*. I Abteilung. Theological und Religionsphilosophische Schriften, ed. K. Goldammer, Wiesbaden 1955.

forms, however, and with different results. The notorious political conflicts generated by Paracelsus, especially those of Basle and Nuremberg, had certain parallels among his followers, particularly in the wake of the Parisian conflicts of the 1590s and 1600s, albeit these latter were not driven by that compulsive pattern of dramatic acceptance, rejection and flight which characterized Paracelsus's own itinerary. Several later Paracelsians, however, including Croll, Severinus, Mayerne and Sendivogius were successful in attaching themselves to princely courts. As a matter of historical development, therefore, the itinerant Paracelsian body also through time advanced from the popular margins of European society, from the streets, highways and inns to the courtly summits. As such, it is a potentially revealing icon of Paracelsianism's social history, a marker of that strategy which sought, with some necessity, sites of protection and power from which to continue and modify the anti-Galenical campaigns, and a marker of that strategy's qualified success.[51]

Paracelsus's own case makes a rather different point concerning the moving body. Aside from Basle, perhaps his worst encounter was the Nuremberg syphilis battle. He had initiated a campaign against two current treatments for syphilis, liquid mercury and fumigation by imported guiac bark. This import was a monopoly, and a reward for financial backing in the election of Charles V to the Imperial throne, granted to the great finance and commercial house of Fugger. When Paracelsus potentially threatened the value of that monopoly, the Nuremberg municipality attempted to ban further works by him on this topic, and to validate their judgement medically, employed the Dean of the Leipzig Medical Faculty to pronounce on Paracelsus's work. The Dean did so negatively, and was also by report a customary owner of cargo shares in the Fugger bark monopoly.[52]

At this stage in European history, commercial houses and Medical Faculties are not usually seen as part of the same field of analysis, seeming perhaps to constitute separate spheres of interest. Yet the Nuremberg affair is revealing firstly because it demonstrates the considerable power wielded by this articulation of major commercial

---

[51] For the way in which Paracelsian itineraries could become political in the sense of being practically involved in Calvinist Reformation politics, see above Chapter 5.

[52] This account of the Nuremberg syphilis battle is drawn from H. Pachter, *Paracelsus: magic into science*, New York 1951, 175–183. The Fuggers' response to Paracelsus's *Three chapters on the French disease*, Nuremberg 1529, was exemplary. They moved successfully to expand their mineral commerce and gained a mercury monopoly.

monopoly and corporate medical monopoly—the sheer scale of that integrated force aroused by Paracelsus is interesting in itself, and an indicator that more than purely orthodox medical interests were threatened by Paracelsian practice. Secondly, however, the outcome is also revealing. In virtue of his printing contacts, Paracelsus could and did publish his new and moderate mercurial therapy, and in virtue of his mobility could seek new venues. In this sense, and it applied to other Paracelsians, in a practice continuously generative of social conflict, mobility could confront established interests, and if thwarted or stymied, could always move on, circumventing those interests, and opening up new fronts of action. Just because for so much of its historical life, Paracelsianism was an adversarial practice, mobility, as well as princely protection, became a significant political advantage for the survival of the movement. The itinerant body of Paracelsian history can therefore usefully supplement that complex history of confrontation, repression, evasion and assimilation, and in such a way as to clarify an ignored, perhaps because almost too obvious condition of that history—motion through politically territorial space.

One useful way of considering alchemy in this period is to think of it as one of the pyrotechnic arts, in that sense a sister-art, though smaller in its laboratory scale, to such arts as metal-refining and pottery.[53] This pyrotechnic identity is an important key to understanding the ideological self-construction of Paracelsianism, once again in often adversarial settings. This self-construction was acutely focused to the alchemist's body, in that it brought together a valorizing of art and handicraft skill, labour and fire, sweat and dirt. Even more than the virtues of itineraries, Paracelsianism advertised the virtues of manual craft, genuine labour productive of real knowledge, the religious sweat of demanding toil, the necessary contact with coal and soot. Paracelsus emphasized the necessity of alchemical skill and its artisanal relation.

> For this reason more diligence should be spent on alchemy, in order to obtain still greater results. Artisans have explored nature and its properties in order to learn to imitate her in all things. . . . Only in

---

[53] See here the work of Paracelsus's contemporary, Georgius Agricola, *De re metallica*, trans H.C. and L.H. Hoover, New York 1912, and the work of Vannochio Biringuccio, *Pirotechnia*, trans C.G. Smith and M.I. Gnadi, New York 1942, 1st ed. 1450.

medicine has this been neglected, and therefore it has remained the crudest and clumsiest of all the arts.[54]

He also evoked both the biblical 'sweat of thy brow', and advised 'In labour and in sweat each man must use the gifts that God conferred upon him . . . as a workman in the smithy, in the mines . . . or in medicine'.[55] The alchemists, he claimed,

> devote themselves diligently to their labours, sweating whole nights and days over fiery furnaces. These do not kill the time with empty talk, but find their delight in their laboratory. They are clad in leathern garments, and wear a girdle to wipe their hands upon. They put their fingers to the coals, the lute, and the dung, not into gold rings. Like blacksmiths and coal merchants, they are sooty and dirty. . . . They perceive the work should glorify the workman, not the workman the work . . . they rejoice to be occupied at the fire and to learn the steps of alchemical knowledge.[56]

This passage has substantial echoes in later chemical writing. Glauber for instance, happy to foreswear universities, 'neither doth it ever repent me, that I have put my hands to the coals, and have by the help of them penetrated into the secrets of Nature.'[57] Earlier, Penotus had claimed, 'I say, every Paracelsian, which doth but only carry coals unto the work, can shew you by eye the three principles of *Theophrastus* Physick'.[58] Both he and Croll were quite content to embrace the derogatory Galenic naming of 'collier physitians'.[59] Skillful, sweating and dirty, the alchemical body was above all productive. In contrast with other and sterile knowledge-disciplinary activities the Paracelsian alchemist produced new items: 'Physick not so learned but with the labour of the hands, practice being workmistresse, where Vulcan day by day doth shew new and pleasant remedies. . . .'[60] Further, in the formulation of Penotus, it produced with Christian charity a 'commodity for all', as opposed to one reserved for a few. This Christian alchemy, with its novel remedies, its fabrial virtue and holy sweat, was counterposed to the 'Heathenish'

---

[54] Paracelsus, *Sämtliche Werke*. I Abteilung, vol. 8 (*Paragranum*), 180.
[55] *Ibid.*, 89, and I Abteilung, vol. 1 (*De honestis utrisque divitiis*), 253–54.
[56] Paracelsus, *Hermetic and alchemical writings*, vol. 1 (*Nature of Things*), 167.
[57] R. Glauber, 'The prosperity of Germany', *The works of J.R. Glauber*, trans. C. Packe, London 1689, 307.
[58] Penotus, 'Apologeticall Preface', 3.
[59] *Ibid.*, 2 and Croll, 'Admonitory Preface', 19.
[60] *Ibid.*, 6.

doctrine of Galen and Avicenna, to the unsullied and idle fingers of College physicians, and their robes to the alchemists' leathern aprons.[61]

Borrowing and adopting a term introduced some time ago by Steven Shapin, but not much noticed since, we may call this the banausic body.[62] As a term, this has the disadvantage of a certain Platonic dismissiveness attached to it, denoting in that sense the merely mechanical. On the other hand, it has a further etymological component which associates the term with oven or furnace, rendering it virtually ideal for this alchemical denotation. It signifies the laborious, skillfull body of the alchemical craftsman, whose knowledge is practice and philanthropy. Its immediate social registration with Paracelsus himself, in terms of occupational or class fraction, is with artisan communities, and perhaps more particularly, one might guess, with those artisanal practices moving away from monopoly or secrecy. Just what dissonances were produced as this ideological association and depiction of practice persisted into the period of Paracelsianism's accession to Court culture is, however, by no means clear, beyond the fact that Croll could give this banausic ideology a chemico-eschatological location in the figure of Elias the Artist, 'who is to restore all things', thereby eliding the banausic with the Protestant revolution's chiliastic projections.[63] The banausic body may finally give partial insight into those often difficult descriptions of Paracelsian knowledge as innate, already engraven within, and drawn forth by ineffable acts of imagination—that is, as inherent in the divine Creation. The key term here is Creation. Paracelsus remarked, with respect to certain kinds of creatures (giants and pygmies), 'As by Art they acquire life, by Art acquire their body, flesh, bones and blood, and are born by Art, therefore Art is incorporated in them, and born with them, and there is no need for them to learn'.[64] That is, such beings apparently carry consciously knowledge of the art of their creation, inscribed in their being. Analogously perhaps, and certainly less consciously, specifically human bodies, created by the

---

[61] Croll, 'Admonitory Preface', 10.

[62] B. Barnes and S. Shapin, 'Head and hand', *Oxford Review of Education*, 2, 1976, 235.

[63] Croll, 'Admonitory Preface', 10. For Paracelsianism in Court culture, see H.R. Trevor-Roper, 'The court physician and Paracelsianism', in V. Nutton (ed.), *Medicine at the Courts of Europe, 1500–1837*, London and New York 1990, 79–94.

[64] Paracelsus, *Hermetic and alchemical writings*, vol. 1 (*Nature of Things*), 125.

skillful hand of God, bear comparably inscribed knowledge: 'Regard-less how we are made—in all our members the hand of God has been directly at work'.[65] Now, if this were the case, it might be pos-sible to understand literally, and not bombastically, how neck hairs, beards and shoe-buckles can contain knowledge, experience and learn-ing. It would be because for Paracelsus, they were made things, bod-ies of knowledge as produced by the banausic art of equally, the Creator and silversmith.

The Paracelsian body has been described as follows. It was semi-otic and temporalized, cosmic in scope, theologically persistent and prolific. In its alchemical practice it was a discriminating sensorium for colour, was politically itinerant, and ideologically banausic. In Paracelsian discourse it was, beyond all this detail, ostentatiously pre-sent, and that is perhaps its overridingly remarkable feature, for as European culture moved into its scientific revolutionary phase, that bodily ostentation of natural philosophical discourse and practice seems substantially to diminish, so that more oblique methods will be required to recover bodily discourse and agency. If we continue to think of the seventeenth century in terms of negative, dis-prefixed words—disenchantment, dissociation of sensibility and the like—it therefore appears as if another such term may need to be added to that lexicon with respect to natural science: disembodiment.

---

[65] Paracelsus, *Sämtliche Werke*. I Abteilung, vol. 9 (*Opus Paramirum*), 115.

CHAPTER THIRTEEN

THE PARACELSIAN KITCHEN

Francis McKee

In this chapter I intend to deal not so much with Paracelsus himself as with the influence of his ideas on the development of digestion theory in the seventeenth century. While this subject has been
touched on before by other scholars it has generally been examined
among other issues within the general evolution of chemical medicine and philosophy. In my examination of several authors interested in Paracelsian ideas I will attempt to suggest a broader social
context in which digestion theory may have played a role, namely
in the changing world of the seventeenth-century kitchen.

For Paracelsus the stomach was of prime importance. In his description of the body he endows each organ with an element he referred
to as the 'archeus', or essential force, which distinguished between
useful and toxic substances. Although each organ has its own archeus,
the most important one was located in the stomach where it worked
as an alchemist, separating life giving nourishment from dross in the
food it received:

> A person eating meat, wherein both poison and nourishment are con-
> tained, deems everything good while he eats. For, the poison lies hid-
> den among the good and there is nothing good among the poison.
> When thus the food, that is to say the meat, reaches the stomach, the
> alchemist is ready and eliminates that which is not conducive to the
> well-being of the body. This the alchemist conveys to a special place,
> and the good where it belongs. This is as the Creator ordained it. In
> this manner the body is taken care of so that no harm will befall it
> from the poison which it takes in by eating, the poison being elimi-
> nated from the body by the alchemist without man's co-operation. Of
> such a nature are thus virtue and power of the alchemist in man.[1]

The process of digestion within the stomach was the most important of many such digestions which were performed by the Archei

---

[1] Paracelsus, *Volumen medicinae paramirum*, trans. and preface by Kurt F. Leidecker,
Supplement to Bulletin of the History of Medicine, No. 11, 1949, 36.

throughout the human body. In turn these digestions were paral-
lelled by those in the natural world according to the Paracelsian concept of the body as a microcosm of the cosmos. This is reflected in
another passage from his work in which he states

> You are aware that the earth exists solely for the purpose of bearing
> fruit and for the sake of man. With the same logic the body also exists
> solely for the same reason. Thus from within the body grows all the
> food which is to be used by the members that belong to the body.
> These grow like the fruit of the earth.[2]

Such descriptions of the body and the digestive process were a radical departure from the Galenic theory of digestion. In the Galenic
tradition, food was ingested and then transformed by heat into chyle,
or the four humours—blood, phlegm, black bile and yellow bile.
This process involved a series of digestions, the first producing the
humours and the second producing the faeces. It was argued that
this series of transformations was caused by a heat which was innate
to the organs of the stomach and the food was cooked in this organic
oven (a process termed 'coction'). In explaining this process Galen
used the metaphor of fermentation, comparing the generation of the
humours to the fermentation of wine, which undergoes alteration
through the agency of its contained heat.

Although Galen employs this metaphor of fermentation it seems
more probable, that he considered fermentation to be a kind of
digestion and never believed that digestion was a kind of fermentation. Later writers, however, such as Fernel, while continuing to compare digestion to the fermentation of wine, began to consider digestion
as a kind of fermentation, particularly when they had abandoned
the concept of innate heat and were casting about for another innate
force that could stimulate digestion.

Paracelsus, then, despite his departure from Galenic tradition, still
held to the belief that heat was the primary agent of digestion although he realised that it was powerfully aided by what he termed
'appetising acids'.

I would now like to move on to the seventeenth century and one
of the most elaborate expressions of digestion influenced by the work
of Paracelsus—Michael Maier's text, *Atalanta Fugiens*. Maier, a court
physician, outlines his theory of Paracelsian medicine in a series of
highly symbolic emblems accompanied by a musical score for a three-

---

[2] *Ibid.*, 29.

part fugue based on Mercury, Sulphur and Salt. A quick glance at many of his emblems will immediately confirm the esoteric quality of the world surrounding chemical medicine in this period, though it is less commonly observed that Maier also respects the value of common, mundane activities. In the third emblem of the book, for instance, he lays emphasis on the need for observation. Beneath an image of a woman washing clothes the verse says

> Let one who loves to study dogmas
> Not fail to take up every helpful hint:
>
> You see a woman, washing stains from sheets,
>
> As usual, by pouring on hot water
> Take after her, lest you frustrate your art,
> For water washes the black body's dirt.[3]

Here Maier is using a realistic image to point out that in the study of alchemy close observation of the mundane, everyday act will be of help. Paracelsus too had said

> A Physitian ought not to rest only in that bare knowledge which their Schools teach but to learn of old Women, Egyptians, and such like persons; for they have greater experience in such things than all the Academicians[4]

In his commentary on the emblem Maier points to the chemical process of cleaning linen, claiming that women learnt this from observing nature and in particular the bleaching of animals's bones. He then compares this to alchemy saying

> The same happens to the philosophical subject: first it is coarse and dirty, but the philosophers cleanse it with philosophical water, till it is white and perfect, the whole process of calcination, ascending, dissolving, distillation, precipitation, coagulation, hardening and the other processes are prepared by one washing . . .[5]

The mundane image reveals a model for one of the vital alchemic processes. For the reader, nature as depicted in the image contains

---

[3] Michael Maier, *Atalanta fugiens: An Edition of the Emblems, Fugues, and Epigrams*, trans. and ed. by Joscelyn Godwin, 1989, 111.

[4] Paracelsus *Sämtliche Werke*. I. Abteilung. Medizinische, naturwissenschaftliche und philosophische schriften, ed. K. Sudhoff, 14 vols. Munich/Berlin 1922–33, vol. 14, 541 (of the Supreme Mysteries of Nature).

[5] H.M.E. De Jong, Michael Maier's *Atalanta fugiens: Sources of an Alchemical Book of Emblems*, Leiden 1969, 67.

a 'signature' of the celestial, which an adept can decipher by close observation.

The image of a woman at household chores is repeated later in Emblem 22. Again it is a realistic and mundane scene, this time of a woman cooking fish. The motto reads: When you have the white lead, do the women's work that is COOK.[6] The commentary goes further and gives a description of steaming fish

> Some people cook fish in the following manner: they use two well-closed pans, one on top of the other, putting the fish in the upper pan and the water in the lower one. When the pans are put on the fire, the vapour of the boiling water rises and the fish get cooked by the hot steam. Now this is the unsurpassed procedure of the Philosophers ... for air is an imperceptible vapour, which ripens the fruit on the trees. ... It is the air, also which dyes and colours the gold apples in the Garden of Hesperides[7]

Again everyday domestic work is used as a model for the alchemic philosopher and physician. Throughout the whole book Maier adopts the familiar image of a woman as the representative of nature, guiding those who would study the secret arts.

The medical benefits of such observation and experience are most clearly expressed in Emblem 28, one of the central images of the book. Here we see a King sitting in a steam bath, sweating out the black bile of melancholy. His physician has evidently learnt the lessons of the washing woman and, in particular, of the woman steaming fish. Maier's commentary on this emblem argues that: In the human body there occur three cooking or consuming processes, namely in the stomach, the liver and the veins.[8] He goes on to outline a chemical version of the digestion process and then extends the metaphor of digestion to discuss the celestial elements saying

> There are just about as many kinds of cooking processes or consuming processes in metallurgy as in the human body; the first process takes place in the great year, that is in the revolution of the uppermost sphaera ...[9]

With this, Maier has moved from domestic cookery through medicine and alchemy to a meditation on the cosmos. Such a sequence

---

[6] Michael Maier, *Atalanta fugiens*, 149.
[7] De Jong, Michael Maier, *Atalanta fugiens*, 198.
[8] *Ibid.*, 206.
[9] *Ibid.*, 207.

of association is to be expected of a physician interested in the work of Paracelsus, though in Maier's case he is careful to emphasise the mundanity of many of the scenes depicted in his work, placing them alongside the more surreal images expected of a musical, emblematical, Rosicrucian Paracelsian physician.

Other emblem books of the same period were also beginning to represent with new theories of digestion. In Theodore de Bry's *Emblemata Saecularia* (1611) emblem 44 depicts the effects of fermentation on the body. The emblem, however, lacks the prose context provided by Maier which would place the theory within a more universal philosophy. It appears simply as one image in a series which have an implicit cosmology. Later in the century another emblem in a book by Jacob Bornitz indicates the popular progress of the stomach as chemist metaphor.

Returning to Maier, then, his work employs the Paracelsian terminology of digestions and cooking. Within *Atalanta Fugiens* food itself is used as a symbolic language, elaborating an already esoteric landscape. But what of the real cooks, working away in their real kitchens? If physicians were rethinking the question of digestion and hence the role of food in the body, then did they have any impact on the actual preparation of a meal? The evidence from François Pierre de La Varenne's *Le Cuisinier Français* published in 1651 suggests that continental cookery was undergoing a major transformation in the first half of the seventeenth century. La Varenne, summarising the evolution of several decades of French cooking, marks a clear shift away from medieval tradition to a new cuisine based on the bouillon and on the addition of sauces to a dish. It is tempting to assume that the vigorous debates on chemical philosophy and the process of digestion may have influenced court cooking. The links between cookery, alchemy and chemistry have always been strong, embodied perhaps by the 'bain marie', named after an alchemist from the middle east. Sadly, La Varenne's insistence on limiting his comments to cookery, however, reduces the argument to mere speculation.

In England, though, the more frequent publication of cookery books in the seventeenth century offers greater insight into the influence of chemical philosophy on the kitchen. The cookery books which began to appear in England at the end of the sixteenth century are notably different from their later French counterparts in that they are aimed at women, and intended to facilitate the running of a large domestic establishment. French cookery books, on the other hand, emphasise court cookery which would inevitably be undertaken by a male chef.

Two of the most influential cookery writers to be published in England in this period are Sir Hugh Plat and Gervase Markham. Plat's works included *The Jewell House of Nature* and *The Delighte of Ladies*, while Markham published *The English House-Wife* in 1615. Plat's *Jewell House* is divided into two sections—the first full of useful household hints and the second entitled Diverse new sorts of Soyle, devoted to agricultural questions. The implication in Plat's work is that cookery and distilling are the woman's domain while gardening and husbandry are the man's responsibility. Gervase Markham reinforces this idea through the publication of a companion volume to the English House-Wife entitled The Compleat Husbandman and the Gentleman's Recreation, or The Whole Art of Husbandry. In all of these works the emphasis is on the practical employment of the texts and to a large degree all are free of esoteric jargon or arcane symbolism.

Both writers, however, were interested in the ideas of Paracelsus and the new chemical philosophy of the early seventeenth century. Plat, in the preface to The Jewell House of Art and Nature, argues for the right to publish his work by comparing himself to Paracelsians:

> Here hence it commeth to passe that the most part of our chimical and paracelsian practisers, not being able to open those fast locked bodies of the mettals, whereby to make them by many rotations so volatile as they ought, do therefore give them in their grosse Natures, with their earthly and poisoned parts, not beeing able to make a trew and philosophicall division of them . . . Seeing then, that al these ancient & new Magicians . . . durst never as yet presume to rase out that old envied sentence Plura latent quam patent, being written in capitall letters, by the hande of Nature . . . why should not I, having spent som of my sweetest hours in reading . . . adventure as boldlie as the rest[10]

He also argues that although his work springs from private endeavour, it has a public good, saying:

> When I consider with my self (righte honourable) that the trew end of all our privat labors and studies, ought to bee the beginning of the publike and common good of our country, wherein we breath and have our being: I holde my self partely bound by the law of nature, & partly by the necessity of the times, to disclose and manifest, even

---

[10] Sir Hugh Plat, *The Jewell House of Art and Nature* (London 1594) B4r–B4v.

those secret and hidden magisteries, both of art and nature, which I had long since enterred in a case of marble and are now (fearing some patent of concealements) ready to breake out of their tombes, and to pleade their owne tenures.[11]

Here Plat manages to combine a sense of the Paracelsian microcosm/macrocosm conception of the world with the urgency of seventeenth-century English politics, where the boundary between private and public had become a volatile issue. Within this context, he presents a series of helpful hints that encompass both food and all other dimensions of domestic life, telling the reader, for instance:

1. How to write a letter secretly
2. How to roast meat more speedilie and with lesse fire
3. [How] to helpe venison that is tainted
4. [How] to steal bees[12]

Plat's book also includes substantial section on cures and medical receipts, a phenomenon typical of seventeenth-century English cookery books. The inclusion of such receipts demonstrates just how blurred the line remained between cookery and simple pharmacy at that time. Take for example Plat's inclusion of a recipe for Stephen's Water which reads as follows:

> Take a gallon of the best Gascoyne wine: then take Ginger, Gallingale, Cinamon, Nutmegs, Graines, Cloves, Anniseedes, Fennell seedes, Carroway seedes, of each of them a dram weight: then take wilde Time, rysop, Lavender, Sage, Mints, red Roses, Garden Time, Pellitory of the wall, and Rosemary, of each of them one good handfull, and [beat] the herbs very small, and stampe the spices all together very small: put all together into the Wine, and close it fast twelve houres, and stirre it divers times: then still it in a Limbeck, and keep the first water, for it is the best: and then keepe the second, for it is good, but not so good as the first[13]

The emphasis on distillation here, however domestic, may be a popularisation of the more esoteric chemical medicine of the Paracelsians—although Charles Webster has rightly pointed out that distillation in England may have been influenced by much broader interests in distillation than the efforts of English Paracelsians alone.[14] In English

---

[11] *Ibid.*, A2r.
[12] *Ibid.*, A3r–A4r.
[13] Sir Hugh Plat, *Delightes for Ladies*, London 1609, 28.
[14] See C. Webster, *The Great Instantation. Science, Medicine and Reform 1626–1660*, London 1975.

cookery books, however, it is the Paracelsians who give it greatest emphasis.

The cookery books of Plat and Markham were published during a period in England when the country house was undergoing radical change. The late Elizabethan and early Jacobean country houses reflected a new emphasis on privacy and a new awareness of the roles of the husband and wife within such a house. Plat and Markham acknowledge these evolving roles in their division of husbandry and cookery, often allying it to allusions of Adam and Eve, a tradition that would continue through to the mid-eighteenth century with the book, *Adam's Luxury, Eve's Cookery* (1747). Their stress on the public benefits of private, domestic management also reconciled these new relationships with the political macrocosm. It was fitting too that these books laid emphasis on one aspect of cookery in particular which had evolved in tandem with the new style of country house—the banquet.

In his book, Life in the English Country House, Mark Girouard briefly outlines the rise of the small banqueting house in the second half of the sixteenth century. He points to the medieval origin of the dessert, or banquet, as a 'voiding'—a small dish to be consumed while the table was being cleared. By the sixteenth century, the dish became more elaborate and eventually stimulated the building of small, intimate rooms designed specifically for the consumption of desserts. These rooms were often situated in towers at the top of the house or in a separate building in the gardens. These developments can be seen in the context of a growing desire for privacy among the higher classes, and Girouard cites Queen Elizabeth's habits as a formative example saying,

> She ate more and more in the privy chamber, at the expense of the presence chamber . . . the royal table was prepared for dinner in the presence chamber, to the accompaniment of all the usual ceremonies laid down in the Harleian and other regulations. The first course was then brought in by forty yeomen of the guard. But the Queen was not in the room and never appeared; she was at a separated table in her privy chamber. Sayes were taken, wine and beer were poured, three courses and a dessert were served, all with full ceremony to an imaginary queen at an empty table.[15]

Within this context of privacy, the banquet assumes a special importance. It could be the final element of a meal but it could also be

---

[15] Mark Girouard, *Life in the English Country House*, Harmondsworth 1980, 110.

an informal picnic-style dish, consumed outside the ceremonies of mealtime—informal but intimate. It was this versatility which allowed the banquet to acquire its unique social and spiritual dimensions.

As we have already seen, the banquets were held in specially designed rooms or buildings. The foods generally used in these meals included 'quince paste, quince cakes, quinces in syrup, hippocras, jelly, leach, gingerbread, marmalade, sugar-plate, spice cakes, jumbals, marchpane, conserves and baked fruit'. This predilection for sweet and spicy foods immediately added a sense of luxury to the occasion and, as a matter of course, the idea of luxury brought with it such ideas as vice and virtue. The banqueting rooms themselves reinforced the notion of spirituality, with several being designed to instill a sense of peace and solitude. Girouard quotes a description of Lady Elisabeth Berkeley's banqueting house which was described as 'the retired cell of her soul's soliloquies to God her creator'. Later he cites Thomas Tresham's Triangular Lodge at Rushton in Northamptonshire which was decorated with mystic signs and numbers in honour of the Holy Trinity.

That food and cookery was used as an ethical system in this period can be seen in Thomas Middleton's play *Women beware Women*, when one of the male characters uses food metaphors while discussing commerce, sex and idleness, saying,

> Those that are wealthy and have got enough, 'Tis after sunset with 'em; they may rest, Grow fat with ease, banquet, and toy and play . . .[16]

Middleton's puritan impulse was not so strictly shared by those who consumed banquets, but religion may have influenced their meal despite this. The message of luxury and ease presented by banquets and, in particular, by the subtleties or moulded sugar figures consumed in the meal was tempered by the emblematic design of much of the food. Sir Hugh Plat gave instructions for the making of marchpane conceits such as the following:

> Take two pounds of Almondes, beeing blaunched and dryed in a sieve over the fire, beate them in a stone mortar, and when they be small mix with the two pound of sugar being finely beaten, ading two or three spoonfulls of Rosewater, and that will keep your almonds from oiling: when your paste is beaten fine, drive it thin with a rowling pin, and so lay it on a bottome of wafers, then raise up a little edge on the side, and so bake it, then ice it with Rosewater and Sugar, then

---

[16] Thomas Middleton, *Women Beware Women, 1622*, London 1968, I, iii, 31–33.

put it into the oven againe, and when you see your ice is risen up
and drie, then take it out of the Oven and garnish it with prettie con-
ceipts, as birds & beastes beeing cast out of standing molds. Sticke
long comfits upright in it, cast bisket and carowaies in it, gild it before
you serve it: you may also print off the Marchpane paste in your
molds for banquetting dishes. And of this paste our comfit makers at
this day make their letters, knots, Armes, escocheons, beasts, birds, and
other fancies.[17]

There was an obvious element of pleasure in constructing such clever
and appealing works and the mention of 'conceits' brings the metaphysical poets to mind. The communal, Hermetic wit of the poets
who passed their manuscripts around is evident in the structure and
enjoyment of a Jacobean banquet.

Furthermore, there was a sense in which the notion of 'you are
what you eat' played a part in these meals. Given the chemical transformation which occurred during digestion, the consumption of a
moulded snake or bird became a spiritual ingestion of that creature.
The consumption of a quince or of a sweet pie could also imbue
the diner with the virtues or vices highlighted by Middleton. In more
elaborate banquets the owner of the country house would construct
small sugar replicas of his possessions or buildings on his estates for
his guests. On one level this is no more than an amusing but triv-
ial conceit. On another level, however, it involves the host and the
guest in a subtle power relationship in which the owner displays his
wealth and the guest acknowledges and confirms it.

In another sense such consumption was a digestion of knowledge as
you interpreted the emblematic conceits of the dish—one author even
suggests making moulds from the corpse of a recently killed animal
such as a rabbit, or hare, and later producing moulded banqueting-
stuff from this shape. There is a certain hunger for accuracy in such
a suggestion as if it was an early gastronomic version of natural
history.

Again from the point of view of religion, the strict anti-iconic spirit
of early seventeenth-century England may have influenced the banquet subtlety. As Reformation ideology continued to hold back English
painting, images flourished in the less obvious areas where it could
be defended as functional decoration if questions were asked.

The dessert or banquet was presented as offering an ethical consumption—it was a culinary form of imitation. One of the central

---

[17] Sir Hugh Plat, *Delightes for Ladies*, London 1609, 28.

literary metaphors of the late seventeenth and early eighteenth century was that of imitation as a kind of digestion. The metaphor flourished just as medical ideas on digestion were being vigourously debated. In the first half of the seventeenth century though, this metaphor was already being enacted in the banquet where, through digestion, you could consume a moral by eating an emblematic sugar work.

By means of the purity and sweetness of sugar it was possible, then, to achieve a modest alchemical or spiritual transformation.

The subtle equation of food, luxury and spirituality was destroyed by the civil war. From 1655 onwards, however, a new wave of cookery books began to appear. These works both looked back to the 'Golden age' of Charles I and, after 1660, pointed towards a new vitality in the Restoration kitchen.

The first of these works to appear—*The Queen's Closet Opened*—was first published in 1655. Again, the work allies itself to the urgency of English politics, declaring in its preface that the reader must 'thank the time, not me, for otherwise these pretious leaves had never beene in common'. The work purported to be taken from the manuscript recipes of Queen Henrietta Maria and, given its date of publication, it must have appeared to be both an elegy for the pre-lapsarian days of Charles I and an act of political subversion under the reign of Cromwell.

Certainly the book became incredibly popular, running through at least five editions between 1660s and the 1680s, inspiring both Hannah Wooley, the first English woman to publish a cookery book— *The Ladies Directory*—and also an anonymous author hoping to profit from imitation with the title, *The Queen-Like Closet*. Most revealingly, the preface of *The Queen's Closet Opened* was changed from the second edition onwards and the following paragraph was inserted, stating that

> in regard of the Benefit which so many have received from these, which we shall now rather call Experiments than Receipts contained therein . . . neither have we known of any that have bought it, who have not testified their high esteem thereof. And indeed, how should it otherwise be, knowing out of what Elaboratories it was produced?[18]

The Queen has now been transformed from cook to chemist through the language of 'experiments' and 'laboratories'. By adding this

---

[18] M.W., *The Queen's Closet Opened*, London 1661, nn.

passage the publishers succeed in reinforcing the links between politics, chemistry and the kitchen in seventeenth-century England. Of
course, it is to be more realistic to assume their motive for this in-
sertion was to cash in on a new desire for all things experimental
among the reading public, but the fact that a cookery book could be
so easily disguised as a book of experiments argues for the continued blurring of distinctions between chemistry, alchemy and cookery.

   Such a blurring of bourdaries occurs in the works of another
author of that period—Sir Kenelm Digby. A Royalist, Digby had
pursued scientific studies while also working for the King as naval
commander and diplomatist. After his death, an influential collection of his recipes was published as *The Closet of the Eminently Learned
Sir Kenelm Digby Opened* (1669). The work included over 100 recipes
for mead and hydromel attributed to various aristocratic Royalists.

   In the year of the Restoration, 1660, Digby was invited to give a
lecture at Gresham College and chose as his subject 'The Vegetation
of Plants'. In this lecture, he promotes a Paracelsian form of husbandry when discussing the planting of a seed or bean, saying:

> This dry shrunk compacted substance, being buryed slightly in the
> moist ground, at a season when the approaching Sun (the great Archaeus
> and the fire of nature) beginning to dilate and sublime up to the
> Superficies of the Earth, that volatile and balsmick salt which his
> remoteness during the Winter had suffered to be shrunk up together,
> and condensed and sunk deeper towards the Center; must of neces-
> sity receive into its substance, that saline humidity which environeth
> it, is contiguous to it, and on all hands presseth upon it:[19]

Digby then goes on to discuss the growth of the bean in terms that
again intimately link food and the politics of England. He says:

> The immediate effect of this humecting of the Bean . . ., must neces-
> sarily be that it swelleth and grow bigger . . . And from thence it will
> follow, that the skin . . . must needs crack and tear to afford way and
> liberty to the dilation of the swelled body . . . and in that little natu-
> rall body, we may read the fate which hangeth over political ones,
> when the inferiour Members that should study nothing but obedience,
> have gotten the power into their hands: for then every one of them
> following their impetuous inclinations, the whole is brought into con-
> fusion; and that is destroyed which everyone in their tumultuary way

---

[19] Sir Kenelme Digby, *A Discourse Concerning the Vegetation of Plants*, London 1661,
8–9.

aimed to gain the Mastery of; unlesse a superiour Architect, as in the present case of our bleeding Nation, do come to draw light and order, out of that darknesse and confusion. It will happen then to this swollen Bean . . . than which followeth, is a totall Putrefaction, Dissolution, and Destruction of the compound: But if it be kept within its due limits, then the body in which it was wrought, is raised to a nobler pitch, and the Ethereall spirits of it are actuated, and put in possession of their native vertue . . .[20]

It is clear from this passage that the Paracelsian concept of micro-cosm and macrocosm is being applied to the relationship between food, the human body and subsequently the body politic of the state of England. Interestingly, a similar application can be found in an-other, more scientific, text published in the same period—*Oriatrike or Physick Refined* (1662), John Chandler's translation of the works of van Helmont.

It was the work of Johannes Baptiste van Helmont in the early seventeenth century which made the decisive break with the Galenist concept of digestion. Van Helmont had rejected the doctrines of Galen and the medieval schools when he was studying the various branches of science. Frustrated by the Galenists he retired to the countryside and turned his back on practising medicine, devoting his energies to chemical experiments. The discoveries made by van Helmont and the theories he outlined were always placed within a larger system of religion and cosmology. This system, like much of his chemical work, was influenced by alchemical concepts and a mystical world-view. Although others in this period were beginning to reject the Galenic idea of digestion and to discover the role of gastric juices and acids, it was van Helmont's work which had the greatest impact. For almost a century after the posthumous pub-lication of his treatise *Heat Does Not Digest Efficiently, but Excitingly*, his ideas on fermentation and digestion found strong support. The reason for this constant support must lie in part in his striking, metaphorical style of writing. Medically, his theories were refined and secularised by the next generation of doctors, most notably Sylvius. His mystical description of fermentation and the links between Man and nature, however, proved deeply attractive to a more general reader. As the influence of Cartesianism and the rise of the mechan-ical school of medicine reduced man to a machine, van Helmont's

---

[20] *Ibid.*, 9–14.

theories linked man to the active principle that governed the universe through the simple act of eating.

Van Helmont began by attacking the Galenic theory of digestion and innate heat in the stomach. He argued that heat could not be the agent of digestion as animals without heat such as fish could digest. Heat, then, did not transform the food digested into another substance, it merely modified the original substance. In digestion it was obvious that food underwent a radical transformation and fire could not achieve this. Van Helmont's observation of the hen's ability to dissolve glass by digestion taught him that an acid must be at work. This was reinforced by a childhood experience when van Helmont was bitten on the tongue by a sparrow and he noticed an intensely acid taste in the bird's throat—a striking example of the importance of bodily agency as outlined by John Christie in Chapter 12. This acid, however, had to have an active agent in order to deal with a wide variety of foodstuffs. Van Helmont decided that this agent was a ferment and that the acid originated in the spleen, though it had no links with the 'black bile' of Galenic medicine. Walter Pagel also suggests that van Helmont knew that this 'acid ferment' in the stomach was hydrochloric acid.

Van Helmont argues that the Galenists did not discover the role of this acid ferment because they were misled by the use of a metaphor. In the opening paragraphs of *Heat Does Not Digest Efficiently, but Excitingly* he states that,

> Because the whole foundation of nature is thought to hang on the hinge of heat, and the Elements, mixtures, and temperaments are already banished far off; therefore to establish the progeny of the Archeus, and vital Spirits, we must hence following speak of digestions: The which, because the Schools have enslaved to heat, I will shew that heat is not the proper instrument of digestion. Indeed, the metaphor of digestion hath deceived the Schools: to wit, it being a Poetical liberty borrowed from a rustical sense, introduced, they have made concoction of the same name with digestion.
>
> And as they knew seething or boyling to be concoction, therfore they translated digestion to be boyling, and on both sides where they though heat to be the natural, total, and one only cause of them: For they saw that by seething, and roasting, very many things waxed tender, and were altered: Therefore a liberty being taken from artificial things, they translated a Kitchin into the amazed transmutations of the bowels and meats: not indeed by way of similitude but altogether properly and immediately, and by thinking, the matter passed over

into a belief, and into a true opinion; and all the offices, and benefits of our nature, they translated into heats, and temperaments, as it were into totall causes . . .[21]

Here, he appears to attack the way in which the metaphor of cookery and kitchens is employed as well as disparaging the theory of digestion by heat. When, however, he feels he has sufficiently proved the fallacy of that theory he recuperates the metaphor, adapting it to his own ideas on fermentation and in fact, expanding it to deal with activities beyond digestion. Setting his own theories of digestion in A sixfold digestion of humane nourishment he remarks that:

the proper Kitchin or Digestion of the stomach is from without to within; but the Kitchin which is made universal in its hollowness, is there also wholly composed and enclosed; And that, lest the digestion of them both should breed confusion. Indeed, there is a two fold Cook in the Stomach; one from the Spleen; and the other being proper to it self sends forth divers digestions.[22]

Here, he not only restates the kitchen/cookery metaphor but surrounds it with linking images by describing it as a 'shop'. The bowels are then described as a 'buttery' and the spleen is linked with the stomach in a 'Duumvirate' or 'Sheriffdom'. The digestive process is represented by these images as a thriving mercantile region where food is the main business, a region in which he says 'the Poets have erected the Golden and prosperous Kingdoms of Saturn, and in pride, the liberal Feasts of Saturn'.

In *Oriatrike*, then, van Helmont's metaphorical landscape equates the human body and the body politic. In fact, with his world of butteries, shops, sheriffdoms and kitchens he has imagined a body politic that is driven by the need to consume and which reflects the process of digestion and consumption at every level.

It may have been simply fortuitous that *Oriatrike*, with its compelling metaphors, was published in the 1660s but its images of cooking and consumption were to have a lasting effect. The later work of Sylvius, Peyer, Brunner, Willis and Borelli all advanced the medical conception of digestion in the seventeenth century but the heated debate on the nature of digestion remained dominated by the meta-

---

[21] John Baptiste van Helmont, *Oriatrike, or Physick Refined*, London 1662, 198.
[22] *Ibid.*, 215.

phors of Paracelsus and van Helmont. This remains true even into the early eighteenth century when the battle is joined by Archibald Pitcairne, Hecquet and Astruc.

Furthermore, as England entered the Augustan era and began to enjoy the first fruits of empire and a growing consumer culture, metaphors of eating, cookery and digestion acquired a central role in debates on the health of the body politic. Tea and coffee became coded references to political parties and roast beef became the emblem of England while physicians such as Bernard Mandeville and George Cheyne attempted to control the diet of an increasingly voracious nation.

I have attempted to show how the metaphors of cookery and kitchens used by Paracelsus continued to evolve in a variety of ways in the work of later physicians such as Maier, Digby and van Helmont. The evolution of these metaphors was accompanied by the emergence of a new style of cuisine and by the emergence of a new literary genre—the cookery book. For medical historians these books represent a potentially rich source of information on food, diet, and domestic remedies. More importantly, perhaps, the wealth of cookery manuscripts from this period offer a detailed picture of the changing food habits of the age. Only a more systematic examination of this material can reveal the true nature of the relationship between chemistry and cookery.

CHAPTER FOURTEEN

'INVISIBLE DISEASES' – IMAGINATION AND MAGNETISM: PARACELSUS AND THE CONSEQUENCES*

Heinz Schott

Some scholars of Paracelsus' work show him as a harbinger of psychosomatic medicine. Thus, they interpret his well known treatise *De causis morborum invisibium* (On the invisible diseases)[1] as an essay pointing to modern theories of medical psychology and psychotherapy, in spite of its occult, magical and even cabbalistic impact.[2] I take the opposite view. I assume that the occult, magical and religious content of Paracelsus' writings is reflected in modern psychosomatic medicine in a secularized form. To this extent, modern concepts, especially the Freudian paradigm, are disguised latecomers from the period of the Renaissance. The currents of the natural philosophy and the specifically scientific approach of the Renaissance are hidden today, but they are still to be found.

When we study the different psychosomatic concepts in the history of medicine, we generally notice the double character of psychosomatic ideas. On the one hand there are ideas, pictures, illusions within a person's mind which may imprint themselves upon his own body or infect other bodies by communication. We may call this the power of imagination (*Vorstellungs-* or *Einbildungskraft*). On the other hand there are energies or natural powers which correlate the individual organism with the whole organism of nature. This we may call the correlation between microcosm and macrocosm. The most essential idea of natural philosophy, from the Stoics up to romanticism, claims that all bodies, including the human organism, are connected by networks of magnetic influence. This concept of magnetism,

---

* Abbreviation: *Paracelsus*, ed. Sudhoff = Theophrast von Hohenheim gen. Paracelsus: *Sämtliche Werke*. 1. Abt. Medizinische, naturwissenschaftliche und philosophische Schriften, ed. Karl Sudhoff. 14 vols. München, Berlin 1929–1933.

[1] 'Paracelsus, ed. Sudhoff, vol. 9, 251–350; complete title: *'de causis morborum invisibilium, das ist, von den unsichtbaren krankheiten und iren ursachen'*.

[2] Cf. e.g. Werner and Annemarie Leibbrand, 'Die "kopernikanische Wendung" des Hysteriebegriffs bei Paracelsus', in *Paracelsus, Werk und Wirkung. Festgabe für Kurt Goldammer*, ed. Sepp Domandl, Wien 1975, 125–132.

especially the concept of sympathetic interaction, covers the energetic problem: the transference of vital powers within the body or
from one body to another.[3]

Imagination plays a great role in the history of medicine. The
images of visualized pictures may represent healing powers (Sigmund
Freud's 'Eros'). Others may represent destructive powers (death in-
stinct, Freud's 'Todestrieb').[4] We know the traditional quasi-scientific
methods within the history of medicine: The mantic methods of
dream interpretation or interpretation of prognostic signs and visions.
The painted images of the saints in the Middle Ages, for example, play an important role in the religious medicine of the Middle
Ages. The power of the icons may be explained by a power exerted
by imagination over the body functions. Evil imaginations, sugges-
tions by the Devil or demons, on the other hand, could produce illness or death. We may think of the imagery of monsters predicting
social disaster.[5]

The idea of magnetism derives from the cosmological concept of
interaction. Occult powers within the natural world influence the
human organism. Magic medicine tries to cure sick persons by so-
called magnetic techniques. They tend to strengthen the vital forces
of the organism: in other words, to accumulate vitality. But there
are also destructive powers of magnetism. They weaken vitality and
take away life energy—like vampires.[6] The long tradition of magical practices and sympathetic cures documents the importance of
magnetic influence as a medical idea.

---

[3] On the concept of sympathy and its metaphoric use in the history of medicine; see Heinz Schott: *Sympathie als Metapher in der Medizingeschichte*, Würzburger
medizinhistorische Mitteilungen 10, 1992, 107–127.

[4] The Freudian terminology is very clearly pointed out by J. Laplanche and
J.-B. Pontalis, *Das Vokabular der Psychoanalyse*. Frankfurt am Main 1973 (suhrkamp
taschenbuch wissenschaft, vol. 7). Cf. the articles on '*Eros*', 143–145 and '*Todestriebe*',
494–503.

[5] The mantic interpretation of monsters (Latin: 'monstra') as signs of sin and
moral decay have an important impact on modern behaviour against children born
with malformations; cf. Heinz Schott, Die Stigmen des Bösen: Kulturgeschichtliche
Wurzeln der Ausmerze-Ideologie', in *Wissenschaft auf Irrwegen: Biologismus-Rassenhygiene-
Eugenik*, ed. by Peter Propping und Heinz Schott. Bonn and Berlin 1992, 9–22.

[6] The term 'Od-vampirism' (*Od-Vampirismus*) describes the negative (weakening)
powers of persons in the middle of the 19th century according to the 'Od' theory of
the German chemist Carl Reichenbach; cf. Karl Spiesberger: Justinus Kerners
'Seherin von Prevorst' in Betrachtung esoterischer Tradition und im Lichte psychischer Forschung, in, Erich Sopp and Karl Spiesberger, *Auf den Spuren der Seherin*,
Sersheim 1953, 64.

Before we deal with Paracelsianism and Mesmerism we should try to construct a rough typology of psychosomatic models. *Firstly*, the *imago* may come from outside into the mind, which takes it up and imprints it on the body. This mechanism is called 'introjection' in psychology. *Secondly*, the *imago* may originate from inside the human organism, for example, by a disorder of bodily function. In this case the psyche takes up the *imago* and regards it as a real phenomenon. This mechanism is called 'projection' in psychology. Both these mechanisms, introjection as well as projection, may support either healing processes or destructive ones.

In a similar way, there are two processes of magnetic activity. *Firstly*, a magnetic influence from outside means an input of energy into the body. It is a positive transfer which may be compared to charging a battery. The flow of energy through the medium of the nervous system, for example, aims (as a healing method) at strengthening the vitality. *Secondly*, there is the model of attraction—of driving out the germ of disease. The magnetic power may attract the pathogenic 'seed' (*Krankheitssamen*) according to Paracelsus. The human organism is considered as a psychosomatic entity into which energy can be introduced (input) or extracted (output) by an outside agent. To this extent the power of magnetism is based on transference of energy.

A special method of prophylaxis is the defense mechanism (a term borrowed from Freud's psychoanalysis).[7] Special practices such as wearing an amulet, for example, are intended to give protection against both bad images and bad magnetic influences.

Often Paracelsus has been admired as a genius who attained new insight into the human body and mind and their disorders, and who gave physicians a philosophical and ethical basis for their practice. But he is by no means the founder of the theory of imagination and magnetism. Rather, he took up fairly common ideas and attitudes of his period and adapted them to his specific purposes. He is a representative of his time.[8] Walter Pagel is the chief among those who have demonstrated the enormous impact of neo-Platonism, alchemy, gnosis, and, last but not least, the cabbala on Paracelsus. He is directly influenced by Renaissance Platonism, especially

---

[7] Cf. Laplanche/Pontalis, 'Abwehrmechnismen', 30–33.

[8] In this regard we may compare him with Sigmund Freud, who represents the spectrum of scientific and cultural currents at the turn of the 19th century.

as represented by Marsilio Ficino (1433–1499) and Giovanni Pico della Mirandola (1463–1494) of the Florentine Academy, as stressed by Pagel.[9]

The influence of the cabbala on Paracelsus has usually been underestimated. The religious mysticism of the Jews, its metaphors and symbols, were generally of great interest in the humanistic period. I mention only Johannes Reuchlin and his fight for the acceptance of the Jewish cabbala.[10] The Christian cabbala developed during the period of the Reformation. Millenianism (chiliasm), Swabian pietism, the Rosicrucians and even romantic natural philosophy and its offshoots (up to and including modern depth psychology) were influenced by cabbalistic elements.[11]

Pagel points out: '. . . even if Paracelsus had no first hand knowledge of cabbalistic ideas and sources, he could not fail to arrive at concordant views in his doctrine as a whole as well as in certain specific points. Such concordances are largely the result of the dominant role played by the theory of Microcosm in both.'[12]

This aspect is often ignored by scholars, at least in the German tradition. It may be a consequence of either open or more subtle antisemitism that they considered Paracelsus to be the 'Luther of physicians' (*Lutherus medicorum*).[13] He appeared as the incarnation of the German art of healing, a genius fighting against un-German trends in medical theory and practice. This interpretation flourished during the Third Reich, a subject recently explored by Udo Benzen-

---

[9] Cf. Walter Pagel, *Das medizinische Weltbild des Paracelsus: Seine Zusammenhänge mit Neuplatonismus und Gnosis*. Wiesbaden 1962; more detailed in Walter Pagel, *Paracelsus. An Introduction to Philosophical Medicine in the Era of the Renaissance*, 2nd revised ed. Basel 1982, 284–289. The importance of Ficino's and Pico's theory for *magia naturalis* is pointed out by Wolf-Dieter Müller-Jahncke, *Astrologisch-magische Theorie und Praxis in der Heilkunde der frühen Neuzeit*, Stuttgart 1985, 33–41.

[10] Cf. Max Brod's introduction to Reuchlin's life and work, *Johannes Reuchlin und sein Kampf. Eine historische Monographie*, Stuttgart 1965. Recently an anthology appeared in print covering the whole topic: *L'Hébreu au Temps de la Renaissance*, ed. Ilana Zinguer. Leiden 1992; see especially the article by Christoph Dröge, 'Quia Morem Hieronymi in Transferendo Cognovi . . .'—Les Débuts des Etudes Hébraiques chez les Humanistes Italiens', 65–88.

[11] Cf. e.g. Volker Roelcke, *Jüdische Mystik in der romantischen Medizin? Kabbalistische Topoi bei Gotthilf Heinrich Schubert* (1991, in press).

[12] Pagel, *Paracelsus*, 214.

[13] This expression appeared as a term of abuse in Basel, where Paracelsus taught at the university in 1527/28; it was also used afterwards in a positive sense; cf. Ernst Kaiser, *Paracelsus, mit Selbstzeugnissen und Bilddokumenten*. Reinbek bei Hamburg (Rowohlt Taschenbuch) 1984, 88.

höfer.[14] Antisemitic and anti-scholastic statements by Paracelsus seemed to prove his independence not only of the Jewish tradition but also of the classical authorities of Galenism and Arabism. Such sentiments, which were not evaluated within their historical context, could be taken to serve as affirmations of nationalistic and imperialistic propaganda. Thus, it was often overlooked 'that Paracelsus was a strong admirer of the Cabalah', as Kudlien put it.[15]

Important concepts of Paracelsus point to cabbalistic sources. I will just hint at his central term *Licht der Natur* (light of nature). In a treatise belonging to the topic of the 'invisible diseases', Paracelsus identifies the cabbalistic art with the adept's discoveries in the 'light of nature' within himself: 'Look at Adam and Moses and others, they searched for that within themselves that is in man and opened it, and it belongs all to cabbala; they knew no strange things from the devil or [evil] spirits, but from the light of nature; that is what they evoked within themselves.'[16] The inward approach to the divine sources of the spiritual light recalls the mystical practices of the cabbala (and other religious subsystems). The successful process depends on a quasi-scientific scholarly self-purification. From the 'Sohar', the holy scripture of the cabbala, we know about the model of the divine light emanating throughout the material world, the famous doctrine of *Sefiroth*.[17]

Material things absorb the divine light, covering it like clothes and producing darkness. The sun, often visualized as the 'eye of God', symbolizes the archaic fount of divine light and wisdom. Like the sun, God sends life energy to all beings on the earth. 'The glamour [created by God] went from one end of the world to the other and

---

[14] Cf. Udo Benzenhöfer (among other articles), 'Zum Paracelsusbild im Dritten Reich unter besonderer Berücksichtigung der Paracelsusfeier in Tübingen/Stuttgart im Jahre 1941', in, *Paracelsus, Theophrast von Hohenheim: Naturforscher-Arzt-Theologe*, ed. Ulrich Fellmeth and Adreas Kotheder. Stuttgart 1993, 63–79.

[15] Fridolf Kudlin, 'Some Interpretive Remarks on the Antisemitism of Paracelsus', in *Science, Medicine and Society in the Renaissance*, ed. by Allen G. Debus, New York 1972, 121–126. Kudlien refers to Walter Pagel's interpretation.

[16] Cf. Paracelsus [*Fragmentum libri de morbis de morbis ex incantatibus et impressionibus inferioribus, das ist von den unsichtbaren krankheiten*], ed. Sudhoff, vol. 9, 360; present author's translation. 'sich Adam an und Moysen und ander, die haben das in inen gesucht, das im menschen war, und das geöffnet und alle gabalischen und haben nichts frembdes kent vom teufel noch von geisten sonder vom liecht der natur; das haben sie gar herfür in inen gebracht'.

[17] Cf. Gershom Scholem, *Zur Kabbala und ihrer Symbolik*, 7th' ed. Frankfurt a.M. 1992, 16–17; 53–54.

then remained hidden', we read in the 'Sohar'.[18] 'The whole of heaven is nothing other than *imaginatio* influencing man, producing plagues, colds, and other diseases', we hear from Paracelsus.[19] The same happens in the microcosm, i.e. within the individual human organism. Paracelsus uses the metaphor of an inner sun: 'Well, what else is imaginatio than a sun within man, having such an effect in his globum [body], that is, where on it shines.'[20] Indeed, there are— according to Pagel—'concordances in detail between the lore of the Cabalah and the teaching of Paracelsus.'[21]

Let us come to the main topic. What is the basic model of imagination and magnetism for Paracelsus? Firstly, the attractive power of the magnet symbolizes the power of imagination, moreover, Paracelsus identifies both powers. 'As the magnet can attract steel, there is also a magnet in the imagination, which also attracts. There is an imaginatio like a magnet, and an impressio like the sun and heaven, making a man by the power vulcani.'[22] Paracelsus gives us an example (*Exempel*), a parable to explain the identity of imagination and magnetism. The magnet is just a metaphor for imagination: 'Without hands and feet, the magnet attracts iron. Like the magnet attracting the visible, the corpora (bodies) are invisibly drawn to the imagination by itself. But it is not the corpus (body) that enters, but what the eyes see and is not palpable. i.e. form and colour . . .'.[23]

There are two steps: the *attraction* (incorporation) of an object (*ding*) by the imagination (a quasi-magnet) is followed by an *impression* of

---

[18] *Der Sohar. Das heilige Buch der Kabbala*, ed. by Ernst Müller. 5. Aufl. München 1991, 50; cf. also 49–52 and 76–78.

[19] '*als der ganz himel ist nichts als imaginatio, derselbige wirket in den menschen, macht pesten, kaltwehe und anderst.*' *Paracelsus*, ed. Sudhoff, vol. 14, 311 (present author's translation to the original quotations).

[20] '*nun was ist imaginatio anderst, als ein sonn im menschen, die dermaßen wirket in sein globum, das ist, do hin sie scheint?*' *Paracelsus*, ed. Sudhoff, vol. 14, 310.

[21] Pagel, *Paracelsus*, They need to be considered by scholars in the future. Recently, such a project—sponsored by the German-Israeli Foundation for Scientific Research and Development—started: 'Jewish and Renaissance Thought in the Works of Paracelsus.'

[22] '*dan kan der magnes an sich zihen stahel, so ist auch ein magnet do in der imagination, wie ein magnet und ein impressio, wie die sonn und wie der himel, der ein menschen macht in der kraft vulcani.*' *Paracelsus*, ed. Sudhoff, vol. 14, 313.

[23] '*der magnet zeucht an sich das eisen on hend und füß. zu gleicher weis wie also der magnet das sichtig an sich zeucht, also werden auch die corpora unsichtig durch die imagination an sich gezogen. nicht das das corpus hinein gang, sonder das get hinein, das die augen sehen und nicht greiflich ist, also die form und die farbe . . .*'; *Paracelsus*, ed. Sudhoff, vol. 9, 290.

this introjected object, similar to the sun and heaven impressing man. 'What climbs up into heaven is imaginatio, and what falls down is impressio born out of the imagination'.[24] This movement describes a sort of reflex action, crossing microcosm *and* macrocosm. A macrocosmic reflex occurs, for instance, when the (evil) imagination of a human individual poisons the stars, which send back the poison to the earth causing plagues and disorders.[25]

In his treatise *De causis morborum invisibilium* (On the invisible diseases) Paracelsus uses the term *imaginatio* to explain the correlation between body and soul.

> The imagination is a master by itself and has the art and all instruments and all it wants to produce, for example as a cellarman, painter, metalworker, weaver etc.; . . . What does imagination need? Nothing more than a globe on which it can work, that is, the screen on which it paints what it wants to paint.

In this way, the imagination of a pregnant woman can express itself directly on the body of the child in the uterus:

> The woman with her imagination is the workmaster and the child is the screen on which the work is perfected. The hand of the imagination is invisible, the instrument also, and both work together. . . . So the imagination does its work at that place, in the way the imagination has decided it.[26]

In this regard, Paracelsus also calls the power of imagination 'belief' (*Glaube*). Belief is 'like a workman's instrument' which can be used for good as well as for bad purposes. Belief can produce all diseases. Paracelsus compares it with a weapon. Disease will be produced when the weapon is active against its own originator. Paracelsus uses the parable of the man with a rifle which exactly describes the reversion of affections (*Affektverkehrung*) in modern psychology:

> We produce our diseases, so we become similar to a man who has got all his weapons and rifles. But when he meets a manikin aiming at him with a ready rifle the big man is anxious about the weapon and is frightened by it—the same happens to us. . . . When we become weak the power of our belief hits us as a shot from a rifle and we have to tolerate and to suffer what we have thrown against us.

---

[24] '*und das herauf kompt in himel, ist imaginatio und wider herab felt, ist impressio, die geboren ist aus der imagination.*' *Paracelsus*, ed. Sudhoff, vol. 14, 314.

[25] Cf. *Paracelsus*, ed. Sudhoff, vol. 14, 317.

[26] *Paracelsus*, ed. Sudhoff, vol. 9, 287.

Belief which is self destructive Paracelsus calls 'despair' (*Verzweiflung*).
It is a reversal of our belief which makes us weak and sick. The
rifle is directed against its owner. The pathological imagination may
even give origin to an epidemic, for example a plague or pestilence.
The most important cause of plague, therefore, is that people in
dispair may 'poison heaven, so some will suffer from plague depend-
ing on their belief.'[27] Imagination becomes a very dangerous phenomenon if it is combined with despair, and so returns to its own
origin. As it was pointed out before, this mechanism constitutes a
sort of a reflex activity.

Paracelsus compares persons in despair also with a thief, who
hangs himself, being in discordance with god and sentenced to self-
hanging. 'They are not worthy to be hanged by another [person].'[28]
The wealthy opposite of despair is 'simplicity' (*Einfalt*), which is a
refuge from self-destruction.[29]

As I mentioned above, the magnet is a symbol or a metaphor for
magnetic healing in the context of *magia naturalis*, natural magic. At
the same time, to Paracelsus it is a real instrument for curing several diseases. The magnet symbolizes the occult powers of natural
bodies, their secret sympathies (attractions) and antipathies (repul-
sions) like those of real magnets. In particular, the interaction between certain bodies can be understood by magnetic techniques. The
modern history of 'magnetism' as one of the most important ideas
of natural philosophy and its medical derivations starts with Paracelsus. In the *Herbarius* Paracelsus describes the application of the
Persicaria. This is a plant with magical healing powers. In the same
way as a magnet 'marvellously attracts the iron', *Persicaria* works
against wounded flesh.

> You may understand the herb, you should know that you have to take
> the herb drawing it through a fresh stream, then you have to place
> it on the part you wish to cure for as long as you need to eat half
> an egg. Then you have to bury it in a humid place so that it can rot,
> and the disorder will heal in the same time. . . . It is not necessary to
> make the sign of the cross over the wound or to pray, because it is
> a natural action, working naturally, not superstitiously or magically
> beyond nature.[30]

---

[27] '. . . *das sie den himel vergiften, das er etlichen pestilenz gibt, nach dem ir glaub ist.*'
Paracelsus, ed. Sudhoff, vol. 9, 280.

[28] '*nicht wert das sie ein ander henk*'; *Paracelsus*, ed. Sudhoff, vol. 9, 358.

[29] Cf. *Paracelsus*, ed. Sudhoff, vol. 9, 357.

[30] '*Damit und ir den brauch des krauts verstanden, so sollent ir wissen, das in der gestalt*

The magnetism of the herb is compared with the interaction between a magnet and a piece of iron. As the piece of iron can be magnetized by passing the magnet along its surface, so the wound can be magnetized by stroking the herb over its surface. In both cases a correspondence will develop between two bodies, ensuring that magnetic interaction occurs. How this 'concordance' works is a miracle, a great work of God (*'magnale'*), a mystery of nature. However, in addition, the magnet is more than a metaphor. It attracts not only iron or steel, but also all 'martial diseases' (which come from the planet Mars). So, it supports the influence of Mars, (e.g. in diarrhoea or the menstrual bleeding). The magnet can draw the *materia peccans* to the right place, so it can be digested and then be driven out at the right time.[31] The uterus, the stomach and the bowels are organs which can be influenced directly by the magnet. If the uterus is displaced upwards, it can be driven back by the magnet. The same is possible in the case of epilepsy (falling sickness, *fallende Sucht*). Some magnets in a certain conformation 'drive the illness from the head to the center (stomach).' The magnet can also cure convulsions, stop bleeding, and heal haemorrhoids. No medical author emphasises the power of the magnet more than Paracelsus.

Imagination and magnetism remained major topics for two or three centuries after Paracelsus's death. The further development of this topic cannot be dealt with in detail here. The dualism between soul and body introduced by René Descartes, the anatomical and physiological research on the nervous system and especially the brain (e.g. by Thomas Willis),[32] the new physical paradigms from Kepler to Newton and the development of the physical and chemical analysis of the human or animal organism all specified the concepts of imagination and magnetism. Imagination was increasingly interpreted as an idea fundamentally affecting psychosomatic interaction. The

---

gebraucht wird, nemlich man nimpt das kraut und zeuchts durch ein frischen bach, demnach so legt mans auf das selbig, das man heilen wil, als lang als einer möcht ein halb ei essen. darnach so vergrabt mans an ein feucht ort, domit das faul werde, so wird der schad gesunt in der selbigen zeit . . . das etlich ein kreuz uber die scheden machen, etlich beten darzu; solch alles ist von unnöten, gehört nit darzu, dan es ist ein natürliche wirkung do, die das natürlich tut, nit superstitiosisch und zauberisch.' *Paracelsus*, ed. Sudhoff, vol. 2, 18.

[31] Cf. the chapter on the magnet in *Herbarius, Paracelsus*, ed. Sudhoff, vol. 2, 49–57.

[32] The reflex model introduced by Descartes and the brain research especially by Willis is clearly analysed and illustrated in Edwin Clarke and Kenneth Dewhurst, *Die Funktionen des Gehirns. Lokalisationstheorien von der Antike bis zur Gegenwart.* München 1973, 69–74.

'invisible diseases' are born of the imagination, explains Paracelsus. The imagination afflicts the spiritual regulation forces, the so-called *archeus* or *archei*. A pathological idea (*idea morbosa*) may infect other human beings and may thus even start an epidemic of disease.[33] The theory of mass psychology is based on the concept of transferable ideas. The image (*imago*) seems to be a contagion, like the germ of an infectious disease.

The magnetic effect gradually became interpreted more and more as a natural law, an analogue to Newton's law of gravitation. Power (*Kraft*) is a universal phenomenon, an active principle, as Newton pointed out. The cosmological ether seems to be the medium of power. It penetrates all matter like subtle rays.[34]

When Franz Anton Mesmer began his 'animal magnetism' in Vienna about 1775, it was obviously not a direct offspring of Paracelsian thought. As a doctor Mesmer was quite up to date with the scientific developments in medicine.[35] Indeed, he was a representative of the Enlightenment, and—as Robert Darnton pointed out[36]—the Mesmerists in Paris played an important role in the French Revolution. The classical concept of Mesmer's animal magnetism was based on the new concept of electricity and its therapeutic application (electrical therapy), and the fashionable use of steel magnets for the cure of diseases in the second half of the 18th century. Mesmer's dogma of a universal fluid (*Allflut, fluide universel*) was nothing other than a credo in Newtonian physics.[37] Mesmer believed in his new foundation of medicine as a natural science. Strictly speaking he was an 'iatrophysicist'. The transfer of energy as a healing power was mediated by the nerves. By his techniques of magnetization (Mesmerization)

---

[33] Cf. *Paracelsus*, ed. Sudhoff, vol. 9, 279–280.

[34] Heinrich Feldt studied the concept of power in regard to the history of magnetism in detail, especially from Kepler and Newton until the 18th century and the concept of mesmerism; cf. Heinrich Feldt, *Der Begriff der Kraft im Mesmerismus, die Entwicklung des physikalischen Kraftbegriffes seit der Renaissance und sein Einfluß auf die Medizin des 18. Jahrhunderts*. Med. Diss. Bonn 1990.

[35] Mesmers scientific ideas are very problematic; cf. e.g. Ernst Florey, Franz Anton Mesmers magische Wissenschaft, in, *Franz Anton Mesmer und der Mesmerismus. Wissenschaft, Scharlatanerie, Poesie*. Gereon Wolters, Konstanz 1988, 11–40. Nevertheless, as a member of the medical faculty in Vienna, Mesmer was well informed about scientific standards.

[36] Cf. Robert Darnton, *Mesmerism and the End of Enlightenment in France*, Princeton 1964.

[37] Cf. Heinz Schott, 'Die Mitteilung des Lebensfeuers. Zum therapeutischen Konzept von Franz Anton Mesmer (1734–1815)', *Medizinhistorisches Journal*, 17, 1982, 195–214.

Mesmer evoked 'crises' (*Krisen*) which today can only be understood as psychosomatic or psychodynamic group phenomena. But in his self-understanding Mesmer found no place for anything called 'soul' or 'mind'. He did not even discuss the theory of imagination. We know that his critics told him that his animal magnetism was nothing more than the effect of the powers of imagination.[38]

Mesmer was a genuine positivist. He systematically ignored the possibility of negative energies or of pathological transfer of the *fluidum*. His magnetic 'manipulations' transferred only the healing power of *fluidum*; they never had to extract pathological complexes or matter. Mesmer never used magnetic 'passes' for exorcistic manipulation like some Mesmerists 30 or 40 years later.[39]

When Mesmerism became an element of the Romantic movement and the natural philosophy of the early 19th century, the power of imagination was rediscovered. The concept of somnambulism shows us a fascinating combination of the concept of the power of imagination and the power of magnetism. The altered state of consciousness experienced in somnambulism revealed the imagination as a manifestation of nature itself. When a somnambulist patient produced daydreams, visions or prophetic ideas, these were understood to be secret messages from hidden (occult) nature. The 'Seeress of Prevorst' (*Die Seherin von Prevorst*), the famous case history of a patient written by the Swabian doctor and poet Justinus Kerner (1786–1862), is a valuable document in the characterization of a concept of the imagination in natural philosophy of the Romantic era.[40]

The scientific explanation followed the anatomical and physiological guidelines of the age. People could be mesmerized by directing

---

[38] See Heinrich Feldt, The 'force' of imagination in the medicine of late eighteenth century Germany, in, *Proceedings of the 1st European Congress on the History of Psychiatry and Mental Health Care*, ed. by Leonie de Goei and Joost Vijselaar, Rotterdam, Erasmus Publishing 1993, 25–31.

Gereon Wolters pointed out the scientific problem of Mesmer's theory refused by two commissions in Paris; he analysed the report at the Royal Academy of Sciences as an epistemological document of the Enlightenment; see Gereon Wolters, 'Mesmer und sein Problem, Wissenschaftliche Rationalität', in, *Franz Anton Mesmer und der Mesmerismus*, 121–137.

[39] On Kerner's exorcistic manipulations see Heinz Schott, Zerstörende und heilende Bestrebungen des 'Magnetischen Lebens': Kerners Forschungsperspektive im Kontext der zeitgenössischen Medizin, in, *Justinus Kerner, Jubiläumsband um 200. Geburtstag*, Part 2. Weinsberg, 443–450.

[40] Justinus Kerner, *Die Seherin von Prevorst. Eröffnungen über das innere Leben des Menschen und über das Hereinragen einer Geisterwelt in die unsere*, 2 parts, Stuttgart 1929.

the vital powers within the nerves from the 'cerebral system' to the 'ganglion system'. In practical terms that means, the vital power has to be pulled down from the head to the stomach (abdomen). That could be managed by magnetic manipulations or it could happen spontaneously. When magnetic life (*magnetisches Leben*) according to Justinus Kerner arose in the Seeress, the interplay of imaginations could flourish: e.g. the vision of a secret language of nature could develop or the spirit of a dead grandmother could appear. Even healing of other patients by praying at a long distance was reported.[41]

Although the Romantic speculations about cosmological and religious dimensions of nature as a whole organism were increasingly rejected by the scientific community in the middle of the 19th century, the Mesmerist concept of somnambulism provided the first modern psychosomatic model. It was based on anatomical, physiological and clinical findings and furnished physicians with both experimental and treatment methods. The research activities of Mesmeristic scholars are fascinating. Here we see the beginnings of modern psychotherapy, medical psychology and psychosomatic medicine.[42]

It is interesting to notice traditional concepts in contemporary medical practise. Parapsychological mediumism uses imagination and visions for practical purposes. The progress of science has not eradicated the human belief that we may call superstition. Today we may also see a type of Mesmerists practise magnetopathy with magnetic 'passes' and the magnetic tub (*baquet*). In 1992 I met a psychiatrist—a medical doctor—at a workshop on hypnosis, and he told me that he successfully uses the magnetic tub for his therapeutic group sessions. During the sessions he imitates Mesmer by wearing a violet robe and applying magnetic 'passes'. The motive for such practices is not, I assume, primarily historical interest. It originates in discontent with the present situation and the hope of coming into contact with the primary natural sources of life.

Today healing methods by 'invisible' powers again are very popular. I refer only to so-called spiritual healing and magnetopathy (*Heilmagnetismus*), with its complex religious, spiritual (and even spirit-

---

[41] See Heinz Schott, 'Der "Okkultismus" bei Justinus Kerner—Eine medizinhistorische Untersuchung', in, *Justinus Kerner: Nur wenn man von Geistern spricht. Briefe und Klecksographien*, ed. Andrea Berger-Fix, Stuttgart 1986, 71–103.

[42] I remember the pioneering work of Henry F. Ellenberger, *The Discovery of the Unconscious*, 2 vols., Bern 1973. Ellenberger shows the importance of mesmerism and somnambulism for the development of modern 'dynamic psychiatry'.

istic), magical and psychological techniques. These phenomena are often condemned as old superstition, but a historical review should take into account their long tradition in the history of medicine and natural (religious) philosophy. The cabbala, for example, played an important role in the transfer of religious mysticism to natural philosophy and science in the Renaissance. So, Paracelsus as a philosopher and alchemist may sometimes resemble a cabbalistic scholar more than a laboratory researcher or natural scientist in the modern sense.

We should realize the unique situation of Paracelsianism at the beginning of the modern era. Natural philosophy and natural science were saturated by religious attitudes and rites. Research in the 'light of nature', e.g. the production of new medicines by alchemy, was at the same time an approach to the light of God, a process of personal purification, and worship. C.G. Jung's concept of individuation has shown its psychological importance.[43] The 'scientific communities', small groups of adepts with more or less secret rules of behaviour, were essential. Moreover, there were possibilities for friendly discussions between Jews, Christians and Muslims without repression—at least, this was an ideal, praised among others by Johannes Reuchlin in the trialogue of his treatise *De arte cabbalistica*.[44]

This intensive communication between mutually respecting scientists strikes me as highly important. Today we need a multi-cultural ('multi-religious') atmosphere in which intellectuals and scientists can exchange their experiences and findings to overcome dangerous prejudices.

Finally, it is very interesting that the theory of imagination and magnetism is traditionally linked with social and political phenomena and tries to explain events of mass psychology, e.g. the attraction a leader exerts on a crowd of people. In this regard Paracelsus again uses the magnet as a metaphor: 'You find a man who knows to speak, so that all the world runs to him and listens. Know, then, that his mouth [*Maul*] is a magnet, powerfully attracting the people.'[45]

---

[43] Cf. e.g. C.G. Jung, Einleitung in die religionspsychologische Problematik der Alchemie, in, C.G. Jung: *Gesammelte Werke*, vol. 12, 17–54. See also Chapter 8 above.

[44] Max Brod emphasized this aspect especially in his sympathetic book, *Johannes Reuchlin*.

[45] *'du findest ein man, der kan reden, das im alle welt zulauf; und hört im zu. nu wiß, das das maul ein magnet ist, zeucht an sich die leut in der kraft.' Paracelsus,'* ed. Sudhoff, vol. 9, 363.

CONSOLIDATED LIST OF LITERATURE

Abbri, F., *Elementi, Principi e Particelle: la teorie chimiche da Paracelso a Stahl*, Turin 1980.
Achelis, J.D., *Paracelsus: Volumen Paraminum (Von Krankheit und gesundem Leben)*, Jena 1928.
Agnew, L.R.C., 'Quackery', in A.G. Debus ed., *Medicine in seventeenth-century England*, London 1974, 313–25.
Agricola, G., *De re metallica*, trans H.C. & L.H. Hoover, New York 1912.
Alexander, F.G. & Selesnick, S.T., *Geschichte der Psychiatrie. Ein kritischer Abriss*, Zurich 1969.
Allen, M.J.B., 'Marsilio Ficino on Plato, the Neoplatonists and the Christian Doctrine of the Trinity', *Renaissance Quarterly*, 37, 1985, 555–84.
Allendy, R., 'La psychiatrie de Paracelse', *Nova Acta Paracelsica*, 2, 1945.
Andersen, A. ed., *Quattuor Centuriæ Epistolarum*, Historisk Samfund for Sønderjylland 1971.
Andersen, J.O., *Holger Rosenkrantz den Lærde*, Copenhagen 1896.
Anderson, W.S., 'The Roman Socrates: Horace and his Satires,' in *idem*, *Essays on Roman Satire*, Princeton 1982, 13–49.
Andreae, J.V., *Ein geistliches Gemälde. Entworfen und aufgezeichnet von Huldrich StarkMann, Diener des Evangeliums. Nach dem wiedergefundenen Urdruck, Tübingen 1615*, edited by R. Breymayer, Tübingen 1991.
Anonymous, 'La Historia de la Ciencia en España como Realidad Marginal en su Organización y Contexto Social,' *Anthropos*, no. 20, 1982, 2–15.
———, introduction, *Anstösse*, 29, 1982, 40.
———, *Thyrus* ναγου *[onagou] In Tergum Georgii Fedronis*, s.l. 1565.
Anthony, M., *The Valkyries: The Women Around Jung*, Devon 1990.
Arndt, *Vier Bücher von wahrem Christenthumb*, Jena 1607.
Arnold, G., *Supplementa der Kirchen-Historie*, Frankfurt 1703.
Artelt, W., 'Wandlungen des Paracelsusbildes in der Medizingeschichte', *Nova Acta Paracelsica*, 8, 1957, 33–38.
Backus, I., 'Valentin Crautwald, Bibliotheca Dissidentium', in A. Sèguenny, ed., *Répertoire des non-conformistes religieux des seizième et dix-septième siècles*, Baden 1985, 9–70.
Bacon, F., *The Works*, eds. J. Spedding et al., 14 vols., London 1857–74.
Baillif, R. le, *Le Demosterion . . . Auquel sont contenuz Trois cens Aphorismes Latins & François. Sommaire veritable de la Medecine Paracelsique, extraicte de luy en la plus part, par le dict Baillif*, Renne 1578.
Bakan, D., *Sigmund Freud and the Jewish Mystical Tradition*, Princeton 1958.
Bakhtin, M., *Rabelais and his World*; original Russian version 1965; English translation by H. Iswolsky, Cambridge, Mass. 1968.
Baldwin, M., 'Alchemy in the Society of Jesus', in Z.R.W.M. von Martels, *Alchemy Revisited: proceedings of the international conference on the history of alchemy in the University of Groningen, 17–19 April 1989*, Leiden, no date, 182–7.
Barker, F., *The tremulous private body: essays on subjection*, London 1984.
Barnes, R.B., *Prophecy and Gnosis in the wake of the Lutheran Reformation*, Stanford 1988.
Barnes, B. & Shapin, S., 'Head und hand', *Oxford Review of Education*, 6, 1975.
Bartholin, C., *De Philosophiae in Medicina Usu et Necessitate*, 17 Nov. 1613, Copenhagen 1613.
———, *Exercitatio Disputationis Secundæ Ordinariæ & Anniversariæ in Academia Regia Hafniensi*, 7 Nov. 1614, Copenhagen 1614.

————, *De Studio Medico*, Copenhagen 1628.

————, *Opuscula Qvatuor Singularia*, Copenhagen 1628.

Bartholin, T., *Cista Medica Hafniensis*, Copenhagen 1662.

Bastholm, E., *Petrus Severinus og hans Idea medicinæ philosophicæ*, Odense 1979.

Bazala, V., 'Paracelsus und die positive Gesundheitslehre' in *Gestalten und Ideen um Paracelsus*, Salzburger Beiträge zur Paracelsusforschung 20, 1972, 27–35.

Becher, J.J., *Chymisches Laboratorium, oder Untererdische Naturkündigung*, Frankfurt/Mainz 1680.

————, *Närrische Weißheit*, Frankfurt/Mainz 1682.

Beckmann, C., *Exercitationes Theologicae. In quibus De argumentis pro vera deitate Christi Servatoris nostri Contra Fausti Socini, Valentini Smalcii, Christophori Ostorodi, Ioannis Crellii Franci, et similium recentissimas molitiones: Ut et De argumentis pro vera humana Natura Christi ejusdem, Contra Mennonem Simonis, Theophrastum Paracelsum, Valentinum Weigelium, Paulum Felgenhauerum et alios huius notae*, Amsterdam 1642.

Behrend, C., 'En dagbog fra en rejse i Denmark i året 1588', *Fra Arkiv og Museum*, vol. 5, (1912–1915), 294–310.

Benedictus, L., *Nucleus Sophicus seu Explanatio in Tincturam Physicorum Theophrasti Paracelsi*, Frankfurt 1623.

————, *Nucleus Sophicus, oder Außlegung in Tincturam Physicorum Theophrasti Paracelsi*, Frankfurt 1623.

Bensaude, B. & Stengers, I., *Histoire de la chimie*, Paris 1993.

Benzenhöfer, U., 'Zum Brief des Johannes Oporinus über Paracelsus. Die bisland älteste bekannte Briefüberlieferung in einer Oratio von Gervasius Marstaller', *Sudhoffs Archiv*, 75, 1989, 55–63.

————, *Zum Paracelsusbild im Dritten Reich unter besonderer Berücksichtigung der Paracelsusfeier*, Tübingen/Stuttgart 1941.

Betschart, I., 'Der Begriff "Imagination" bei Paracelsus', *Nova Acta Paracelsica*, 6, 1952.

————, 'Paracelsus und die moderne Psychologie', *Nova Acta Paracelsica*, 8, 1957.

————, 'Die Signaturenlehre des Paracelsus', *Nova Acta Paracelsica*, 9, 1977.

Bianchi, M.L., *Signatura Rerum: Segni, Magia e Conoscenza da Paracelso a Leibniz*, Rome 1987.

————, 'Occulto e manifesto nella medicina del Rinascimento Jean Fernel e Pietro Severino' in the *Atti e Memorie dell'Accademia Toscana di Scienza e Lettere: La Colombaria*, 47, (Nuova Serie—33), 185–248.

Biegger, K., 'De Invocatione Beatae Mariae Virginis. Paracelsus und die Marienverehrung'. *Kosmosophie*, VI, Stuttgart 1990.

Birchler, L., 'Lionardo und Paracelsus', *Nova Acta Paracelsica*, 5, 1948.

Biringuccio, V., *Pirotechnia*, trans. C.G. Smith & M.I. Grudi, New York 1942, 1st ed. 1540.

Bittel, K., 'Die Kindheit Theophrats in Einsiedeln', *Nova Acta Paracelsica*, 1, 1944, 37–44.

————, 'Ein Sozial-Programm bei Paracelsus', *Nova Acta Paracelsica*, 3, 1946, 77–85.

Blaser, R., 'Paracelsus als Aushängeschild' in *Die ganze Welt ein Apotheken. Festschrift für Otto Zekert*, Salzburger Beiträge zur Paracelsusforschung, 8, Vienna 1969, 1–6.

————, *Paracelsus in Basel, Sieben Studien über Werk, Wirkung und Nachwirkung des Paracelsus in Basel*, Basel 1979.

Bloch, E., *Vorlesungen zur Philosophie der Renaissance*, Frankfurt 1972.

Boerhaave, H., *A new method of chemistry*, trans. P. Shaw & E. Chambers, London 1727.

Bogner, R.G., 'Das Judicium des Elias Schade (1589). Ein Frühes Zeugnis der Verketzerun Theophrast von Hohenheims, in J. Telle ed. *Parerga Paracelsica*, Heidelberger Studien zur Naturkunde der Frühen Neuzeit, III, Stuttgart 1992.

Bornkamm, H., 'Äußerer und innerer Mensch bei Luther und den Spiritualisten', in: *Imago Dei, Festschrift für Gustav Krüger*, Gießen 1932, 85–109.

Bostock, R., 'The Difference betwene the Auncient Phisicke, first taught by the godly forefathers, consisting in unitie, peace and concord; and the latter Phisicke procedding from idolators, ethnickes and heathen: as Gallen and such other... London 1585.

Bourdieu, P., Language and Symbolic Power, ed. J.B. Thompson, trans. G. Raymond & M. Adamson, Cambridge, Mass. 1991.

Braun, L., Paracelsus und die Philosophiegeschichte, Salzburger Beiträge zur Paracelsusforschung 5, Vienna 1965.

———, 'Paracelsus und der Aufbau der Episteme seiner Zeit' in Festschrift für Otto Zekert, Salzburger Beiträge zur Paracelsusforschung, 8, Vienna 1969, 7–18.

———, Paracelsus. Alchemist—Chemiker—Erneuerer der Heilkunde. Eine Bildbiographie, Zurich 1990.

Breger, H., Elias artista—A Precursor of the Messiah in Natural Science, in E. Mendelsohn & H. Nowotny eds., Nineteen Eighty Four: Science between Utopia and Dystopia (Sociology of the Sciences, vol. 8), Dordrecht, Boston, Lancaster 1984, 49–72.

Brinckmann, D., 'Paracelsus und die Seele der Technik', Nova Acta Paracelsica, 2, 1945, 129–71.

———, 'Paracelsus und das anthropologische Problem der Übertragung', Nova Acta Paracelsica 8, 1957.

Brock, W.H., The Fontana history of chemistry, London 1992.

Brod, M., Johannes Reuchlin und sein Kampf. Eine historische monographie, Stuttgart 1965.

Broeckx, C., 'Notice sur le manuscript Causa J.B. Helmontii, déposé aux Archives Archiépiscopales de Malines', Annales de l'Académie Royale d'Archéologie de Belgique, 9, 1852, 277–327.

Bruck, van den, A.M., Verschwärmte Deutsche, Die Deutschen, vol. 3, Minden 1905.

Brunn, von, W.A.L., Paracelsus und seine Schwindsuchtslehre, Praktische Tuberkulose-Bücherei 26, Leipzig 1941.

Bunners, M., Die Abendmahlsschriften und das medizinisch-naturphilosophische Werk des Paracelsus, Theol. diss., Berlin 1961.

Burgess, R., Portraits of Doctors and Scientists in the Wellcome Institute of the History of Medicine, London 1973.

Burnet, T., The Theory of the Earth: Containing an Account of the Original of the Earth..., London 1684.

Bynum, W.F. & Porter, R., Medical Fringe and Medical Orthodoxy 1750–1850, London 1987.

Campbell, B.F., Ancient Wisdom Revived: A History of the Theosophical Movement, California 1980.

Catalogue from the 19th Exhibition of the Council of Europe, Christian IV og Europa, Denmark 1988.

Chamberlain, H.S., Die Grundlagen des neunzehnten Jahrhunderts, 2 vols., Munich 1909.

Chandler, J., translated Oriatrike or Physick Refined. The Common Errors therein Refuted. And the whole Art Reformed & Rectified. Being a New Rise and Progress of Phylosophy and Medicine, for the destruction of Diseases and Prolongation of Life, London 1662.

Christie, J.R.R., 'Bad news for the body', Art History, 9, 1986, 263–71.

———, 'Historiography of chemistry in the eighteenth century: Herman Boerhaave and William Cullen', Ambix, 41, 1994, 4–19.

Clark, C., The Vulgar Rabelais, Glasgow 1983.

Clarke, E. & Dewhurst, K., Die Funktionen des Gehirns. Lokalisationstheorien von der Antike bis zur Gegenwart. München 1973.

Clericuzio, A., 'Robert Boyle and the English Helmontians', in Z.R.W.M. von Martels, Alchemy Revisited: proceedings of the international conference on the history of alchemy in the University of Groningen, 17–19 April 1989, Leiden, no date, 192–199.

Clowes, W., A Right Frutefull and Approoved Treatise for the Artificiall Cure of that Malady called in Latin Struma, London 1602.

Comenius, J.A., Opera omnia, vol. 15/I, Prag 1986.

Cook, H.J., 'The new philosophy and medicine in seventeenth-century England', in D.C. Lindberg & R.S. Westman eds., *Reappraisals of the Scientific Revolution*, Cambridge 1990.

Copenhaver, B.P., 'Natural magic, hermetism and occultism in early modern science', in D.C. Lindberg & R.S. Westman eds., *Reappraisals of the Scientific Revolution*, Cambridge 1990, 261–301.

Cosmopolita, A.P., *Nuncius Olympicus Von etzlichen geheimen Bücheren, und Schrifften/so ein fürnehmer Gottesgelehrter und Philologia, durch viel beschwerliche Reisen vnnd grosse Vnkostung/Ecclesiae vnd Reip[ublicae] literariae commodo zusammen gebracht/darin die gröste Himlische vnnd Jrrdische Weißheit begriffen ist [. . .]*, Amsterdam 1626.

Croll, O., 'Admonitory Preface', in *Philosophy reformed and improved in four profound tractates*, transl. H. Pinnell, London 1657.

Crowther, J.G., *British scientists of the nineteenth century*, London 1935.

Curry, P., 'Revisions of Science and Magic', in *History of Science*, 23, 1985, 302–325.

———, *A Confusion of Prophets: Victorian and Edwardian Astrology*, London 1992.

D'Aubigné, A., *'Memoires'* ed. L. Lalaune, Paris 1869.

———, *'Histoire Universelle'* ed. A. de Ruble, *Société de l'Histoire de France*, IX, 1886–96.

D.O.M.A. Alchemia Andreae Libavii . . ., Francofurti: Iohannes Saurius, impensis Petri Kopffij, 1597.

D.O.M.A. Alchymia Andreae Libavii, Recognita, Emendata, et aucta, tum dogmatibus et experimentis nonnullis; Tum Commentario Medico Physico Chymico . . ., Francofurti: Iohannes Saurius, impensis Petri Kopffij, 1606.

D.O.M.A. Wolmeinendes Bedencken von der Fama und Confession der Bruderschafft dess Rosen Creutzes . . ., Frankfurt, Egenolff Emmeln in verlegung Petri Kopffij, 1616.

Daems, W.F., 'Die Ideen der heilpflanze bei Paracelsus', *Nova Acta Paracelsica*, New Series 3, 1988.

Daniélou, J., *From Shadows to Reality. Studies in the Biblical Typology of the Fathers*, London 1960.

Darnton, R., *Mesmerism and the End of Enlightenment in France*, Princeton 1964.

De Jong, H.M.E. *Michael Maier's Atalanta fugiens: Sources of an Alchemical Book of Emblems*, Leiden 1969.

De Telepnef, B., 'Glossen zum Paragranum oder Viersäulenbuch', *Nova Acta Paracelsica*, 3, 1946.

Debus, A.G., *The English Paracelsians*, London 1954.

———, 'Solution analysis prior to Robert Boyle', *Chymia*, 8, 1962, 41–62.

———, 'Sir Thomas Browne and the study of colour indicators', *Ambix*, 10, 1962, 29–36.

———, 'Robert Fludd and the Use of Gilbert's "De Magnete" in the Weapon Salve Controversy', in *Journal of the History of Medicine and Allied Science*, 19, 1964, 389–417.

———, 'Mathematics and Nature in the Chemical Texts of the Renaissance,' *Ambix*, 15, 1968, 1–28.

———, *The Chemical Philosophy: Paracelsian science and medicine in the sixteenth and seventeenth centuries*, 2 volumes, London 1972.

———, 'Peter Severinus' in *Dictionary of Scientific Biography*, 14 vols., New York 1970–80.

———, 'Mysticism and the Rise of Modern Science and Medicine,' *Studies in History of Medicine*, 4, 1980, 199–213.

———, *Thomas Sherley's Philosophical Essay* (1672): Helmontian Mechanism as the Basis of a new Philosophy, *Ambix*, 27, 1980, 124–135.

———, *Science and History: A Chemist's Appraisal*, Coimbra 1984.

———, 'Chemistry and Iatrochemistry in Early Eighteenth-Century Portugal: A Spanish Connection' in A.V. Marques ed., *História e Desenvolvimento da Ciência em Portugal*, 2 vols., Lisboa 1986, 2, 1245–62.

————, *The French Paracelsians: the chemical challenge to medical and scientific tradition in early modern France*, Cambridge 1991.

Descartes, R., *Oeuvres*, eds. Adam/Tannery, vol. 2, Paris 1898.

————, *Oeuvres*, vol. 6, eds. Adam/Tannery, Paris 1965, nouvelle édition.

Dessenius, B., *Meicinae veteris et rationalis adversus oberronis cuiusdam mendacissimi atque impudentissimi Georgii Fedronis, ac universae Secta Paracelsicae imposturas, defensio*, Cologne 1573.

Die Geschichte der Physik, vol. 2, Braunschweig 1884.

Diesner, P., 'Der elsässische Arzt Dr. Helisaeus Röslin als Forscher und Publizist am Vorabend des dreißigjährigen Krieges', *Jahrbuch der Elsaß-Lothringischen Wissenschaftlichen Gesellschaft zu Straßburg*, 11, 1938, 192–215.

Digby, K.A., *Discourse Concerning the Vegetation of Plants*, London 1661.

Dilg-Frank, R., 'Paracelse, philosophe de la nature et de la religion: Bibliographie 1960–1980', in *Paracelse—Cahiers de l'Hermétisme*, Paris 1980, 269–80.

Dobbs, B.J.T., 'From the Secrecy of Alchemy to the Openness of Chemistry', in T. Frängsmyr ed., *Solomon's House Revisited: The Organization and Institutionalization of Science*. Canton Mass. 1990, 75–94.

Domandl, S., 'Agrippa von Nettesheim, Faust und Paracelsus—drei unstete Wanderer'. *Salzburger Beiträge zur Paracelsusforschung*, 26, 1988, 9–15.

Donne, J., 'Ignatius His Conclave' (1610) in *Complete Poetry and Selected Prose*, London 1936.

Dopsch, H., 'Humanismus, Renaissance und Reformation—Paracelsus und die geistigen Bewegungen seiner Zeit', in H. Dopsch et al. eds., *Paracelsus (1493–1541) 'Keines anderen Knecht...'*, Salzburg 1993, 249–58.

Dorn, G., *De naturae luce physica ex Genesis desumpta iuxta sententiam Theophrasti Paracelsi Tractatus. Cui annexa est modesta quaedam admonitio ad Thomam Erastum*, Frankfurt 1583.

Dreyfus, H.L. & Dreyfus, S.E., *Mind over Machine*, New York 1986.

Duchesne, J., (Quercetanus), *Ad Iacobi Auberti de ortu et causa metallorum Explicationem [. . .] Responsio*, Lyon 1575.

————, (Quercetanus), *Le Povrtraict de la Santé . . .* S. Omer: Charles Boscart 1618.

Dunk, E., *The Copy of a Letter written by E.D. Doctour of Physicke to a Gentleman, by whom it was published*, 1606.

Dyk, A., 'Zur Krise unserer Gegenwart', *Salzburger Beiträge zur Paracelsusforschung* 25, 1987.

Eamon, W., 'From the Secrets of Nature to Public Knowledge: The Origins of the Concept of Openness in Science', *Minerva* 23, 1985, 321–347.

————, *Science and the secrets of nature. Books of Secrets in medieval and early modern culture*, Princeton 1994.

Eckhart, von, J.G., 'Lebensbeschreibung des Freyherrn von Leibnitz', in G. von Murr, *Journal zur Kunstgeschichte und zur allgemeinen Litteratur*, part 7, Nürnberg 1779, 198.

Elkhadem, H., 'Du Latin a l'Arabe: Introduction de la Doctrine Medico-Chemique de Paracelse en Orient au XVIIIᵉ Siècle', *Civilisations*, *38*, no. 1, 53–73.

Ellenberger, H.F., *The Discovery of the Unconscious, Die Entdeckung des Unbewussten*, 2 vols., Bern/Stuttgart/Vienna 1973.

Elmer, P., 'Medicine, Religion and the Puritan Revolution', in R. French & A. Wear eds., *The Medical Revolution of the Seventeenth Century*, Cambridge 1989.

Englert, L., *Paracelsus. Mensch und Arzt*, Berlin 1941.

Erastus, T., *Disputationum De Medicina Nova Philippo Paracelsi Pars Prima—Quarta*, Basel [1571] 1573.

Esquire, R.B., [R. Bostocke], *The difference betwene the auncient Phisicke, first taught by the godly forefathers, consisting in vnitie peace and concord: and the latter Phisicke proceeding from Idolaters, Ethnikes, and Heathen: as Gallen, and such other consisting in dualitie, discorde, and contrarietie . . .*, London 1585.

Evans, R.J.W., *Rudolf II and His World: A Study in Intellectual History*, Oxford 1973.

Fairclough, H.R., English Translation *Ars Poetica or Epistle to the Pisos* in *Horace: Satires, Epistles and Ars Poetica*, Cambridge Mass. 1991 [first published, 1926].

Febvre, L., 'Aux origines de l'esprit moderne: Libertinisme, naturalisme, mécanisme', in his *Au coeur religieux du XVIe siècle*, Paris 1957, 337–58.

Feldt, H., *Der Begriff der Kraft im Mesmerismus. die Entwicklung des physikalischen Kraftbegriffes seit der Renaissance und sein Einfluß auf die Medizin des 18. Jahrhunderts*. Med. Diss. Bonn 1990.

———, The 'force' of imagination in the medicine of late eighteenth century Germany, in L. de Goei and J. Vijselaar eds., *Proceedings of the 1st European Congress on the History of Psychiatry and Mental Health Care*, Rotterdam 1993, 25–31.

Fellmeth, U. & Kotheder, A., eds., *Paracelsus, Theophrast von Hohenheim: Naturforscher-Arzt-Theologe*. Stuttgart 1993.

Ficino, M., *De vita libri tres*, Venice, 1498, reprint Hildesheim and New York 1978.

———, *Three Books on Life: A Critical Edition and Translation, with Introduction and Notes* by C.V. Kaske and J.A. Clark, New York 1989.

Figala, K. & Neumann, U., 'Michael Maier (1569–1622): New Bio-Bibliographical Material', in Z.R.W.M. von Martels, *Alchemy Revisited: proceedings of the international conference on the history of alchemy in the University of Groningen, 17–19 April 1989*, Leiden, no date, 34–50.

Figulus, B., *Pandora Magnalium Naturalium aurea et Benedicta. De Benedicto Lapis Philosoph[orum] Mysterio*, Strassburg 1608.

———, *Thesaurinella Olympica*, Frankfurt/Mainz 1608.

Fjeldstrup, A., *Dr. Peter Payngk: Kong Christian IV's Hofkemiker*, Copenhagen 1911.

Florey, E., 'Franz Anton Mesmers magische Wissenschaft', in G. Wolters, *Franz Anton Mesmer und der Mesmerismus. Wissenschaft, Scharlatanerie, Poesie*. Konstanz 1988, 11–40.

Foster, W., *Hoplocrisma-spongus; or, A sponge to wipe away the Weapon-salve. A Treatise wherein it is proved that the cure . . . is Magicall and Unlawfull*, London 1631.

Foucault, M., *The Order of Things. An Archaeology of the Human Sciences*, London 1970.

———, *The birth of the clinic*, London 1973.

———, *Discipline and punish: the birth of the prison*, London 1979.

Frei, P.G., 'Parapsychologisches bei Paracelsus', *Nova Acta Paracelsica* 7, 1954, 121–32.

French, P.J., *John Dee. The World of an Elizabethan Magus*, London 1972.

Frühsorge, G. & Strasser, G.F., *Johann Joachim Becher (1635–1682)*, Wiesbaden 1993.

Frye, N., *The Great Code: the Bible and Literature*, New York 1982.

Gaberel, J., *Histoire de l'Eglise de Genève*, 2 vols., Geneva 1858–62.

Galluzzi, P., 'Motivi paracelsiani nella Toscana de Cosimo II e di Don Antonio dei Medici: alchimia, medicina "chimica" e riforma del sapere' in *Scienza, credenza occulte, livelli di cultura*, Firenze 1982, 31–62.

Garin, E., ed., G.P. della Mirandola, *De dignitate hominis*, Bad Homburg 1968.

Garnier, A., *Agrippa d'Aubigné et le Parti Protestant*, Paris 1928.

Garstein, O., *Cort Aslakssøn*, Oslo 1953.

Gause, U., *Paracelsus (1493–1541). Genese und Einfaltung seiner frühen Theologie*, Tübingen 1993.

Gessner, K., *Bibliotheca Universalis, siue Catalogus omnium scriptorum locupletissimus, in tribus linguis, Latina, Graeca et Hebraica: extantium et non extantium veterum ac recentiorum in hunc usque diem doctorum et indoctorum, publicatorum et in Bibliothecis latentium*, Zürich 1545.

Geyer-Kordesch, J., 'Cultural habits of illness. The Enlightened and the Pious in eighteenth century Germany', in R. Porter ed., *Patients and Practitioners*, Cambridge 1985.

Gibson, T., 'A Sketch of the Career of Theodore Turquet de Mayerne,' *Ann. Med. Hist.*, New Series, 5, 1933, 315–26.

Gilly, C., 'Zwischen Erfahrung und Spekulation. Theodor Zwinger und die religiöse und kulturelle Krise seiner Zeit', *Basler Zeitschrift für Geschichte*, 1977, 77, 57–137 and 1979, 79, 125–223.

———, *Johannes Valentin Andreae (1586–1986). Katalog einer Ausstellung in der Bibliotheca Philosophica Hermetica*, Amsterdam 1986.

———, *Iter rosicrucianum. Auf der Suche nach unbekannten Quellen der frühen Rosenkreuzer, Das Erbe des Christian Rosenkreuz, Vorträge gehalten anlässlich des Amsterdames Andreae-Symposiums*, Amsterdam 1988.

———, *Das Sprichwort 'Die Gelehrten die Verkehrten' oder der Verrat der Intellektuellen im Zeitalter der Glaubensspaltung, Forme e destinazione del messaggio religioso. Aspetti della propaganda religiosa nel Cinquecento*, ed. A. Rotondò, Florence 1991.

———, 'Das Bekenntnis zur Gnosis von Paracelsus bis auf die Schüler Jacob Böhmes', in G. Quispel ed., *De hermetische Gnosis in de loop der eeuwen*, Baarn 1992.

———, *Adam Haslmayr. Der erste Verkünder der Manifeste der Rosenkreuzer*, Amsterdam 1994.

Girouard, M., *Life in the English Country House*, Harmondsworth 1980.

Givry, G. de, *Oeuvres Complètes de Paracelse, Traduites pour la Première Fois du Latin et Collationnées sur les Editions Allemandes*, 2 vols., Paris 1913–4.

Glauber, J.R., *Theutschlands Wohlfahrt*, part 1, Amsterdam 1656.

———, *Von den drey anfangen der Metallen*, no place, 1666.

———, *Glauberus concentratus*, Amsterdam 1668.

Glauber, R., 'The prosperity of Germany', *The works of J.R. Glauber*, trans. C. Packe, London 1689.

Glebe-Møller, J., 'Socialetiske Aspekter af Niels Hemmingsen's Forfatterskab', *Kirkehistoriske Samlinger*, 1979, 7–56.

Godwin, J., translated and ed. M. Maier, *Atalanta fugiens: An Edition of the Emblems, Fugues, and Epigrams*, London 1989.

Goldammer, K., ed., *Paracelsus. Sozialethische und sozialpolitische Schriften*, Tübingen 1952.

———, *Paracelsus. Natur und Offenbarung*, Heilkunde und Geisteswelt 5, Hannover 1953.

———, ed., *Paracelsus, Die Kärntner Schriften*, Klagenfurt 1955.

———, ed., *Paracelsus, Sämtliche Werke. I Abteilung. Theoligical und Religionsphilosophische Schriften*, Wiesbaden 1955.

———, ed., *Religiöse und sozialphilosophische Schriften in Kurzfassungen*, Wiesbaden 1973.

———, *Paracelsus in der deutschen Romantik. Eine Untersuchung zur Geschichte der Paracelsus-Rezeption und zu geistesgeschichtlich Hintergründen der Romantik*, Salzburger Beiträge zur Paracelsusforschung, Vienna 1980.

———, 'Paracelsus-Bild und Paracelsus-Forschung. Wissenschaft und populäre Elemente in der Literatur', *Nova Acta Paracelsica*, 10, 1982, 109–27.

———, *Paracelsus in neuen Horizonten: Gesammelte Aufsätze*, Vienna 1986.

———, 'Aufgaben der Paracelsusforschung', in J. Telle ed., *Parerga Paracelsica. Paracelsus in Vergangenheit und Gegenwart*, Heidelberger Studien zur Naturkunde der frühen Neuzeit 3, Stuttgart 1992.

Golinski, J.V., 'Hélène Metzger and the Interpretation of Seventeenth Century Chemistry', *History of Science*, 25, 1987, 81–97.

———, 'Chemistry in the Scientific Revolution: Problems of Language and Communication', in D.C. Lindberg & R.S. Westman eds., *Reappraisals of the Scientific Revolution*. Cambridge 1990, 367–396.

Goltz, D., 'Die Paracelsisten und die Sprache', *Sudhoffs Archiv* 56, 1972, 337–352.

———, Naturmystik und Naturwissenschaft in der Medizin um 1600, *Sudhoffs Archiv*, 60, 1976, 45–65.

Görlich, E., *Leibniz als Mensch und Kranker*, Dissertation Medical College Hannover 1987.

Granjel, L.S., *Francisco Suarez de Rivera: Médico salamantino del siglo XVIII*, Salamanca 1967.
Greiner, K., *Paracelsus im Lande seiner Väter*, Salzburger Beiträge zur Paracelsusforschung 2, Salzburg 1961.
Grell, O.P. & Scribner, B. eds., *Tolerance and intolerance in the European Reformation*, Cambridge 1996, 1–12 and *passim*.
Grell, O.P. & Cunningham, A. eds., *Medicine and the Reformation*, London 1993.
Grell, O.P., 'Caspar Bartholin and the Education of the Pious Physician', in O.P. Grell & A. Cunningham eds., *Medicine and the Reformation*, London 1993, 78–100.
———, 'The Reception of Paracelsianism in Early Modern Denmark: from Peter Severinus, The Dane, to Ole Worm', *Medical History*, 1995, 39, 78–94.
Grensemann, J., *Der arzt Polybos als Verfasser hippokratischer Schiften*, Mainz 1968.
Guerlac, H., 'Guy de la Brosse and the French Paracelsians', in A.G. Debus ed., *Science, Medicine and Society in the Renaissance: essays to honour Walter Pagel*, 2 vols.: London 1972, vol. I, ch. 16.
Guggisberg, H.R., 'Castellio and der Ausbruch der Religionskriege in Frankreich. Einige Betrachtungen zum Conseil à la France désolée', *Archiv für Reformationgeschichte*, 68, 1977, 253–267.
———, 'The Defence of Religious Toleration and Religious Liberty in Early Modern Europe: Arguments, Pressures and some Consequences', *History of European Ideas*, 4, 1983, 35–50.
———, *Religiöse Toleranz. Dokumente zur Geschichte einter Forderung*, Stuttgart 1984.
———, 'Sebastian Costellio and the German Reformation', *Archiv for Reformation History*, Special Volume, *Reformation in Germany and Europe: Interpretations and Issues*, 1993, 325–343.
Gundolf, F., *Paracelsus*, Berlin 1927.
Guterman, N., trans. *Theophrastus Paracelsus: Lebendiges Erbe, Zurich 1942*, Princeton 1951, second edition 1958, reprinted 1959.
Haberlandt, H., 'Paracelsus im Lichte moderner naturwissenschaftlicher Forschung,' *Nova Acta Paracelsica*, 7, 1954.
Hall, A.R., *Isaac Newton: Adventurer in Thought*, Oxford, Cambridge, Mass. 1992.
Halleux, R., 'Helmontiana', *Academiae Analecta. Mededelingen van de Koniklijke Academie voor Wetenschappen, Letteren en Schone Kunsten van België*, 45, 1983, 33–63.
Hamilton, A., 'The Book of "vaine fables": the reception of 2 Esdras from the fifteenth to the eighteenth century', *Kerkhistorische opstellen aangenboden aan Prof dr. J. van den Berg*, Kampen 1987, 45–61.
Hammer, K., 'Der Reformer Oekolampad, 1482–1531' in H. Oberman ed., *Reformiertes Erbe*, 1, Zurich 1992, 157–170.
Hannaway, O., *The Chemists and the Word: The Didactic Origins of Chemistry*, London 1975.
———, 'Laboratory Design and the Aim of Science: Andreas Libavius and versus Tycho Brahe', *Isis*, 77, 1986, 585–610.
Harrer, G., 'Paracelsus und das Ganzheitsdenken in der modernen Medizin, *Salzburger Beiträge zur Paracelsusforschung*, 12, 1974, 53–54.
———, 'Paracelsus und die Psychopharmaka', *Salzburger Beiträge zur Paracelsusforschung*, 22, 1981, 163–68.
Hartmann, F., 'Paracelsus und die heutige Medizin', *Anstösse*, 2, 1982.
Hartmann, H., *Paracelsus—eine deutsche Vision*, Berlin/Vienna 1941.
Hartmann, R.J., *Theophrast von Hohenheim*, Stuttgart/Berlin 1904.
Helk, V., *Laurentius Nicolai Norvegus S.J.*, Copenhagen 1966.
———, *Dansk-Norske Studierejser fra Reformationen til Enevælden 1536–1660*, Odense 1987.
Helmont, van, J.B., *Oriatrike, or Physick Refined*, London 1662.
———, *Ortus medicinae. Id est, initia physicae inaudita. Progressus medicinae novus, in morborum ultionen ad vitam logam*, Amsterdam 1648; reprinted Brussels 1966.
Hemleben, J., *Paracelsus. Revolutionär, Arzt und Christ*. Frauenfeld/Stuttgart 1973.

Henry, J., 'Doctors and healers: popular culture and the medical profession', in S. Pumfrey, P.L. Rossi & M. Slawinski, *Science Culture and Popular Belief in Renaissance Europe*, Manchester 1991, 191–221.

Herholdt, J.D. & Mansa, F.V. eds., *Samlinger til den danske medicinal-Historie*, 2 vols., Copenhagen 1833–35.

History of the Royal Society of London, London 1667.

Hoffmannus, N., *De Igne Naturae . . .* in *D.O.M.A. Syntagmatis Arcanorum Chymicorum Tomi Secundi . . .* Francofurti: impensis Petri Kopffij, 1613.

Hogenson, G.B., *Jung's Struggle with Freud*, Indiana 1983.

Hovesen, E., *Lægen Ole Worm*, Århus 1987.

Howard, R., 'Guy de La Brosse: Botanique et chimie au début de la révolution scientifique,' *Revue d'Histoire des Sciences*, 31, 1978, 301–26.

———, 'Guy de La Brosse and the Jardin des Plantes in Paris' in H. Woolf, ed. *The Analytic Spirit: Essays in the History of Science in Honor of Henry Guerlac*, Ithaca 1981, 195–224.

Howe, E., *Urania's Children: The Strange World of the Astrologers*, London 1967.

Hubicki, W., 'Libavius (or Libau), Andreas', in C.C. Gillispie ed. *Dictionary of Scientific Biography*, vol. 8, New York 1970–76, 309–312.

———, 'Paracelsists in Poland', in Allen G. Debus, *Science, Medicine and Society in the Renaissance: Essays to honour Walter Pagel*, 2 vols. London 1972, vol. 1, 167–176.

Hull, R.F.C., trans. *Psychologische Betrachtungen: Eine Auslese aus den Schriften von C.G. Jung, Zurich 1945; second edition 1949*, London 1953.

———, *The Spirit in Man, Art and Literature*, London 1966.

Hunninus, N., *Gründtlicher Beweiss wie Theophrastus Paracelsus, Weigel, Felgenhauer, Teting und andere [. . .] mit falschen Weissagungen umbgehen*, s.l. 1634.

Hunter, M. & Wootton, D. eds, *Atheism from the Reformation to the Enlightenment*, Oxford 1992.

Huygens, *Oeuvres complètes*, vol. 8, Thee Hague 1899.

Imbach, R. & North, J.D., 'Dante Alighieri und V. und VI.', *Lexikon des Mittelalters*, III cols. 553–59, Munich and Zurich 1991.

Irtenkauf, W., 'Abraham Schnitzer, der gelehrte Scharlatan. Leben und Werk eines Bergmeisters im 16. Jahrhundert', *Veröffentlichungen des Tiroler Landesmuseum Ferdinandeum*, 64, 1984.

Jacobi, J., *Complex/Archetype/Symbol in the Psychology of C.G. Jung*, original German edition, Zurich 1957, English translation by R. Manheim, New York 1959.

Janicola, R., *Strena [. . .] Was von den newen Paracelsischen Propheten/vnd Thurneuserischen Warsagern zu halten*, Hamburg 1601.

Jobe, T.H., The Devil in Restoration Science: The Glanvill-Webster Witchcraft Debate, *Isis*, 72, 1981.

Johannes, S. ed., Paracelsus, *Philosophia de limbo aeterno perpetuoque homine novo secundae creationis ex Iesu Christo Dei filio*, Magdeburg 1618.

Jouanna, J., *Hippocrate: La nature de l'homme*. Edité, traduit, et commenté, Berlin 1975.

Jung, C.G., Einleitung in die religionspsychologische Problematik der Alchemie, in C.G. Jung: *Gesammelte Werke*, vol. 12, 17–54.

———, *Paracelsica. Zwei Vorlesungen über den Arzt und Philosophen Theophrastus*, Zurich/Leipzig 1942.

———, *Mysterium Coniunctionis: An Inquiry into the Separation and Synthesis of Psychic Opposites in Alchemy*; first German edition 1955, 1956; English translation by R.F.C. Hull, Princeton 1963, repr. 1977.

———, *Memories, Dreams, Reflections*, orig. German edition 1962; tr. by R. & C. Winston, London 1983.

Kaiser, E., *Paracelsus, mit Selbstzeugnissen und Bilddokumenten*, Hamburg 1984.

Kämmerer, E.W., *Das Leib-Seele-Geist-Problem bei Paracelsus und einigen Autoren des 17. Jahrhunderts*, Kosmosophie 3, Wiesbaden 1971.

Kapferer, H., *Die Werke des Hippokrates. Die hippokratische Schiftensammtung in nevier deutscher Übersetsung*. Stuttgart/Leipzig 7, 1934.

Karcher, H., 'Paracelsus. Stadtarzt von Basel', *Nova Acta Paracelsica*, 1, 1944.

Kayser, H. ed., *Schriften Theophrasts von Hohenheim gennant Paracelsus*, Leipzig 1921.

Kerner, J., *Die Seherin von Prevorst. Eröffnungen über das innere Leben des Menschen und über das Hereinragen einer Geisterwelt in die unsere*, 2 parts, Stuttgart 1929.

Kerners, J., 'Seherin von Prevorst' in Betrachtung esoterischer Tradition und im Lichte psychischer Forschung, in, E. Sopp & K. Spiesberger, *Auf den Spuren der Seherin*, Sersheim 1953.

Klenk, H., 'Ein sogenannter Inquisitionsprozess in Gießen anno 1623', *Mitteilungen des Oberhessischen Geschichtsvereins*, NF, 49/50, 1965, 39–60.

Kocher, P.H., 'Paracelsian Medicine in England: the First Thirty Years (ca. 1570–1600)', *Journal of the History of Medicine*, 2, 1947, 451–480.

———, 'John Hester, Paracelsian (fl. 1576–93)' in J.G. McManaway, G.E. Dawson & E.E. Willoughby eds., *Joseph Quincy Adams Memorial Studies*, Washington 1948.

Kohut, H., *The Analysis of the Self*, New York 1971.

Kolbenheyer, E.G., *Paracelsus. Romantrilogie*, Munich 1941.

Kolding, N.N., *De besynderligste Historier...*, Copenhagen 1567.

Kollitz, J., *Gegenbericht von der Panacea Amwaldina... autore Andrea Libavio...* Frankfurt: verlegung Petri Kopffij, 1595.

Kornerup, B., *Hans Poulsen Resen*, 2 vols., Copenhagen 1928 & 1968.

———, *Ribe Katedralskoles Historie*, 2 vols., Copenhagen 1947 & 1952.

Korshin, P.J., *Typologies in England 1650–1820*, Princeton 1982.

Kristeller, P.O., *Eight Philosophers of the Italian Renaissance*, London 1965.

———, *Studies in Renaissance Thought and Letters*, Rome 1956; offset reprint Rome 1969.

———, *Philosophie des Marsilio Ficino*, Frankfurt 1972.

Kudlin, F., 'Some Interpretive Remarks on the Antisemitism of Paracelsus', in ed. A.G. Debus, *Science, Medicine and Society in the Renaissance*. New York 1972, 121–126.

Kühlmann, 'Oswald Crollius und seine Signaturenlehre. Zum Profil hermetischer Naturphilosophie in der Ära Rudolphs II', in A. Buck ed., *Die okkulten Wissenschaften in der Renaissance, Wolfenbütteler Abhandlungen zur Renaissanceforschung*, 12, Wiesbaden 1992.

Kusukawa, S., 'Aspectio divinorum operum. Melanchton and astrology for Lutheran medics', in O.P. Grell & A. Cunningham eds., *Medicine and the Reformation*, London 1993, 33–56.

La Fontenelle Vaudoé et Auguis, ed., *Memoires et Correspondance de Philippe du Plessis Mornay*, Paris 1824, vols. x–xii.

Laarmann, M., 'Limbus patrum/L. puerorum', *Lexikon des Mittelalters*, V, Munich and Zurich 1991.

Laplanche, J. & Pontalis, J.-B., *Das Vokabular der Psychoanalyse*. Frankfurt/Main 1973.

Leibbrand, W. & A., 'Die "kopernikanische Wendung" des Hysteriebegriffs bei Paracelsus, in S. Domandl, ed., *Paracelsus, Werk und Wirkung. Festgabe für Kurt Goldammer*, Wien 1975, 125–132.

Leibniz, G.W., *Philosophische Schriften*, ed. Gerhardt, vol. 7, Berlin 1890.

———, *Sämtliche Schriften und Briefe* (Academy edition), Berlin, Leipzig 1950, series I, vol. 4.

———, *Sämtliche Schriften und Briefe* (Academy edition), series III, vol. 2 & 3, Berlin 1991.

Leidecker, K.F., 'Paracelsus, Volumen medicinae paramirum', *Bulletin of the History of Medicine, Supp.*, 11, 1949, 36.

Lejeune, F., *Theophrast von Hohenheim. Paracelsus*, Berlin 1941.

Levack, B., *The Witch-hunt in Early Modern Europe*, London 1987.

Libavius, A., *Andreae Libavi Halensis Sax. Med. D. Po. Laur. Physici Rotenburgici ad Tubarim, Neoparacelsica*, Francofurti: Ioannes Saur, impensis Petri Kopffij, 1594.

Lindberg, D.C. & Westman, R.S. eds., *Reappraisal of the Scientific Revolution*, Cambridge 1990.

Linden, S.J., 'Alchemy and eschatology in seventeenth-century poetry', *Ambix*, 31 1984, 102–124.

Lindroth, S., *Paracelsismen i Sverige till 1600-tallets mitt*. Lychnos Bibliotek, no. 7, Uppsala 1943.

List, M., 'Helisäus Röslin—Arzt unt Astrologe, Schwäbische Lebensbilder', in H. Haering & O. Hohenstatt, *Schwäbische Lebensbilder*, Stuttgart 1942, 468–480.

Loch, W., 'Identifikation und Projektion', in *Über Begriffe und Methoden der Psychoanalyse*, Bern/Stuttgart/Vienna 1975, 71–90.

Long, P.O., 'The Openness of Knowledge: An Ideal and Its Context in 16th-Century Writings on Mining and Metallurgy', *Technology and Culture*, 32, 1991, 318–355.

López Piñero, J.M., 'La Carta Filosofica-Medico-Chymica (1687) de Juan de Cabriada, Punto de Partida de la Medicina Moderna en España,' *Asclepio* 17, 1965, 207–12.

———, 'El "Dioalogus" (1589) del paracelsista Llorenç Coçar y la cátedra de medicamentos químicos de la Universidad de Valenica (1591)' in the *Cuadernos Valencianos de Historia de la Medicina y de la Ciencia XX (Serie B—Textos Clásicos)*, Valencia 1977.

———, 'La Ciencia en la España de los Siglos XVI y XVII' in vol. 5, *La Frustración de un Imperio (1476–1714)* of Manuel Tuñon de Lara, *Historia de España*, Barcelona 1981, 357–427.

Lübbers, A., *De Oldenborgske Kongers Sygdomme og Død*, Copenhagen 1906.

Ludwig, G., *Ehre Des Hoch-Fürstlichen Casimiriani Academici in Coburg, oder Desselben vollständige Histories*, 2 vols., Coburg 1725.

Lyby, T. & Grell, O.P., 'The consolidation of Lutheranism in Denmark and Norway', in O.P. Grell ed., *The Scandinavian Reformation. From evangelical movement to institutionalisation of reform*, Cambridge 1994, 114–43.

M.W., *The Queen's Closet Opened*, London 1661.

Magnus, H., *Paracelsus, der Überarzt. Eine kritische Studie*. Abhandlungen der Medizin 16, Breslau 1906.

Mahuet, J. de, 'Limbes', *Catholicisme*, 7, cols. 792–800.

Maier, M., *Tractatus Posthumus sive Ulisses ... Una cum annexis Tractatibus de Fraternitate Roseae Crucis*, Frankfurt 1624.

Marcel, R., ed., *Marsile Ficino. Théologie platonicienne de l'immortalité des âmes*, Paris 1964–70.

Marstaller, G., *Oratio Theophrasto Paracelso*, n.p. 1570.

Marty, P., 'Paracelsus, der Retter der Geistesumnachteten. Ein paar Gedanken zum Hohenheimer als Psychopathologen', *Nova Acta Paracelsica*, New Series 1, 1987.

Matthießen, W. ed., *Paracelsus, Theologische und religions-philosophische Schriften*, Munich 1923.

Mattioli, M.P.A., 'Medecin Senoys', *Les Commentaires ... sur les six liures des Simples de Pedacius Disocoride Anazarbeen*, Lyon 1561.

Medicus, F., 'Paracelsus in der philosophischen Bewegung seiner und unserer Zeit'. *Nova Acta Paracelsica*, 1, 1944, 53–61.

———, 'Das Problem der Erkenntnis bei Paracelsus', *Nova Acta Paracelsica* 5, 1948, 1–17.

Meisner, B., *In Systematis theologici partem primam generalem De Religione et ejus articulis [...] Disputato XVI. De Religione Fanatica [...] [respondit] Johann Spleiß*, Wittenberg 1626.

Merenne, M., *La verite des sciences. Contre les septiques ou Pyrhonniens*, Paris 1625; Reprint, Stuttgart/Bad Cannstaat 1969.

Merkel, I. & Debus, A.G. eds., *Hermeticism and the Renaissance: Intellectual History and the Occult in Early Modern Europe*, London 1988.

Mertz, G., *Das Schulwesen der deutschen Reformation im 16. Jahrhundert.* Heidelberg 1902.

Metzke, E., 'Erfahrung und Natur in der Gedankenwelt des Paracelsus' (1939) in *Coincidentia oppositorum. Gesammelte Studien zur Philosophiegeschichte*, Forschung und Berichte der Evangelischen Studiengemeinschaft, 19, Witten 1961, 20–58.

Middleton, T., *Women Beware Women*, London 1622, reprinted London 1968.

Miekle, H.P., 'Schwenckfeldianer im Hofstaat Bischof Marquards von Speyer (1560–1581)', *Archiv für Mittelrheinische Kirchengeschichte*, 28, 1976, 77–83.

Miller-Guinsburg, A., 'Von Paracelsus zu Böhme: Auf dem Wege zu neuen Bestands-aufnahmen in der Beeinflussung Böhmes durch Paracelsus,' *Paracelsus in der Tradition, Vorträge/Paracelsustag 1978, Salzburger Beiträge zur Paracelsusforschung*, Folge 21, Vienna 1980, 96–118.

———, Die Ideenwelt des Paracelsus und seiner Anhänger in Hinsicht aut das Thema des Christlichen Magus und dessen Wirken, in, *Salzburger Beiträge zur Paracelsusforschung*, 22, 1981, 27–54.

———, Paracelsian Magic and Theology. A Case Study of the Matthew Commentaries, in Kreatur & Kosmos, *Internationale Beiträge zur Paracelsusforschung*, Stuttgart-New York 1981, 125–139.

Milt, B., 'Conrad Gesner und Paracelsus', *Schweizerische Medizinische Wochenschrift*, 59, 1929, 486–509.

Moffett, T., *De Ivre et Praestantia Chymicorum Medicamentorum Dialogus apologeticus*, Frankfurt 1584.

Montanari, F., 'Limbo', *Enciclopedia Dantesca*, 3, 651–54.

Montanus, J.B., *In nonum librum Rhasis ad R[egem] Almansorem lectiones restitutae a Ioanne Cratone*, Basel 1562.

Moran, B.T., 'Court Authority and Chemical Medicine: Moritz of Hessen, Johannes Hartmann, and the Origin of Academic Chemiatria', *Bulletin of the History of Medicine*, 63, 1989, 225–274.

———, 'Prince-practitioning and the Direction of Medical Roles at the German Court: Maurice of Hesse-Kassel and his physicians', in V. Nutton ed., *Medicine at the courts of Europe, 1500–1837*, London 1990, 95–116.

———, *Chemical Pharmacy Enters the University: Johannes Hartmann and the Didactic Care of Chymiatria in the Early Seventeenth Century*, Madison 1991.

———, *The alchemical world of the German court: occult philosophy and chemical medicine in the circle of Moritz of Hessen (1572–1632)*, Sudhoffs Archiv, Beihefte H.29, Stuttgart 1991.

Morsius, J., *Nuncius Olympicus Von etzlichen geheimen Bücheren und Schriften*, Philadelphia 1626.

Mühler, R., 'Paracelsus und E.T.A. Hoffmann', *Salzburger Beiträge zur Paracelsusforschung*, 11, 1972, 117.

Müller, E., ed., *Der Sohar. Das heilige Buch der Kabbala*, München 1991.

Müller, K. & Krönert, G., *Leben und Werk von Leibniz*, Frankfurt/Main 1969.

Müller-Franke, W.-D. & Telle, F. *Analecta Paracelsica Studien zum Nachleben Theophrast von Hohenheim im dentschen Kultutgeibiet der frühen Neuzeit*, Stuttgart 1994.

Müller-Jahncke, W.-D., *Astrologisch-magische Theorie und Praxis in der Heilkunde der frühen Neuzeit*, Stuttgart 1985.

Müller-Salzburg, L., 'Faust und Paracelsus', *Nova Acta Paracelsica*, 10, 1982, 133.

———, 'Der Teil und das Ganze in Hohenheims Gedankenwelt', *Salzburger Beiträge zur Paracelsusforschung*, 25, 1987, 146–79.

———, 'Paracelsisches bei Goethe', *Salzburger Beiträge zur Paracelsusforschung* 26, 1988.

Multhauf, R., 'Medical Chemistry and "The Paracelsians"', in *Bulletin of the History of Medicine*, 28, 1954, 101–25.

———, 'The Significance of Distillation in Renaissance Medical Chemistry, in *Bulletin of the History of Medicine*, 30, 1956, 327–345.

————, *The origins of Chemistry*, London 1966.

Netzhammer, R., *Theophrastus Paracelsus. Das Wissenswerteste über dessen Leben, Lehre und Schriften*, Einsiedeln/Waldshut/Cologne 1901.

Newton, I., *Certain philosophical questions: Newton's Trinity Notebook*, eds. J.E. McGuire & M. Tamny, Cambridge 1983.

Nicholl, R., *The Chemical Theatre*, London 1980.

Nollius, H., *Parergi Philosophici Speculum*, Gießen 1623.

Ong, W.J., *Rhetoric, Romance, and Technology: Studies in the Interaction of Expression and Culture*, Ithaca and London, 1971.

Opel, J.O., *Valentin Weigel. Ein Beitrag zur Literatur- und Kulturgeschichte Deutschlands im 17. Jahrhundert*, Leipzig 1864.

Ormsby-Lennon, H., 'Rosicrucian Linguistics' in I. Merkel & A.G. Debus eds., *Hermeticism and the Renaissance: Intellectual History and the Occult in Early Modern Europe*, London 1988, 315–332.

Ottmann, J., 'Erinnerung an Libavius in Rothenburg ob der Tauber', *Verhandlungen der Gesellschaft Deutscher Naturforscher und Ärzte*, 65, 1894, 79–84.

Oxford Encyclopedia of the Reformation, 4 vols., Oxford 1996.

Ozment, S., *When Father's Ruled: Family Life in Reformation Europe*, Cambridge, Mass. 1983.

Pachter, H.M., *Paracelsus: Magic into Science*, New York 1951.

Pagel, W., *Das medizinische Weltbild des Paracelsus: Seine Zusammemhänge mit Neuplatonismus und Gnosis*. Wiesbaden 1962.

————, Helmont, in J.B. van Helmont, *Aufgang der Artzney-Kunst*, vol. 2, München 1971, Appendix XIII.

————, 'Van Helmont's Concept of Disease—To Be or not to Be? The Influence of Paracelsus', *Bulletin of the History of Medicine*, 46, 1972, 419–454.

————, *Joan Baptista van Helmont: reformer of science and medicine*, Cambridge 1982.

————, *Paracelsus. An Introduction to Philosophical Medicine in the Era of the Renaissance*, Basel, 1958; Second edition, Basel et al., 1982.

————, *Religion and Neoplatonism in Renaissance Medicine*, ed. M. Winder, London 1985.

Paracelsus, *Hermetic and alchemical writings of Aureolus Phillippus Theophrastus Bombast, of Hohenheim called Paracelsus the Great*, 2 vols., London 1894.

Paracelsus in der Bibliotheca Philosophica Hermetica, Amsterdam 1993.

Partington, J.R., *A History of Chemistry*, London 1961.

————, *The Fontana History of Chemistry*, London 1992.

Passions and the Interests, Princeton 1977.

Patai, R., *The Jewish Alchemist*, Princeton 1994.

Paulus, J., 'Alchemie und Paracelsismus um 1600. Das Verzeichnis spagyrischer mediziner des Augsburger Stadtarztes Kard Widemann. Kritische Edition und Kommentar', *Frühneuzeit-Info*, 1992, 3, vol. 2, 48–72.

Peickert, W.-E., *Das Rosenkreuz*, Berlin 1973.

Penotus, B.G., *Apologiae in duas parses divisa ad Iosephi Michelii Middelburgensis Medici scriptum [. . .] Adjuncta est [. . .] Epistola Bernardi Penoti ad D. Andream Libavium*, Frankfurt 1600.

————, 'An Apologeticall Preface' to the *One Hundred and Fourteen Experiments and Cures of the Famous Physitian Theophrastus Paracelsus*, in L. Phioravant (Fioravanti), *Three Exact Pieces of Leonard Phioravant Knight and Doctor in Physick . . . Whereunto is Annexed Paracelsus his One hundred and fourteen Experiments: With certain Excellent Works of B.G. à Portu Aquitans*, London 1652.

Perier, G., 'La vie de Monsieur Pascal', in *idem B. Pascal, Oeuvres*, vol. 1, Paris 1908, 69–70.

Peuckert, W.-E., *Theophrastus Paracelsus*, Stuttgart and Berlin 1941.

Pfefferl, H., *Die Überlieferung der Schriften Valentin Weigels* (doctoral dissertation, partly published), Marburg/Lahn 1991.

Pharmacopoeia Londinensis of 1618 Reproduced in Facsimile with a Historical Introduction by George Urdang, Hollister Pharmaceutical Library, Number Two, Madison 1944:

Pilpoul, P., *La Querelle de l'Antimoine (Essai historique)*. Thèse pour l'Doctoral en Médecine, Paris 1928.

Plat, H., *The Jewell House of Art and Nature*, London 1594.

——, *Delightes for Ladies*, London 1609.

Polanyi, M., *Personal Knowledge*, London 1962.

Porter, R., 'The language of quackery in England 1660–1800', in P. Burke & R. Porter eds., *Language and Society*, Cambridge 1986.

Poynter, F.N.L., 'Nicholas Culpeper and the Paracelsians', in A.G. Debus, *Science, Medicine and Society in the Renaissance: Essays to honour Walter Pagel*, 2 vols., London 1972.

Price, F.N. trans. *The Fame and Confession of the Fraternity of the Fraternity of R.C. commonly of the Rosie Cross*, Margate 1923.

Pumfrey, S., 'William Gilbert's Magnetic Philosophy 1580–1684: the Creation and dissolution of a discipline'. Unpublished Ph.D. dissertation, University of London 1987.

Rattansi, P.M., 'Paracelsus and the Puritan Revolution', *Ambix*, 10, 1963.

——, The intellectual origins of the Royal Society, *Notes and Records of the Royal Society of London*, 23, 1968, 129–143.

——, 'Art and Science: the Paracelsian vision', in J.W. Shirley ed., *Science and the Arts in the Renaissance*, London 1985.

Rees, G., 'Francis Bacon's Semi-Paracelsian Cosmology', *Ambix*, 22, 1975, 81–101.

Reinhardt, *Briefe an Ehrenfried Walther von Tschirnhaus von Pieter van Gent*, Freiberg 1911.

Reitz, A., *Die Welt des Paracelsus. Leben und Gedanken des ausgezeichneten Doktors der Medizin Theophrastus von Hohenheim, genannt Paracelsus*, Stuttgart 1937.

Reussner, B., *Ein kurtze Erkelrung un Christliche widerlegung, Der unerhörten Gotteslesterungen und Lügen, welche Paracelsus in den dreyen Büchern Philosophie ad Athenienses had außgeschüttet*, Görlitz 1570.

Ribera, F.S. de, *Anatomica Chymica, Inviolable, y Memorable*, Madrid 1743.

Roelcke, V., *Jüdische Mystik in der romantischen Medizin? Kabbalistische Topoi bei Gotthilf Heinrich Schubert*, 1991.

Rommel, von, C., *Correspondance de Henri IV avec Maurice le Savant, Landgrave de Hesse*, Paris 1840.

Rørdam, H.F., *Kjøbenhavns Universitets Historie fra 1531 til 1621*, 4 vols., Copenhagen 1868–74.

——, ed., *Danske Kirkelove*, 3 vols., Copenhagen 1883–89.

——, 'Breve til og fra Holger Rosenkrands', *Kirkehistoriske Samlinger*, Series 3, vol. 6, 1887–89, 35–36.

Röslin, H., *De opere Dei creationis seu de mundo Hypotheses orthodoxae quantumvis paradoxae: continentes summa summarum artium principia, Physices, Chymiae, Medicinae, Astronomiae, Atrologiae, Metaphisices: nec non praecipua fundamenta Philosophiae et veteris et novae*, Frankfurt 1597.

——, *Mitternächtige Schiffarth/ Von den Herrn Staden in Niderlanden vor XV Jaren vergebenlich fürgenommen [. . .] Ein künstlicher Philosophischer Tractat*, Oppenheim 1611.

——, *Prodromus Dissertationum Chronologicarum*, Frankfurt 1612.

Rosenberg, A., *Der Mythos des 20. Jahrhunderts. Eine Wertung der seelisch-geistigen Gestaltenkämpfe unserer Zeit*, 5th ed., Munich 1933.

Rosner, E., *Hohenheims Weg von St. Gallen nach Ausburg (1531–1536)*, Vienna 1977.

——, Studies zum Leben und Wirken des Paracelsus in St. Gallen 1977, *Nova Acta Paracelsica*, New Series 3, 32, 1988.

Rotondò, A., *Studi e ricerche di storia ereticale italiana del Cinquecento*, Turin 1974.

——, 'Pietro Perna e la vita culturale e religiosa di Basilea fra il 1570 e il 1580', in *idem, Studi e ricerche di storia ereticale italiana del Cinquecento*, Turin 1974.

Rott, E., *Histoire de la representation diplomatique de la France auprès des cantons suisses*, II, Berne and Paris 1902.

Rudd, N., 'Horace', in E.J. Kenney & W.V. Clausen ed., *The Cambridge History of Classical Literature*, *II*, *Latin Literature*, Cambridge 1982, 370–404.

Rudolph, H., 'Theophrast von Hohenheim (Paracelsus). Arzt und Apostel der neuen Kreatur', in H.-J. Goertz, *Radikale Reformatoren*, Munich 1978.

———, 'Kosmosspekulation und Trinitaetslehre. Ein Beitrag zur Bezichung zwischen Weltbild und Theologie bei Paracelus', *Saltzburger Beitrage Zur Paracelsusforschung*, 21, 1980, 32–47.

———, 'Einige Gesichtspunkte zum Thema Paracelsus und Luther' in *Archiv für Reformationsgeschichte*, 72, 1981, 34–54.

———, 'Paracelsus' Laientheologie in traditionsgeschichtlicher Sicht und in ihrer Zuordnung zu Reformation und katolischer Reform', in P. Dilg & H. Rudolph eds., *Resultate und Desiderate der Paracelsus-Forschung*, Stuttgart 1993, 79–98.

Rupp, G., *Patterns of Reformation*, London 1969.

Saint-Simon, L. de, *Mémoires complets*, ed. La Bédollière, vol. XIII, Paris 1856.

Samso, J., 'A proposito de dos libros recientes sobre las relaciones culturales entre España y Tunez,' *Ethica*, 9, Barcelona 1975, 243–54.

Sandler, J. ed., *Projection, Identification, Projective Identification*, London 1989.

Santillana, G. de, *The Crime of Galileo*, Chicago 1955.

Schad, M., *Paracelsus. Sein Ringen um eine wirklichkeitsgemässe Medizin*, Vorträge Urachhaus 38, Stuttgart 1987.

Schefer, H.U., *Das Berufsethos des Arztes Paracelsus*, Gesnerus, Supplement 42, Aarau/ Frankfurt/Salzburg 1990.

Scheller, E.F., *Langlebigkeit mit Paracelsus-Arzneien. Versuch einer Geriatrie nach Paracelsus*, Heidelberg 1977.

Schepelern, H.D., *Museum Wormianum*, Odense 1971.

Schiffer, I., *Charisma. A psychoanalytic look at mass society*, Toronto 1973.

Schipperges, H., *Paracelsus im Licht der Natur*, Stuttgart 1974.

———, 'Paracelsus. Arzt in seiner Zeit—Arzt an der Grenze der Neuzeit', *Anstösse*, 2, 1982, 40–46.

———, *Paracelsus. Das Abenteuer einer sokratischen Existenz*, Freiburg 1983.

———, *Die Entienlehre des Paracelsus. Aufbau und Umriss seiner Theoretischen Patologie*, Veröffentlichungen aus der Forschungsstelle für Theoretische Pathologie der Heidelberger Akademie der Wissenschaften, Berlin/Heidelberg 1988.

Schlegel, E., *Paracelsus in seiner Bedeutung für unsere Zeit. Heilkunde, Forschungsprinzipien, Religion*, Munich 1907.

Schneider, H., 'Johann Arndts Studienzeit', *Jahrbuch der Gesellschaft für Niedersächsische Kirchengeschichte*, 89, 1991, 133–176.

Schnizlein, A., 'Andreas Libavius und Seine Tätigkeit am Gymnasium zu Rothenburg', *Beilage zum Jahresbericht des Kgl. Progymnasiums Rothenburg ob der Tauber für das Schuljahr 1913/1914*. Rothenburg 1914.

Schoeps, H.J., *Philosemitismus im Barock*, Tübingen 1952.

Scholem, G., *Zur Kabbala und ihrer Symbolik*, 7th ed. Frankfurt 1992.

Schott, H., 'Die Mitteilung des Lebensfeuers. Zum therapeutischen Konzept von Franz Anton Mesmer (1734–1815)', *Medizinhistorisches Journal*, 17, 1982, 195–214.

———, 'Der "Okkultismus" bei Justinus Kerner—Eine medizinhistorische Untersuchung', in A. Berger-Fix ed., *Justinus Kerner: Nur wenn man von Geistern spricht. Briefe und Klecksographien*, Stuttgart 1986, 71–103.

———, 'Die Stigmen des Bösen: Kulturgeschichtliche Wurzeln der Ausmerze-Ideologie', in P. Propping & H. Schott ed. *Wissenschaft auf Irrwegen: Biologismus— Rassenhygiene—Eugenik*, Bonn and Berlin 1992, 9–22.

———, *Sympathie als Metapher in der Medizingeschichte*, Würzburger medizinhistorische Mitteilungen, 10, 1992.

Scriba, 'The autobiography of John Wallis', *Notes and Records of the Royal Society of London*, 25, 1970, 42–43.

Senn, W., 'Adam Haslmayr. Musiker, Philosoph und "Kertzer"', in *Festschrift Leonhard C. Frantz*, Innsbrucker Beiträge zur Kulturwissenschaft, 11, Innsbruck 1965, 379–400.

Sennert, D., *De chymicorum cum Aristotelicis et Galenicis consensu ac dissensu Liber*, Wittenberg 1619 and 1633.

Severinus, P., *Idea Medicinæ Philophicae fundamenta continens totius doctrinæ Paracelsicæ, Hippocraticæ, & Galenicæ*, Basle 1571.

Shackelford, J.R., 'Paracelsianism in Denmark and Norway in the 16th and 17th centuries', dissertation, University of Wisconsin 1989.

Shackleford, J., 'Paracelsianism and Patronage in Early Modern Denmark', in B.T. Moran ed., *Patronage and Institutions: Science, Technology and Medicine at the European Court, 1500–1750*, New York 1991, 85–110.

———, 'Tycho Brahe, Laboratory Design, and the Aim of Science: Reading Plans in Context', *Isis*, 84, 1993, 211–230.

Shapin, S. & Schaffer, S., *Leviathan and the Air Pump. Hobbes, Boyle and the Experimental Life*, Princeton 1985.

Skinner, Q., 'Meaning and Understanding in the History of Ideas', *History and Theory*, 8, 1969, 3–52.

Snorrason, E., *Danskeren Johan Rhode i det 17. århundredes Padua*, Copenhagen 1965.

Solomon, H.M., *Public Welfare, Science and Propaganda in Seventeenth Century France: The Innovations of Théophraste Renaudot*, Princeton 1972.

Sperber, J., *Von dreyerley Seculis oder Hauptzeiten, Tröstlicher Prophecey und Weissagung. Von der zunahenden güldenen als der Dritten und Letzten Zeit und dem gantzen zustande derselben*, Amsterdam 1663 (Mss. in Wolfenbüttel, 772 Helmst., ff. 173–287, and in the Heimatmuseum Köthen).

Spunda, F., *Paracelsus. Menschen, Völker, Zeiten. Eine Kulturgeschichte in Einzeldarstellungen*, vol. 6, Vienna/Leipzig 1925.

———, *Das Weltbild des Paracelsus*, Vienna 1941.

Stadler, F., 'Paracelsus und die Musik in Salzburg', *Salzburger Beiträge zur Paracelsusforschung*, 23, 1984, 118–27.

Stenglin, L., *Apologia adversus Stibii spongiam a Michaële Toxite aeditam*, Augsburg 1569.

Stickofer, G., *Paracelsus. Ein Lebensbild*, Nova Acta Leopoldina, New Series, 66, Halle 1941.

Stokes, T.M., 'Walter Pagel as an historian of medicine', unpublished M. Phil. essay, Cambridge Wellcome Unit.

Strauss, G., *Luther's House of Learning: Indoctrination of the Young in the German Reformation*, Baltimore and London 1978.

Strebel, J., *Paracelsus. Zur vierten Jahrhundertfeier seines Todes 1541–1941*, Luzern 1941.

———, 'Stand und Aufgaben der schweizerischen Paracelsus-Forschung', *Nova Acta Paracelsica*, 1, 1944.

———, 'Nachwort mit Kommentaren zu Hohenheims erster Monographie in der Weltliteratur über Gewerbe-Krankheiten und Gewerbe-Hygiene,' *Nova Acta Paracelsica*, 5, 1946.

———, 'Paracelsus als Begründer der allgemeinen und speziellen Balneologie. Ein Kommentar zur paracelsischen Lehre von den Heilquellen (De Thermis)', *Nova Acta Paracelsica*, 5, 1948, 121–34.

———, 'Über Heilpflanzen und Heilbäder in der Balneologie Hohenheims und über seine korrigierenden Zusätze zu den Heilbädern', *Nova Acta Paracelsica*, 5, 1948, 135–38.

Strunz, F., *Theophrastus Paracelsus. Idee und Problem seiner Anschauung*, Deutsche Geistesgeschichte, vol. 2, 2nd ed., Salzburg/Leipzig 1937.

———, *Beiträge und Skizzen zur Geschichte der Naturwissenschaften*, Hamburg/Leipzig 1909, rep. Leipzig 1972.

Sucker, H., 'Wie finden wir einen Weg zu einer neuen Chemie und Pharmazie', *Nova Acta Paracelsica*, New Series 3, 1988, 13–25.

Sudhoff, K., *Versuch einer Kritik der Paracelsischen Schriften*. vol. II, Berlin 1899.

——— ed., *Theophrast von Hohenheim, gen. Paracelsus: Sämtliche Werke. 1. Abt. Medizinische, naturwissenschaftliche und philosophische Schriften*, 14 vols. München, Berlin 1929–1933.

———, *Paracelsus. Ein deutsches Lebensbild aus den Tagen der Renaissance*, Leipzig 1936.

Taylor, T., *Christ Revealed: Or . . . A Treatise of the Types and Shadows of our Saviour*, London 1635: reprint ed., New York 1979.

Telle, J., 'Kurfürst Ottheinrich, Han Kilian und Paracelsus. Zum pfälzischen Paracelsismus im 16. Jahrhundert', in *Von Paracelsus zu Goethe und Wilhelm van Humboldt*, Salzburger Beiträge zur Paracelsusforschung, 22, Vienna 1981, 130–146.

———, 'Die Schreibart des Paracelsus im Urteil deutscher Fachschriftsteller des 16. und 17. Jahrhunderts', *Medizinhistorisches Journal*, 16, 1981, 78–100.

———, 'Die Schreibart des Paracelsus im Urteil deutscher Fachschriftsteller des 16. und 17. Jahrhunderts', in R. Dilg-Frank ed., *Kreatur und Kosmos. Internationale Beiträge zur Paracelsusforschung*, Stuttgart/New York 1981.

———, 'Johann Huser in seinen Briefen', in *Parerga Paracelsica*. Heidelberger Studien zur Naturkunde der Frühen Neuzeit, III, Stuttgart 1992.

Temkin, O., 'The elusiveness of Paracelsus', *Bulletin of the History of Medicine*, 1952, 26, 201–217.

———, *Galenism: Rise and Decline of a Medical Philosophy*, Ithaca and London 1973.

Thiel, R., *Männer gegen Tod und Teufel*, Berlin 1936.

Thoren, V.E., *The Lord of Uraniborg: a biography of Tycho Brahe*, Cambridge 1990.

Török, S., *Die Religionsphilosophie des Paracelsus und ihr zeitgeschichtlicher Hintergrund*, Theol. diss., Vienna 1946.

Trevor Roper, H.R., 'The Sieur de la Rivière, Paracelsian physician of Henry IV' in A.G. Debus ed. *Science, Medicine and Society in the Renaissance. Essays to Honor Walter Pagel*, 2 vols., New York 1972.

———, 'The Paracelsian Movement,' in *idem, Renaissance Essays*, London 1985, 149–99.

———, 'The court physician and Paracelsianism', in V. Nutton ed., *Medicine at the Courts of Europe, 1500–1837*, London and New York 1990, 79–95.

———, *From Counter-Reformation to Glorious Revolution*, London 1992.

Trigg, J.W., *Origen: The Bible and Philosophy in the Third Century*, London 1985.

Turnbull, G.H., *Hartlib, Dury and Comenius*, London 1947.

Ullman, M., *Die Medizin im Islam*, Leiden 1970.

Valverde, J.-L., *La Farmacia y las Ciencias Farmaceuticas en la Obra de Suarez de Rivera*, Salamanca 1970.

Veibel, S., *Kemien i Danmark*, Copenhagen 1937.

Vickers, B., 'Epideictic and Epic in the Renaissance', *New Literary History: A Journal of Theory and Interpretation*, 14, 1982–83, 497–537.

——— ed., *Occult and Scientific Mentalities in the Renaissance*, Cambridge 1984.

———, *In Defence of Rhetoric*, Oxford 1988.

Vogdt, A., *Theophrastus Paracelsus als Arzt und Philosoph*, Stuttgart 1956.

Waite, A.E., trans. *The History of Magic, Including a Clear and Precise Exposition of its Procedure, its Rites and its Mysteries*, London 1913.

———, *Shadows of life and thought*, London 1938.

———, *The Hermetic and Alchemical Writings of Aureolus Philippus Theophrastus Bombast, of Hohenheim, called Paracelsus the Great, Now for the First Time Faithfully Translated into English*, 2 vols., London 1894, repr. New York 1967.

Walker, J., *Lectures on geology*. ed. H. Scott, Chicago 1966.

Wall, C., Cameron, H.C. & Underwood, E.A., *A History of the Worshipful Society of Apothecaries of London*, Oxford 1963.

Walsch, J.G., *Historische und Theologische Einleitung in die Religions-Streitigkeiten außer der Evangelisch-Lutherischen Kirche, Jenna 1733–1736* (Facsimile reprinted Stuttgart 1985).

Waltershausen, von, S., *Paracelsus am Eingang der deutschen Bildungsgeschichte*, 2nd ed., Leipzig 1942.

Webb, J., *The Flight from Reason* (*The Age of the Irrational*, vol. 1), London 1971.

Weber, E., *Johann Arndts Vier Bücher vom wahren Christentum als Beitrag zur protestantischen Irenic des 17. Jahrhunderts, Eine Quellenkritische Untersuchung*, Hildesheim 1978.

Weber, R., 'Reformatio Medicinae und die Heilkunst des Volkes', *Nova Acta Paracelsica*, 8, 1957.

Webster, C., *The Great Instauration. Science Medicine and reform 1626–1660*, London 1975.

——— ed., *Health, medicine and mortality in the sixteenth century*, Cambridge 1979.

———, 'Essay Review', *Isis*, 1979, 70, 591.

———, *From Paracelsus to Newton: Magic and the making of modern science*, Cambridge 1982.

———, 'The nineteenth century afterlife of Paracelsus', in R. Cooter, ed., *Studies in the History of Alternative Medicine*, London 1988, 79–88.

———, 'Paracelsus: medicine as popular protest', in O.P. Grell & A. Cunningham eds., *Medicine and the Reformation*, London 1993, 57–77.

———, 'Paracelsus Confronts the Saints: Miracles, Healing and the Secularization of Magic', in *Social History of Medicine*, 1995.

Weimann, K.-H., *Paracelsus-Bibliographie 1932–1960 mit einem Verzeichnis neu entdeckter Paracelsus-Handschriften (1900–1960)*, Kosmosophie 2. Wiesbaden 1963.

Weinhandl, F., *Paracelsus-Studien*, ed. S. Domandl, Salzburger Beiträge zur Paracelsusforschung 10, Vienna 1970.

Werle F., 'Die kosmische Weltanschauung des Paracelsus', *Nova Acta Paracelsica*, 4, 1947, 12–29.

Werner, H. ed., *Mikrokosmos und Makrokosmos. Okkulte Schriften von Paracelsus*, Munich 1989.

Westman, R.S., 'Proof, poetics, and patronage: Copernicus's preface to *De Revolutionibus*', in D.C. Lindberg & R.S. Westman, *Reappraisals of the Scientific Revolution*, Cambridge 1990, 167–205.

———, 'Nature, art and psyche: Jung, Pauli, and the Kepler-Fludd polemic' in B. Vickers ed., *Occult and Scientific Mentalities in the Renaissance*, Cambridge 1984, 177–229.

Weuthen, A., 'Zum Paracelsus-Bild des 20. Jahrhunderts', *Beiträge zur Geschichte der Pharmazie*, 38, 1986, 58–60.

Weyer, J., *De praestigiis Daemonum et incantationibus ac ueneficiis libri sex*, Basel 1566, 1568, 1577, 1583.

———, *Witches, Devils and Doctors in the Renaissance: Johann Weyer, De Praestigiis daemonum*. Transl. J. Shea. In *Medieval and Renaissance Texts*, vol. LXXIII, Binghampton, N.Y. 1991.

Wollgast, S., *Philosophie in Deutschland zwischen Reformation und Aufklärung 1550–1650*, Berlin 1988.

Wood, P.B., 'Methodology and Apologetics: Thomas Sprat's "History of the Royal Society"', *British Journal for the History of Science*, 13, 1980, 1–26.

Worm, O., *Oratio Inauguralis de Fratrum R, C. Philosophiam Reformandi Conatu*, 10 May 1619, Copenhagen 1619.

———, *Controversiarum medicarum exercitatio II*, Copenhagen 1626.

———, *Exercitatio IV*, Copenhagen 1630.

———, *Exercitatio XII*, Copenhagen 1644.

Yates, F.A., *The Rosicrucian Enlightenment*, London 1972.

Zanier, G., 'La Medicina Paracelsiana in Italia: Aspetti di un'accoglienza Particolare,' *Rivista di storia della filosofia*, no. 4, 1985, 627–53.

Zekert, O., *Paracelsus in der Zeit*, Salzburger Beiträge zur Paracelsusforschung 1, Vienna 1960.

Zeller, E., *Paracelsus. Der Beginn eines deutschen Arzttums*, Halle 1935.

Zeller, W., *Theologie und Frömmigkeit. Gesammelte Aufsätze*, ed. by B. Jaspert, Marburg 1971.

Zetzner, L., *Alchymia Ratione et Experientia ita Demum Viriliter Impugnata et Expugnata unâ cum suis Fallaciis et Deliramentis Quibus Homines Imbubinârat ut Numquam in Posterum se Erigere Valeat*, Argentorati 1603.

Zinguer, I. ed., *L'Hébreu au Temps de la Renaissance*, Leiden 1992.

Zwinger, T. ed., *Theatrum humanae vitae*, Basel 1571.

INDEX OF NAMES

INDEX OF PLACES

INDEX OF SUBJECTS

Studies in the History
of Christian Thought

EDITED BY HEIKO A. OBERMAN

46. GARSTEIN, O. *Rome and the Counter-Reformation in Scandinavia.* 1553-1622. 1992
47. GARSTEIN, O. *Rome and the Counter-Reformation in Scandinavia.* 1622-1656. 1992
48. PERRONE COMPAGNI, V. (ed.). *Cornelius Agrippa, De occulta philosophia Libri tres.* 1992
49. MARTIN, D. D. *Fifteenth-Century Carthusian Reform.* The World of Nicholas Kempf. 1992
50. HOENEN, M. J. F. M. *Marsilius of Inghen.* Divine Knowledge in Late Medieval Thought. 1993
51. O'MALLEY, J. W., IZBICKI, T. M. and CHRISTIANSON, G. (eds.). *Humanity and Divinity in Renaissance and Reformation.* Essays in Honor of Charles Trinkaus. 1993
52. REEVE, A. (ed.) and SCREECH, M. A. (introd.). *Erasmus' Annotations on the New Testament.* Galatians to the Apocalypse. 1993
53. STUMP, Ph. H. *The Reforms of the Council of Constance (1414-1418).* 1994
54. GIAKALIS, A. *Images of the Divine.* The Theology of Icons at the Seventh Ecumenical Council. With a Foreword by Henry Chadwick. 1994
55. NELLEN, H. J. M. and RABBIE, E. (eds.). *Hugo Grotius – Theologian.* Essays in Honour of G. H. M. Posthumus Meyjes. 1994
56. TRIGG, J. D. *Baptism in the Theology of Martin Luther.* 1994
57. JANSE, W. *Albert Hardenberg als Theologe.* Profil eines Bucer-Schülers. 1994
59. SCHOOR, R.J.M. VAN DE. *The Irenical Theology of Théophile Brachet de La Milletière (1588-1665).* 1995
60. STREHLE, S. *The Catholic Roots of the Protestant Gospel.* Encounter between the Middle Ages and the Reformation. 1995
61. BROWN, M.L. *Donne and the Politics of Conscience in Early Modern England.* 1995
62. SCREECH, M.A. (ed.). *Richard Mocket, Warden of All Souls College, Oxford, Doctrina et Politia Ecclesiae Anglicanae.* An Anglican Summa. Facsimile with Variants of the Text of 1617. Edited with an Introduction. 1995
63. SNOEK, G.J.C. *Medieval Piety from Relics to the Eucharist.* A Process of Mutual Interaction. 1995
64. PIXTON, P.B. *The German Episcopacy and the Implementation of the Decrees of the Fourth Lateran Council, 1216-1245.* Watchmen on the Tower. 1995
65. DOLNIKOWSKI, E.W. *Thomas Bradwardine: A View of Time and a Vision of Eternity in Fourteenth-Century Thought.* 1995
66. RABBIE, E. (ed.). *Hugo Grotius, Ordinum Hollandiae ac Westfrisiae Pietas (1613).* Critical Edition with Translation and Commentary. 1995
67. HIRSH, J.C. *The Boundaries of Faith.* The Development and Transmission of Medieval Spirituality. 1996
68. BURNETT, S.G. *From Christian Hebraism to Jewish Studies.* Johannes Buxtorf (1564-1629) and Hebrew Learning in the Seventeenth Century. 1996
69. BOLAND O.P., V. *Ideas in God according to Saint Thomas Aquinas.* Sources and Synthesis. 1996
70. LANGE, M.E. *Telling Tears in the English Renaissance.* 1996
71. CHRISTIANSON, G. and T.M. IZBICKI (eds.). *Nicholas of Cusa on Christ and the Church.* Essays in Memory of Chandler McCuskey Brooks for the American Cusanus Society. 1996
72. MALI, A. *Mystic in the New World.* Marie de l'Incarnation (1599-1672). 1996
73. VISSER, D. *Apocalypse as Utopian Expectation (800-1500).* The Apocalypse Commentary of Berengaudus of Ferrières and the Relationship between Exegesis, Liturgy and Iconography. 1996
74. O'ROURKE BOYLE, M. *Divine Domesticity.* Augustine of Thagaste to Teresa of Avila. 1997
75. PFIZENMAIER, T.C. *The Trinitarian Theology of Dr. Samuel Clarke (1675-1729).* Context, Sources, and Controversy. 1997
76. BERKVENS-STEVELINCK, C., J. ISRAEL and G.H.M. POSTHUMUS MEYJES (eds.). *The Emergence of Tolerance in the Dutch Republic.* 1997
77. HAYKIN, M.A.G. (ed.). *The Life and Thought of John Gill (1697-1771).* A Tercentennial Appreciation. 1997
78. KAISER, C.B. *Creational Theology and the History of Physical Science.* The Creationist Tradition from Basil to Bohr. 1997
79. LEES, J.T. *Anselm of Havelberg.* Deeds into Words in the Twelfth Century. 1997
80. WINTER, J.M. VAN. *Sources Concerning the Hospitallers of St John in the Netherlands, 14th-18th Centuries.* 1998

81. TIERNEY, B. *Foundations of the Conciliar Theory*. The Contribution of the Medieval Canonists from Gratian to the Great Schism. Enlarged New Edition. 1998

82. MIERNOWSKI, J. *Le Dieu Néant*. Théologies négatives à l'aube des temps modernes. 1998

83. HALVERSON, J.L. *Peter Aureol on Predestination*. A Challenge to Late Medieval Thought. 1998. ISBN 90 04 10945 5

84. HOULISTON, V. (ed.). *Robert Persons, S.J.: The Christian Directory (1582)*. The First Booke of the Christian Exercise, appertayning to Resolution. 1998

85. GRELL, O.P. (ed.). *Paracelsus*. The Man and His Reputation, His Ideas and Their Reputation. 1998

Prospectus available on request

BRILL — P.O.B. 9000 — 2300 PA LEIDEN — THE NETHERLANDS